From the West Coast to the Western Front

From the West Coast

to the Western Front

BRITISH COLUMBIANS AND THE GREAT WAR

3853D

38056

Mark Forsythe and Greg Dickson

Harbour Publishing

Harbour Publishing Co. Ltd.
P.O. Box 219, Madeira Park, BC, V0N 2H0
www.harbourpublishing.com

Editing by Maureen Nicholson
Text and cover design by Roger Handling/Terra Firma Digital Arts
Additional image credits: (Top front cover and pages 2-3) "Curtiss" J.N. 4-D above the clouds, CWM 19940003-714, George Metcalf Archival Collection, © Canadian War Museum. (Front cover, inset) Hat badge of the BC Regiment, courtesy of Greg Dickson. (Front cover bottom) Nursing Sisters of the Canadian Overseas Expeditionary Force with soldiers, courtesy of Marianna Harris. (Back cover) Canadian troops at Vimy, 1917, City of Vancouver Archives, LP 61.2.
Indexed by Ellen Hawman

Printed and bound in Canada

Harbour Publishing acknowledges financial support from the Government of Canada through the Canada Book Fund and the Canada Council for the Arts, and from the Province of British Columbia through the BC Arts Council and the Book Publishing Tax Credit.

Cataloguing data available from Library and Archives Canada

ISBN 978-1-55017-666-7 (paper)
ISBN 978-1-55017-667-4 (ebook)

CONTENTS

INTRODUCTION

IF MEN COULD LEARN FROM HISTORY, WHAT LESSONS MIGHT IT TEACH US?
—*SAMUEL TAYLOR COLERIDGE*

One hundred years ago this year, the Great War broke out, unleashing a slaughter unimaginable to a world that seemed to be on the road to progress and peace. In fact, Canadians were about to celebrate a hundred years of peace with the US since the end of the War of 1812. But instead memorials to that peace were put on hold. By 1919, we were building cenotaphs to commemorate the more than sixty-six thousand Canadians killed in a war Canada was drawn into as part of the British Empire.

Those cenotaphs we built in our towns and cities include the names of over six thousand men and women from British Columbia. The war touched families in every corner of our province. Farm boys from the Okanagan and nurses from Vancouver Island faced indescribable horrors—gas, gangrene and machine guns. And the war left a mark on the generations to come.

When the authors sat down early in 2013 for a coffee, we were both on personal quests to find out more about our family members who went to the Western Front. We wanted to know what motivated them and how the march to war changed them—and where they died. With the hundredth anniversary of the war fast approaching, we quickly realized that other British Columbians might be on this same quest. It dawned on us that a book would be a fitting tribute to those who served, those who opposed and even those who were deemed unwelcome or enemy aliens.

British Columbia was far from the front lines in 1914, but in a sense we were at the centre of the passions that swept the world into the conflict. Our premier, Richard McBride, was a staunch imperialist, and our province was full of recent immigrants from Great Britain,

The hat badge of the BC Regiment—6,225 British Columbians were killed before the war was over.
Courtesy of Greg Dickson

Europe and Asia. Their feelings about the war were inextricably linked to the countries they left behind. Many rushed to take part when war was declared late in the summer.

Canadians had experienced one brief exposure to modern warfare—in South Africa at the turn of the twentieth century. But our romantic illusions about the nature of battle were still intact. And the war was going to be over by Christmas. All the better reason to enlist before it was over and be part of the excitement. The BC economy was reeling from a recession, jobs were scarce for young men and a few months in Europe seemed like a welcome tonic.

Just that summer, our little Pacific naval fleet (represented by an aging cruiser called HMCS *Rainbow*) was making headlines, turning back the *Komagata Maru* in Vancouver Harbour. Aboard the *Komagata Maru* were 376 passengers, mostly Sikhs, but also Muslims and Hindus. They were British subjects from India who by rights should have been able to settle anywhere in the British Empire. White British Columbians thought differently and, after a standoff, turned them away. Within a year, British Empire Indians would be fighting and dying alongside their Canadian comrades on the Western Front.

Our wartime history is the story of contradictions like that: strange turns and unexpected consequences. Imagine a time when our women could not vote. Neither could Japanese or Chinese Canadians or our First Nations. And yet they all served along with those who did have the franchise. By the end of the war, the government needed female votes to survive and many women were able to cast a ballot. Ethnic minorities waited much longer.

British Columbians served not only on the Western Front but also in East Africa, Russia, Greece and Mesopotamia, on the seas and in the air. We here in BC supplied the food, the raw materials and even the submarines that made the war possible. Tinned salmon from BC was shipped overseas. Our Sitka spruce was used to build fighter aircraft.

We joined up at the highest per capita rate in Canada. Few spoke out against the war. Those who did risked arrest or even death. Albert "Ginger" Goodwin, a labour activist, was gunned down in one of those manhunts near Cumberland on Vancouver Island in 1918.

Those who went willingly were sometimes incredibly brave in adversity. Our province produced many heroes, such as General Arthur Currie from Victoria; Raymond Collishaw, the second-highest-ranking Canadian flying ace; and over a dozen Victoria Cross recipients,

WHEN STEVE'S PARD JOINED UP

By Tom Cottrell

From the popular *Canada in Khaki* book series. Western Canadians expected their talents would be well used.
From *Canada in Khaki*, 1917

including Gordon Flowerdew from Walhachin, who died in the last cavalry charge of the war. Aboriginal vets like George McLean were decorated for valour and so were Japanese Canadians like Masumi Mitsui.

Private Thomas Moles of the 54th Kootenay Battalion was court-martialled for desertion and executed by firing squad at 05:30 on October 22, 1917. He is buried at Ypres, one of over twenty Canadians sentenced to death for leaving the battlefield.

Some found love amid the carnage. Dr. Howard Burris from Kamloops was working with Nurse Robina Stewart from Manitoba in a Canadian hospital in Salonika, Greece. Their courtship continued when they were reposted to Liverpool and they married there in 1919 before returning to Kamloops to raise a family of doctors and nurses.

The war also produced an outpouring of novels, poetry, plays and art. One of British Columbia's first successful writers, Frederick Niven, wrote a poem about the strange Christmas Truce of 1914, when soldiers on the Western Front laid down their guns and met together in no man's land. It includes these lines:

> Between the trenches then they met
> Shook hands, and e'en did play
> At games on which their hearts were set
> On happy Christmas Day.

Lieutenant Allan Brooks from Vernon served as a sniper on the Western Front but devoted the rest of his life to ornithology and drawing and painting birds. Pierre Berton, Hubert Evans, John Gray and Jack Hodgins all wrote about the Great War. Berton's *Vimy*, Gray's *Billy Bishop Goes to War* and Hodgins's *Broken Ground* became classics.

The event that started the war in the first place had an eerie link to British Columbia.

Right: After the German army rolled through Belgium, graphic drawings were part of an information campaign on the home front to rally support for Canada's entry into the war.
Courtesy of Don Stewart

Far right: A children's story written in 1910 that later raised money for Belgian children early in the war.
Courtesy of Don Stewart

THE TALE OF A BELGIAN HARE

BY
FRANCES EBBS - CANAVAN
AND
LILLIAN CLARKE SWEENEY

When the Archduke Franz Ferdinand was gunned down by an assassin in Sarajevo on Sunday, June 28, 1914, a few BC old-timers must have remembered his hunting trip to the province in 1893. The archduke travelled incognito, touring Stanley Park and then setting off along the Dewdney Trail with a large retinue, including a personal taxidermist. The great white hunter would later be hunted himself.

These are some of the stories we will tell in the pages ahead. We'll include many of the generous offerings from CBC listeners along the way. In many respects, the personal stories are the best. We set out to find how the Great War had touched British Columbians, and CBC listeners responded by going into their attics and basements to find diaries, letters, photos and memorabilia from a hundred years ago. Thank you for playing such an important part in this project.

Proceeds from this project will benefit the Canadian Letters and Images Project at Vancouver Island University in Nanaimo. Dr. Stephen Davies started the project over a decade ago to preserve the stories of ordinary Canadians and the richness of their wartime experiences. With this help, we hope Professor Davies will be able to enlist more history students to help transcribe letters and scan photographic images to add to the collection.

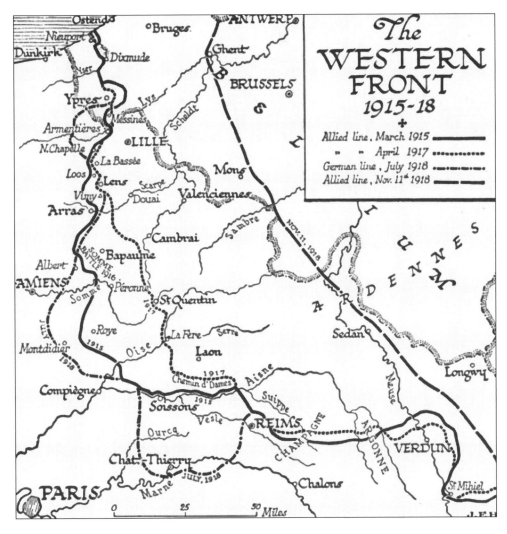

Some of the key battles on the Western Front, which hardly moved over the course of the war.
From *The Outline of History*, H.G. Wells, 1921

Our World at War

1914

June 28	Archduke Franz Ferdinand and his wife assassinated in Sarajevo
July 23	*Komagata Maru* escorted out of Vancouver Harbour by HMCS *Rainbow*
Aug. 4	Great Britain declares war on Germany after its invasion of neutral Belgium. As a former colony and now self-governing dominion, Canada automatically involved
Aug. 4	Agents for Premier Richard McBride inspect and purchase Seattle-built submarines for over one million dollars
Aug. 5	Canada commits to send infantry division of twenty-five thousand men
August	Troops entrain for basic training at Valcartier, Quebec
Sept. 18	Vernon Internment Camp opens for Germans, Austro-Hungarians and Ukrainians
October	First contingent arrives in Britain/Salisbury Plain
Oct.–Nov.	The first Battle of Ypres, Belgium. Trench warfare begins on the Western Front
Nov. 1914	Colonel Henry Seymour Tobin organizes and commands the 29th (Vancouver) Battalion, known as "Tobin's Tigers." One of their members, Bob Hanna, earns the Victoria Cross for exceptional bravery
Dec. 25	The Christmas Truce—British, German and French troops celebrate together

1915

1915	Aboriginal Canadians enlist—four thousand serve (one in three able-bodied Native men)
February	Canadians are deemed ready to proceed to France
March 26	Cyclone Taylor leads the Vancouver Millionaires to the Stanley Cup at the Denman Arena
April	British Pacific Construction and Engineering, a Seattle company, builds submarines for the Russians at secret plants in Burnaby and Vancouver to avoid violating American neutrality
April 22	Ypres gas attack
April 24	Edward Bellew of Kamloops sees action at Ypres, later earns VC
July	Ukrainian Canadian Filip Konowal enlists, later earns VC
Dec. 8	"In Flanders Fields" appears anonymously in *Punch*
Dec. 15	BC premier McBride resigns and moves to London

1916

Jan. 21	Victoria's John Sinton earns VC in Mesopotamia
March	Battle of St. Eloi
June 16	Battle of Mount Sorrel

July 1	The Somme—Newfoundland Regiment slaughtered
Sept. 1	Japanese Canadian Masumi Mitsui travels to Calgary to enlist after being turned away by BC regiments
Sept. 14	Provincial election—Conservatives defeated, Liberals elected
Sept. 15	Canadians attack at Courcelette
Sept. 15–16	Nursing Sisters Elsie Collis and Ethel Morrison join Canadian Army Medical Corps
Sept.–Oct.	Battle of Regina Trench
Oct. 9	Chilliwack Piper James Richardson (VC) killed in action

1917

April 6	United States joins the war effort
April 9–12	Battle of Vimy Ridge—a defining moment for the Canadian Corps
April	George McLean, BC Native soldier, awarded DCM for bravery at Vimy
August	Billy Bishop receives VC
Aug. 6	Premier Richard McBride dies in London, England, of Bright's disease
Aug. 15–17	Vancouver's Michael O'Rourke earns VC at Hill 70
Aug. 21	Abbotsford's Robert Hanna earns VC at Battle of Hill 70
Aug. 29	Conscription introduced by the *Military Service Act*
Oct.–Nov.	Battle of Passchendaele
Nov.	Strange flu symptoms reported in China, later identified as "Spanish flu"
Dec. 6	Halifax explosion
Dec. 17	Nursing sisters and women with relatives in the military vote in the federal election

1918

Jan. 24	First woman to run (and be elected)—Mary Ellen Smith—in a Vancouver by-election. First time women vote in a BC provincial election
Feb.20	Wee Tan Louie of Kamloops rides a horse across the Rockies to enlist in Calgary
March 31	Walhachin VC recipient Gordon Flowerdew dies of wounds received in the last great cavalry charge of the war
April 21	Red Baron shot down
May 9–10	Victoria's Rowland Bourke earns VC for action in Royal Navy Reserve
Aug. 8–18	Battle of Amiens (Last Hundred Days campaign)
Sept. 27– Oct. 11	Canal du Nord and Cambrai
Sept. 29– Oct. 3	Powell River's John MacGregor earns VC at Cambrai
Nov. 11	Armistice

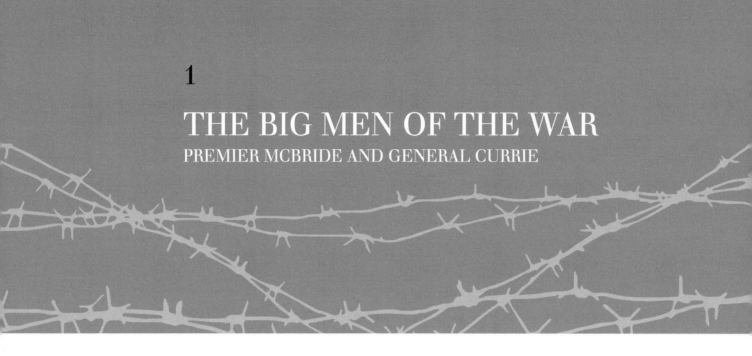

1

THE BIG MEN OF THE WAR
PREMIER MCBRIDE AND GENERAL CURRIE

Two leaders, more than all the others, personified British Columbia's wartime spirit. Richard McBride was the province's most successful politician. Arthur Currie has been hailed as Canada's greatest battlefield general. (In fact, Britain's wartime prime minister, David Lloyd George, believed Currie was the best general in the British Empire.)

Both men were living in Victoria when the war broke out. McBride was premier of the province, at the pinnacle of his power. Currie was a struggling real estate agent, laid low by the recession. Both were big men, over six feet tall. Both displayed an instinctive talent for leadership. But it was Currie who would soon shine the brightest. McBride, though no one realized it at the time, was on his way out.

Our Dick

It was said that no man was as wise as Dick McBride looked. That was a bit of a backhanded compliment, but McBride's looks were political gold through four elections. His image was even featured on cigar boxes. He was "Our Dick" and he was amazingly popular as long as the economy boomed. And boom it did between 1903 and 1912. BC went from one railroad—the venerable CPR—to three, or was it four? It was hard to keep count as McBride shuffled investors in and out of his office in Victoria.

While he promoted railroads at home, McBride preached imperialism abroad. He made annual trips to London to make his case for a strong naval presence on the West Coast. In 1912, he provided reporters in London with his perspective:

> This is a matter which closely affects British Columbia. Since the withdrawal of the Pacific squadron, we have been left practically defenceless on the Pacific Coast. We have been greatly impressed with the vigour and strength of Hon. Winston Churchill's naval policy and we have hope and confidence that any naval scheme in which he and the Canadian Government concur will restore to British Columbia a full and fair measure of naval protection.

Above: Men of the 104th New Westminster Fusiliers depart for the front. In August of 1914, everyone expected soldiers to be home by Christmas, but the brutal conflict did not end until November 1918. Canada lost 61,966 lives in the "war to end all wars."
Courtesy of Don Stewart

Left: Premier Richard McBride in his heyday. Governor General Earl Grey described him as a "picturesque buffalo."
British Columbia Electric Railway Company photo, City of Vancouver Archives, LGN 952

Opposite: British Dreadnoughts. These state-of-the-art warships were the pre-eminent symbols of national power.
From *The Graphic Magazine*, June 15, 1918

McBride and Churchill were cronies and on the same page on naval matters. In Canada, McBride advanced Churchill's dreadnought plans. In Britain, Churchill returned the favour, including McBride in his influential social circle (which included the royal family) and helping him get a knighthood in 1912.

McBride loved to play on the imperial stage. But by 1913, things were going wrong at home. The recession was taking its toll. The British investment that had fuelled the good times dried up. The railways that once seemed to be the symbol of progress started to falter. McBride's era of prosperity was coming to an end.

Currie's Early Struggles

Arthur Currie had come west from Ontario in 1894 to seek his fortune. He was trained as a schoolteacher and taught for a time in Sidney. But he switched to real estate when he saw the McBride economic boom was making people around him rich. He too did very well for a while, and then the bottom fell out and he was in deep trouble.

He came from Irish stock like McBride and both men listed their religion as Anglican. But Currie was a Liberal politically, which put him at odds with the predominantly Conservative establishment led by McBride. This streak of independence would also mark his approach to military affairs. He had the courage to defy superiors who could break him in order to press for his own views. And the military was his passion. He was president of the BC Rifle Association and served with the 5th Regiment Canadian Garrison Artillery for more than a dozen years before the war broke out.

Who's Who and Why

Both McBride and Currie appeared in the 1913 edition of *Who's Who and Why*. The thick red volume captured all the big men of Western Canada. Some paid for their entries: aspiring lawyers, businessmen and real estate agents. But a few prominent men in public life were given a full page. BC's premier made good copy and his larger than life reputation inspired Governor General Earl Grey to call McBride "a picturesque buffalo."

A popular postcard. Premier McBride visits with 30th and 31st BC Horse in 1912.
Courtesy of Greg Dickson

On the other hand, readers of *Who's Who* could be forgiven for missing the 1913 entry for real estate agent Arthur Currie. He submitted a photo of himself in uniform hoping an appeal to military service might turn his struggling business around. The outbreak of war was the best thing that ever happened to him.

Although they weren't political bedfellows, McBride and Currie knew each other and there is every indication they liked each other. McBride even put in a good word when Currie was up for promotion to command the Canadian Corps in 1917. Both men were ardent imperialists at a time when it was a great thing to be an imperialist. And they were happy warriors. Ready for the fight.

Still, that recession was hitting the little guy pretty hard. Unemployment was high. With jobs in short supply and wages under pressure, men were looking for better prospects wherever they could be found. Immigrants who might drive wages even further down or take scarce jobs were not welcome.

Some young men headed for the States looking for work. Theo Dickson, the son of a struggling real estate agent from Vernon, headed for Montana but found he was even worse

Tom Anderson.
Courtesy of Christopher Anderson Arnett

From Our Listeners: My Grandfather Tom Anderson

By Christopher Anderson Arnett, Salt Spring Island

My grandfather Tom Anderson never offered to talk about the war. As with most men of accomplishment he wasn't forthcoming about his experience in war or in his career as Vancouver's longest-serving city fireman. As a child I didn't know the right questions to ask. In his undershirt, he'd point to the scar on his upper right arm where shrapnel hit him. In the garage of his Vancouver Island retirement home, he had a huge jackknife—his "trench knife." A drawer held a dud hand grenade, but my favourite thing was his long steel bayonet with leather scabbard and webbing which I wore as a sword when playing pirates with my cousins on the sand cliffs of South Saanich.

I asked where he fought and he said, "Lens," a name with no historical resonance. "What was the name of your unit?"

"The 47th Battalion," he said. Someone told me something about "that corporal who took out a machine-gun nest and won the Victoria Cross" and that Grandad "should have got one too." A scar, some cool stuff, a place name, a military unit, some action, but not much else. No one ever asked him about the details. Long after he passed away, old photos and archival records told more of the story.

Born in Vancouver in 1895 of Norwegian immigrants, Grandad joined the active militia in 1913 and served in the 18th Field Hospital of the 6th BC Regiment (The Duke of Connaught's Own), Vancouver's oldest military unit. When the war broke out in 1914 he did not rush to enlist. He was a city fireman in an essential service. Two years later when his militia unit raised an overseas battalion (the 158th) Grandad, then newly wed, joined up with his younger brother Paul on March 7, 1916. Old photos show him at Vernon with his platoon—a group of twenty-one-year-olds clowning around and preparing for the adventure of their lives. Upon arrival in England the 158th was absorbed into a pool of bodies to replenish the high casualties of units already at the front. Drafted to "B" Company of the 47th (New Westminster) Battalion, he joined his unit on June 24, 1917, near Vimy Ridge

and the occupied French coal-mining city of Lens, more than a year after enlisting in Vancouver.

On the night of August 17, the 47th relieved the 75th Battalion at the Cité du Moulin, a shattered suburb south of Lens where, in the battle for Hill 70, the CEF had fought for the first time under a Canadian command in a set-piece battle designed not only to take and hold opposing trenches but to kill as many of the enemy as possible.

A few days following this strategic victory a less successful attack was ordered on a heavily fortified, ruined coal mine on the city's southern outskirts. In the early hours of August 21, Grandad, with the rest of "B" Company, advanced through a maze of destroyed houses, billowing smoke and a hail of machine gun, rifle, artillery and chemical weapons fire. Most of the officers and NCOs were killed or wounded outright and command fell to a corporal, Filip Konowal, who led his men into what has been described as the fiercest hand-to-hand urban fighting of the war. Konowal took out two machine-gun nests and personally killed sixteen enemy soldiers, many with the bayonet. The war diary of the 47th Battalion records that the fighting was "most severe" and that "the situation made it unwise to take many prisoners." Konowal was awarded a Victoria Cross but the attack failed in its objectives and cost 1,108 Canadian casualties. All Grandad told me about this fight was that he hadn't noticed his wound until a relief officer drew his attention to his blood-soaked uniform sleeve and sent him to a field hospital. Invalided to England, he recovered and spent the remainder of the war as an army fitness instructor.

The Christmas before he died he presented me with a very special gift—the bayonet he used in the fight over the ruins of the Cité du Moulin. I knew he wouldn't be with us much longer and decided only then to ask him more direct questions about his experience for the benefit of the gathered family. "Hey Grandad, I was wondering if you could tell us a bit about the war?"

He looked at me and said, "None of it made any sense."

off than back home in the Okanagan. He wrote to his younger brother, Ted, to warn him the bad times were everywhere:

> I would not come to the States because it's a hard world over here. I am working on a ranch at present earning $1.25 a day and have only earned $5.60 so far. In a few days I lose my job but will soon land something else. I had a pretty hard time of it for a while without any money or a thing to eat.

Embattled Immigrants, Labour Strife

In Vancouver, the bleak job picture turned ugly when news spread that a ship carrying South Asian immigrants was on the way. When the *Komagata Maru* tried to land its passengers in Vancouver on May 23, 1914, the ship's captain met stiff resistance. The passengers were British subjects and felt they had a right to disembark. But the authorities called in HMCS *Rainbow* and would not let any passengers come ashore. The standoff lasted for two months. On July 23, the *Komagata Maru* was forced to leave Vancouver Harbour under naval escort. Only a few passengers were allowed to disembark.

The aging cruiser HMCS *Rainbow* watches over the *Komagata Maru* in Vancouver Harbour, July 1914.
Leonard Frank photo, Vancouver Public Library 6229

McBride no doubt supported the outcome. He was a firm believer in a white Canada. "Another facet of McBride's imperialism was his fear of Asiatic immigration," said former BC Attorney General Brian Smith, who wrote a highly respected study of McBride.

In peacetime, both the navy and the militia could be depended on to serve their political masters. As a militia officer in Victoria, Arthur Currie too got the call in 1913—in his case to police a Vancouver Island coal strike.

The Nanaimo strike of 1913–14 was a bitter, class-riven dispute that dragged on and on. In August 1913, fearing violence, the BC attorney general called out the militia. The headline in the August 15 edition of the Victoria *Daily Colonist* read, "Military Forces to Bring Order Out of Anarchy at Vancouver Island Coal Mines."

Members of the Victoria militia sailed for Nanaimo with two Maxim guns. "The mission of the soldiery is not to kill," warned one of the officers, "but as you can see we have guns with us."

Colonel Currie was in charge of the 5th Regiment and he was in a difficult place. He hadn't signed on to shoot civilians. But he came out of this police action with his self-respect intact. The militia was able to move in and defuse the situation. Currie got some of the credit for working with the strikers. He must have been buoyed by an editorial in the Victoria *Daily Colonist:*

> The militia at Nanaimo today represents each one of us, whether we sympathize with the miners or not. It is asserting the supremacy of what we have declared to be the law; of the law that protects both the rich man with his hoarded wealth and the penniless agitator for new social conditions... The militia is not a tool in the hands of capital as some profess to believe. It is the guardian of the liberty of the people.

Currie made more headlines just a year later when the British government declared war. He might be a failed real estate agent to his neighbours, but in the military community he was already recognized as one of its most promising militia officers.

1914 and War

"Despite struggling daily with his financial woes," wrote Currie biographer Tim Cook, author of *The Madman and the Butcher*, "Currie, a towering figure at over 6'2 and 250 pounds, was recognized as one of the best militia commanders in the country."

It should be remembered that Canada went to war with what was essentially a civilian army. About six hundred thousand enlisted from across the country. But they were not professional soldiers. Some had served in local militias but many had no previous military experience. Over four hundred thousand went overseas and almost all were civilian soldiers: bank clerks, loggers, miners, farmers and real estate agents like Currie.

Currie had proved himself to be good at commanding a few hundred men. Canada's minister of militia and defence, the erratic and egotistical Sam Hughes, decided Currie was capable of greater things. From obscurity, he picked him to be one of just a few brigadiers to command the first infantry brigades taking shape at the new training camp at Valcartier, Quebec. Currie was thirty-eight years old and was now in charge of four thousand men. Within just a few years, he would command the entire Canadian Corps on the Western Front.

The Generals—Lions or Donkeys?

After the war, it was said of our soldiers that they were "lions led by donkeys," the suggestion being that British generals in particular were throwbacks to a different era, arrogant old men in jodhpurs who thought of the men as nothing more than cannon fodder. That view has been coming under reconsideration as historians look back a hundred years and learn more about what actually happened.

"It's a myth that the generals on both sides were heartless effete aristocrats who sipped champagne behind the lines while they pondered, unsuccessfully, the challenges of modern industrial war," historian Margaret MacMillan wrote recently in the *Guardian* newspaper. "Nor were they all from the upper classes. General Erich Ludendorff, one of the most successful of the German generals, was middle class, while General Arthur Currie, arguably the most competent of the British Empire's generals, was (in civilian life) an unsuccessful salesman."

MacMillan and other historians think the generals deserve more credit. Certainly Currie stands apart, a citizen soldier who learned on the job and kept improving his understanding of trench warfare and tactics. In an interview with *Canada's History* magazine, biographer Tim Cook said that is what makes Currie a truly outstanding Canadian:

> He never claimed to be brilliant. He never claimed to have all the answers. And how could he? How do you defeat barbed wire, and trenches and machine gun positions and artillery and poison gas and everything else? But he was willing to learn, he was willing to apply himself to try to understand how to break through the terrible stalemate on the Western Front. And he always did so with the soldiers' lives in mind.

McBride's Sad End

For a man who succeeded so well and at such a young age, it was a terrible shock for McBride when it all started to unravel. The first shock was the recession. And then the public started to question how a man who had seemed to be so brilliant could be left holding the bag when the bill came due for all the over-extended railroads and other projects. He promoted all these railroads and guaranteed them, but they were unsustainable when recession hit. The editor of the *Grand Forks Sun* (a Liberal newspaper) put it bluntly:

> We give him credit for being a shrewd and successful politician but maintain that he lacked the essential sagacity of a statesman. He rode on a wave of marvellous prosperity while in power and acted as if those days of inflated values were endless. Had he been gifted with a deeper foresight, he would have foreseen that the conditions which produced the prosperity were transitory, and would have governed the province less recklessly than he did.

Top: General Currie reviews his battle plan.
From *Canada in Khaki*, 1917

Above: The National Hero: General Currie signed this photo for an admirer.
Courtesy of Don Stewart

Politics aside, the recession and war years were hard for the newspaper business as well. Many closed as advertising dried up. McBride too knew when the game was up. In late 1915, sensing that he could not win another election, he gave up the reins to Attorney General William Bowser and left for his beloved London to take up the post of Agent General. Bowser was left to clean up the mess and suffer defeat when an election was finally held in September 1916.

In London, McBride's star recovered some of its lustre. His friendship with Churchill gave him an influence beyond his modest status. Historian Margaret Ormsby wrote in *British Columbia: A History*:

> Once arrived in the British capital, Sir Richard found companionship in the stimulating little group of Canadians who had already established themselves there in positions of influence...At just the right moment, McBride was able to put in a word on behalf of General Sir Arthur Currie, a fellow Irish-Canadian, whom he had known in Victoria...His influence helped to win for Currie the command of the Canadian Corps in June 1917, in succession to Sir Julian Byng.

For McBride, the year ahead was not good. He had become ill with Bright's disease and it proved fatal. When he realized the end was near, McBride appealed to the new Liberal government back in British Columbia for financial aid to come home. They provided funds but McBride died before he could sail on August 6, 1917.

Under the banner headline "Richard McBride Is Dead," the *Vancouver Province* reminisced:

Sir Richard...during the boom days of the province in the past decade was an unbeatable leader. He was a man of broad vision and imperial views. In going to England, he felt he would be able to do British Columbia a valuable service in an imperialistic way...Sir Richard McBride was once described by Premier Borden as a brilliant young Canadian whose name in British Columbia means to the people of that province much, if not all, that the name of Sir John A. Macdonald meant, and still means to Eastern Canada. And Hon. Winston Churchill...spoke of him at the dinner given in his honor in London as having "high destinies" written in his face.

McBride was just forty-seven. His body was brought back to BC and his public funeral in Victoria was a major event. But he died financially insolvent, putting a lie to suggestions that he had personally benefitted from all the railway expansion that he promoted. According to Patricia Roy in *Boundless Optimism: Richard McBride's British Columbia,* McBride wrote an epitaph of sorts shortly before resigning as premier:

For my own part, I have tried to do my little best and to serve the Province first and the party next. Possibly I may have attempted too much in the end, however, all of the policies I have espoused are bound to reflect creditably on the country.

Currie's Rise

While he was not in command of the Canadian Corps at Vimy Ridge, General Currie was certainly instrumental in the planning that led to a victory there in April 1917. Victoria bombardier Thomas Baxter of the 10th Battery at Vimy remembers Currie's audacity. His interview was put online as part of the project "A City Goes to War" from the University of Victoria Special Collections:

Sending letters home was a ritual for many soldiers.
City of Vancouver Archives, LP 202

General Currie from Victoria was in charge of the Canadian troops. I said to him, "Will the Canadians capture Vimy Ridge?" He said, "I'll try if you'll give me 700 field guns." And they [military headquarters] said, "Where are we going to get 700 field guns?" He says, "I don't know.

If you can't do it, I'm not going to do it." Well, he was very clever, because usually they just had one row of field guns. Well, when you advance, you've got to stop firing and go ahead. When you do that, you let the enemy dig in. His idea was that they have two rows of guns. I was in charge of a gun in the back row. And they fired. And when they were told to stop and go ahead, the other row started firing. So there were shells dropping on the German front lines all the time. We made bridges to get our guns over the German front lines but when we got there, it was so badly blown up, they weren't long enough and we had to detour the long way around. And I only saw one dead Canadian soldier and that amazed me.

That "creeping barrage" made all the difference at Vimy. It pulverized the enemy and prevented machine gunners from setting up again to cut down the Canadian troops. Currie was putting what he was learning into practice, and he was getting noticed. In June 1917, McBride was still alive and his endorsement helped Currie to get full command of the Canadian Corps.

In August, Canadians fought at Hill 70 and in October they went through the horror of Passchendaele. Conscription passed into law that year and Currie had more manpower but he no longer had a strictly volunteer army. In December the federal election brought a Unionist government to power, saving Prime Minister Robert Borden from defeat but not the condemnation that would result from conscription.

In the meantime, Currie carried on. Biographer Tim Cook, in an interview with *Canada's History* magazine, said that Currie was a workaholic:

I don't think anyone would have predicted in 1914 that he would become Canada's greatest battlefield general. He fought under extremely difficult conditions. He was a man who pushed himself relentlessly. He put in 16 and 17 hour days. He barely slept. He was killed by the war ultimately. It shortened his life.

In March 1918, the Germans launched one last major offensive and overran many of the battlefields where Canadians had fought hard to gain ground. Currie wrote to his troops on March 27:

Looking back with pride on the unbroken record of your glorious achievements, asking you to realize that to-day the fate of the British Empire hangs in the balance, I place my trust in the Canadian Corps, knowing that where Canadians are engaged, there can be no giving way. Under the orders of your devoted officers in the coming battle, you will advance, or fall where you stand, facing the enemy.

To those who fall, I say: "you will not die, but step into immortality. Your mothers will not lament your fate, but will be proud to have borne such sons. Your names will be revered forever by your grateful country, and God will take you unto Himself."

Canadians, in this fateful hour, I command you and I trust you to fight as you have ever fought, with all your strength, with all your determination, with all your tranquil courage. On many a hard-fought field of battle, you have overcome this enemy, and with God's help, you will achieve victory once more.

(Sgd.) A.W. Currie, Lieut. Gen., Commanding Canadian Corps

It was cold comfort for Canadian soldiers, and there were reports that copies of the order were thrown aside in disgust. But the Canadians did overcome. The Germans overextended themselves, and with the entry of more Americans into the war effort that summer, the tide gradually turned.

In August, when the picture was a little brighter, Currie delivered his assessment of the work ahead to an audience in London. The speech reflects the feelings of hatred and revenge that reached their zenith in 1918:

Personally, I think that the factor that can be turned in our favour is this: If we stop and fight the Boche, we will kill a sufficient number to make him silly, while America develops enough strength to turn the man power in our favour...Our men do not regard the Boche as a superman; and, remembering the crimes they have committed, we shall never take such delight in killing them as when we next meet them. Germany is simply a mad dog that must be killed, a cancerous growth that must be removed.

After four years of war, the image of Canadians as amateur soldiers was gone and Currie spoke about that to his London audience:

When we came to England first, we were not regarded as the finest fighting soldiers. We had many things said about us unjustly; and suggestions were put about that it was improbable we should ever become good soldiers. Everywhere today, at General Headquarters and all other places, it is recognized that Canadian soldiers are fit to take their place beside the veteran soldiers of the British Army, with whom we are proud to serve.

The same could be said of Currie. It was rumoured that Prime Minister Lloyd George was preparing to put him in charge of all British forces. The war would end before that could happen. But there was still plenty of fighting left in 1918.

Currie led the Canadians through the last hundred days, first at Amiens, then at Canal du Nord, Cambrai, and on the eve of the Armistice, at Mons, retaking the city where British forces first faced the Germans in 1914. After Armistice, Currie exhorted his troops to take no personal vengeance against the civilian population as they marched into Germany:

Some of you have already commenced, while others are about to march on the Rhine, liberating Belgium in your advance. In a few days, you will enter Germany and hold certain parts, in order to secure the fulfilment of the terms of armistice preliminary to the peace treaty. The rulers of Germany, humiliated and demoralized have fled...It is not necessary to say that the population and private property will be respected. You will always remember that you fought for justice, right, and decency, and that you cannot afford to fall short of these essentials, even in the country against which you have every right to feel bitter. Rest assured that the crimes of Germany will receive adequate punishment.

Historian J.L. Granatstein wrote in the *Globe and Mail* that while Canadians should be appalled by the death toll, they should also recognize that those victories shortened the war:

The Hundred Days, that short period running from Aug. 8, 1918, to the armistice on Nov. 11, saw the Canadian Corps score victory after victory against the toughest German defences on the Western Front. The Hundred Days was unquestionably the most decisive campaign ever fought by Canadian troops in battle.

As others have pointed out before us, the sacrifice in blood and treasure was shocking. Sixty thousand Canadians, over six thousand British Columbians among them, killed out of a national population of eight million. Tim Cook did the math and estimated the equivalent death toll today would be 250,000 Canadians killed over a four-year period. That is a staggering figure.

Currie came out of the war on top. But the death toll would come back to haunt him. And so would his clumsy attempts to salvage his real estate business before the war by "borrowing" money that should have paid for militia uniforms. More on that in our concluding chapter.

From Our Listeners: Constance Philip, A Heroic Nursing Sister

By Marianna Harris

My grandfather's cousin, Constance Sarah Young Philip, served in the Canadian Overseas Expeditionary Force as a nursing sister. She was born in Scotland, came to Canada and enlisted on February 24, 1915. She was awarded three medals for her contributions in France, including at Abbeville Hospital. In the fall of 1916 Constance was admitted to hospital herself, then transferred to a sisters' convalescent home. After spending time in hospitals in England, she returned to Canada in 1919 living in West Vancouver and died in 1950 in Essondale. It is my suspicion that she was suffering from dementia also brought on by her service overseas.

Nursing Sister Constance Philip, third from left, with soldiers.
Courtesy of Marianna Harris

From Our Listeners: Major G.D. (Paddy) Cameron, Military Cross

By Lorraine Cameron

My grandfather, Paddy Cameron, joined up in August 1914 at the age of twenty-two years. As a consummate horseman he joined British Columbia Horse in Kelowna. Before very long they were sent to Vernon and then on to Valcartier by train with their horses.

Once there, despite the best efforts of Lieutenant Pyman to get the group from Vernon into a battalion as a platoon, the recruits were told to individually sign up wherever they could. Paddy and several others went to the Lord Strathcona's Horse Regiment. Two of his friends had joined a highland regiment but changed their minds and came with him to the Straths. He recalled how they had done their riding tests in kilts!

Transport overseas was by convoy. The horse boat for the regiment was SS *Monmouth,* the slowest in the convoy. There were five hundred horses on board and Paddy was pleased to say that theirs was the only deck which didn't lose a horse. When horses aren't working and moving much they don't need a lot of grain. Apparently not all those in charge of feeding knew that and a number of horses on the other decks succumbed to colic and were buried at sea.

The regiment spent the balance of 1914 in tents with their horses picketed at Pond's Farm on Salisbury Plain in the south of England. After the New Year they went into billets in a nearby town. On May 4, 1915, the Straths went to France as infantry, leaving the horses in England.

Paddy never spoke about the circumstances in which he distinguished himself and for which he was awarded the Military Cross. Instead his war stories involved funny things that happened to him well away from the front lines. He recalled having two wisdom teeth extracted by an apprentice dentist. It was a bit gory and the apprentice fainted.

At one point he was wounded, it was a single gunshot wound through the calf of his right leg. This brought to an end about thirty-six hours of intensive activity. While he was being transported back from the front lines in a train full of wounded, Paddy fell fast asleep and could not be wakened. The attendant, noting his apparently comatose condition and the large blood stain on his blanket courtesy of the badly wounded German prisoner in the bunk above, labelled Paddy as "gravely wounded."

That phrase was included in the message his mother, at home in Kelowna, received.

While Paddy was recovering at Orpington Hospital just outside London, a friend who was a doctor came to visit at the bidding of Mrs. Cameron. She apparently didn't believe her son when he said it wasn't as serious a wound as first thought. Dr. Campbell managed to get Paddy released for a short time so they could go into London.

Before he left the hospital, a nurse carefully sewed a blue band on the sleeve of his uniform. This was a signal to barmen that the soldier was convalescing and was not to be served a drink. On reaching a hotel in the city, the two young Canadians slipped into the men's room where Dr. Campbell quickly set about snipping off the blue band with his scissors so Paddy could have a drink with him. He was still at his task when a brigadier from the British Army entered the restroom.

Both boys thought as soon as the officer figured out what they were doing, they would be in trouble and likely their evening of fun was over before it really began.

Instead the brigadier, in a very posh accent, said, "I say, would you mind removing mine too?" Needless to say, they were relieved and Dr. Campbell was only too happy to cut off the brigadier's blue band as well.

Paddy felt that being wounded actually saved his life because the Canadian casualties were enormous in the months that followed. His younger brother, Ian, all of twenty-three years, lost his life at Vimy Ridge in April 1917.

When Paddy returned home to Guisachan, the family farm, his dog was waiting for him at the end of the drive where she had been every day for nearly five years. He lived and farmed at Guisachan until shortly before his death at ninety-two in December 1984.

He enlisted as a trooper in 1914 and was discharged as a captain in 1918. During peacetime and World War II he commanded a militia company, having attained the rank of major.

2

OFF TO WAR
TRAINING AND TRENCHES

In September 1914, a story appeared in the *Vernon News* with the headline "Good Riflemen Wanted—Kitchener Would Prefer That Recruits Be Good Shots Rather Than Well Drilled."

"Never mind whether they know anything about drill," Lord Kitchener wrote to his officers. "It does not matter if they don't know their right foot from their left. Teach them how to shoot and do it quickly."

Only weeks into the war, the Western Front was proving to be a bloodbath where conventional armies were quickly swallowed up by the slaughter. Kitchener needed more men who could shoot and fight, not just march and polish badges. British Columbia's soldiers seemed to have the right stuff.

In a CBC Vancouver interview in 1998, Pierre Berton, the author of *Vimy,* said this about the recruits from Western Canada:

The dusty hills of Vernon Camp were the main training grounds for soldiers from around the BC interior region.
Courtesy of Don Stewart

There was a large number who were outdoors people. There were people used to sleeping out in the rain, or digging the equivalent of trenches, or living in sleeping bags or blankets. They were good horsemen—very good at riding. They were good shots...They shot rabbits and squirrels—and some things larger—They knew how to use a gun.

Men who enlisted in BC went for training at a number of camps around the province. Vernon Camp in the north Okanagan drilled many of the men from regiments in the Interior.

Letters from Training Camp

Hubert Evans, who would become one of the province's best-known novelists, joined the 54th Kootenay Battalion in 1915. By June he was training at Camp Vernon.

The young newspaperman wrote back to Nelson, BC, with his observations already showing a literary flair:

Since the day our long train of 15 coaches drew into Vernon station, we have had little time to read the ancient philosophers or study French. It was a very ordinary trip from the region of stern

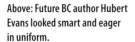

Above: Future BC author Hubert Evans looked smart and eager in uniform.
Courtesy of Touchstones Nelson Museum of Art and History

Left: Postcards were popular with soldiers training at Camp Vernon in the Okanagan. This one shows the Rocky Mountain Rangers tents and insignia.
Courtesy of Greg Dickson

mountains of rock to this place among the milder rolling hills. Undoubtedly you want some news of the camp, and especially of the 54th battalion. Some fatigue uniforms have been served out, and you would not know your old friends now. Everyone is tanned brown, and though the men higher up may not agree with us, we think that some day in the not too distant future, we will be real soldiers.

I will someday send a postal card which will show the camp spread out on a plain between two great hills, with its symmetrical lines of white tents. We were inspected by Col. Davis this afternoon. By "us" I mean the whole battalion. About every other man in A company seems grieved that he didn't make a better showing: but you know how that is—all the same as the blushing soloist at the amateur concert who knocks her act but gets supremely sore when anyone else does the same. *The Vernon News*, I heard someone say, ran a story the other day saying the men of the 54th were

Stories of Camp Life from the *Vernon News*

Thanks to Lorne Adamson at the Vernon Museum for these transcriptions

August 13, 1914: 30th BC Horse Busy Mobilizing

Orders were received last evening by Col. Bott to prepare at once for call for active service—expect to be ready tonight. The big armoury on Mission Hill was a scene of feverish activity this morning...The wished-for news was at once telephoned and telegraphed up and down the valley to the Kelowna, Enderby, Armstrong and Lumby contingents, and already out-of-town detachments were coming in.

Although disappointed at the order that they should mobilize as unmounted troops, the officers and men of the 30th had taken hold of the work with enthusiasm...Nobody knows what their movements will be: but it is hoped by them all that they will be called upon to cross the sea and take part in the great conflict as soon as possible. The men of the Okanagan have given their supreme pledge of devotion to their flag and country by enrolling for service. Their great desire now is for an opportunity to render that service in the most effective manner possible.

June 10, 1915: Well-Behaved Men

Nearly every day sees some fresh arrivals at the camp, and there are now about 2,000 men under canvas on the hill. Two hundred recruits from Vancouver for the 47th arrived yesterday, and 1,000 men of the 54th are expected to reach here from Kootenay on Saturday.

Any apprehension that may have existed in certain quarters that the advent of such a large number of men would create disturbing problems as to the moral welfare of the town must have been pretty well removed by this time. A more orderly or well conducted crowd than the soldiers who throng the city streets in the evenings could not be desired. It is inevitable, of course, that among the thousands of soldiers who will train here, a few turbulent and unruly spirits may be found but we believe that the proportion of these is greatly less than among the same numbers of civilians. These men are here to prepare themselves for service, and they evidently fully realize this fact. They have offered the supreme sacrifice of self-devotion to their country's cause in enlisting to face the foe, and to them soldiering is no pastime or child's play. They are a cheerful and happy looking crowd, but we believe that behind smiling faces is a grim determination to do their best when the time arrives, and an ardent desire to reach the scene of conflict and get into grips with the enemy at the earliest possible moment.

June 29, 1915: No Hard Liquor

Soon after his arrival here the Commandant held a meeting with the license commissioners and hotel men, at which he stated that he would tolerate no excessive use of liquor among the troops under his command. He was here, he said, to see that they were trained for efficient service as quickly and thoroughly as possible, and he would not permit this duty to be hampered in any way by over-indulgence, in intoxicants by either officers or men under his control. He suggested that if possible the hotel keepers would co-operate with him to the extent of seeing that men in uniform were served with nothing stronger than beer. Under this arrangement no liquors except beer and soft drinks are served in any bar during the hours that the soldiers are down town. In order that no invidious distinction should be apparent the rule applies to civilians and soldiers alike, and between the hours of 4:30 and 9 p.m. nobody can obtain a drink of anything stronger than beer in any Vernon hotel.

July 15, 1915: Mobilization Camp

Citizen soldiers encamped at the Central Mobilization Camp on Mission Hill are rapidly rounding into that magnificent condition which has characterized their fellows on the battle line in France, and brought forth considerable praise from British army officers.

Route marches, continual drills, lectures in musketry and machine gun practice, the disposition of forces, first aid work, trench digging and bayonet fighting pack the soldiers' days with incessant activity.

November 18, 1915: Such Fine Troops

His Royal Highness the Duke of Connaught is not wont to deal in superlatives and is noted as being a man of few words, yet this experienced soldier stated most emphatically during his visit here last summer that in all Canada he had not reviewed such fine troops and had seen no camp offering so many advantages for training as the one in Vernon. Major-General Lessard and Colonel J.A. Currie were equally emphatic in expressing their approval and the Camp Commandant, Colonel J. Duff Stuart, after a visit to Sewell and Sarcee, had no hesitation stating that the site and the climate here were greatly superior to those which came under his observation elsewhere.

very well behaved, which might imply that some others were not. Really I think the fellows are "jake" and can be compared with an equal number of civilians with credit.

Everyone is anxious to have the Kootenay battalion canteen opened. A regimental fund for this and other purposes has been started and we look for big things from it. The 47th battalion and the 11th CMR's each have one. Of course they are dry, but all sorts of eats are sold, and both are well patronized by us.

Heading Overseas for Training Camp and Leave in London

When our men got to England, the British military establishment was of the view that many were not yet ready to fight. So there was more training in the muddy fields of the Salisbury Plain and in Kent. The hardship of unremitting rain and living in tents actually killed some men before they made it to the front. Disease spread easily, and the men were vulnerable physically and mentally. It was a sad way to die, though it saved some from the horrors of the trenches.

Private Theo Dickson Writes Home from England

March 18, 1916 (West Sandling, Kent): The first thing we did here was get ready for drill which we did, and we have drilled ever since. It mostly consists of practice and musketry from 8 am to 5:30, then supper and as a rule we sit around and smoke and talk till bed time at 9:30. We all have six days off and free tickets to anywhere in England and Scotland, but I will just see London this trip.

Theo Dickson of Vernon was just 22 years old when he died from illness at a training camp in England.
Courtesy of Greg Dickson

Below: The YMCA provided a home away from home for soldiers on leave in London.
Courtesy of Greg Dickson

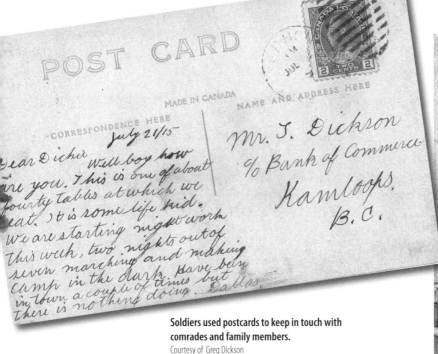

Soldiers used postcards to keep in touch with comrades and family members.
Courtesy of Greg Dickson

April 23, 1916: I just arrived back from London after four days of real pleasure. I spent [one] morning up at the West End checking over the Bank of England and St. Paul's and London Bridge... and it was all grand. After dinner I started out for Westminster Abbey and was just in time to see a society wedding pulled off there, and then I went into the Abbey and as they were holding a service I had to sit down and wait until they were finished. I had the pleasure of meeting one of the most beautiful girls who sat beside me. And I asked her if she would mind showing me through. My good looks must have got her because she did, and she showed me her uncle's grave in there also. So I guessed she must be some society girl which she turned out to be. She was a dream. She took me over to Buck Palace, Hyde Park, Piccadilly and all around, and I took her to a big theatre and it cost me 10. Next day, she came around to the YMCA [where Theo was staying] with her car and took me all over London. Best of it was she ran the car herself. So we were all alone and saw all the different gardens...and stopped at a beautiful house which was her home and had dinner and spent the evening there. Her mother was awful nice to me and they both smoked lovely cigarettes, and I was wishing, "if my mother could only see me now." I was about broke so I said farewell and said I was going home to camp on the morning train. So Miss Eleanor took me back to my YMCA in her car and when I said farewell, she let me hold her dear little hand a few moments longer than was good for me.

June 2, 1916: I have been down to the range again all this week and we start early in the morning and arrive home about 8 pm. I hear from Ted [his brother who was at the front] quite often and he always tells me not to come over to France. Poor kid, I suspect he is afraid I'd get hit, but with you people all praying for us, why we should be ready to meet any danger. My throat and neck are pretty well swollen up and I'm afraid it's mumps...

July 10, 1916 (in hospital): My mail has all gone astray since [my unit] went over to France. I received a couple of letters from the boys over there and the fellow who took my place in the section where I should have been has been killed. So I guess it was God's will that I should go to hospital instead of France. By the time you get this I will be out of hospital. I am sick of England and its beauty. It gets on one's nerves...but I am awful anxious to get home and down to something else. One gets tired of this life but I guess I will be lucky if I get a chance to get over to France as we all expect to be home for Xmas but perhaps not.

Private Theo Dickson died in hospital of spinal meningitis on July 23. He was twenty-two years old.

Westerners at the Front

It must have been a shocker to go from the tedium of a farm or office in British Columbia to a muddy trench in Flanders, surrounded by rats and lice, under enemy fire, your nose constantly assaulted by the stench of dead men and animals. But that was what most recruits faced once the stalemate of trench warfare took hold in the fall of 1914.

Soldiers were loath to share the sorrows of trench life with the folks back home, and most letters contain only veiled references to the horrors they faced. It was not until after the war that more realistic narratives started to surface. Even the newspapers and pictorial magazines contained a whitewashed version of the Western Front. Photographs were staged, or sanitized drawings were used to illustrate articles.

Some newspapers published letters from the front lines because real news of life at the front was hard to come by. The casualty lists and medical reports speak eloquently about the toll that bullets, shrapnel, machine guns and gas took. And through postwar interviews with soldiers, we can piece together a clearer picture of what those young British Columbians faced.

Dolph Browne at Ypres, the Somme and Vimy Ridge

As told to grandson Jeremy Webber

Dolph Browne was an Irishman who had immigrated to Alberta and British Columbia about 1912. In January 1916, he signed up with the 5th University Company, reinforcing the Princess Pats Canadian Light Infantry, and saw action at Ypres, the Somme and Vimy Ridge.

In 1970, his grandson Jeremy Webber interviewed him for a school project. Browne first saw action at Ypres:

> The Ypres Salient was a bulge into the German lines and they held all the hills and we were down in the hole so that you had fire coming in from all directions. And there, our rations and our water had to be carried in every night. If the shelling was too bad, you didn't get any rations or water. The water table was up within three feet of the surface of the ground so that you couldn't make any dugouts. You had to throw up breastworks for trenches. And we just slept in the bottom of the trench when we were in the line.

The Ypres Salient was a ghastly place where the Canadians were exposed all the time. To Browne it seemed hopeless:

> I think the Ypres Salient was the dirtiest place that I ever fought because we would go on the line for five days and lose 90 men and we hadn't done one thing except hold the line. When we went down to the Somme, there we were in two attacks and then we were in supports on attack on the Regina Line. There was a lot more satisfaction to that because you were accomplishing something.

But conditions at the Somme weren't much better:

> Well, at the Somme, we had no shelter at all. You just slept outside because we were pushing the Germans back and you just didn't have any shelter and you just slept outside. As far as the fighting was concerned, it was alright. The things that bothered us most was the wet, and the dirt and the rats and the lice because we didn't have any spray or powder to deal with them.

For an Irishman, used to getting potatoes each day, the food was pretty grim:

> In France, well we usually got a loaf of bread to three men, sometimes four. At breakfast time we had one piece of bacon. At noon, we got mulligan, but it was usually just meat and water with Italian chestnuts thrown in. For months, we didn't see a potato. Then at night, we just had our bread and some jam and tea. In other words, what we got for 24 hours was less than what we would eat in one meal in civil life.

Dolph Browne told his story of the war to a grandson in 1970.
Courtesy of Greg Dickson

Canadian troops in action.
City of Vancouver Archives, LP 61.2

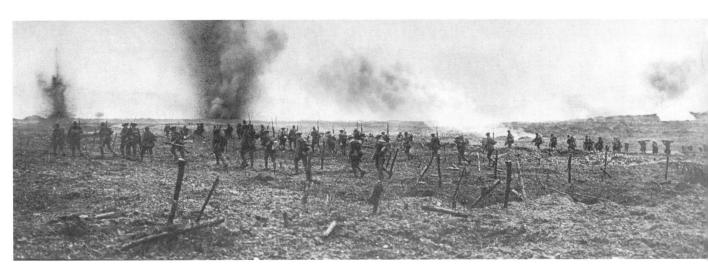

Moving ammunition up to the front line.
From *Canada in Khaki*, 1917

There were iron rations for emergencies. But they weren't much use:

Well, the original iron rations were a can of bully beef, and two hard tack biscuits. But the bully beef wasn't practical because your iron rations were supposed to be used in an emergency. Well when you were in a spot that was an emergency, you didn't have any drinking water. And only a fool would eat highly salted corned beef. In the fall of 1916, they issued a chocolate ration which was very, very highly concentrated. And it was so rich, that it was in a tin. It was impossible to eat a third or at the outside a half of it at one time.

If they took prisoners, they had to feed them out of their own food supply:

Well, the customary thing was that they were fed out of our rations for the first day after they were captured. This didn't always apply if you could get them off your hands quickly but that was the rule. Of course, you didn't take too many prisoners unless you were attacking and advancing.

Sometimes you went into battle without anything to eat:

The night we went in on the attack by Courcelette we had no lunch. We were just going to be served with supper when the order came to fall in and we went around the shoulder of a hill and over the top. And we didn't have any supper. Then we were in there for two nights and day without food or water except what we had in our own water canteen or what we could pick up from men who had been killed.

When soldiers went in on the attack, there was supposed to be a carefully timed artillery barrage but sometimes, things didn't work out as planned:

It was getting dusk and we moved forward to take [a German] trench. It was very strongly held and of course we had lost a lot of men and our commanding officer decided that we weren't strong enough to take it so the order came to retire. I was on the left and there were six bombers covering our flank and when the order came to retire, I walked out about sixty yards to try and contact these bombers and tell them to retire and I couldn't find them. As it happened, they had gone into the

Battle of Passchendaele—wounded Canadians and Germans at a dressing station. Canada suffered close to a quarter of a million casualties during the war.
CWM 19930013-473, George Metcalf Archival Collection, © Canadian War Museum

German trench and they stayed there with the Germans on both sides of them. They stayed there all night and all the next morning. And then about two o'clock in the afternoon, there was a bunch of bombs exploding and the Germans started to pour out over the trench and it looked like an attack. But (actually) the Germans had decided to bomb the six bombers out and instead of that the bombers bombed the Germans out. And when we saw these Germans pouring out over the trench, we opened up with everything we had until they started waving white handkerchiefs and we realized that they wanted to surrender. And if my memory serves me correctly, we took 272 prisoners.

So things were going pretty well for the Princess Pats, but they were a little too far ahead of schedule:

The plan was that, when they last told us to retire the night before, the plan was that they were going to have an artillery barrage on this trench at 20 minutes to 5 in the afternoon and that at 5 o'clock we would go over and take it. So of course, we went over and took it at 2:15 when these Germans were surrendering and they sent two runners back for to call off this barrage. The one runner was evidently killed by shellfire because he was never heard of again. And we heard of the second one about two days later when he was in hospital in England. In other words, they never got there. We went into the trench and were straightening it up and at 20 minutes to 5 when our own guns opened up and gave us an awful pasting. We didn't have any shelter, and it was worse than any German artillery fire that I had ever been in up until that time. I don't know how many men that we lost from our own barrage but when we went in on the attack we had somewhere between 1,000 and 1,100 men and when we came out two days later we had 163.

In October 1916, Browne's unit marched to Vimy Ridge to prepare for the most sophisticated attack the Canadians had been involved in up to that time:

Well of course, we went to Vimy—we got there in the latter part of October. The dugouts were excellent because it was a chalk country and you could dig deep dugouts. We were there all winter because the Vimy attack didn't come until April 9, 1917. And when you're in one location for a matter of five or six months, you can do quite a lot of things to make yourself comfortable.

NOTHING is to be written on this side except the date and signature of the sender. Sentences not required may be erased. If anything else is added the post card will be destroyed.

I am quite well.

I have been admitted into hospital

{ sick. } and am going on well.
{ wounded } and hope to be discharged soon.

I am being sent down to the base.

I have received your { letter dated _____
{ telegram " _____
{ parcel " _____

Letter follows at first opportunity.

I have received no letter from you
{ lately.
{ for a long time.

Signature only.   W. E. Huck

Date Aug 17th

[Postage must be prepaid on any letter or post card addressed to the sender of this card.]

(08871) Wt. W3497-293 4,500m. 7/16 J. J. K. & Co., Ltd.

Communication from the battlefield was often limited to prescribed postcards, like this one from W.E. Huck, who was killed two years into the war. The postcard and death notice arrived back at home at the same time.
Courtesy of Don Stewart

In Loving Memory of

CORP. W. E. HUCK

Who Died for His King and Country

October, 1916

Asleep in Jesus! blessed sleep,
  From which none ever wakes to weep
A calm and undisturbed repose,
  Unbroken by the last of foes.
Asleep in Jesus! far from thee
  Thy kindred and their graves may be,
But thine is still a blessed sleep,
  From which none ever wakes to weep

From Our Listeners: Passing the Eye Test

By Peter Burton, Vancouver

Harry Robert Burton, my father, was born in 1896 and joined the Canadian Army in 1916. He said it was because he was going to fail calculus in his first year of engineering at University of Toronto and the university would promote a student who enlisted to the next year.

My father went to France in 1917 after a year in England and was demobbed in 1919, having ended up in Germany. He was in the Signal Corps but never in the front lines. I am reasonably convinced that any assignment to the front lines was prevented by an important officer, Colonel Elroy Forde (a building is named after him at the Royal Military College in Kingston), who was married to one of my father's aunts.

My father was shortsighted. At the time you could not enlist if you required glasses, but you could wear glasses once you had completed your enlistment.

Sounds a bit like a minor Catch-22. My father said that he had failed the eye test administered by one of his professors. The test was rescheduled for a week subsequent. On the retest he was left to memorize the chart for an hour and then passed the test the second time.

My father also served for six years in World War II, but not overseas, instead serving at Pettawawa, where, among other things, he commanded a unit guarding interned Germans, Ukrainians, Russians, Italians and Canadian communists.

I went to Ypres and Vimy Ridge a couple of years ago. I found it all very moving. While I don't support the Harper government's glorification of Canadians as "warriors," I do think projects like this are very important, particularly with the reflection on the lives of those in Canada and the domestic impact of the war and its aftermath.

When the attack at Vimy finally came in April 1917, Browne was hit before he could put up much of a fight:

> We attacked right from the position we had been holding for six months. Up in front of Neuville St. Vaast. I didn't see much of the fighting because we moved off on the attack about 20 minutes to 5 and I got over about a mile and a quarter and I got hit in the foot with a spent bullet and had to crawl back. I had to crawl back a mile and a quarter to our own line, and when I got there, our colonel quizzed me on what had been happening and then he went out and got four German prisoners and made them pack me back on a stretcher to the light railway. At the base near Mt. St. Eloi, they had a field ambulance and we were lying on stretchers on the ground and they picked us up with ambulances and took us back to the railhead. And sometime late that afternoon we were put on the train for Boulogne. And the next morning I was operated on at the Boulogne Hospital and two days later moved to England.

That was the last time he saw action:

> I was in the Norfolk and Norwich Hospital for about seven weeks and then was sent to the convalescent camp at Epsom, and from there I got passed as fit to train for France again. And after spending a leave at my old home in Ireland, I came back to Seaford and put in one morning on the parade ground and was back in hospital for four and a half months.

Ted Dickson joined the Canadian Army Medical Corps and became a stretcher bearer.
Courtesy of Greg Dickson

Ted Dickson, Stretcher Bearer in the Canadian Army Medical Corps

Ted Dickson signed up in Vernon in September 1915. He was eighteen years old and was soon working as a stretcher bearer with the 1st Canadian Army Field Ambulance on the Western Front. He kept a trench diary in 1916 and early 1917, which was discovered in his papers many years later. While at the front, he learned that his older brother Theo had suddenly died at a training camp in England.

> August 16, 1916: Heard of the death of my dear brother Theo. He died on the July 23rd Sunday which I shall never forget. Poor kid. The people at home must [have] suffered a lot from the shock and sorrow.

The next month, he found himself in a German trench and was impressed with the work the Germans had done to make themselves comfortable:

Above: Men gathered for drills in Hastings Park in Vancouver.
Stuart Thomson photo, Vancouver Public Library 8730

Left: A standard kit for a British Columbia soldier.
Harold Smith photo, Vancouver Public Library 18400

September 8, 1916: Up the line is a German dugout which the Australians took and then the Canadians relieved them. They certainly do nice dugouts, soft as can be made, step down and about forty feet below the ground. This one has wallpaper in it. It's some joint. One would think they were going to stay here for keeps.

In April 1917 he was at Vimy for the big attack:

April 4, 1917: Spent the morning going for water about a mile away. Coming back, Fritz put one about ten yards ahead [a shell or grenade], and trench mortars, and killed a man right in a dugout. One fellow was standing on top. He was going through the air. I was behind a plank and shrapnel was coming all around me. [Another soldier] was ahead of me, and then he beat it around a corner and I followed down a dugout. We got half buried because Fritz puts one in the doorway. Ten minutes after, we beat it for our dugout and then we had five stretcher cases. We got about fifty yards from our dressing area ramps and Fritz blew up some more trench mortars—and also a bridge. A very exciting time.

Ted Dickson survived Vimy but that was the last diary entry from the front. Years later, one Sunday morning, he sat down and wrote an unusual letter to his maker in which he described another incident at Vimy:

What about that time at Vimy Ridge after we delivered the stretcher case and they started shelling? And the shells started exploding around me and I jumped in a hole, and a rat was a foot away from my face, and he was wounded and bleeding. And [through] the light of shells exploding I could see I had a friend, and that minute I knew you were there with me and the rat.

Exploding shells were powerful enough to gouge deep holes into the ground, like the ones seen here.
E.T. Sampson photo, City of Vancouver Archives, Gr War P18

From Our Listeners: Surviving the Trenches

By Michael Kew, Vancouver, with help from Eileen (Kew) Seale, Quesnel

James Edward Kew was born December 23, 1897, in Beamsville, Ontario. He attended the local school and assisted his older brothers and sisters in the operation of the family farm and orchard. Like other patriotic youth, James joined one of many informal militia camps which sprang up after war broke out in August 1914. According to his sister, Anna, their mother thought James—then just sixteen—was simply continuing on with something like Boy Scouts.

On November 5, 1914, the 4th Canadian Mounted Rifles was formed and assigned to the Canadian Expeditionary Force. Recruitment of twenty-eight officers and 577 men from existing cavalry units and their informal militia began, and James joined the 4th CMR. The regiment was billeted in the Canadian National Exhibition grounds in Toronto. Seven hundred horses were assigned and training began.

In May 1915, the regiment responded positively to a request to volunteer for overseas service as a dismounted unit. On July 18, the 4th CMR sailed and arrived July 29, moving immediately to training camps in South England. On October 24, 1915, James joined "Battalion in Field," and in December 1915, the regiment experienced its first tour of duty in trenches in Belgium.

At the end of May 1916, the unit participated in the Battle of the Somme, taking over trenches at Sanctuary Wood. At sunrise on June 2, they suffered one of the most intensive bombardments of the war. The Canadian front line trenches and connectors were demolished by shells and a mine which exploded just after noon. On June 4, three officers out of twenty-two, and seventy-three men out of 680 in the 4th CMR answered to their names. The 1st and 5th CMR were equally devastated, and the survivors were withdrawn to Divisional Reserve and into billets at Steenvoorde. Empty ranks were refilled and by July 23, the reconstituted 4th CMR relieved the 5th CMR in the old battle lines of June 2.

> *Mike Kew: While I was driving Mom and Dad from their rented condo in Vancouver up to the Cariboo, the year he died [1968], as we approached Lytton, one of them said, "It's June 2nd." Dad said they always made a point of remembering this date because of his escape from disaster, and then I heard for the first and only time about his experience. He said that he and a chum, who had been together since joining up, survived the first blast of shells which destroyed everything around them. They decided to run to the rear by following successive blasts which passed them over, so they ran as hard as they could toward each blast to their rear. Dad said they were both young and in good physical shape and both arrived safely in the rear positions beyond the shelling. They survived by running out of it.*
>
> *Eileen Seale: When I was a grown woman, one day in early November, Dad and I were sitting outside enjoying the afternoon sun of the late fall. I asked him, "Dad, what was it like in the war? He looked away, was very quiet, then said softly, "I can never tell you."*

James remained with the 4th CMR throughout their service in the Somme (1916), Vimy Ridge (1916–17), Passchendaele (1917), the German Offensive (1917–18) and Cambrai and Mons (1918). On February 14, 1919, they returned to England. James Kew was among the thirty-two original men and officers who returned with the unit.

The battalion arrived in Halifax, March 17, 1919, and Toronto three days later. They were "dismissed" and James returned to his family in Beamsville, being "struck off strength" and discharged on May 17, 1919.

> *Mike: James's older sister Marie told me that he spent the summer and winter of 1919–20 living at home and recovering his health. He himself told me he had "trench mouth" and what he thought was scurvy, for his teeth were loose and slow to recover. Marie also said he drank all of his brother Victor's hard cider that winter (after the rum rations of the trenches and country wines, dry towns like Beamsville must have been hard to accept).*

In or about 1920, James left Beamsville and headed west. He may have joined one of the groups of unemployed men who were offered free or cheap rail transportation to the prairie provinces to assist with grain harvest. He is known to have worked in CNR bridge construction in Saskatchewan, and also spent time as an assistant to a blacksmith and as a telephone lineman near Banff.

> *Mike: I never asked how long Dad had been at Banff, but when the job on the telephone line concluded, as with most such short-term summer projects, the men would have been laid off. I suspect it was at this point that Dad decided to take a CPR train westward. In any case he did tell me that he and another chap got off the train in Ashcroft, picked up their packs and set off for the goldfields of the Cariboo.*
>
> *I believe Dad worked at various mines in the area, at Keithley Creek, perhaps. He probably did not stay long there, for he and another backpacker decided to cross over the Snowshoe Plateau to Barkerville where Dad stayed for several years.*

In the late twenties, he met Beatrice Strand of Quesnel, whom he married in 1931. In 1936, James Kew was appointed federal fisheries inspector for the Cariboo, a position he held until his retirement in 1964. The Bowron Lake property and cabin that Jim and Bea established in the 1940s remains in the family, maintained, enjoyed and appreciated by their descendants.

> *Eileen: Dad's work as fisheries inspector took him away for days at a time—sometimes weeks—working alone in the bush checking salmon streams, counting fish, clearing logjams and navigating stormy lakes. We used to worry about him getting sick or hurt, or encountering an angry moose or grizzly. He did carry a firearm, but no communications device. Whatever potential hazards and dangers were out there, they must have seemed nothing to him, compared to the World War I horrors he could not speak about.*

Trench journals were popular with the troops because they were written mostly by soldiers.
Courtesy of Don Stewart

Trench art made from a shell from the BC Regiment Collection.
Courtesy of Greg Dickson

THE·LISTENING·POST

BRITISH COLUMBIA

6ᵗʰ Duke of Connaught's Rifles | 11ᵗʰ Irish Fusiliers | 88ᵗʰ Victoria Fusiliers
102ⁿᵈ Rocky Mountain Rangers | 104ᵗʰ New Westminster Fus | West Kootenay Rifles
Reinforcing — Battalions — 11ᵗʰ. 30ᵗʰ. 47ᵗʰ

CANADA

PRINTED BY KIND PERMISSION OF LT. COL. ODLUM, OFFICER COMMANDING 7TH CANADIAN INFANTRY BATTALION
CENSORED BY CHIEF CENSOR. IST . CAN . DIV.. — CAPT W. F. ORR. EDITOR I/CPL. H. MAYLOR. NEWS EDITOR.

Nᵒ 7   **BRITISH EX. FORCE, FRANCE OCT 29. 1915.**   **PRICE 1 d.**

Why Listening Post ?

Neither has it any connection with the comfortable lucrative appointment, (in better English "cushy job") you hope to enjoy when you've ceased to sweat your soul case out on the plains of Flanders.

Well what the H... is it then? What the H... Bill. What the H... I beg your pardon I was still thinking of the gluttonous British Householder with the morning paper, his asthmatic spouse and his bacon and eggs. I'm trying to put him off, until he's got his mouth empty, and can get some of his teetotal ideas off the hooks.

It is not true that we've been accused of having for one man in the firing line, ten behind. The people who are supposed to have said it are fas too polite. Personally we believe that one well fed man is as good as three half starved. Also we would institute a special pluperfect particular Rum Corps, who would see we got our three ha'pennoth regularly. All t e excellent blundering, misinformed, busybodies who would preach teetotalism at 4am. on the parapet, have no idea what it is like to be in a British trench in the "wee sma' hoors" when the vital tide is at its lowest abb. There are no teetotalers in the trench at that hour, when the rum comes round.

We were in the trench at Fleurbaix time 4 am. We walked along slipping on the muddy boards, at times a puddle taking us well over the boot tops. The sentry gazing through a drizzle of misty rain, grunted an verbose response to our morning salutation. Everyone was depressed, and the world seemed sad slushy and sunk in a sea of mud and dispendency.

Then someone passed carrying a pannikin, he was followed by another. In the east a grey sorrowful dawn was struggling with the dismal desolate darkness. Then someone commenced to whistle, and further off a few words of a song rose in the gloom. Down the trench three figures round an object on the ground were laughing. As I approached a voice said " have some rum Old Dear?" The object on the ground was a rum bottle. We declined not because we didn't want it but because it was now required in the trench. As we left the trench the day was brightening in the east, and the whole trench was singing. And as we crawled into our dug-out we reflected that after all good wine gladeneth the heart,

All this is not explaining what a Listening Post is. A Listening Post may be described as a verbulous non-luminosity of intense optic and acoustic acuity. I dont know what this means and Archbishop W......s says it sounds like swearing.

Over in front of the parapet of our trench lies what the poetic call No Man's Land, It has been aptly described as the only neutral country in Europe.

Now although this country is neutral, we and the gentle Germaus have to find out what is the state of affairs pertaining to this spot, as is the fashion with other neutral countries. Therefore we send out our listening posts. As with other ambassadors, pleinpotenticous (that takes some spelling and the editor says its rubbish. however I think it looks poetry good, and after all I m writing the " leader ") and enough extraordinaires, ours has to be a diplomatist.

He wears no diplomatic service uniform, he speaks not meaning one thing with his lips another with his eyes. He talks but that in whispers and always to the point, his dress is khaki and mud and mainly the latter.

Our envoy does not spend his days in a foreign clime, hung round with dispatch boxes and foreign decoctions. His hours are those of the Tom cat from dusk to dawn, his pleasure to arrive as far towards the gentle Germans as possible and his only decoration is his rifle.

As others play with cypher and code, so he has his own private wire. Tied to his little finger or toe according to taste.

One Pull.	The Boots.
Two Pulls.	The Chambermaid
Three Pulls.	The Bell Hop
Four Pulls.	Send up the drinks
Five Pulls.	And more.

(To be continued)

Hotel Grandevue de la Hun

Aug. 28th.   *DAILY BULLETIN*   8 a.m.

A Daylight Robbery took place sometime yesterday afternoon when a light fingered gentleman passing down. Humble Str. at a time when it was comparatively deserted stole our advertisement off the boarding. In consideration of the fact that it had no commercial value we believe this gentleman must have been paid to destroy our advertising matter by the manager of the " Hirsch Hotel". Anyway last evening when the manager of that hotel and some of his friends had occasion to pass nur doors they were noticed to have very happy countenances. Of course such an act of spite as this evidently was, cannot possibly benefit them very much. However we have decided to employ two experts to run the perpetrators to earth.

12.30 p.m.

Our two experts Messrs Davis and Ormrod, both famous for their ability in running to earth and for their connection with the Med. Profession, report that, after a minute examination of the nails, which they evidently forgot to take, they have come to the conclusion that the thief must have been under the influence of Chlorinated water. There was also a strong smell of B. S. a very powerful drug used in the manufacture of No. 9's. Evidently the plot thickens. Messrs Davis and Ormrod are working on the clue and expect to

Extra, Extra! Get Your Trench Journal!

The military drew from all walks of life, including journalists, poets and cartoonists. It wasn't long before this brain trust produced various news sheets and magazines right from the trenches. Some were even crafted aboard the troop ships. They were created by soldiers for soldiers and often featured satirical prose, poetry, complaints, regimental sporting news, honour rolls, military decorations and jokes along the lines of "Don't put your rum issue in your tea. You might spill the tea." Or "First soldier: Do you think we're winning the war? Second soldier: I don't know. I haven't seen the paper today." Most of these sheets disintegrated in the muddy trenches, but some were sent home and collections are now housed in the Canadian War Museum.

Here are some of our favourite trench journal titles, where dark humour and irony are on full display:

The Brazier at the Front—16th Battalion Canadian Scottish (includes the Seaforth Highlanders from Vancouver)

The Canadian Machine Gunner—Canadian Machine Gun Corps

The Dead Horse Corner Gazette: A Monthly Journal of Breezy Comment—4th Battalion

In and Out—Canadian Field Ambulance

The Message from Mars—4th Canadian Division

The Western Scot—Victoria's Western Scots 67th Battalion

The Whizz Bang—207th Battalion

The Shell Hole Advance

The Briny—*Somewhere in the Atlantic*

M & D (Medicine & Duty)—Victoria, 11th Canadian Field Ambulance

The Busy Beaver—Royal Canadian Engineers

The Listening Post—7th Canadian Infantry (1st British Columbia Regiment)

Prime Minister Robert Borden sent a letter to the *Listening Post* on its second anniversary in May 1917:

From time to time I have had the privilege and pleasure of reading this very interesting paper established and conducted under such novel and remarkable conditions, and I have been struck by the ability and wit displayed by the contributors. To the men at the front it must be a great source of interest and diversion; to those at home in Canada it is in itself a message telling of the splendid cheerfulness and indifference to hardship with which our gallant men are defending our institutions and our liberties.

Above: The mud that soldiers experienced while training in Vernon was nothing like what they would soon face in the trenches and on the battlefields of the Western Front.
Courtesy of Don Stewart

Left: Troops transfer a mountain of gear from Kamloops to training camp at Vernon.
Courtesy of Don Stewart

3

ORDINARY MEN, EXTRAORDINARY COURAGE
OUR VICTORIA CROSS RECIPIENTS

Leaf through this chapter. Look at the faces. Some are grown men. Some look like kids. British Columbia regiments and British Columbia men were put in some very hot spots during the war. They did their best and many died trying. At least sixteen Victoria Crosses can be linked in one way or another to our province. The recipients served in the infantry, as stretcher bearers, in the Royal Navy Reserve, in cavalry units, as pipers, and in the regiments of other Allied countries.

They earned their honours at sea, on the Western Front, and in Mesopotamia. Some were killed in action. Others lived to tell their grandchildren about events half a world away. Some went on to distinguished careers after the war. At least one ended up broke on skid row.

Some of BC's Victoria Cross recipients displayed on a Beatty Street mural in Vancouver.
Courtesy of Greg Dickson

They came back to the cities and small towns of Western Canada and their acts of valour were often forgotten. But after all they'd been through, some even served again in World War II.

Here are the remarkable sixteen.

Holding Back the Enemy at Ypres: Captain Edward Bellew, 7th Battalion (BC Regiment)

Captain Edward Bellew was born on the high seas in 1882, according to his attestation papers. He attended the Royal Military College at Sandhurst, served with the Royal Irish Regiment around the turn of the century and then emigrated to Canada in 1903 to work with the Department of Public Works as a civil engineer. When war broke out in 1914, he was already an experienced military man. Like many other British nationals, Bellew was among the first to sign up in September 1914 and joined the 7th Battalion (BC Regiment).

Most men thought the war would be over quickly and Bellew confidently left his wife behind in North Vancouver while he went overseas to mop things up. He was thirty-one, over six feet tall and in fine fighting form. By April 1915, he was in the thick of the action at Ypres. His machine-gun post came under overwhelming attack and his sergeant was killed. Bellew was wounded but fought on until his ammunition ran out and he was captured. He spent the rest of the war as a prisoner.

The Canadians were hit with gas at Ypres and Bellew's medical records show he had gas poisoning. In 1917 he was moved to internment in Switzerland. He was finally released in December 1918. In 1919, his valour at Ypres was recognized with the awarding of the Victoria

Captain Edward Bellew won his Victoria Cross at Ypres.
Courtesy of the Department of National Defence

Many soldiers adopted pets like these to provide some comfort far from home.
CWM 19920085-199, George Metcalf Archival Collection, © Canadian War Museum

Cross. Bellew returned to Canada where he continued to work in surveying and construction. He retired to Monte Creek near Kamloops where he spent his last years, living on until 1961. Heroism ran in the family. A second cousin from Scotland also won the VC.

Citation: For most conspicuous bravery and devotion to duty near Keerselaere on 24th April, 1915, during the German attack on the Ypres salient. Capt. (then Lieut.) Bellew, as Battalion Machine Gun Officer, had two guns in action on the high ground overlooking Keerselaere. The enemy's attack broke in full force on the morning of the 24th against the front and right flank of the Battalion— the latter being exposed owing to a gap in the line. The right Company was soon put out of action, but the advance was temporarily stayed by Capt. Bellew, who had sited his guns on the left of the right Company. Reinforcements were sent forward but they in turn were surrounded and destroyed. With the enemy in strength less than 100 yards from him, with no further assistance in sight, and with his rear threatened, Capt. Bellew and Serjt. Peerless, each operating a gun, decided to stay where they were and fight it out. Serjt. Peerless was killed and Capt. Bellew was wounded and fell. Nevertheless, he got up and maintained his fire till ammunition failed and the enemy rushed the position. Capt. Bellew then seized a rifle, smashed his machine gun, and fighting to the last, was taken prisoner.—*London Gazette*, no. 31340, May 15, 1919

Determined to Do His Part: Rowland Bourke, Royal Naval Volunteer Reserve

This mild-mannered Kootenay fruit farmer was rejected by all three arms of service because of his eyesight, but Rowland Bourke persisted until he found a place in Royal Naval Volunteer Reserve working on motor launches. His Victoria Cross came in 1918 when he worked tirelessly to rescue men from ships sunk in a blockade effort in Belgium (for the whole story, see Chapter 4).

Citation: Volunteered for rescue work in command of *Motor Launch 276,* and followed *Vindictive* into Ostend, engaging the enemy's machine guns on both piers with Lewis guns. After *ML 254* had backed out, Lieut. Bourke laid his vessel alongside *Vindictive* to make further search. Finding no one, he withdrew, but hearing cries in the water, he again entered the harbour, and after a prolonged search, eventually found Lieutenant Sir John Alleyne, and two ratings, all badly wounded, and in the water, clinging to an upended skiff, and he rescued them. During all this time the motor launch was under very heavy fire at close range, being hit in fifty-five places, once by a 6 in. shell—two of her small crew being killed and others wounded. The vessel was seriously damaged and speed greatly reduced. Lieut. Bourke, however, managed to bring her out and carry on until he fell in with a Monitor, which took him in tow. This episode displayed daring and skill of a very high order, and Lieut. Bourke's bravery and perseverance undoubtedly saved the lives of Lieut. Alleyne and two of the *Vindictive's* Crew.

The Last Great Cavalry Charge: Lieutenant Gordon Flowerdew, Lord Strathcona's Horse

Gordon Flowerdew once confided to a friend that the bar was so high for winning the Victoria Cross that it would probably cost the recipient his life. That proved to be the case when Flowerdew led one of the few cavalry charges of the war at Moreuil Wood in 1918. He was killed in action and awarded the Victoria Cross posthumously (for more on Flowerdew and his roots in Walhachin, see Chapter 7).

Walhachin's Gordon Flowerdew was killed while leading one of the last cavalry charges in 1918.
Courtesy of the Department of National Defence

Citation: For most conspicuous bravery and dash when in command of a squadron detailed for special service of a very important nature. On reaching the first objective, Lieutenant Flowerdew saw two lines of the enemy, each about sixty strong, with machine guns in the centre and flanks, one line being about two hundred yards behind the other. Realising the critical nature of the operation and how much depended upon it, Lieutenant Flowerdew ordered a troop under Lieutenant Harvey, VC, to dismount and carry out a special movement while he led the remaining three troops to the charge. The squadron (less one troop) passed over both lines, killing many of the enemy with the sword; and wheeling about galloped at them again. Although the squadron had then lost about 70 per cent of its numbers, killed and wounded, from rifle and machine-gun fire directed on it from the front and both flanks, the enemy broke and retired. The survivors of the squadron then established themselves in a position where they were joined, after much hand-to-hand fighting, by Lieutenant Harvey's party. Lieutenant Flowerdew was dangerously wounded through both thighs during the operation, but continued to cheer on his men. There can be no doubt that this officer's great valour was the prime factor in the capture of the position.—*London Gazette,* no. 30648, April 24, 1918

Capturing Hill 70: Sergeant Major Robert Hanna, 29th Battalion (Tobin's Tigers)

Robert Hanna, one of Tobin's Tigers, earned his VC at Hill 70.
Courtesy of the Department of National Defence

Robert Hanna's tight-lipped grin stands out among the band of brothers that grace the mural on Vancouver's Beatty Street. He was one of the lucky Victoria Cross recipients to live a long life, passing on in Mount Lehman in 1967. Hanna was an Irishman, born in County Down. He came out to Canada in the early 1900s and was nearly thirty when he joined up in November 1914 at Vancouver. He listed his trade as lumberman. Hanna caught the German measles in 1916. But there are no indications he suffered any other injuries. He earned his Victoria Cross at Hill 70 in August 1917 by capturing a fortified machine-gun post that had repelled several other attacks with heavy casualties. Hanna led the team of men who finally took the position and used his bayonet to kill three of the enemy. It was a bloody affair under desperate circumstances. But persisting after seeing other men mowed down must have taken courage.

> Citation: For most conspicuous bravery in attack, when his company met with most severe enemy resistance and all the company officers became casualties. A strong point, heavily protected by wire and held by a machine gun, had beaten off three assaults of the company with heavy casualties. This Warrant Officer under heavy machine gun and rifle fire, coolly collected a party of men, and leading them against this strong point, rushed through the wire and personally bayoneted three of the enemy and brained the fourth, capturing the position and silencing the machine gun.
>
> This most courageous action, displayed courage and personal bravery of the highest order at this most critical moment of the attack, was responsible for the capture of a most important tactical point, and but for his daring action and determined handling of a desperate situation the attack would not have succeeded.
>
> C.S./M. Hanna's outstanding gallantry, personal courage and determined leading of his company is deserving of the highest possible reward.
>
> —*London Gazette,* no. 30372, November 8, 1917

He Chose War over Homesteading: Private John Chipman "Chip" Kerr, 49th Batallion (Edmonton Regiment)

TOLD WITH HELP FROM GRANDSONS IAN AND GRAHAM KERR

John Chipman Kerr was a lot like other young Canadians who signed up in the early years of the war. He was toughened by his experiences in the bush of Western Canada and he was ready for something more exciting. Born in Nova Scotia, Kerr came to British Columbia to work as a lumberjack in the Kootenays. Then he and his brother Roland decided to give homesteading a try and found a place in Spirit River, Alberta. They stuck to it for a while, but

Chip Kerr captured dozens of prisoners under heavy fire.
Courtesy of the Department of National Defence

by September 1915 they had had enough. As the story goes, they closed up the cabin and headed for Edmonton to enlist, leaving only a terse message on the cabin door: War is Hell, but what is homesteading?

That sums up pretty well the motivation of a lot of young Canadians. Farming or working in a bank was tedious compared to the glamour of London or Paris and deeds of valour at the front. The farming brothers were soon in the thick of battle, serving with the 49th Edmonton Battalion.

Chip Kerr's moment of glory would come at Courcelette in September 1916, where the British first introduced tanks into battle. Kerr was twenty-nine years old and spoiling for a fight. He got his wish. The citation for his Victoria Cross captures the action well.

Citation: For most conspicuous bravery. During a bombing attack he was acting as bayonet man, and, knowing that bombs were running short, he ran along the parados under heavy fire until he was in close contact with the enemy, when he opened fire on them at point-blank range, and inflicted heavy loss. The enemy, thinking they were surrounded, surrendered. Sixty-two prisoners were taken and 250 yards of enemy trench captured. Before carrying out this very plucky act one of Private Kerr's fingers had been blown off by a bomb. Later, with two other men, he escorted back the prisoners under fire, and then returned to report himself for duty before having his wound dressed.—*London Gazette*, no. 29802, October 26, 1916

The German trenches that Kerr was ordered to take were heavily fortified. The new tanks added to the general confusion. The British and Canadians had the advantage. But 250 yards of trench proved to be more resistant. It fell upon Chip Kerr and his men to take that stretch.

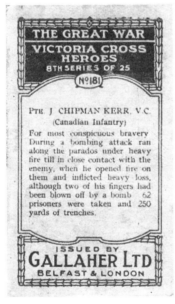

Victoria Cross recipient Chip Kerr was the subject of a popular cigarette card series.
Courtesy of Ian Kerr

They jumped in and started working their way along it until they encountered a sentry who threw a grenade. Kerr put up his hand to protect his face and the explosion took off his finger. Then both sides started bombing each other and it became difficult to see a way forward. At that point, Kerr jumped out of the trench and made his way along the top of the back wall—the parados. According to some accounts, his rifle jammed so he took the rifle of his second bayonet man and kept firing. Finally, deciding that all was lost, the enemy soldiers surrendered and Kerr was able to get some treatment for his damaged hand.

"Chip lost a part of his little finger on his left hand in the attack," grandson Graham told us. "It didn't seem to slow him up much."

Kerr received British Columbia's third Victoria Cross in the war. And Kerr, just a regular guy, was a national hero. His portrait was painted by A.Y. Jackson, his face appeared on cigarette cards, and he earned a lifetime annuity along with his decoration. Chip survived the war but his brother Roland wasn't as lucky. He was killed in 1917 at Passchendaele.

John Chipman Kerr returned to his homestead and raised a family. He never did enjoy farming much and worked in the oil fields and as a forest ranger. His cabin still stands in Spirit River. A mountain in the Rockies was named after him. And during World War II, he re-enlisted, returning to British Columbia where he worked as a service policeman. He told the family at one point he had spotted a Japanese sub lading water in a remote inlet. Paddling out in a small boat to drive the sub away, he was surprised when the Japanese crew invited him on board and served him a meal. According to Chip, they let him return to shore, confident that he was not a threat.

After the war, he retired to Port Moody, BC. On February 19, 1963, he died at age seventy-six and was buried in Mountain View Cemetery, Vancouver.

Fighting for a Country That Interned His Countrymen: Corporal Filip Konowal, 47th Battalion (Westminster Regiment)

BC was not a friendly place for Ukrainian Canadians in 1914. They were considered enemy aliens, citizens of the Austro-Hungarian Empire, even though their natural allegiance did not lie there. Many were interned in camps across the province, and even in the camps they were second-class citizens, forced to do heavy labour building roads and breaking rock. So the fact that Filip Konowal served and served with such distinction is an incredible story. There is a plaque dedicated to his accomplishments outside the drill hall in New Westminster, the home of the regiment he served in. As it says, he was personally awarded the Victoria Cross by King George V in London for valour at Hill 70 in 1917. He killed at least sixteen of the enemy in the assault. He was severely wounded but went on to fight with the Siberian Canadian Expeditionary Force when the war was over. He died in Ottawa in 1959. We'll tell more of Konowal's story in Chapter 14.

Filip Konowal

Born in Urkaine, Filip Konowal emigrated to British Columbia in 1913. While serving as a Corporal with the 47th Battalion of the Canadian Expeditionary Force, he fought with exceptional valour in August 1917, near Lena, France. For this, His Majesty King George V personally conferred the Victoria Cross on Konowal, in London, on 15 October 1917, stating " Your exploit is one of the most daring and heroic in the history of the army. For this, accept my thanks." Konowal also served with the Canadian Siberian Expeditionary Force, finally returning to Vancouver in June 1919, having served three years and 357 days. He died in Ottawa in 1959.

Citation: For most conspicuous bravery and leadership when in charge of a section in attack. His section had the difficult task of mopping up cellars, craters and machine-gun emplacements. Under his able direction all resistance was overcome successfully, and heavy casualties inflicted on the enemy. In one cellar he himself bayonetted three enemy and attacked single-handed seven others in a crater, killing them all.

On reaching the objective, a machine-gun was holding up the right flank, causing many casualties. Cpl. Konowal rushed forward and entered the emplacement, killed the crew, and brought the gun back to our lines.

The next day he again attacked single-handed another machine-gun emplacement, killed three of the crew, and destroyed the gun and emplacement with explosives.

This non-commissioned officer alone killed at least sixteen of the enemy, and during the two days' actual fighting carried on continuously his good work until severely wounded.—*London Gazette*, no. 30400, November 26, 1917

Top: A Ukrainian Canadian hero, Filip Konowal. King George V personally conferred the Victoria Cross in 1917.
Courtesy of the Department of National Defence

Above: The Ukrainian community erected this plaque at the New Westminster Drill Hall.
Courtesy of Greg Dickson

Courage at Canal du Nord: Lieutenant Graham Tomson Lyall, 102nd Battalion

Lieutenant Graham Lyall was born in Manchester and moved to Ontario but signed up in 1914 when the war broke out and ended up with the 102nd Battalion, a northern BC unit. His Victoria Cross came at Canal du Nord in 1918 when he overran a heavily defended position and captured dozens of prisoners. He returned to England in 1919 and eventually served again

Graham Lyall captured dozens of prisoners at Cambrai and put nine machine guns out of action.
Courtesy of the Department of National Defence

in World War II, rising to the rank of colonel. In 1941, he died of a heart attack in Egypt, where he is buried.

> Citation: For most conspicuous bravery and skilful leading during the operations north of Cambrai.
>
> On September 27th, 1918, whilst leading his platoon against Bourlon Wood, he rendered invaluable support to the leading company, which was held up a by a strong point, which he captured, by a flank movement, together with thirteen prisoners, one field gun and four machine guns.
>
> Later, his platoon, now much weakened by casualties, was held up by machine guns at the southern end of Bourlon Wood. Collecting any man available, he led them towards the strong point, and springing forward alone, rushed the position single-handed and killed the officer in charge, subsequently capturing at this point forty-five prisoners and five machine guns. Having made good his final objective, with a further capture of forty-seven prisoners, he consolidated his position and thus protected the remainder of the company.
>
> On October 1st, in the neighbourhood of Blecourt, when in command of a weak company, by skilful dispositions he captured a strongly defended position, which yielded eighty prisoners and seventeen machine guns.
>
> During two days of operations Lt. Lyall captured in all 3 officers, 182 other ranks, 26 machine guns and one field gun, exclusive of heavy casualties inflicted. He showed throughout the utmost valour and high powers of command.—*London Gazette*, no. 31067, December 14, 1918

Canada's Most Decorated Soldier: Lieutenant-Colonel John MacGregor, 2nd Canadian Mounted Rifles

Granddaughter Jaye Roter wrote to us:

John MacGregor was trapping and fishing near Prince Rupert when the war broke out.
Courtesy of the Department of National Defence

> He was a great man, and I am very proud of what he did for our country. Not having met my grandfather, I am not completely sure what gave him his toughness. I do know, however, that my dad had that same toughness, and must have got his personality traits from his dad. Both men had a strong code of honour and great pride. If you set out to do something, you did it to the very best of your ability. There was no doing things halfway—it was all or nothing. There was great "MacGregor" pride, and yes, the MacGregors were descendants of Rob Roy!

John MacGregor was from Cawdor, near Nairn. He was living on a croft and it is said that he left Scotland because he didn't want to be beholden to the local laird. After his father died, he decided to emigrate to Canada—a land of opportunity and open space. That was 1909. In 1912, he was in the Prince Rupert area, where he learned to trap and fish and build his own cabin. News travelled slowly in the bush and it wasn't until about six months after the war began that MacGregor learned of it. After a long trek out, he arrived at Prince Rupert looking pretty grim. Recruiters in Prince Rupert wouldn't have him so he headed for Vancouver, where he was able to sign up in March 1915. He listed his trade as carpenter and mentioned previous military experience at the Nairn Garrison.

MacGregor made it home to Cawdor for a short visit with his family before heading for Ypres and then the Somme. In April 1917, he was at Vimy. He was rising through the ranks, to sergeant, lieutenant and then captain. He was wounded twice and came down with influenza and pleurisy as well. In 1917, he was awarded the Distinguished Conduct Medal for single-handedly capturing an enemy machine gun, "undoubtedly saving his company from many casualties." In January 1918, he was awarded the Military Cross to which he later added a Bar. It was in late 1918, during the last hundred days, that he again braved machine gun fire at Cambrai, and carried on after being wounded to overtake an enemy position.

Citation: For most conspicuous bravery, leadership and self-sacrificing devotion to duty near Cambrai from 29th September to 3rd October, 1918.

He led his company under intense fire, and when the advance was checked by machine guns, although wounded, pushed on and located the enemy guns. He then ran forward in broad daylight, in face of heavy fire from all directions, and, with rifle and bayonet, single-handed, put the enemy crews out of action, killing four and taking eight prisoners. His prompt action saved many casualties and enabled the advance to continue.

After reorganising his command under heavy fire he rendered the most useful support to neighbouring troops. When the enemy were showing stubborn resistance, he went along the line regardless of danger, organised the platoons, took command of the leading waves, and continued the advance. Later, after a personal daylight reconnaissance under heavy fire, he established his company in Neuville St. Remy, thereby greatly assisting the advance into Tilloy. Throughout the operations Capt. MacGregor displayed magnificent bravery and heroic leadership.—*London Gazette,* no. 31108, January 6, 1919

MacGregor came home to Canada in 1919, but his story doesn't end there. He married in 1924 and moved the family to Powell River to be part of the paper mill operation there. His strict integrity during the Depression put him out of work when he refused to give the foreman a kickback to keep his job. He wouldn't play the "VC card" to keep his job but was later reinstated when the truth became known.

MacGregor re-enlisted in World War II as a private, but when fellow VC General George Pearkes came to inspect his unit, he was found out and was made company commander. He spent most of his time on the home front because of health issues. MacGregor went back to work as a carpenter after the war and died in 1952 in Powell River.

"One thing I always remember my dad telling me," says Jaye Roter, "is that he once asked his dad which accomplishment he was most proud of. My grandfather's response was 'My Canadian Citizenship.'"

"Mickey": Private Michael O'Rourke, 7th Battalion (BC Regiment)

Michael O'Rourke was front-page news when he died in Vancouver in December 1957. Seven Victoria Cross winners were his pallbearers at Holy Rosary Cathedral, among them Sergeant Robert Hanna, Chip Kerr and Lieutenant-Colonel Robert Shankland, who also served in the Great War.

"It was a requiem mass unique in Vancouver history," read the *Vancouver Province,* "not only because the casket was flanked by seven members of the commonwealth's highest award, but because it was attended by people from every walk of life."

Generals, judges, aldermen and other dignitaries flocked to the cathedral to pay their respects. "But most of the 200 mourners were Mickey's old pals from the 7th Battalion," said the *Province* reporter, "... and the grey and grizzled dockworkers and homeless old timers from Powell and Main streets who knew Mickey in his days as a longshoreman."

Michael O'Rourke was a tough Irish Catholic from Limerick who came to Canada to blast tunnels and build railways. Mickey was older than most, thirty-six when he signed up in March 1915. He told recruiters that he had already served in the Royal Munster Fusiliers in the old country. But he wasn't starry-eyed about military life. In July, while still training, he was written up for drunkenness and abusive language. He was on his way to France later that year. In June 1916, he was again disciplined for drunkenness. A few months later, he was awarded the Military Medal for bravery at the Somme after leading a counterattack on

Michael O'Rourke was "a brawler and a boozer," but also incredibly brave.
Courtesy of the Department of National Defence

enemy trenches at his own initiative. In August 1917, serving as a stretcher bearer during the battle of Hill 70, he was awarded the Victoria Cross for "conspicuous bravery and devotion to duty."

"He was a brawler and a boozer," says historian Kevin Dooley, who has written extensively about O'Rourke. "But he was also very calm under fire as well as very tough."

During his years in the trenches, O'Rourke had been gassed and hit by shrapnel, and by the end of the war was no longer fit for service. But the brawling Irishman from Limerick received his VC at Buckingham Palace, which must have been a bit of a hoot. O'Rourke's discipline issues meant he was still a humble private—albeit with a lifelong Victoria Cross annuity. He was also eligible for a minimal disability pension.

"He suffered from neurasthenia [shell shock] and severe ulcers," says Kevin Dooley. "It took him many years of struggle to earn a 40 percent pension."

After the war, O'Rourke travelled around the West for a while and then returned to Vancouver, where he served as a night watchman on the waterfront. In 1935, he was back in the headlines, leading a waterfront strike protest parade wearing his medals. "The Battle of Ballantyne Pier" ended with tear gas and a police charge on horseback.

"Scores of men including fourteen police officers were injured," says Dooley. "O'Rourke was not a labour leader but he agreed to lead the parade in 1935 with other vets, and that was a pretty courageous act."

Friends pulled him out of the action before any heads were broken and he earned the eternal gratitude of waterfront workers. Those were the kind of men who showed up at his funeral in 1957, honoured to have known Mickey, a man of the people.

> Citation: For most conspicuous bravery and devotion to duty during prolonged operations.
>
> For three days and nights, Private O'Rourke, who is a stretcher-bearer, worked unceasingly in bringing the wounded into safety, dressing them, and getting them food and water.
>
> During the whole of this period the area in which he worked was subjected to very severe shelling and swept by heavy machine gun and rifle fire. On several occasions he was knocked down and partially buried by enemy shells. Seeing a comrade who had been blinded, stumbling around ahead of our trench, in full view of the enemy who were sniping him, Private O'Rourke jumped out of his trench and brought the man back, being himself heavily sniped at while doing so. Again he went forward about 50 yards in front of our barrage under very heavy and accurate fire from enemy machine guns and snipers, and brought in a comrade. On a subsequent occasion, when the line of advanced posts was retired to the line to be consolidated, he went forward under very heavy enemy fire of every description and brought back a wounded man who had been left behind.
>
> He showed throughout an absolute disregard for his own safety, going wherever there were wounded to succour, and his magnificent courage and devotion in continuing his rescue work, in spite of exhaustion and the incessant heavy enemy fire of every description, inspired all ranks and undoubtedly saved many lives.—*London Gazette,* no. 30372, November 8, 1917

A Career Soldier: Major General George Pearkes, 5th Canadian Mounted Rifles

George Pearkes was born in England and came to Canada in 1906 where he joined the Royal North West Mounted Police. In 1915, he enlisted in the Canadian Expeditionary Force, later commanding the 5th Canadian Mounted Rifles. His Victoria Cross came at Passchendaele in 1917.

> Citation: For most conspicuous bravery and skilful handling of the troops under his command

during the capture and consolidation of considerably more than the objectives allotted to him, in an attack.

Just prior to the advance, Maj. Pearkes was wounded in the left thigh. Regardless of his wound, he continued to lead his men with the utmost gallantry, despite many obstacles.

At a particular stage of the attack his further advance was threatened by a strong point which was an objective of the battalion on his left, but which they had not succeeded in capturing. Quickly appreciating the situation, he captured and held this point, thus enabling his further advance to be successfully pushed forward.

It was entirely due to his determination and fearless personality that he was able to maintain his objective with the small number of men at his command against repeated enemy counter-attacks, both his flanks being unprotected for a considerable depth meanwhile.

His appreciation of the situation throughout and the reports rendered by him were invaluable to his Commanding Officer in making dispositions of troops to hold the position captured. He showed throughout a supreme contempt of danger and wonderful powers of control and leading.—*London Gazette,* no. 30471, January 11, 1918

Pearkes was a career soldier and held major commands during World War II. After retiring from the army, he ended up on Vancouver Island and entered federal politics as a Conservative. He was elected four times to the House of Commons (1945, 1953, 1957 and 1958). Pearkes served as minister of national defence in Prime Minister John Diefenbaker's Cabinet from 1957 until 1960. In 1961, he was appointed lieutenant-governor of British Columbia, a position he held until 1968. He died in 1984 in Victoria.

George Pearkes became a National Minister of Defence in the Diefenbaker government and later a lieutenant-governor of BC.
Courtesy of the Department of National Defence

He Feared Nothing: Lieutenant-Colonel Cyrus Peck, 16th Battalion

Cyrus Peck was not a kid when he enlisted in November 1914. He was forty-three and a big burly man, over two hundred pounds. In Prince Rupert before the war, he ran a fish cannery. But he hit his stride once in uniform. His wartime record was impressive: mentioned in dispatches at least five times, awarded the DSO twice, wounded twice and then gassed in 1918. In November 1916, Peck was promoted to command the 16th Infantry Battalion. His VC came late in the war when he was forty-seven years old. It was in 1918 during the fighting for the Drocourt-Quéant Line, near Cagnicourt in France.

Citation: For most conspicuous bravery and skilful leading when in attack under intense fire.

His command quickly captured the first objective, but progress to the further objective was held up by enemy machine-gun fire on his right flank.

The situation being critical in the extreme, Colonel Peck pushed forward and made a personal reconnaissance under heavy machine-gun and sniping fire, across a stretch of ground which was heavily swept by fire.

Having reconnoitred the position he returned, reorganised his battalion, and, acting upon the knowledge personally gained, pushed them forward and arranged to protect his flanks. He then went out under the most intense artillery and machine-gun fire, intercepted the Tanks, gave them the necessary directions, pointing out where they were to make for, and thus pave the way for a Canadian Infantry battalion to push forward. To this battalion he subsequently gave requisite support.

Above: Cyrus Peck was elected to parliament for Skeena while serving overseas.
Courtesy of the Department of National Defence

Left: Peck's gravestone at the Fraser Cemetery in New Westminster.
Courtesy of Greg Dickson

> His magnificent display of courage and fine qualities of leadership enabled the advance to be continued, although always under heavy artillery and machine-gun fire, and contributed largely to the success of the brigade attack.—*London Gazette,* no. 31012, November 15, 1918

In 1917, while he was still overseas, Peck was elected to the House of Commons as the member of parliament for Skeena during the khaki election. He was defeated in 1921 but went on to serve as an member of the legislative assembly on Vancouver Island during the 1920s. He died in 1956, well into his eighties, and has a gravestone in New Westminster, though some of his ashes were also scattered at Metlakatla Pass near Prince Rupert. Someone said of him, "He feared nothing that walked or talked."

Hero of Arras: Private Walter Rayfield, 7th Battalion (BC Regiment)

Walter Rayfield won his VC for "indomitable courage" at Arras.
Courtesy of the Department of National Defence

Walter Rayfield was born in England and was working as a lumberjack when he signed up in Victoria in July 1917 with the Forestry Depot. He was later transferred to the 7th Battalion. It was during the last hundred days at Arras that Rayfield displayed "indomitable courage" in rushing an enemy trench under sniper fire. For capturing forty prisoners, he was awarded the VC. He was also made a member of the Royal Order of the Crown of Belgium by the Belgian government. He died in Toronto in 1949.

> Citation: For most conspicuous bravery, devotion to duty, and initiative during the operations east of Arras from 2nd to 4th September, 1918.
>
> Ahead of his company, he rushed a trench occupied by a large party of the enemy, personally bayoneting two and taking ten prisoners.
>
> Later, he located and engaged with great skill, under constant rifle fire, an enemy sniper who was causing many casualties. He then rushed the section of trench from which the sniper had been operating, and so demoralised the enemy by his coolness and daring that thirty others surrendered to him.
>
> Again, regardless of his personal safety, he left cover under heavy machine-gun fire and carried in a badly wounded comrade.
>
> His indomitable courage, cool foresight, and daring reconnaissance were invaluable to his Company Commander and an inspiration to all ranks.—*London Gazette,* no. 31067, December 14, 1918

A Storm of Lead: Piper James Cleland Richardson, 16th Infantry Battalion

Piper James Richardson played his troops over the top, but died in the battle.
Courtesy of the Department of National Defence

He is one of Chilliwack's most cherished sons. Piper James Cleland Richardson was killed at the Somme in 1916 and awarded the Victoria Cross for his rare act of bravery. He was just seven weeks shy of his twenty-first birthday when he perished.

Born in 1895, James was the eldest of eight children and immigrated to Canada with his family from Scotland in 1913 when his father was hired as chief of police in Chilliwack. A driller by trade, James served with the cadet corps of the Seaforth Highlanders and worked at a factory on Vancouver's False Creek, where he was credited with attempting to save the life of a young boy who fell into the water and drowned. James was also a noted piper who won his share of competitions here in BC.

When the war arrived he wasted no time enlisting as a piper with the 16th Infantry Battalion (the Canadian Scottish CEF) in September 1914. His battalion was involved in the attack on Regina Trench, north of Courcelette, and his Victoria Cross citation tells the story of his selfless actions:

Citation: For most conspicuous bravery and devotion to duty when, prior to attack, he obtained permission from his Commanding Officer to play his company "over the top."

As the company approached the objective, it was held up by very strong wire and came under intense fire, which caused heavy casualties and demoralised the formation for the moment. Realizing the situation, Piper Richardson strode up and down outside the wire, playing his pipes with the greatest coolness. The effect was instantaneous. Inspired by his splendid example, the company rushed the wire with such fury and determination that the obstacle was overcome and the position captured.

Later, after participating in bombing operations, he was detailed to take back a wounded comrade and prisoners.

After proceeding about 200 yards Piper Richardson remembered that he had left his pipes behind. Although strongly urged not to do so, he insisted on returning to recover his pipes. He has never been seen since, and death has been presumed accordingly owing to lapse of time.—*London Gazette*, no. 30967, October 22, 1918

Piper Richardson's enduring story was also recounted by Colonel C.W. Peck, the former commander of his 16th Battalion, in the book *Piper Richardson VC, An Untold Tale of Heroism and Sacrifice:*

Suddenly the whole scene changed. Young Richardson took in the situation. Danger seemed to stimulate and accentuate the Scotch intellect. For some reason, he hadn't been allowed to play up to this point. Turning to the sergeant major in the shellhole beside him, he said, "Will I gie 'em wind?" "Aye mon, gie 'em wind," was the laconic reply. Good God! Look at that! There was a young, smooth-faced boy coolly playing up and down the wire in that hail storm of lead.

James Richardson's pipes were found in the Somme mud and taken to Scotland in 1917, where they remained at a local school until 2003. Once the pipes were identified, the efforts of many individuals and organizations brought them home. The pipes are now on display at the BC legislature.

A statue of Piper Richardson created by master sculptor John Barney Weaver has a prominent place in front of Chilliwack's museum. It was unveiled to the skirl of pipes from the Canadian Scottish Regiment (Victoria), Seaforth Highlanders (Vancouver) and Chilliwack and District Pipe Band. Some thirty members of the Richardson family were on hand for the ceremony in fall 2003.
Courtesy of Mark Forsythe

Robert Shankland won the VC in WW I and served again in WW II.

Courtesy of the Department of National Defence

A Splendid Example and Inspiration: Captain Robert Shankland, 43rd Battalion

Robert Shankland was born in Scotland and was an unmarried clerk when he signed up in Winnipeg in December 1914. He was in his twenties and had previous military experience. He wasn't a big man, only about five foot four. But he was brave. He earned a Distinguished Conduct Medal in 1916 after volunteering to join a party of stretcher bearers under heavy shellfire, bringing in men who had been wounded and partially buried. His military records say, "His courage and devotion to duty were most marked." He was wounded at Passchendaele in October 1917 when under attack but rallied his men to defend their position. He moved to Victoria after the war and served again in World War II. Shankland died in Vancouver in 1968.

Citation: For most conspicuous bravery and resource in action under critical and adverse conditions.

Having gained a position he rallied the remnant of his own platoon and men of other companies, disposed them to command the ground in front, and inflicted heavy casualties upon the retreating enemy. Later, he dispersed a counter-attack, thus enabling supporting troops to come up unmolested.

He then personally communicated to Battalion Headquarters an accurate and valuable report as to the position on the Brigade frontage, and after doing so rejoined his command and carried on until relieved.

His courage and splendid example inspired all ranks and coupled with his great gallantry and skill undoubtedly saved a very critical situation.—*London Gazette*, no. 30433, December 18, 1917

A Distinguished Career: John Alexander Sinton, Indian Medical Service, Indian Army, VC, FRS, OBE

John Alexander Sinton was born in Victoria in 1884 but his family returned to Ulster when he was young. He studied medicine at Queen's and joined the Indian Medical Service in 1911. He was a captain in the Indian Army after the war. Sinton was mentioned in dispatches four times and served in Mesopotamia (Iraq), where he was severely wounded in action but continued to help others.

Citation: For most conspicuous bravery and devotion to duty. Although shot through both arms and through the side, he refused to go to hospital, and remained as long as daylight lasted, attending to his duties under very heavy fire. In three previous actions Captain Sinton displayed the utmost bravery.—*London Gazette*, June 21, 1916

When the war was over, Sinton continued with a distinguished career in medicine, becoming an expert in tropical diseases. He served again as an officer in World War II and was given the Order of St. George. He was elected a Fellow of the Royal Society in 1946. Sinton died in Northern Ireland in 1956.

Died in the Line of Duty as a Vancouver Policeman: Lance Corporal Robert McBeath

Robert McBeath earned his VC in the British Army and didn't emigrate to Canada until after the war. He won honours for action at the Battle of Cambrai in November 1917.

Citation: For most conspicuous bravery when with his company in attack and approaching the final objective, a nest of enemy machine-guns in the western outskirts of a village opened fire both on his own unit and on the unit to the right. The advance was checked and heavy casualties resulted.

When a Lewis gun was called for to deal with these machine-guns, L/Corpl. McBeath

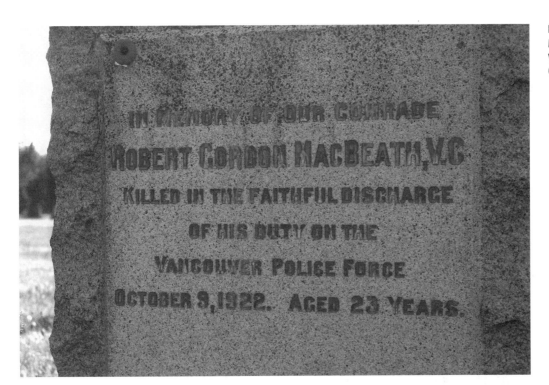

Robert McBeath's grave in Mountain View Cemetery in Vancouver.
Courtesy of Greg Dickson

volunteered for the duty, and immediately moved off alone with a Lewis gun and his revolver. He located one of the machine guns in action, and worked his way towards it, shooting the gunner with his revolver at 20 yards range. Finding several of the hostile machine-guns in action, he, with the assistance of a tank, attacked them and drove the gunners to ground in a deep dugout.

L/Corpl. McBeath, regardless of all danger, rushed in after them, shot an enemy who opposed him on the steps, and drove the remainder of the garrison out of the dug-out, capturing three officers and 30 men. There were in all five machine-guns mounted round the dug-out, and by putting them out of action he cleared the way for the advance of both units. The conduct of L/Corpl. McBeath throughout three days of severe fighting was beyond praise.—*London Gazette,* January 11, 1918

When McBeath moved to Vancouver after the war, he joined the BC Provincial Police and then the Vancouver Police Department. In October 1922, while trying to make a routine arrest, he and a fellow officer were both shot. McBeath's partner survived, but he was killed. He was twenty-three and his grave at Mountain View Cemetery in Vancouver reads as an impressive monument to service: Killed in the faithful discharge of his Duty on the Vancouver Police Force.

From Our Listeners: A Montenegran-Canadian Hero—Sergeant Valisa Bogichevich

By Peter Broznitsky, Pacific Coast Branch of the Western Front Association

Valisa Bogichevich was born probably in Danilovgrad, Montenegro, on September 20, 1886. It's possible he arrived in Canada as early as 1904, at the age of eighteen. Valisa was a member of the active militia, probably the Duke of Connaught's Own Rifles or perhaps the Irish Fusiliers. He stated his occupation as labourer at the time of enlisting in Vancouver into the 29th Battalion on November 9, 1914, and he belonged to the "Montenegrin Church," likely the Serbian Orthodox Church. His next of kin was given as his sister in Danilovgrad. As a 29th original, his attestation paper was signed by Lieutenant-Colonel H.S. Tobin. At twenty-eight years of age and with militia experience, he rose through the ranks in Tobin's Tigers to sergeant. He received a rare combination of gallantry awards: a Military Medal (MM), a Bar to the MM, and the Distinguished Conduct Medal.

Having survived action as a private soldier with the 29th at St. Eloi and Ypres in mid-1916, his first Military Medal was awarded for his bravery on the Somme on September 16, 1916, when he carried *matériel* and messages under intense shellfire to the new front-line trenches in Courcelette. Then on September 26, Valisa volunteered to go under very heavy fire two hundred yards in front of the Canadian line to a detached post and brought back several wounded. This deed brought him the Bar to the MM.

After Courcelette, Valisa fought with the Tigers on Vimy Ridge, Lens/Hill 70 and Passchendaele in 1917. In the early morning of June 3, 1918, he won the DCM during a night raid south of Arras. He led his section against three strong hostile posts, clearing each out and overcoming heavy resistance. He personally accounted for five of the enemy and captured two prisoners, as well as accounting for an unknown number of the enemy in a large dugout with Stokes bombs. An after-action report stated that:

Sergeant Valisa Bogichevich was one of Tobin's Tigers in the 29th (Vancouver) Battalion. He was killed in action in 1918.
Courtesy of Peter Bronitsky

> Sgt. Bogichevich shouted down the tunnel and two men answered the call and were taken prisoner. These men said there were still 8 down below. A light was seen in the tunnel and as no other Huns came out, Mills bombs, cylindrical sticks and Stokes mortar bombs were thrown down the tunnel. In the words of the gallant leader of the party, "De candle, she go out." The party then proceeded along the trench searching out funk holes. A Hun was found hiding in one who refused to come out. Again, in the words of the leader of the party, "I shoot my bolt and on I go."

Sergeant Bogichevich finally fell for his adopted country, instantly killed by enemy fire, just at the "jumping off" line, on August 9, 1918. He is buried in Rosieres Cemetery, the Somme, France. It is possible that his relatives were never officially informed of his death. The Canadian government ordinarily sent documents to the next of kin. But because of the uncertainty of delivery to Montenegro, the forms instead went to Montreal to the Royal Consul General for Serbs, Croats and Slovenes. The whereabouts of Valisa's medals remain unknown.

Peter Broznitsky's grandfather fought with Bogichevich. Peter is a Ladner historian and chair of the Pacific Coast Branch of the Western Front Association. He is currently researching Russians and Ukrainians who served in the Canadian Expeditionary Force (CEF). You'll find more on his project at www.russiansinthecef.ca.

From Our Listeners: Remembering Ernest Edward Woodley

Told by Phyllis Lindsay, Charlie Lake

He was 102 when he was awarded the Knight of the Order of Legion of Honour, the highest decoration in France. Ernest Edward Woodley was born in 1897 in Reading, Berkshire, England, to Edward Woodley and Ellen Fisher. The family of six came to Canada in 1911 and settled in Victoria.

A plumber, he enlisted at Esquimalt in 1916 at age nineteen, serving with the Royal Canadian Regiment in various battles, including Vimy. His niece Phyllis Lindsay wrote, "Uncle Ernest never told we nieces about his war service...except one of his jobs was to bring the deceased soldiers to the medical tents and make sure their tags were carefully kept. He spoke of going 'over the top' of the trenches in many battles, and was in Mons when the war ended. He was shot in the foot and always suffered with 'trench feet.' We had a great celebration for his hundredth birthday. At age 102 he received the Legion of Honour presented by the French consul general. Other than being a bit hard of hearing, his general health was great—and he was a grand fellow. I am the daughter of his youngest sister, Edith May Woodley."

Ernest Woodley died in January 2000.

From Our Listeners: My Father's Story

By Ken Campbell, Kelowna

Kenneth Alexander Campbell enlisted with the rank of private in the 231st Battalion of the Canadian Expeditionary Force in Vancouver on April 17, 1916. When the 231st Battalion arrived in Britain in the spring of 1917, it was assigned to the 72nd Canadian Infantry Battalion known as the Seaforth Highlanders of Canada and later departed for France. In the summer of 1917 the 72nd Battalion was in the front lines during an Allied offensive in France near Avion.

The Battle of Passchendaele, referred by the soldiers as the Battle of Mud, took place on the Western Front between June and November 1917. On November 24, Kenneth Campbell was promoted to lance corporal. The March 13, 1918, edition of the *London Gazette* carried a list of soldiers singled out for courageous behaviour. Private K.A. Campbell was among those who had been awarded the Military Medal. On May 10, 1918, Kenneth Campbell accepted the rank of corporal and on August 22, 1918, his rank was elevated to sergeant.

In the fall of 1918 Sergeant Campbell was awarded the Distinguished Conduct Medal during the Battle of Arras. Sergeant Campbell led Private T. Nelson and Private F. McPherson in a bold initiative on the Arras–Cambrai–Hendecourt–Dury crossroads. The three men cleared a machine-gun defended section of the road and captured no fewer than fifty German prisoners in the process. The events are well documented in the archives of the 72nd Battalion. On November 1, 1918, Sergeant Campbell was wounded by shrapnel. Fortunately the deadly force of the shrapnel was blunted when it impacted the stainless steel shaving mirror in his breast pocket. Sergeant Campbell was hospitalized in France and later transferred to Seaford in Sussex, England.

Kenneth Campbell was discharged in Vancouver on March 3, 1919. In 1922 he married Marguerite Mack and went on to raise a family of three daughters and one son in Port Coquitlam, BC. During World War II Kenneth served as a corporal with the Pacific Coast Militia Rangers.

From Our Listeners: A Sketch of Geoffrey Murray Downton

By Nick Walton, United Kingdom

Geoffrey Murray Downton liked to think of himself as an ordinary man. While serving with the Canadians in the trenches, he wrote a poem about men in the trenches: "...but we are very ordinary men." In a letter to the young girl who was to become his wife, he described himself in the same way. But "ordinary" was not a good way to describe his distinguished war service. He enlisted on February 1, 1915, and was demobilized in March 1919.

Geoff's first experience of trench warfare came the month he arrived at the front, starting service in the Ypres Salient in March 1916 after thirteen months of various types of training in Canada and then in the UK. As a member of the 3rd Pioneer Battalion (building and repairing trenches), he was indirectly involved in the Battle of Mount Sorrell (June 1916), which started with a successful attack by the Germans on the Canadian sector and finished with an equally successful Canadian counterattack ten days later, with no shortage of action in between. He saw service at the Battles of the Somme in the summer of 1916, though not in the front line. When the Canadian Corps stormed over Vimy Ridge in April 1917, he was given an order to make good a tactically important road over the ridge to help bring up supplies. Unfortunately the road was one that was clearly marked on German maps and he found himself and his men working amid an artillery barrage. With shells exploding all around ("a tiresome time" he called it in his journal), one would expect the ordinary man to take cover and abandon the task till the danger was over. However, Geoff realized the importance of what he was doing and doggedly persisted in finishing the job he was given. He records that a shell landed only a few feet away. "We would have been blown to atoms but fortunately it turned out to be a dud and did not go off." On that occasion his luck held. His courage and persistence were noticed and he was awarded the Military Cross.

In August 1918, having been transferred to the machine gunners, he led his machine guns into action at the Battle of Amiens and here again he was lucky to survive a shell burst close by which killed two of his men and took out their gun. After Amiens the Canadians advanced steadily eastward in varying degrees of fierceness of action, with Geoff's machine guns much in evidence. From Amiens it was northeast to Arras, then east to Cambrai and to Valenciennes. Almost exactly three months later they spent the last day of the war fighting a duel with a German gun shelling the farm that they had occupied just outside the Belgian city of Mons. At eleven o'clock the next morning, November 11, the time of the official ending of hostilities, he made his way into Mons, arriving just too late for the ceasefire celebrations.

Having survived the slaughter of the 1914–18 war, he found it a heartbreaking experience to lose his only son in the blazing wreck of a Wellington bomber just outside the city of Exeter, United Kingdom, in January 1943.

Submitted by Geoffrey's nephew Darren Asher of Penticton.

4

BC'S NAVAL LEGACY
IMPROVISING TO PROTECT THE WEST COAST

British Columbians had a swagger about them as they entered the war. But they felt vulnerable about their virtually undefended coastline. For decades, the Royal Navy at Esquimalt had been a comforting presence. After Britain began vacating Esquimalt Naval Base in the early 1900s, there was widespread anxiety about attack or invasion.

At first the Canadian Department of Marine and Fisheries took up the slack, and then the Naval Service of Canada, which became the Royal Canadian Navy in 1911. But in an era when mighty dreadnoughts represented the *ne plus ultra* of naval technology, the fledgling Royal Canadian Navy was royal in name only.

In January 1912, the BC legislature took up the fight, urging the federal government to address naval concerns on the West Coast. Prime Minister Robert Borden's naval policy was floundering. He couldn't get the money to build a robust Canadian Navy and he couldn't convince his political opponents to back a timely contribution to the British Navy's dreadnought program. As a *Vancouver Province* account of the debate in the legislature explained, a lot was at stake:

> There were movements of great importance in the world...which made it imperative that something should be done to defend a coastline stretching from Puget Sound to Alaska and indented in many sounds and inlets which some future enemy might easily utilize for strategic purposes.

The major fear in British Columbia in 1912 was not the German Navy but the rise of China and Japan, two countries that actually ended up sending men to fight alongside us. One newspaper account picked up on the legislative debate, sounding alarms about Japan and China:

> One of the first things an Oriental nation did in adopting western methods was to establish an army and navy, and these two nations were already looking for some place where they could transfer the people from their overcrowded lands, and no place was so convenient as Canada.

As mentioned in the opening chapter, Premier McBride travelled to London in the spring of 1912, and while naval matters were clearly not within his jurisdiction, he met with

Winston Churchill and told the press that British Columbia had been left defenceless by the withdrawal of the Royal Navy. Canada, he insisted, must co-operate in maintaining British naval supremacy. On his return to Canada, McBride met with Prime Minister Borden and delivered Churchill's views. There was no time to lose.

Two years later, when war broke out—not with Japan but with Germany—British Columbia was no better off and the Royal Navy was needed in European waters where it concentrated most of its efforts. As it turned out, Japan was one of Britain's naval allies and ended up with the responsibility for defending Canada's West Coast. This was a shock to McBride, who had done little to foster good relations with the Japanese. Soon Victoria would be entertaining visiting Japanese naval delegations!

The aging cruiser HMCS *Rainbow* was the Royal Canadian Navy's only serious weapon against at least one and maybe two modern German cruisers operating on the west coast of North America. Our strategically important Vancouver Island coal fields, the Vancouver and Victoria harbours, and the fishing fleet looked like sitting ducks for a German attack. McBride thought something needed to be done to bolster the navy's strength. And he set in motion one of the most audacious schemes in the history of provincial politics.

McBride and the Submarines

AN INTERVIEW WITH HISTORIAN PATRICIA E. ROY

Patricia E. Roy: There were rumours days before the war broke out that part of the German fleet was sailing for the North Pacific. Victoria in particular was almost totally lacking in defences. The Royal Canadian Navy had been created in 1911 but for political reasons had not amounted to very much. So when war seemed imminent, the base at Esquimalt had

The best we had on the West Coast—the aging Cruiser HMCS *Rainbow*, here seen leaving Portsmouth for Canada.
City of Vancouver Archives, LP 21

one cruiser, the *Rainbow*. Two small British sloops that had been stationed off Mexico were heading toward Esquimalt—and they were tiny. That was about it.

Premier McBride happened to hear—he was having lunch at the Union Club, the story goes, and a fellow who ran a shipyard in Seattle was also having lunch—and word got around that this shipyard had two submarines, ready to go. It had built them for the Chilean navy. There are conflicting stories about Chile rejecting them because they weren't up to specifications, or Chile simply not having the wherewithal to pay for them.

In any case, the Seattle shipyard had them for sale. So McBride went ahead and bought them. I hasten to add, he did notify the federal government. He sent a telegram off to Prime Minister Borden and Martin Burrell, a federal cabinet minister who happened to be in Victoria at the time, and he consulted with him. Ottawa approved, but 1914 is before the days of instant tellers and wiring money by mail, and the Seattle shipyard said it was strictly a cash-and-carry deal. McBride wrote a cheque for just over a million dollars for the two submarines.

One of the nice things about Victoria is you can always find retired experts on almost anything, and McBride did find a retired Royal Navy submarine expert and sent him and a couple of other people with some naval knowledge down to Seattle along with the cheque. Haste was essential because once Britain was at war, Canada was at war. And once war was declared the Americans would be neutral. With their neutrality legislation in effect, they would not be allowed to sell war materials to a belligerent.

McBride's team rushed out to near international waters. A quick inspection was made. The submarines passed muster. The cheque was handed over and they sailed back toward Esquimalt. By this time the army had gun emplacements at Fort Rodd Hill. They were ready to fire when someone realized that, yes, those were submarines, but if they were enemy submarines they would be coming in from the ocean rather than heading in the other direction. So they phoned Esquimalt, and Esquimalt said, yes, they're our friendly submarines. So don't fire. And they arrived safely in Esquimalt.

Mark Forsythe: Is it true that the torpedoes were in Halifax—that they didn't have torpedoes?

Patricia: They had torpedoes here, but they weren't of the right size. What we really depended on for our defence at the time was the Imperial Japanese Navy, because under the Anglo-Japanese Alliance, Japan and Britain had an agreement whereby they would help each other out in time of warfare. There were two Japanese naval officers based at Esquimalt.

Mark: The threat did pass in the Pacific. What happened to the subs?

Patricia: They were here for a year or so and then they were transferred to Halifax and apparently it was a rather harrowing journey and one of them had a lot of engine trouble. They never had to use them.

Patricia Roy is professor emerita of history at the University of Victoria and author of many books on BC history, including Boundless Optimism: Richard McBride's British Columbia *(UBC Press).*

Top Secret—We Built Submarines in Burnaby

It is one of the better-kept secrets of BC history. Not only did BC purchase two Seattle-built submarines in 1914, but we went on to build submarines for export to the Russians at a hidden factory at Barnet in Burnaby. Nothing remains of the factory now other than a creek named in its honour, but in its heyday, safely concealed beside the CP rail line on Burrard Inlet, the

From Our Listeners: Acts of Memory

By Don Stewart, Vancouver

My earliest memories to do with the Great War were of my mother yelling at my grandfather to stop him from beating me on the head. The pain of being hit combined with her raised voice ("Don't you ever hit little Don again") made the memory stick. I was four years old; it was 1955, forty years after the events that left my grandfather with what we now know as post-traumatic stress disorder.

My grandfather Don Stewart (same name as my father and me) had joined the 28th BN CEF in 1914 and gone overseas where he served as a sniper and acting sergeant until wounded in 1916, after which he was in reserve in England.

When I was eight, on a family visit to Vancouver my father left me with the car in the parking lot at Essondale (Riverview) while he visited his father, who had developed early dementia. My grandfather thought his visitor son was an army buddy from World War I.

I connected with the war in another way at the age of ten. My father was showing me his father's medals, photos in uniform and dog tags, with them a small square of Scottish tartan. His father told him that as his platoon advanced to recover lost ground they came across the bodies of about ten massacred Canadian Scottish who had been shot by Germans after surrendering. His platoon all cut small squares from their kilts to pin on their own uniforms and vowed to take no German prisoners.

As a child of the fifties and young man of the sixties, I would from time to time encounter some of the ruined veterans of the war, men in their sixties and seventies with burned faces or missing limbs, sometimes on an outing from a veterans' hospital.

When I was twelve and wasting a summer, my father, knowing my interest in history, gave me a project to catalogue my grandfather's military medal collection. It rested in a cabinet in a corner of the living room. I was quickly drawn to these mementos of Napoleonic, Victorian, Edwardian campaigns and the two world wars. As I read up on the background of these mementos and the men who received them, my interest grew.

As a bookseller dealing in used and rare books, photographs and manuscripts for the past four decades I have continued to follow these interests.

About twenty years ago I began putting a collection together with the name "The Culture of World War I." It consists of several thousand pieces of war propaganda, art and art books, charity gift books, photographs, posters, postcards, Christmas cards, soldier mail, prisoner mail, window stickers, letters, welcome home programs, novels, poetry, drama, sheet music of patriotic songs and entertainments both war and postwar, and documents for soldiers, civilian war workers, enemy aliens and conscientious objectors.

I see them as acts of memory keeping intact archives left behind by people for whom they were so important. Some commemorate acts of courage and others are remembrance of those who died in war and the families they left behind.

One example is a recently acquired archive of the Nicholson family. W.E. Nicholson was a printer who joined the 196th Western Universities Battalion, CEF. He was transferred to the 46th Battalion and killed in action at Vimy Ridge. The archive includes the telegram sent to his wife Mary, his CEF death certificate, burial report and a long correspondence through the 1920s relating to his headstone and inscription, ending with photographs of his wife at his grave in 1928. Her acts of remembering included large framed photographs of him in uniform. She never remarried.

Another example is a copy of Maple Leaves in Flanders Fields by Herbert Rae (pseudonym of Dr. George Gibson). This novel of the 7th Battalion was annotated by the battalion commander, Victor Odlum, with the actual names of all the characters.

A third example is a large archive of a boy soldier, Corporal H.D. Hodgins of the 15th Battalion. As a schoolboy at the beginning of the war he made his own comic books, then joined the cadets, enlisted by lying about his age, was sent overseas to England and by 1918 was a signaller in France. He kept hundreds of pieces of paper to do with his service and return home.

Image courtesy of Don Stewart

British Pacific Construction and Engineering Company was a going concern.

The man behind the company was James Venn Paterson, the same man who headed the Seattle shipyard and smuggled submarines across the international border for Premier McBride in 1914.

Submarines were built for the Russian Navy at a secret plant in Burnaby in 1917.
City of Burnaby Archives, Photo ID 466-016

Burnaby seems an odd place to build submarines for the Russian Navy. And the story is a strange one. Our allies, including the Russians, were anxious to buy submarines wherever they could find them. The Americans could build them but couldn't sell them directly without contravening their own neutrality laws. So Paterson's Seattle shipyard started looking for ways to build subs to their own patented specifications in Canada. To keep the business, they set up the British Pacific Construction and Engineering Company at Vancouver. The company then found a quiet stretch of shoreline in Burnaby where they could build subs without attracting attention.

The site was closely guarded and the crews sworn to secrecy. And the work started. The design was good and the subs were built to be dismantled and shipped by rail or sea to customers who could then reassemble them closer to the theatre of war where they were needed.

"The works are surrounded by a high barbed wire fence," a secret report stated, "...and search lights are being erected on the machine shops. There is a military guard of nine men there loaned by the Military, and already five submarines are laid down and well underway." Over two hundred men were soon at work and that grew to over 450 working day and night shifts.

Russia needed subs to defend itself against the German Navy and its Turkish allies in the Baltic and Black Seas. It was a long way from BC, but European shipyards couldn't help, and British Columbia was glad to assist. The subs were to be shipped to Vladivostok, and then to travel by Trans-Siberian rail to Petrograd where they would be assembled for service in the Baltic. Three subs were shipped in December 1916. Eventually five would reach Russia.

As if getting submarines across Russia wasn't complicated enough, in 1917 Russia was shaken by revolution. The submarines were caught up in the chaos as the Russian Imperial Navy crumbled away.

"Their careers were brief," wrote historian William Kaye Lamb in *BC Studies* (Autumn 1986). "The *AG-14* was lost with all hands in 1917, and the other four were all scuttled early in

April 1918 at their base in Finland to prevent them from falling into the hands of the advancing Germans."

If you want to find one of the Burnaby-built submarines, you might try travelling to the Baltic Sea. In June 2003 a diving company found the *AG-14*. The team was actually searching for a missing Swedish DC-3 that was shot down by the Russians in 1952 over the Baltic. They recovered the plane and also located the *AG-14*, missing since 1917.

It turns out that the captain of the *AG-14* was none other than Antonius Essen, the only son of the Russian Admiral Nikolai Essen, head of the Russian Baltic Sea Fleet. Admiral Essen died suddenly of pneumonia in 1915. His family received another shock when son Antonius went down with his crew when the *AG-14* hit a mine two years later.

The Essens were actually ethnic Germans who for two centuries served loyally with the Russian Imperial Navy. Seven family members had been awarded the Order of St. George, Russia's highest military decoration.

Back in Burnaby our submarine industry dreams came to an end when the Americans entered the war in 1917. Freed from the constraints of neutrality, submarine manufacturers could move back across the border. The secret Barnet factory was dismantled, leaving little behind but bits of wood and rusty metal.

Canada's First Submariners Were British Columbians

By Julie H. Ferguson

A middle-aged man with piercing blue eyes scrutinized Canada's first submarines, *CC1* and *CC2*, as they crept alongside in Esquimalt following their clandestine departure from Seattle. It was breakfast time on August 5, 1914, the day after World War I was declared. "Barney" Johnson was a master mariner of considerable repute from Vancouver whom the BC Pilotage Authority had "lent" to the Royal Canadian Navy.

No naval band played "Heart of Oak" to mark the historic birth of the Canadian submarine service, but British Columbia's Premier McBride proudly greeted the two boats he'd purchased to defend his province from German cruisers threatening the Pacific coast.

Built for Chile, the first Canadian submarines were spirited out of their Seattle dockyard in the dead of night on August 4, 1914, to circumvent the American neutrality laws about to be enacted. One of these subs is seen here in Seattle before it sailed for Esquimalt.

Library and Archives Canada / E-41068

Top left: First Lieutenant Willie Maitland-Dougall with the crew of D3 that he later commanded. This photo was taken in 1916 or 1917.
Royal Navy Submarine Museum

Top right: HMS *H6* to *H10* fitting out in Montreal, June 1915. They sailed together to the UK and were among the first submarines to make a trans-Atlantic passage. Johnson commanded *H8* and Maitland-Dougall was the navigator in *H10*.
Royal Navy Submarine Museum

The two submarines changed Johnson's life irrevocably, as well as the life of another British Columbian. Willie Maitland-Dougall, from Vancouver Island, was posted to them a few days later. The men were in marked contrast—one was a reservist, too old for submarines, the other a career officer and nineteen; one was trained by experience, the other in the classroom.

In the turmoil of the outbreak of war, Lieutenant Johnson, RCNR, became the first lieutenant (executive officer) of *CC2* and quickly mastered the art of navigating in three dimensions instead of two. Less than a year later, when the German threat evaporated, Johnson transferred to the Royal Navy's H class submarines then being built in Montreal.

The RN appointed him as commanding officer of HMS *H8* and he sailed her across the Atlantic, a feat only just accomplished by *H1-5.* Johnson was the first reserve officer to captain a submarine in the British Empire and he paved the way for other colonial reservists to command them in both world wars.

In March 1916, Johnson's brilliant seamanship brought *H8* home after a mine blew off most of her bow near Holland, earning him a DSO.

Soon Maitland-Dougall joined him in his new command, HMS *D3*, as his first lieutenant. They made a good team in the Western Approaches, claiming one U-boat sunk and another damaged.

As a fifteen-year-old, Maitland-Dougall had joined the first term of cadets at the Royal Navy College of Canada in Halifax. He was a good candidate—intelligent, energetic and resourceful. He became the midshipman on *CC1* and cheerfully learned about submarines, standing watches on the surface and submerged.

Like Johnson, Maitland-Dougall also moved over to the RN—the two navies shared personnel between them. He soon volunteered for submarines, as they were the best option for a promising officer eager for rapid promotion and early command.

Maitland-Dougall sailed across the Atlantic in HMS *H10*, in convoy with *H8*, and aced the new basic submarine course in Portsmouth as the first Canadian. After a stint in the North Sea and now a sub-lieutenant, he rejoined Johnson. Together they ran HMS *D3* without a third hand.

The RN had earmarked the youngster as a prospective submarine captain, and Maitland-Dougall soon bade Johnson goodbye to attend the first class of the newly established Periscope School in Portsmouth. Known as Perisher, the course taught the science and art of submerged attack for command. After passing, he returned to *D3* as her captain.

Above left: Both Johnson and Maitland-Dougall commanded *D3*, an older but bigger class than the more popular H boats. Their primitive periscopes made attacking difficult.
Courtesy of Julie Ferguson

Above: Barney Johnson's bell commemorating his fifty years in the navy still has pride of place on the wardroom bar at HMCS *Discovery* in Stanley Park and reminds all reservists of his legacy.
Courtesy of Julie Ferguson

Opposite bottom: After Johnson and *H8*'s crew returned safely to Harwich in March 1916, they discovered the true extent of the damage—shattered foreplanes, exposed firing pistols and a ripped-open main ballast and trim tank. Johnson's seamanship and a watertight bulkhead aft of the torpedoes had saved them.
City of Vancouver Archives, CVA 582-003

The two British Columbian submarine officers in the Great War: Lt. Willie Maitland-Dougall, RCN (top) and Lt. Barney Johnson, RCNR, DSO (bottom).
Courtesy of Julie Ferguson and the Maitland-Dougall Collection

Commander Rowland Bourke won the VC in WW I and served in the navy until 1950.
Courtesy of the CFB Esquimalt Naval & Military Museum

He inherited a happy and efficient crew that he knew well and they began patrolling the English Channel.

These patrols were shorter but more hectic than in the Atlantic off Ireland. The heavy shipping in restricted waters complicated matters, and *D3* was frequently attacked by her own side.

On March 7, 1918, Lieutenant Maitland-Dougall, RCN, took *D3* to patrol off Le Havre, France. He was in high spirits—it would be a short patrol and he would be ashore in time to celebrate his twenty-third birthday. But *D3* did not return.

The Royal Canadian Navy has never officially recognized Maitland-Dougall's accomplishments, then or now. Indeed, few modern submariners have even heard his name. Maitland-Dougall was the first and only Canadian submarine commanding officer to be lost in action. He also remains the youngest to pass Perisher and earn command at twenty-two.

Johnson survived the Great War and served in World War II with distinction both at sea and ashore as a commander, but not in submarines. A ship's bell given to Johnson by his shipmates still rests on the wardroom bar at HMCS *Discovery* in Stanley Park. It commemorated his fifty years as a naval reservist and he treasured it all his life.

Julie H. Ferguson is the author of Through a Canadian Periscope: The Story of the Canadian Submarine Service. *The second edition celebrates the centenary of the service in 2014 and records in detail the adventures of Johnson and Maitland-Dougall, among those of many other submariners. Julie invites you to visit www.CanadianPeriscope.ca and www.facebook.com/ CanadianPeriscope.*

A Legacy of Heroism at Sea

Many British Columbians served with distinction in the Royal Canadian Navy, the British Navy and the Royal Naval Volunteer Reserve. They found themselves in some tight spots a long way from home.

Here are some more stories of men who served with distinction at sea.

Eager to Serve: Commander Rowland Bourke, VC, DSO

By the CFB Esquimalt Naval and Military Museum

At the start of World War I, few people might have guessed that a quiet, introverted rancher from the interior of British Columbia would soon become one of only four Canadian naval Victoria Cross winners. Ironically, Commander Rowland Bourke almost didn't make it to active duty.

Commander Bourke was born in London, England, in 1885. At seventeen, he came with his family to Nelson, BC. When World War I broke out, he left the family fruit farm and volunteered to enlist in the Canadian forces but was rejected in all three arms of service because of defective eyesight. Undaunted, he returned to England at his own expense and successfully joined the Royal Naval Volunteer Reserve to serve on the motor launches.

In April 1918, raids were arranged to block the Belgian harbour of Zeebrugge-Ostend, most heavily defended of all the German U-boat bases. Bourke, a lieutenant at the time, immediately volunteered his vessel for the rescue of crews whose ships were sunk in the blockade effort. He was again rejected because of his poor eyesight. Despite being told most of the men would not make it back, Bourke persisted in offering his motor launch as a standby in case one of the chosen rescue motor launches was disabled.

As a result, on the night of April 23, Bourke's launch picked up thirty-eight sailors from the sinking blockship HMS *Brilliant* and towed the crippled *ML 532* out of the harbour. For this latter achievement Bourke was awarded the Distinguished Service Order.

When the second operation against Zeebrugge-Ostend was called, Bourke's motor launch was found to be too damaged for the work. But Bourke was so eager to take part that he offered to give up his command in order to participate in the operation on another vessel, *ML 254*. Finally, however, his own ML was accepted as a standby. Bourke had just twenty-four hours to completely refit his vessel and find a new volunteer crew.

He succeeded, and on May 9 and 10, Bourke's ML followed the blockship HMS *Vindictive* into the Belgian harbour. While backing out after the raid, he heard cries from the water. Bourke made a prolonged search of the area amid very heavy gunfire at close range. He found a lieutenant and two ratings from the RN ship badly wounded in the water. Bourke's own launch was hit fifty-five times and two of the crew were killed. Nevertheless, he managed to bring out his vessel in one piece.

For this action, King George V decorated Bourke with the Victoria Cross. He was also presented with the French Legion of Honour. With characteristic modesty, Bourke asked his family not to inform the press of his achievements.

After the war the reluctant hero returned to Nelson and married. In 1932 he and his wife moved to Victoria and Bourke started work at HMC Dockyard in Esquimalt as a civilian clerk.

He was instrumental in organizing the Fishermen's Reserve, a West Coast patrolling operation, just before World War II. He also served as a recruiting officer for a time, but in 1941 he again became an active serviceman, this time with the Royal Canadian Navy Volunteer Reserve. He served as commander at HMCS *Givenchy*, Esquimalt, and Burrard, Vancouver.

In 1950 Bourke ended his long and dedicated career with the navy, retiring as supervisor of civilian guards. He died in August 1958 and was buried with full military honours. Bourke willed his VC and other medals to the National Archives in Ottawa.

Commander Norman McCrae Lewis: Q-Boat Captain, German POW, Peacemaker

Commander Lewis was one of a group of retired British Army and Navy officers who surfaced in the Boundary country around Rock Creek before the war. They were involved in the Kettle Valley Fruit Lands, a scheme to attract English gentry to settle newly developed irrigated lands. The Glossops (mentioned in Chapter 11) were also prominent in this scheme. Fruit farming had a strange allure for British gentry and retired military families. But like many other investment schemes, the Kettle Valley Fruit Lands did not succeed. At the outbreak of war, Commander Lewis, now almost forty, returned to England to re-enlist in the Royal Navy.

Lewis ended up in command of a British Q-ship, innocuously named HMS *Tulip*. Q-ships were built for a special purpose: to deceive the enemy. They were "flower class" vessels, hence the botanical name. Crews dubbed them "cabbage class" and sometimes "herbaceous borders." But they could be deadly and were the bane of the German U-boat fleet.

Q-ships were essentially wolves in sheep's clothing, dressed up to appear like normal merchant vessels. But behind an array of screens, they were actually heavily armed with artillery and machine guns intended to blow German U-boats out of the water. It was said that First Sea Lord Winston Churchill had devised the scheme to even some scores on the high seas.

Germany was behind a strangling naval blockade, but U-boats penetrated the blockade and attacked merchant ships ferrying supplies to England. They would occasionally surface to order a merchant crew to abandon ship before they sank the ship. At that stage, according to the plan, the Q-ship would reveal its true identity and open fire.

On April 30, 1917, HMS *Tulip* encountered *U-62*, a notoriously successful U-boat that had been sinking an average of one merchant ship each day it was at sea. The suspicious German commander set upon the *Tulip*. The first torpedo almost split the *Tulip* in half, killing all twenty men in the engine room. The rest of the crew took to the lifeboats.

Lewis's account of what happened next appears in Robert Jackson's book, *Behind the Wire: Prisoners of War 1914–18*.

> My crew in their disguises as merchant seamen looked a sorry enough collection, in dirty clothes, rakish caps and unshaven chins, but none presented such a disreputable appearance as myself, the "skipper"—collarless, tieless, coatless and hatless, wearing only a grimy jersey, a pair of old blue trousers and slippers—and it was with shamefaced reluctance that I admitted to being the captain of the ill-fated vessel. However, I was taken aboard after bidding farewell to my men in the boats and led down through the conning-tower into the presence of the captain—Captain Ernst Hashagen. I began to wonder what my fate would be as I faced this tall, clean-shaven, pleasant looking officer with the Iron Cross. One was well aware in those days that the operations of "Q" ships were proving a very painful thorn in the flesh of the Germans, and that little mercy had been shown to the personnel of "Q" ships on those few occasions recently when they had fallen into the hands of the enemy.

The HMS *Prize* was another example of a Q-ship. She looked harmless but was heavily armed and sank at least one U-boat while the crew pretended to abandon ship.
Library of Congress, Prints & Photographs Division, Charles Pears drawing, LCUSZ62-69228

Mercifully, the crew who were left behind in lifeboats were picked up later by a British destroyer. And while Lewis feared the worst for his fate, to his surprise, once aboard the *U-62*, he was offered a friendly drink. He spent the next three weeks aboard the U-boat as she tracked other merchant vessels, continuing her deadly spree. Lewis continued to be treated well, dining with the officers, drinking their wine and liqueurs, and smoking their cigarettes. When the *U-62* arrived back at her German base, Lewis was sent to a prisoner of war camp at Karlsruhe and later Freiburg where he spent the rest of the war.

Upon his return to England after the Armistice, he was greeted by his wife, Margaret. They returned to Canada and Rock Creek in early 1919 where he tried to resume his life as a gentleman fruit farmer. But there was no comfortable fortune to be made and Lewis eventually headed home to England.

Lewis became an advocate for the League of Nations and efforts to make a lasting peace with Germany. He befriended his old nemesis, Captain Hashagen, and their families became friends, exchanging Christmas cards. Lewis went on tour with his story, speaking to schools and meetings. In 1931, in a talk at Solihull School in the West Midlands, he told students, "The Great War broke out because no one minded its coming, and the majority welcomed it as something romantic and glorious.

"There is absolutely no justification for so-called civilised countries killing, burning, and starving each other in millions," said Lewis. "There is no romance or glory in war.

"Peace cannot become a reality if people are content merely to do nothing," Lewis went on. "Everyone has his or her task to fulfil. The League of Nations Union takes upon itself the task of educating public opinion, and it is the duty of everyone who wants the League to succeed to join the Union."

Sadly, Lewis's wish that another world war could be averted was dashed. He died in Kent in 1965.

A Small Navy That Did Its Part

The Q-ship strategy was a mixed success. HMS *Tulip* went to the bottom along with hundreds of merchant vessels. The ships of the Canadian Navy fared much better. All except HMCS *Galiano*. This is her story.

HMCS Galiano: *Canada's Lone Great War Loss*

BY DAVID W. GRIFFITHS

Jutland, Coronel, Falklands and Dogger Bank are a few of the great sea battles of World War I, fought between the Imperial German Navy's High Seas Fleet and the Royal Navy's Grand Fleet across the far-flung oceans of the world.

In a number of these actions, ships of the fledgling Royal Canadian Navy distinguished themselves, but none were ever lost.

Indeed, the only Canadian naval casualty to occur during the Great War happened right

HMCS *Galiano* aground at Esquimalt Lagoon.
Courtesy of the Royal BC Museum, BC Archives B-03998

The ship's company of the HMCS *Galiano*.

Courtesy of the Royal BC Museum, BC Archives a-00219

As this Naval Service pamphlet attests, fish were another staple in the home diet. Tinned BC salmon also made a perfect ration and was shipped to the troops.

Courtesy of Don Stewart

here off the coast of British Columbia, less than two weeks before the signing of the Armistice.

She was the former Dominion Government Patrol Vessel *Galiano,* pressed into service with the RCN in late 1917.

Built in 1913 at Dublin, Ireland, the *Galiano* and her sister ship *Malaspina* arrived at Esquimalt via Cape Horn in February 1914, just six months before the outbreak of hostilities, to take up their duties in fishery patrol and protection.

At 162 feet in length and a top speed of eleven knots, both vessels were armed with a single six-pound, bow-mounted cannon.

Once requisitioned by the navy for war service, both the *Galiano* and the *Malaspina* patrolled a virtually undefended Pacific coast, continuing with her civil duties while undertaking minesweeping training as well as servicing and supplying strategic lighthouses and radio stations.

It was just before departing on one of these resupply runs that the *Malaspina* damaged her bow in a hard landing at a dockyard jetty.

The *Galiano* was quickly readied for sea, despite having only recently returned from the Queen Charlottes, being in need of repairs to both her boiler and main bearing, and being shorthanded because of the Spanish flu.

On October 27, 1918, under the command of Lieutenant Robert Pope, and with a crew of thirty-eight, the *Galiano* steamed out of Esquimalt Harbour, bound for the radio and light stations on Triangle Island, off Cape Scott, and the Ikeda Cove wireless station, at the south end of the Charlottes.

Just two days before the *Galiano*'s departure the CPR steamer *Princess Sophia* had been lost with almost 350 passengers and crew, in a blinding snowstorm, after grounding in Lynn Canal, Alaska.

Northern waters were still churning in the throes of that southeast gale on the afternoon of October 29 as the *Galiano* finished unloading fuel and stores at Triangle Island, embarked the station's housekeeper, Emma Brunton, for passage back to Victoria and headed out for the crossing of Queen Charlotte Sound, bound for the Ikeda Station.

At three the following morning, the wireless operators at both Triangle Island and Bamfield picked up a message from the *Galiano:* "Hold's full of water. For God's sake, send help." This was the last that was ever heard from her.

The rescue and later the recovery effort lasted for more than a week. Only three bodies of the forty souls aboard were ever found, along with two skylights and the portside lifeboat.

Speculation about the cause and location of the loss continues to this day. Most theories agree that the *Galiano* was most probably in sight of the light at Cape St. James when she foundered, but whether she shipped a rogue wave, experienced mechanical failure or struck offshore rocks remains a mystery.

In World War I, a total of 422 men of the Canadian Navy and Reserve died while on active service.

The *Galiano* was the only Canadian vessel lost and her sacrifice is commemorated with a memorial in Victoria's Ross Bay Cemetery.

David Griffiths is a Vancouver Island maritime historian.

From Our Listeners: Two Families, One War

It was not uncommon for men from the same family to serve on opposite sides. Sometimes, marriage after the war brought together families with roots in different camps. One of our Chilliwack listeners sent this example.

By Olaf Frost, Chilliwack

My father's mother, Freda Sewell, was in a poorhouse in Rye, Sussex, with one of her brothers when they were sent as teens to Canada in 1914. But her older brother Albert was in the Royal Navy and wrote letters to her. Albert didn't say what he did on his ship but he said that he hoped the war would end and peace would come. He heard and hoped that he would get up to ninety pounds bonus pay after the war. And he told his sister of escorting the captured German fleet to Scapa Flow, Scotland. I never found out if that bonus pay ever came.

On the other side of the family, my mother's mother, Maria, was married in her German village and had two daughters before the Great War. But her first husband died in the war. My mother's father, Eberhard Grafenschaefer, was from the same village and was captured by the French at Verdun and spent four years as a POW in a coal mine. In 1920, Eberhard got home and married Maria and they had two boys and two girls. They all survived World War II. My mother, Klara, and her first brother, Eberhard, were the last two survivors of the original family. Eberhard avoided being a POW but his brother was a prisoner of the French for four years, which turned out better than being in the hands of the Russians or Americans.

Above: Charles, Albert and Freda Sewell visiting in 1922 in Lucan, Ontario.
Courtesy of the Frost family

Left: Eberhard Grafenschaefer as a prisoner of war in France, 1918.
Courtesy of the Frost family

The Gift of Salmon

British Columbia's salmon producers were facing stiff competition from the US and Japan as war erupted. A recession had also created an oversupply of canned salmon, and the warehouses were filling up. As Geoff Meggs wrote in his book *Salmon: The Decline of the British Columbia Fishery*, the war generated a new demand from the British Army, creating opportunity for BC companies: "The First World War assured the canners the abundant profits of guaranteed markets, so they spent the time in intensive expansion, undertaking a new rush for the largely unharvested stocks of chum and pink salmon in the waters north of Johnstone Strait."

During construction on the CNR in 1913 a disastrous rock slide at Hell's Gate restricted Fraser River sockeye from moving up the river to spawn. It had an immediate impact on sockeye numbers and on the stocks four years later. The industry began chasing more pinks and chum to meet this sudden demand. Another challenge was getting the product to market. Many commercial freighters were seconded for the war effort, and prowling German submarines made shipping routes dangerous. This also increased the cost of getting cases of salmon across the Atlantic.

BC salmon was already a well-known commodity in Britain; companies had been shipping tinned salmon to workers since the 1870s, and by 1914 canned salmon was an important part of the British diet. It was also an ideal army ration. Precooked protein ready to eat right from the can. At the war's onset, the provincial government donated 25,827 cases of pink salmon to the imperial authorities. In late 1914 British Columbia's commissioner of fisheries reported this gift of salmon would pay dividends:

Although the salmon had been designed by the Imperial Government for use in the relief of distress in the crowded industrial centres of the Old Country, after the usual strict inspections by British analysts and food inspectors, the War Office asked that 10,000 cases be placed at its disposal for rations for the troops. Letters from the trenches to the Department testify to the appreciation by the soldiers of this change of diet.

The War Office soon ordered another ten thousand cases. BC premier McBride also promoted salmon sales during his frequent journeys to England and by war's end the sockeye, pink and coho fish pack had doubled in size and value. The fishery had also expanded dramatically, moving farther up the coast to Rivers Inlet, the Skeena and Nass Rivers and Vancouver Island.

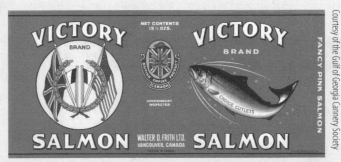

Courtesy of the Gulf of Georgia Cannery Society

From *Canada in Khaki*, 1917

Early in the war, Scottish immigrant Henry Bell-Irving, manager of Anglo-British Columbia Packing Company, was worried about an inadequate naval presence on the West Coast. There was only one coal-burning cruiser called the *Rainbow*, which was long in the tooth and short on crew, and two newly acquired submarines were having mechanical problems. Rumours of German cruisers lurking off the coast had many people nervous. Bell-Irving offered up three of the company's vessels to the British Admiralty: *Holly Leaf, Ivy Leaf and Laurel Leaf*. They soon steamed to Esquimalt, were outfitted to launch torpedoes, then motored to Alert Bay where they patrolled the entrance to Johnstone Strait for the next nine months. The crew on each vessel consisted of the captain, engineer, cook, torpedoman and a signalman.

By war's end a record eighty-seven packing plants were operating in BC. Many returning soldiers found work in the industry, but soon another recession hit and the industry took a nosedive. Some companies went out of business, others were bought by the handful of large companies that dominated the industry. However, British Columbia's abundance of wild salmon provided sustenance when and where British, Canadian and Allied troops needed it most: in the trenches of a gruesome, relentless war.

There is more to be found about the salmon story at the Gulf of Georgia Cannery National Historic Site in Steveston (http://gulfofgeorgiacannery.com).

Courtesy of the Gulf of Georgia Cannery Society

5

OUR FLYING ACES
DARING YOUNG MEN

There has always been something magical about the flying aces of the Great War. While Canadian soldiers struggled in the muddy trenches below, the pilots of the Royal Flying Corps and the Royal Naval Air Service seemed to lead charmed lives in the skies above. "The air was the theatre for tens of thousands of troops watching the sky," said Nanaimo-born flying ace Raymond Collishaw.

"Collie": Maybe the Best Who Ever Flew—Sixty Victories

Raymond Collishaw always lived in the shadow of Ontario's Billy Bishop. Bishop claimed seventy-two victories in the air and won the Victoria Cross. He dined with royalty and had a good war. But "Collie" was the better pilot and might have been the greatest of them all. His sixty victories were undisputed. And while he served most of the war in the less well known Royal Naval Air Service, he was highly decorated and became a true leader of men.

The propaganda experts back in Canada needed a dashing young hero to splash in the newspapers and Bishop was their man. But Collishaw kept quietly racking up victories. After 1918 he fought in ten more small wars before commanding air operations in North Africa in World War II.

Raymond Collishaw was born in Nanaimo in 1893. In 1914, his plan was to join the Canadian Navy. But while he was waiting for a response, he caught the flying bug.

One of Canada's greatest flying aces, Nanaimo's Raymond Collishaw.
Department of National Defence / Library and Archives Canada / PA-002788

"Oh, I wanted to fly!" he told a CBC documentary team in 1969. "We all had to pay four hundred dollars out of our own pocket to pay all the [flying school] living expenses. We got nothing in terms of allowance or any pay for the first months that we were in the game learning to fly."

"Generally speaking, showmanship or any trickery didn't enter into the field at all," said Collishaw. But to survive, you needed some breaks. "It was straightforward duelling. And the best man, the luckiest man, won. It was more luck than anything else."

One of Collishaw's favourite planes—the Sopwith Triplane. German ace Baron von Richthofen liked triplanes too. His was red. Collishaw's was black. Despite its unusual appearance, the triplane was very agile. One wag observed that it looked like "a drunken flight of steps."
Department of National Defence / Library and Archives Canada / PA-006395

Collishaw qualified as a Royal Naval Air Service pilot in 1916. And he was good. Very good. His description of a dogfight captures the element of performance:

"It was a sporting affair because there was a fifty–fifty chance for each. And there would be cheering going on in the trenches as one side or the other side overcame his adversary. The Germans were all watching their boy wearing their national colours. And on the English side, again they would say, that's our boy. In those conditions, with the tremendous audience, each pilot wearing the colours of his country, he couldn't very well run away even if he wanted to with this tremendous mass of people watching him. So it was a fight to the finish. It took quite a different kind of character to suffer that kind of terrible ordeal."

Collishaw had that character. Fellow flying ace Bill Alexander described Colliishaw as irrepressibly upbeat.

"That is Collishaw right through. I have never known anyone more—what is the word?— ebullient. I never saw him depressed in all the months I was flying with him. He was an excellent squadron man."

Group Captain Gerry Nash, who also flew with Collishaw in the Royal Naval Air Service, said he stood out as a leader of men.

"He was a man's man, and one of the boys," says Nash. "There was a great spirit of camaraderie between himself and the other members of the squadron."

"I always think of myself as most successful as a squadron commander," Collishaw said when he was in his seventies. "In the first war, I commanded three fighter squadrons successively, which I think no one else in the world did at that time."

How did he do it? The life expectancy for pilots was dismally short. So Collishaw knew he needed to inspire his officers—and distract them from the constant reminders of mortality.

"I deliberately adopted a policy of trying to make everybody happy. Some young fellows have a tendency to go to their cabins and mope and think about the dangers of tomorrow whence they might be wounded or killed. So I deliberately developed a policy to see to it that all the officers went into the mess and had a jolly good time there, sing song and drinking. And it worked too!"

Gradually Collishaw's accomplishments became better known. His flight group's Sopwith Triplanes became not only famous, but infamous.

"Each flight had its own colours. One was blue and one was red. And in my particular case, it was black. The engine cowling and wheel covers were black. And as they were coloured black, the men began to call the flight 'the black flight.' Then when the flight became more famous, the newsmen picked the idea up."

Gerry Nash called his machine *Black Sheep*. Collishaw's plane was *Black Maria*, a popular name for police paddy wagons. Black humour indeed.

King George V came to inspect Collishaw's squadron in 1918. He was impressed. Not bad for a bunch of colonials from Canada. Collishaw was starting to have a good war.

"My generation had an excellent time, because when I was a boy, Canadians never went abroad. And when they went to the first war, it was the first major occasion when a vast number of Canadians really saw the world as it was rather than what they heard about in their schoolrooms."

Away from home, and faced each day with death, British Columbia's young pilots cut loose when they had time to spare. Collishaw laughed when he remembered some of the binges they went on.

"Every fighter squadron was given a half day off a week. And on that half day, these kids went wild. They would go into some big town and paint the town red. They'd get back in, say two or three in the morning—maybe four—pie-eyed, and roll into bed. The orderly would come in and wake the fellow up. He'd turn himself out of bed, get up and washed, get dressed and go out [to fly again]. You see, there was something peculiar about the air. As soon as you got out into the fresh air, it cleared your brain. They'd be quite normal after fifteen or twenty minutes. But at first you couldn't get any sense out of them. Hah, hah!"

Once in the air, it was serious business.

"One of the most terrible things that could happen to a fighter pilot was to get locked in a deadly embrace—in what was known as a waltz, where you went round and round and round, making continuous, endless turns, each opponent trying to get on the tail of the other fellow. And, of course, the other fellow was very anxious to see he didn't do that. If your aircraft was getting onto the tail of the other fellow, you could see what you were doing with the nose of your aircraft by watching the other fellow's face. His face showed that his time had come."

Collishaw survived the war and went on to fight in the air over Russia during the revolution.

"I took part in ten small wars between the two big ones. And we found out in the small wars that a pilot can get killed just as dead as he can in a big war!"

The death of a fellow pilot during the Great War brought him in contact with the pilot's sister in New Westminster. And that meeting eventually led to marriage.

"My wife had three brothers who were fighter pilots, and all three were killed. One in 1916, one in 1917 and one in 1918. And so because of my close association with her brother, I naturally met her in 1917. And then we were engaged for six years. I didn't want to get married because I was keen on adventure and I realized that marriage would tether my activities as an adventurer. And so we hung fire on our engagement for six years and then we got married."

A tribute to the Trapp brothers at Fraser Cemetery in New Westminster.
Courtesy of Greg Dickson

Opposite: An aerial battle at sea. Armed seaplanes fought it out in the air and on water.
From *The Graphic Magazine*, Sept. 21, 1918

Collishaw received many honours, including the Croix de Guerre, Companion of the Order of the Bath, the Distinguished Service Order and Bar, Officer of the Order of the British Empire, Distinguished Service Cross, and the Distinguished Flying Cross—by one count over twenty-five honours. He was mentioned in dispatches repeatedly. Replicas of his decorations are on display at the Vancouver Island Military Museum in Nanaimo, part of an impressive display on a local boy. He died in 1976.

His widow, Neita Trapp, outlived him, dying in 1989. The cemetery in New Westminster has a special monument to the three brothers she lost in the war. Stanley Trapp died in France in 1916, George Trapp died in Belgium in 1917 and Donovan Trapp died in France in 1918.

Thanks to Colin Preston, CBC archivist in Vancouver, who found the Collishaw documentary for us.

From Our Listeners: Flying Boat Pilot Claude Chester William Purdy

By Dianne Rabel, Prince Rupert

Dianne Rabel is a Prince Rupert teacher who has visited the Great War battlefields and researched the war. She took a class to Vimy Ridge in 2012 and continues to research the impact of the war on BC's northwest.

Claude Purdy is remembered as the pilot of the ill-fated Curtiss Flying Boat on which Al Sturtevant, son of privilege, Yale graduate and noted athlete, lost his life. Sturtevant was the first American airman to die in combat in the Great War; consequently his death received much attention. But it was Prince Rupert bank accountant Claude Purdy who was at the controls on February 15, 1918, when they and two British crewmen were shot down over the North Sea.

Claude was the eldest son of Ontario-born Dr. Alexander DeForest Purdy and his wife Henrietta. He was born in 1888 in East Selkirk, Manitoba, but within a few months the family moved to Bellingham, Washington, where Dr. Purdy practised medicine for about twelve years until his death. In 1901 Henrietta and her children were back in Canada and living at 1158 Melville Street, Vancouver.

The next few years Claude spent in school and then embarked on a banking career in 1910. He and his brother Fred, two years his junior, supported their widowed mother and younger brother Herbert on their salaries as bank accountant and railway clerk.

In 1914 Claude completed a banking course at Queen's University in Kingston, Ontario, then continued his banking career at the Canadian Bank of Commerce in the young, bustling city of Prince Rupert, BC. He appears to have taken the city by storm, and the local newspaper carried dozens of reports of his social activities and community service. One of the city's most eligible bachelors, Claude was reported at dances, fundraisers and every event of note. He served as treasurer of St. Andrew's (Anglican) parish, entered his garden produce in the fall fair and participated in whatever was at hand. We know he made numerous excursions on the coastal steamer because at that time the comings and goings of first-class passengers and hotel guests were front-page news! In late 1915 he signed up with the local Earl Grey's Own Rifles as lieutenant.

But Claude was obsessed with aviation. While others rolled bandages, he started an aviation fund and gave the *Prince Rupert Daily News* regular updates of donors and their contributions. So it came as no particular surprise in 1915 when Claude announced his intention of becoming a flyer himself.

Claude left the north coast in May 1916 to study aviation at the Glenn Martin School near Los Angeles, California. By fall he was on his way back to Vancouver and thence to Britain to join the Royal Naval Air Service.

His flying career began at Sleaford in Lincolnshire as flight sub-lieutenant. In time he was transferred to Felixstowe and promoted to flight lieutenant. By 1917 the end of the war was in sight and American aviators, notably the famous Yale "Millionaires' Unit," joined the British, Canadians, Australians, New Zealanders and South Africans who were already there.

Purdy wrote to the bank:

Am here taking some special work on large sea-planes which will be able to stay out at sea on patrol much longer than the ordinary ones. Our special object is to sink submarines…There were four of us chosen last week for this job. One of our bunch out on patrol this morning brought down a Zeppelin. I should like to have an opportunity to get one as this has been my ambition ever since I came over…We have some very fine machines, some of which I should say are the largest in the world. It seems wonderful that such a large structure can possibly get into the air at all. Patrols, of course, go on in all kinds of weather, and we have to be pretty good at navigation, as there is very little in the air to go by when it is foggy; in fact it takes some pretty good work to steer through clouds, and fog is much worse. The whole thing has to be done by instruments by which one can tell the speed through the air, climbing and gliding angles, and the position laterally. There are also a dozen other things which require attention, and which help to keep the course and to keep the station at home posted on one's movements. It is very interesting indeed to go sailing through the air with anything from five hundred to nine hundred horse-power behind one in the shape of engines.

Early on the morning of February 15, 1918, Purdy, along with a South African pilot in a second flying boat, was scheduled to escort a shipment of beef between Britain and Holland. One of the Yale flyboys was slotted as Claude's co-pilot that day, but Sturtevant wanted more flying hours and persuaded his friend to trade shifts. According to the South African, the two aircraft were each pursued by several German planes. The other pilot managed to elude his attackers and make his way back to base, but once he left, all the aircraft pursued Purdy, forcing him farther south, away from the coast. Then, as in a bad dream, German air ace Friedrich Christiansen came from another direction and downed his plane. (Christiansen was credited with the hit, but other accounts give it to Urban and Ehrhard.)

When Al Sturtevant's heartbroken father went to the Baltic coast to try to find out what happened to his son, Christiansen told him that after the crash he had circled back to look for survivors. He saw three men clinging to the wreckage, waving frantically. He said he considered rescuing them, but thought his own situation too precarious, so did not. By the time Felixstowe realized there was a problem, all but one aircraft were out on missions. The single plane left at the base attempted a search but was damaged on takeoff, thus Purdy and his crew were left to perish in the icy waters. No trace of plane or crew was ever found.

Interestingly, Claude's younger brother Herbert became an American flyer and was credited with a U-boat sinking in 1918.

A full account of Purdy's final flight is published in Marc Wortman's The Millionaires' Unit: The Aristocratic Flyboys Who Fought the Great War and Invented American Airpower.

Major Donald Roderick MacLaren—Forty-Eight Victories

"No more romantic figure emerges from the records of British aviation than that of Major Donald MacLaren of Vancouver." So wrote George Drew in his groundbreaking 1930 book, *Canada's Fighting Airmen.*

MacLaren stood alone as a latecomer to the war effort, rapidly scoring victories in the air in the last year of hostilities. He left a fur trading post in the Peace River Country to enlist in the Royal Flying Corps in spring 1917 and didn't arrive in France until late that year. In the short time that remained, he attained the position of fourth-highest-scoring Canadian ace.

The MacLaren family arrived in 1911 in Vancouver where Donald studied electrical engineering. He and his brother Roy decided to go into the fur business with their father and ended up in a remote part of the Peace River. "The war seemed very remote," wrote George Drew, "...and months passed into years without their realizing the extent to which Canada had become involved in the vast conflict." But when it finally sunk in, Donald, Roy and their father all headed south to enlist.

Flying turned out to be something that Donald MacLaren was very good at. He had very little time to excel, but his list of citations kept piling up.

Donald MacLaren left a fur trading post for the Royal Flying Corps.
From *Canada's Fighting Airmen,* 1930

June 22, 1918, awarded the Military Cross: For conspicuous gallantry and devotion to duty. On one occasion, when on low bombing work he bombed a long-range enemy gun, 9,000 yards behind the lines, obtaining from a height of 200 feet two direct hits on the gun track and two on the railway track alongside. When returning to our lines he encountered a hostile two-seater machine, which he shot down to the earth. He then attacked a balloon, which burst into flames, and finally, observing another two-seater plane, he engaged it and eventually succeeded in crashing it to the earth. He set an example of gallantry and skill to his squadron.

September 16, 1918, awarded the Bar to Military Cross: For conspicuous gallantry and devotion to duty as a fighting pilot. He has recently destroyed no less than nine enemy machines and proved himself a brilliant fighting pilot against enemy aircraft often far superior in number. He has done magnificent service and set a splendid example to his patrol.

September 21, 1918, awarded the Distinguished Flying Cross: Accompanied by two other pilots, this officer attacked four enemy aeroplanes; all of these were destroyed; he himself fought two down within 200 feet of the ground, destroying both. The two pilots who were with him each accounted for one of the remaining two. It was a well-conceived manoeuvre ably carried out, reflecting credit on all concerned. This officer has in four-and-a-half months accounted for thirty-seven hostile aircraft and six balloons, displaying great resolution and exceptional tactical ability.

February 8, 1919, awarded the Distinguished Service Order: Bold in attack and skilful in manoeuvre, Captain MacLaren is conspicuous for his success in aerial combats. On 24th September he and his patrol of three machines attacked a formation of six enemy scouts, although the latter were protected by sixteen other enemy aircraft at a higher altitude. Firing a burst at point-blank range, this officer shot down one in flames. In all he has accounted for forty-eight enemy machines, and six kit balloons.

MacLaren was also awarded the Legion of Honour and Croix de Guerre. He stayed with the Royal Air Force for a few years after the war, but in 1921 he was back in Vancouver where he organized Pacific Airways Limited, one of the country's first successful commercial airlines. He died on July 4, 1988, aged ninety-six.

Captain Frederick McCall—Thirty-Seven Victories

Frederick McCall was born in Vernon in 1896 and enlisted with 175th Battalion in early 1916. But "Freddie" caught the flying bug and transferred to the Royal Flying Corps in March 1917, proceeding to France in December of that year. A month later he brought down his first enemy machine while flying a cumbersome two-seater reconnaissance plane. He won the Military Cross in March. "He has set a fine example of courage and determination on all occasions," read the citation, "and has rendered most valuable service."

McCall was active in the great German offensive in the spring of 1918, attacking fast-moving troops on the ground with bombs and machine-gun fire. He also shot down four more planes and added a Bar to his MC at a special investiture with the king.

In the dying days of the war, McCall drove up his tally of victories earning the DSO. "His courage and offensive spirit have inspired all who serve with him," read the citation.

In September 1918, at twenty-two years of age, he sailed back to North America aboard the *Scotian.* He settled back in Calgary, Alberta, and founded his own company, Great Western Airways, becoming good friends with fellow aviation pioneer Donald MacLaren. McCall died in Calgary on January 22, 1949, at the age of fifty-two. Calgary airport was named for him for a time but later became Calgary International Airport.

Capt. Frederick McCall was born in Vernon and went on to found his own airway, Great Western.
From *Canada's Fighting Airmen,* 1930

Captain Charles Robert Reeves Hickey—Twenty-One Victories

Charles Hickey, like fellow Nanaimo flying ace Raymond Collishaw, flew with the Royal Naval Air Service. He was just eighteen when he signed up in March 1916, a farm boy with no previous military experience. He and his father both served in the Canadian Mounted Rifles before he decided to join the RNAS. He flew a Sopwith Camel and transferred to the Royal Air Force when it was formed in 1918. After scoring an astounding twenty-one victories, he was killed in a mid-air collision with another Sopwith Camel in October 1918.

His citation in November 1918 for the Distinguished Flying Cross with Bar read:

A very determined air fighter who has destroyed seven enemy machines and brought down nine completely out of control during the past three months. His skill and initiative as a flight commander have made his flight very successful. Last month he destroyed two machines and brought down two more out of control in one day, and the remainder of his flight, at the same time succeeded in disposing of several more enemy aircraft without sustaining any casualties.

Major Alfred Williams Carter—Seventeen Victories

Alfred Carter was another one of the Royal Naval Air Service boys. Raised in Alberta, he enlisted in 1915 and was a respected flight commander with the RNAS by 1917. He flew Sopwith Pups and Sopwith Triplanes and later a Camel.

His citation for the Distinguished Service Cross read:

This officer has at all times led his patrols with great courage, skill and pertinacity, often engaging superior numbers of hostile aircraft. On 22 July 1917, he engaged, single-handed for half an hour, five enemy scouts which he prevented from carrying out a reconnaissance. On 24 July 1917, with one other pilot, he attacked four enemy aircraft, one of which he drove down completely out of control.

In a 1969 CBC documentary, he described how he recovered a souvenir from one of the enemy aircraft he shot down:

I got the German fighter started down and I stayed right on his tail until he crashed in the canal. And I went up to the front where he was and got this rudder off the aircraft and brought it back to the squadron and eventually I had it crated up in a small crate and brought it home to Canada with my luggage.

After the war, Carter ran a car dealership in Victoria (A.W. Carter Ltd.) and then rejoined the air force, rising to the rank of air marshall. He died in Vancouver in 1986.

Willie Hilborn in his Sopwith Camel.
Courtesy of Pat (Hilborn) Sexsmith

The Hilborn Brothers of Quesnel

TOLD WITH HELP FROM WILLIAM HILBORN'S NIECE, PAT (HILBORN) SEXSMITH, PRINCE GEORGE

William and Clarence Hilborn were big men, well over six feet, men who would stand out in a crowd. They came from a big family too—eight children. Their mother Josephine was from a pioneer stock in Barkerville. Their father was a respected farmer and a skilled tradesman who built many buildings in Quesnel.

Willie and Clarence were close in age and interests. And when the war broke out, they both wanted more than anything to fly. So they paid for their own flying lessons and stuck with it as long as the money lasted. The brothers graduated as Royal Flying Corps pilots within weeks of each other in the summer of 1917.

Willie Hilborn was the better pilot and more effective in combat. But he had one problem. He was prone to airsickness. He wrote to his brother in 1918, "I am starting to feel sick again. It is my stomach that bothers me. I would like to quit about the end of August."

Even with the airsickness, Willie proved to be leadership material. He rose to the rank of captain and served as a wingman for one of Canada's greatest aces, William Barker, who won the VC. They served together on the Italian front, conducting dogfights with Austro-Hungarian pilots who were just as proficient as the more famous German aces.

Willie scored seven victories in Italy, a significant accomplishment for a flyer who came into the war late. And he was rightfully proud of his accomplishments. He wrote to Clarence, "I have put more time in than any other officer since we came to Italy. I did six hours last week in one day. That was three patrols. I have a great machine...about the best in the squadron."

He loved his Sopwith Camel even though he was a pretty big man to squeeze into the cockpit. And his success in the air attracted attention. "I was recommended for the DFC a couple of days ago," he wrote to Clarence. "I am not supposed to know but somebody told me that knew. It will come through in a few days for sure. Decorations are very nice for sure, but I don't believe in taking foolish chances to get them. I have just gone along, and done my work, and with a little luck have done pretty well."

The Hillborn brothers with their family in Quesnel.
Courtesy of Pat (Hilborn) Sexsmith

His Distinguished Flying Cross citation read: "An excellent patrol leader who on all occasions displays courage, endurance and skill."

While Willie tried not to take chances, his superiors were the architects of a plan that would cost him his life. They determined that his squadron should start flying at night, a risky business in the primitive fighter planes of the day.

On August 31, Clarence received a telegraph at his hotel in London: "Deeply regret to inform you that Capt. W.C. Hilborn, Royal Air Force, is reported to have died of wounds on August twenty sixth. The Air Council express their sympathy. Sincerely, Air Ministry."

On August 16, just a few months before the war ended, Willie had collided with a tree while practising night flying.

"After the crash, he lived for a while," niece Pat Sexsmith told us. "He was scalped by the tree, and then died of infection."

Back home in Quesnel, his mother took the news hard. She wrote to Clarence:

Last Saturday we got the news of our dear son Willie's death. I could not write then. Oh, I can't tell you how we feel and I'm sure your own dear heart aches too. But we believe he has gone to a better world where there is no war and no more pain. Where everything is bright. He was a good boy and so brave and we are all proud of him. Only we wanted him home again, it was such a shock to us all. We must try and be brave.

Pat Sexsmith says her grandmother never forgot or forgave the air force for the loss:

I know how it affected my grandmother Josie. My grandfather Stephen of Quaker stock, accepted tragedies with more equanimity, but my grandmother was very bitter. She refused to go to the cenotaph with the rest of the Hilborns. As a Girl Guide attending the ceremonies, I felt honoured to have a family member who gave his life so we could have peace in Canada. It bothered me that grandmother wouldn't honour his memory too. She hid his DFC. It was never found.

Willie Hilborn is buried at the Montecchio Precalcino Communal Cemetery in Italy. His brother Clarence made it home safely and became a building contractor in North Vancouver.

The Bell-Irving Boys

The Bell-Irving family served with distinction during the Great War. Four of the boys accounted for nine awards for gallantry: Henry Beattie Bell-Irving of the RCN, who served in the Dover Patrol (Distinguished Service Cross and Bar); Roderick Ogle Bell-Irving, who served in the 16th Battalion, Canadian Scottish (Distinguished Service Order [Posthumous] and Military Cross); Malcolm (Mick) McBean Bell-Irving, who served in the Royal Flying Corps (Distinguished Service Order and Military Cross); and Alan Duncan Bell-Irving, who served in the Royal Flying Corps (Military Cross and Bar as well as the Croix de Guerre).

The fighting Bell-Irvings made quite a splash in England. In 1916, the *London Daily Express* described them as "all red-blooded, red-haired and red-fibred, with grit marked all over them."

Duncan could not obtain a commission, so he went to Europe as a private with his own motorbike and for the first year of the war was a dispatch rider. Mick went to England and took private flying lessons before joining the Royal Flying Corps. Both boys became distinguished flyers. Duncan Bell-Irving scored seven victories, earning a place among British Columbia's flying aces.

He was a good shot and a good flyer, later becoming an instructor. But in September 1915, Duncan was shot down. He miraculously survived. Then he was wounded in December. He was shot down again in October 1916 and again wounded in November. With those injuries (and a little luck) he was appointed to a leading position at a flying school in Gosport, England.

Duncan's citation for the MC with Bar read: "For conspicuous gallantry in action. He displayed great courage and skill when escorting a bombing raid. He engaged several enemy machines and drove them off. Afterwards, although his own machine was damaged, he continued to fight against superior numbers of the enemy."

Duncan went on to serve in the RAF in World War II and died in 1965.

Brother Mick was also a fighter with an incredible ability to survive. In December 1915 he was wounded within days of his brother Duncan. Both were both transferred to London to a private hospital run by Lady Ridley in her large house, where they recovered.

In early July 1916 Mick was wounded again, this time in the head while on a photo-reconnaissance flight. He passed out, regaining consciousness just in time to crashland inside the British lines. His observer was also wounded and died soon after. The bullet had entered Mick's skull and lodged in the brain. Unbelievably, no vital parts were touched though he suffered some memory loss. He was nursed by his sister Isabel who had joined the nursing staff at Lady Ridley's and he recovered sufficiently to return to Canada. Having been awarded a DSO and an MC, he was given a hero's welcome.

While he was in Canada, the bullet in his brain shifted, causing blackouts and some loss of peripheral vision. He was sent to Johns Hopkins Hospital in Baltimore where Dr. William Dabney successfully removed the bullet.

In January 1918 Mick was involved in another flying accident. After the successful removal of the bullet in his brain he was given command of one of the first Canadian RFC squadrons at Camp Borden, though he was not yet allowed to fly. Later he returned to Britain and was appointed liaison officer with responsibility for all matters affecting Canadians in the RFC. On a visit to Gosport he persuaded Duncan's successor to let him take the special advanced flying course. While performing a difficult stunt, his plane crashed and he was badly injured, once more to his head. One leg was so badly smashed that it was amputated above the knee. From this time Mick's flying days were over and as soon as he was sufficiently recovered, he returned to Canada. He died in 1942.

With excerpts from Ray Eagle's In the Service of the Crown: The Story of Budge and Nancy Bell-Irving.

The Bell-Irving family in London in 1918. Back row, left to right: Malcolm, Aeneas, Roderick and Duncan. Front row, left to right: Dick, H.O. and Henry.
Courtesy of the Bell-Irving family, Harbour Publishing Archives

Flight Lieutenant Harwood James Arnold

Dianne Rabel from Prince Rupert wrote:

Harwood was well known and admired on the north coast according to the *Prince Rupert Daily News*. He worked as a wireless telegrapher in a number of places including Triple Island and Ikeda on the Queen Charlotte Islands. He was working on the QCI when war broke out and he had the idea he could combine his wireless skills with aviation. He went directly to Vancouver to make his way to England to sign up with the Royal Naval Air Service. In July 1915 he was awarded a DSO for his part in the Königsberg incident in German East Africa. There are varying accounts of his death in 1918, but seems it was accidental.

His citation for the Distinguished Service Order read:

Flight Commander Cull and Flight Sub-Lieut. Arnold were spotting on the 11th July, under fire in a biplane, when the enemy's fire damaged it, so that it descended in a quarter of an hour from

3,200 feet to 2,000 feet. During this time no attempt was made to return to Headquarters at Mafia, although it was obvious that this could not be done unless a start was made at once. Flight Sub-Lieut. Arnold continued to send spotting signals the whole time, and when a quarter of an hour later, the machine was again hit and forced to descend, Flight Commander Cull controlled the machine and Flight Sub-Lieut. Arnold continued to send spotting corrections to the last, after warning the monitors that they were coming down and would endeavour to land near them. The aeroplane finally came down in the river, turning over and over. Flight Commander Cull was nearly drowned, but was assisted by Flight Sub-Lieut. Arnold, and both were rescued by a boat from the Mersey.

According to the book *Collishaw and Company,* Arnold returned to England in 1916 to take pilot training and became a flying instructor at Eastchurch. He married in England in 1917 but was killed accidentally in 1918 in a target shoot when a student's bullets hit his propeller and caused the craft to catch fire and crash.

Captain Bernard Paul Gascoigne Beanlands—Thirteen Victories
BY BILL HOWSON, WEST YORKSHIRE

Paul Beanlands was born in Victoria on September 9, 1897. He was the son of the late Canon Arthur Beanlands. Canon Beanlands had been in Victoria since 1884 and was rector and canon in residence at Christ Church Cathedral, Victoria. Beanlands entered Oundle School while his parents were still resident in Canada but later his family returned to England and settled at Wickhurst Manor, Weald, Sevenoaks.

Beanlands was entered at Sandhurst on August 22, 1914, and after three months of instruction passed out and was then sent on a special course in machine gunnery, which he passed with 100 percent. He was then commissioned to the 3rd Battalion of the Hampshire regiment on December 23, 1914, at Gosport. On January 23, he was in France with the 1st Hampshires, stationed near "Plug Street." When his colonel found out how young he was, he and his staff from the sergeant major upward co-operated in guiding him along the path of a good soldier. This he never forgot.

The infantry were having a gruelling time in the Ypres salient because there was a lack of artillery and ammunition. Beanlands, along with other young soldiers, had long periods of trench warfare with little relief. He was a good shot and had hoped to be a member of the team from Oundle to shoot at Bisley in 1914. At the front he was a useful sniper. He had a good eye and a remarkably steady hand, and later became a very good marksman as his friends used to testify.

By a coincidence Beanlands was detailed to help instruct the 1st Battalion British Columbian Regiment in trench warfare and was recognized by Canadian friends from Victoria. Later, having just been relieved from the trenches himself, he volunteered to guide the Canadian Expeditionary Force on a very dark night to their trenches. He returned safely himself, but it was that fatal month of May when the Canadians were so badly gassed.

Beanlands had always wanted to fly. His letters home from the trenches to his father had been full of the delights of flying and its possibilities. On December 23, 1915, he was seconded to the Royal Flying Corps and sent to Reading for his theoretical training. He passed out 3rd and went on to Shoreham to learn to fly. He was now six feet three-and-a-half inches tall, and to the dismay of his instructors too big to fit into the first two classes of planes. He returned to France on August 23, 1916, and was promoted to flight commander on December 1. On December 13 he won his MC for bringing down three German planes the same day. He returned to England in February 1917.

It must have been sometime between May and June 1916 when Beanlands flew over to Oundle to see a cricket match and was warmly welcomed by Mr. and Mrs. Sanderson (the headmaster and his wife) and the whole school. The event was commemorated by a postcard of himself and his mechanic standing by the plane.

During one of his flights reconnoitring early one morning over Lens, the interrupter on his plane froze and his gun missed firing between the revolutions of the propeller and blew off a blade. He was fifteen thousand feet up over the German lines and continued to fly in ever-widening circles until he was able to land behind his own lines without mishap to his observer or himself. The whole plane disintegrated from the strain of the heavy vibration and fell to pieces on landing. His men presented him with the hub and remaining blade of his propeller with an inscription of the event.

In 1918 he was acting squadron leader when he was seriously wounded near St. Quentin during the great retreat. He was returning to his base and saw our men being hard pressed in the trenches. He flew low, firing at the German lines. A bullet pierced through one leg and glanced off a piece of metal in his plane back into the other leg. Realizing he had been wounded, he made for his base but found he was bleeding profusely and flew into the grounds of a hospital, where he landed only just in time to be evacuated by the last of the staff to the railway station. After a wait of many hours, he was put in the last train from that district before it was overrun by the Germans.

It was some months before Beanlands recovered from his wounds. Then, just before his twenty-first birthday, he was made a captain in the RAF. On December 10, 1918, he was appointed examining officer to the 18th Wing, which entailed the testing of instructors and pupils of the London District and their planes. It was while he was testing a plane on May 18, 1919, just before taking up pupils, that he was killed at the age of twenty-one years and eight months. He was buried at Sevenoaks.

Paul Beanlands was a nephew of Bill Howson's great-grandmother.

A postcard of Paul Beanlands (right) when he returned to his school.
Courtesy of Bill Howson

From Our Listeners: A Zeppelin Pilot's Story

Told by Henning Graf von Platen-Hallermund, 108 Mile

Henning Graf von Platen-Hallermund operates the Arcona House B&B at 108 Mile and one day two guests from Yarmouth, England, noticed an oil painting on the wall. As he told us, this painting connected them in a very unusual way.

> They were sitting at the breakfast table and they looked at one particular oil painting in my living room—my grandfather is driving four beautiful horses. And they said: "Well, who is that?"
>
> I said, "Well, that's my grandfather."
>
> And in that very moment they realized that they didn't have any idea what my name was, so they asked me. I said the name of that gentleman is Count von Platen-Hallermund, and that's my name too.
>
> These two guests were from Yarmouth and when they heard the name of this person in the picture, and were informed by me that this person did indeed have a brother named Magnus, they said, "We know a gentleman by that title and name who was flying a zeppelin in the First World War and bombarded Yarmouth!"
>
> The gentleman then looked at his wife and said, "That was when grandmother just barely made it. She was somewhere in the port facilities of Yarmouth. She barely got away on her bicycle."
>
> Here they were, two people from Yarmouth whose grandmother was bombarded by the brother of my grandfather.
>
> We had another toast or something like that. We were all very moved I must say. Magnus was shot down a couple of times and never really recuperated from it. Terrible.

As Henning says, Count Magnus von Platen-Hallermund led quite a life. Two German Zeppelins, the L4 and the L3, were part of a January 1915 mission to attack industrial and military sites in Humberside. The weather was bad and they changed their plans. The L3 found Great Yarmouth and dropped its bombs, killing a civilian who was believed to be the first British civilian to be killed by aerial bombardment. Others were killed as more bombs were dropped. The L4 bombed Sheringham and Kings Lynn, killing two people. The L4 was under the command of Kapitanleutnant Count Magnus von Platen-Hallermund. Von Platen-Hallermund was in command when the L4 went down over Denmark in February 1917. He escaped death but was taken prisoner.

Von Platen-Hallermund later escaped and was reported to be fighting in Finland. He survived World War I and was killed during an air raid on Hamburg on July 21, 1943.

A painting that started an interesting conversation.
Courtesy of Henning Graf von Platen-Hallermund

Sitka Spruce

By D.E. Hatt

Sitka Spruce is fine of grain,
And Sitka Spruce is tough,
To carry weight and stand the strain
There grows no better stuff;
It thrives upon Queen Charlotte Isles
And lifts its head on high,
When summer's sun upon it smiles
Or winter rages by.

Sitka Spruce is straight and clear,
And Sitka Spruce is light,
That aviator knows no fear
It girds into the fight;
For borne on wings that tire not,
He hurtles on the foe
Until he finds a vital spot
And sends him down below.

Sitka Spruce the Allies need,
And Sitka Spruce must get;
The loggers answer: "With all speed
This need shall now be met."
And when the logger speaks his mind
It is not empty boast—
The Allied nations soon shall find
The thing they need the most.

From Sitka Spruce: Songs of Queen Charlotte Islands, *R.P. Latta and Company Printers, 1918 (Don Stewart collection)*

Airborne with Sitka Spruce

Strong, light and flexible, Sitka spruce *(Picea sitchensis)* was instrumental in taking the war to the skies. Its traditional uses by indigenous people included ropes, fishing spears and even vitamin C, but during the Great War the wood's long, tough fibres made it ideal for airplane construction. And perhaps more importantly, Sitka spruce didn't splinter when struck by a bullet. The Allies' demand for spruce exceeded supply, and as British airplane losses mounted, Harvey Reginald MacMillan was called upon to marshal the British Columbia harvest, much of it from the Queen Charlotte Islands/Haida Gwaii. The Yale-educated MacMillan was a rising star, who by age twenty-seven was BC's first chief forester. As the late Ken Drushka wrote in his prize-winning biography, H.R. MacMillan rose to this new challenge and far exceeded expectations.

His task was to secure vast quantities of airplane quality spruce as quickly as possible, and to do this he had to "organize from scratch" what Drushka describes as "the biggest logging show anyone ever attempted to put together." A tentative objective of three million board feet per month was reached in July 1918, and this had been tripled by the end of the war.

Even today some people on the Queen Charlottes/Haida Gwaii lament the "slash and dash" measures used to harvest these trees.

After the war H.R. MacMillan built one of the country's biggest lumber companies and again served as an administrator during World War II. (Sitka spruce was also used during this war to build the famous Mosquito bomber or "Wooden Wonder.") The industrialist and philanthropist was awarded the Order of the British Empire for his wartime contributions, followed by the Order of Canada. Sitka spruce is still prized for construction, fine interior finishes, masts and decking; the wood has strong acoustical properties, which also makes it popular for building guitars, violins and pianos.

The ninety-six-metre Carmanah Giant on Vancouver Island is four hundred years old and identified as the tallest tree in the country.

May this Sitka spruce stand tall for centuries yet.

BC's Other Flying Aces

James Alpheus Glen, schooled in Enderby: RNAS, fifteen victories

George Thomson, a printer from Celista: RAF, fourteen victories

Harold Byron Hudson, Vancouver: RFC, thirteen victories

Art Duncan, Vancouver Millionaires Hockey player: RFC, eleven victories (see Chapter 15)

William Henry Brown, born in Victoria: RFC, Military Cross, nine victories

Leonard Arthur Christian, born near Armstrong: RNAS, nine victories

George Leonard Trapp, Collishaw's brother-in-law, New Westminster: RNAS, six victories, killed in action 1917

Joseph Hallonquist, born Mission: RFC, five victories

6

JOURNEY TO VIMY
CANADA'S SOLDIERS COME OF AGE

Passengers are quietly chatting and sipping coffee aboard our high-speed train as it slices through the French countryside. Fields are a green blur, cattle stand like statues and traffic on the A1 Autoroute appears to be crawling as our TGV train sneaks up behind vehicles, leaving them behind. As the Forsythes hurtle northward from Paris to Arras, a small city in the Pas-de-Calais region, time seems to slow, then shift into reverse. We are approaching the Western Front.

I try to imagine the reality of this bucolic place almost a hundred years ago during the Battle of Arras. Troops from Britain, Canada, Australia, New Zealand and Newfoundland had dug in for the spring offensive with the goal of punching through German lines. Armies were locked in a terrible stalemate, facing constant shellfire, snipers, relentless mud and a fear that surely gnawed at each man on both sides of the conflict. The Canadians were focused on Vimy Ridge, and among the soldiers amassed was my great-uncle Albert Ernest Rennie, a farm labourer from Ontario. He would survive the Vimy assault, serving with the 18th Battalion, but he was killed just four months later during preparations for the Hill 70 assault.

Our train pulls into Arras at midday. A war memorial dominates a plaza across from the train station. The city was only three kilometres from the front lines and heavily bombarded during the war; the names of civilians and enlisted men killed are etched into cold, grey stone. This journey to Vimy Ridge begins with a slight detour to my great-uncle's grave. My wife and I rent a car and drive just beyond Vimy to Lens, then weave westward to the small mining village of Sains-en-Gohelle. Archives available on the internet have helped pinpoint my great-uncle's grave: Row D. Grave 17. Plot 2. Technology has also allowed me to gaze down via satellite images to this very row of headstones.

The cemetery sprawls behind a red brick wall in the centre of the village. French tricolours shift in the breeze. Hundreds of Canadian, British and Chinese Labour Corps workers are buried here in precise rows, grass neatly clipped to the edge of the headstones. To my knowledge I'm the first from my family to stand at Albert's grave. It is difficult to articulate the

Opposite: Vimy Monument, Vimy Ridge National Historic Site of Canada.
Courtesy of Mark Forsythe

hollow, empty sensation that creeps over me, but a man I knew very little about has become all the more real to me. We locate a flower shop, purchase one red and one white blossom, then stab them into the soil in front of Albert's marker. I write a message in a registry tucked behind a small brass door, a small gesture to honour Albert Ernest Rennie's sacrifice, and a life cut so very short at age twenty-one.

We are back on the road, winding southward now toward the Vimy Monument. Turning a corner in the village of Givenchy-de-Gohelle we see the monument perched on the ridge above us. This was a prime strategic location that the Germans had seized just three months into the war. From here they could see everything moving on the Artois and Douai Plains, and spent the next two years building forts, tunnels and machine-gun bunkers and stringing miles of barbed wire. It was truly a fortress. British and French troops tried to dislodge them in 1915 and 1916 at a horrific cost of 190,000 lives. Numbers beyond our ken.

Now it was the colonials' turn and for the first time all of the corps fighting together. Four Canadian divisions, some hundred thousand men—with help from the British 5th Division—began arriving in the fall of 1916 to begin preparations under Commander Julian Byng, who had tasked General Arthur Currie (at the time the 1st Division Commander) to analyze what had gone wrong during battles at the Somme and Verdun. One thing was certain: the Canadians were highly innovative, rehearsing their attacks so that each soldier knew his part in the battle. Individual soldiers were also issued maps, not just the officers and NCOs. They practised on large-scale replicas of German defences, pursued trench raids to capture prisoners and gather intelligence information, and used aerial photos to learn more about the enemy's intricate trench systems. Lieutenant-Colonel Andrew MacNaughton drew on new optical and acoustical sciences to pinpoint German field guns to be destroyed in order to help clear the way for the infantry.

Almost six miles of new tunnels were built; "saps" or dead-end subways were also extended beneath German positions to eavesdrop and to plant explosives. The skills of Canada's loggers, miners and railway builders were of critical importance to help build the infrastructure necessary to bring in men, supplies and munitions for the elaborate and highly detailed attack. A week before the main event, the largest artillery barrage ever unleashed began to soften defences. A million shells were fired, a hellish noise heard clear across the English Channel in London. The Germans later described this as the "Week of Suffering."

Cold rain mixed with a slushy blizzard ushered in Easter Monday, April 9, 1917. When "Zero Hour" arrived at 5:30 a.m., Canadians began storming the ridge, aided by a creeping artillery barrage that advanced a hundred yards every three minutes. Timing was critical. By that afternoon the Canadians had seized three of the four main objectives. Hill 145, the highest point on the ridge, offered the most resistance and was taken three days later. The Canadians defied the naysayers and delivered the first significant breakthrough of the war. The French press called it "Canada's Easter Gift to France."

Standing at the base of the Vimy Monument, I turn my back to April winds ripping across the Douai Plain. I search countless rows of soldiers' names etched into the base of the monument, looking for my friend Bill Ferrer's great-uncle. He was among 11,168 Canadians reported missing in action in France whose remains were never found; their names memorialized in these marble slabs that cleave the sky. One of the young Canadian interpreters says the remains of soldiers still emerge from nearby farmers' fields. The earth gives them back up to the living, and in some cases remains have been identified through DNA testing and these

soldiers receive military burials with full honours. I eventually locate Bill's great-uncle, run my hand across the letters, Frank Ferrer.

Canada's victory at Vimy came at a horrific cost: 3,598 killed and 7,004 wounded. Today that would be like eliminating the entire population of Port Hardy, BC, and maiming everyone living in Sechelt, BC. Vimy was the first significant British victory in thirty-two months, regarded by many Canadians as a watershed moment in the country's development. No longer was Canada a mere colony or dominion of Britain; its citizens stepped forward and exceeded expectations, setting the stage for further military achievements. Hill 70, Passchendaele and the Hundred Days Campaign followed; British Prime Minister David Lloyd George called Canadians the "Shock Troops of the Empire." This contribution warranted Canada a separate signature at the Treaty of Versailles at war's end.

Above left: Albert Rennie's grave at Sains-en-Gohelle, France. This Commonwealth War Graves Commission cemetery is kept in immaculate condition.
Courtesy of Mark Forsythe

Above: The Arras Memorial commemorates 34,785 killed soldiers with no known graves.
Courtesy of Mark Forsythe

From Our Listeners: Private Buddy McKie of No. 3 Company

With all four Canadian divisions at Vimy, many of our CBC listeners trace their family members to this battle.

By Richard McKie, Richmond

If it wasn't for the Great War, I wouldn't have been born, making me a war baby, one generation removed. My grandfather, William John (Buddy) McKie, was born in the gritty coal-mining community of North Shields, England. As a youth he immigrated to North America in search of a better life.

Buddy landed in Halifax and made his way across the continent, eventually settling in Spokane, Washington, where he was taken in by the Fogelquist family, prosperous owners of a department store. Dewey Fogelquist supported Buddy while he attended Lewis and Clark High School, giving him the education to make him successful. This was put to use soon enough, for when Britain declared war on Germany Buddy went north to Nelson, BC, where he joined the 102nd Battalion, Canadian Expeditionary Force. The was the Comox–Atlin Battalion, soon to become the North British Columbia Regiment, which was commanded by Lieutenant-Colonel J.W. Warden.

The colonel valued an educated man and soon promoted Buddy to the rank of sergeant. Slightly built, Buddy found himself in command of a platoon of rough and ready loggers and miners, as the 102nd was described in their regimental history as "The biggest, heaviest Battalion in the Empire." Finding he was unable to handle his rambunctious charges, Buddy asked to be reduced in rank back to private. His commander in No. 3 Company, Major James Skitt Matthews (later to become the long-serving archivist to the City of Vancouver), accepted his resignation and Buddy resumed the rank of private.

Soon enough the battalion marched out of Comox to travel by ship, train, then ship again to the south of England, where they continued their training, then headed off to the trenches of France. The battalion first saw battle at St. Eloi, where they suffered their first casualty, followed by the bloody campaign of the Somme, culminating in the Battle of Courcelette, where No. 3 Company went over the top for the first time. They took their objective but suffered heavy casualties, including Major Matthews, who was badly wounded.

Buddy came through unscathed and carried on with No. 3 Company, eventually joining in the assault on "The Pimple" at the Battle of Vimy Ridge. By some miracle Buddy was one of the few members of the 102nd who came through the battle physically unscathed. When he revisited the ridge some thirty-five years later, he said that it "smelled like death." The famous place had left its mark on Buddy.

After the battle for Vimy Ridge the battalion fought in a series of smaller actions, culminating in a nasty scrap called "The Second Triangle" fought in the coal mining area around Courcelette. The main objectives were a destroyed sugar refinery and brewery.

It was during this action that Buddy was wounded by the concussion of an artillery shell and his lungs were badly burned by poison gas. His injuries were severe enough to take him out of action and have him sent to England to recuperate. The hospital was in the well-to-do Sussex town of Horsham. The soldiers were encouraged to spend their convalescence in the local park as fresh air and sunlight were considered very beneficial to their recovery.

It was in the park that Buddy met a young children's nanny who went there to walk her young charges. Her name was Dorothy Hedger, and the young Canadian soldier must have impressed her, as a November 1917 entry in Buddy's service record recorded, "Granted permission to marry." Buddy and Dorothy were wed and went on to settle in Vancouver and become the parents of seven children and many grandchildren, one of whom was me, born in 1956.

Buddy had a rough time after the war as his injuries made it difficult to work and he didn't receive a disability pension until the 1930s. Fortunately he was remembered by his old company commander, Major Matthews, who used his infamous networking skills to help Buddy get by. They became lifelong friends and both lived until the 1970s when they finally joined their 102nd comrades and "went west."

McKie is third from right. Buddy visited Spokane on a Red Cross drive and participated in the Washington's Birthday Parade with a contingent of returned Canadians. The yearbook describes "Sergeant McKie arriving at the school in a large limousine."
Courtesy of Richard McKie

The Vimy Myth

The late historian and author Pierre Berton traced the Vimy battle in his highly popular book, Vimy, which was told through the voices of the men who experienced it. During one of Berton's visits to Vancouver, Greg Dickson spoke with him about why Vimy took on mythic status with many Canadians:

> Vimy was a myth because, first of all, we won. Dieppe is also a myth because we lost. But it's better to have won than to have lost. But it was really the only time that the Canadian Corps was together, advancing in line up that precipitous hill. From the point of view of the war, it didn't really mean a hell of a lot. It gets about one line in most of the histories, but for Canada it was everything. First we had done something that nobody else thought we could do. The Germans didn't think so; they said there would be enough left to go home in a boat. And the French didn't think so; they tried. And the English didn't think so; they tried and failed. It was a combination of good generalship, tough soldiers, but above all very careful preparation. We had something nobody else had...it's why we lorded over the Americans. Don't forget, it was the first Allied victory of the war, and this is 1917 and the war started in 1914. So people are hungry, especially in this country, hungry for a victory. It brought people together. It gave us a myth and legend, and that's why we celebrate it still. That's why schools and streets are named Vimy. The word is part of the Canadian lexicon.

Keeping Vimy Alive

By Cameron Cathcart

Cameron Cathcart is a former broadcaster and television producer with a career spanning forty years, including thirty years with the Canadian Broadcasting Corporation. As chair of the Vancouver Remembrance Day Committee since 2003, he leads a team that organizes and conducts the annual November 11 ceremony at Victory Square. A keen amateur historian, he initiated in 2010 the annual Vimy Day Commemoration at Victory Square, developing the "Generation to Generation" ceremony at the Vancouver Cauldron a year later. In 2012 he set in motion the formation of the all-cadet Vancouver Flag Party.

In 2009 he was awarded the prestigious Minister of Veterans Affairs Commendation for his outstanding service in promoting awareness of veterans' issues in Canada. In 2013 he received the Queen Elizabeth II Diamond Jubilee Medal for his "dedicated service to his peers, the community and to Canada."

We asked him about his own journey to the Vimy Monument and about the meaning of this battle in our history.

Vimy. It is an iconic name and place that resonates deeply with Canadians today. Has done among the older generation for much longer. My personal awareness of Vimy was not fully realized until recently.

World War I was unknown to me as a child, perhaps because none of my family was involved. Whereas World War II left an imprint because my parents occasionally hosted young men from Commonwealth countries training to be pilots and my father was always listening to the radio for news from the front.

As I got older my interest in military history focused on the Second War, which seemed more relevant to me. I was appalled by the senseless causes, questionable leadership, miserable trench warfare and tragic loss of life that was the legacy of the First War. It solved nothing and led to the next war.

I now have a better understanding of Canada's decision a hundred years ago to be involved

This forest has grown on what was once a landscape blown apart by bombs and mines.
Courtesy of Mark Forsythe

Some of the preserved trenches at Vimy National Historic Site.
Courtesy of Mark Forsythe

in the First War, the terrible price of lives lost, and how by our actions we emerged at the end with greater political independence. To widen my interest I decided to take a first-hand look and joined a tour of First War battlefields in the fall of 1981.

From the highway in the broad valley below, Vimy appeared impressive yet lonely. I could see the ridge rise steeply eastward and tried to visualize the relentless artillery barrage before thousands of troops found their footing and charged up the ridge, many to their deaths and, for most, victory.

Driving into the vast Vimy battlefield park deeded by France to Canada as a "free gift in perpetuity," I was primed on the carefully rehearsed preparations for the great battle, but those details were quickly put aside as the Vimy Monument, magnificent with its twin pillars reaching skyward, came into view.

The road leading to it cuts through a cratered battlefield. Sheep were scattered among the pines, planted in the 1920s, grazing to keep the grass neatly trimmed and preventing humans from injury or death if they ignore posted warnings of unexploded bombs and shells.

Farther along, preserved trenches laced a field with sand-bagged walls, duckboards and machine-gun firing points so that visitors could "feel" the experience of trench warfare. I lingered for some time trying to confront the terror of war without success.

Extensive tunnelling took place before the Battle of Vimy Ridge, used by Canadian troops as they prepared to attack enemy defences above. Remnants of these, dug into ancient chalk beds, have been reopened. As I moved along the tunnels dozens of names of soldiers and regimental badges were carved into the walls, as if frozen in time, the authors long dead.

Approaching the monument itself I felt a mix of excitement and emotion. It is a stunning commemoration of one of the most hard-fought battles of the First War, which Canadian historians call a "turning point in our history."

The monument has no fewer than nineteen statues, carved individually or in clusters. The iconic pillars stand as sentinels but equally compelling to me was *Canada Bereft* gazing down the slope of Hill 145 where the Canadian infantry charged up the ridge through bitter rain and sleet early on April 9, 1917.

Before the Battle of Vimy Ridge a soldier named William Grey wrote home. A poignant line from his letter reads: "If you get word I'm missing just make up your mind that I'm gone, as usually one is never found." He survived.

I've read that one of the ironies of the First War was that it took more than twice as long as the war itself to finish burying the dead. I faced the wall where the names of 11,285 Canadian soldiers are inscribed. I began to comprehend the overwhelming numbers of those who didn't survive, are lost forever, and who left someone to grieve at home.

It has been said the most powerful act of remembrance of Canada's dead in the First War was the engraving of those names. I agree. The Vimy Monument does not glorify war. It is a memorial of national respect.

From Our Listeners: Lieutenant Jack Hudgins

By Janet Hudgins, Vancouver
Janet Hudgins writes of the tragic cost of war for individuals and families, and our collective responsibility to assist those who put themselves in harm's way.

This is my father, Jack, an officer in the First War (and the next one as well). He was at Vimy, where his brother still lies in the mud somewhere, and was in the midst of about eight other major battles. It must have destroyed him as he rose from a ploughboy to a lieutenant in a few years, but when I knew him he just let life happen. The government offered him nothing and he asked for nothing. He seemed to think that was the proud thing to do. He had believed the propaganda, put on a kilt and took up arms because he had been convinced it was the right thing to do.

Somehow, at his best he persuaded my mother to leave Aberdeen, Scotland, and go to a hamlet in Nova Scotia where she was a bright light and he was never seen.

Wars not only destroy the immediate victim but generations thereafter. All during my adult life I have written to ministers to take care of vets, properly recognizing the depth of the damage and the cost to these people. There is a little of that now, all these years later, with beds available at UBC and, I think, three others in the country. But it's the tip of the iceberg. As long as governments deny the destruction of war to human beings, they can rely on the false bravado told from the front for their rhetoric and call vets up again when the whim arises.

I went to Vimy and found my uncle's name on the fabulous monument there. I'll never forget it because it was so stunningly beautiful that I immediately understood it was a peace icon. It was also a very cold day in April, the month in which my father arrived there, with hard driving rain in my face. I could sense in my bones what it must have been like in the trenches and it made me weep.

Jack Hudgins rose from ploughboy to lieutenant with the 85th Highlanders. His youngest brother Major was killed in the fighting. Jack's family said his body came back after the war, but his mind never did.
Courtesy of Janet Hudgins

From Our Listeners: Joseph Buchan, Vimy Trench Survivor

By Linda Pearce, Ocean Park, Surrey
Linda Pearce writes about her grandfather Joseph Buchan's experiences at Vimy and its impact on his life and on those around him. She also honours him with a pencil drawing.

My grandfather Joseph Buchan smelled of pipe smoke. After lunch he would clip his trouser leg, mount his old black bicycle and ride off to his allotment. There he grew pansies and what seemed an almost endless supply of my rhubarb. As child I was a little afraid of him and Granny often entertained us in a separate room. I knew he had been wounded. His wrist was scarred and wouldn't bend. Later I saw him as a sweet and quiet man and remember him telling me once with a twinkle in his eye, "Never do today what you can put off 'til tomorrow."

In his youth he was an athlete and champion swimmer, once swimming around the coast of Northern Ireland. His wish to live in Canada brought him from a fishing community in Peterhead, Scotland, to Toronto and work for a wool merchant. When war broke out he initially felt removed by the distance, but on hearing that Scottish herring boats had been caught in an attack in the North Sea, it came closer.

His attestation papers were signed on November 10, 1914, and he joined the 19th Battalion of the CEF, which sailed on SS *Scandinavia* from Montreal to England. Then on September 14, 1915, they embarked for Boulogne. His war records show that he remained in France until June 1916 when he was sent to Surrey, England, to recover from severe influenza. He suffered other conditions while in France including trench fever, an intense fever caused by infected lice feces entering open wounds.

Other accounts have described the interminable mud, rats and disease-infested conditions in the trenches. Like many men who experienced the trauma of that time, it was later in life that he felt able to share any of his personal memories. Then after his evening glass of whiskey he told his youngest daughter he recalled hearing German

Linda Pearce drew this portrait of her grandfather Joseph Buchan. After being hit by shrapnel, he lay in a trench all night before being rescued.
Drawing by Linda Pearce

boys talking to each other when all was quiet. He also remembered that when a concert party came to entertain the troops "we thought we were in heaven."

When the Battle of Vimy Ridge began he talked about creeping along the trench, throwing grenades. My cousin wrote, "Having visited Vimy some years ago I saw how the trench system zigzagged along the ridge very close to the German trenches, it must have been terrifying."

He was hit by shrapnel on the first day of the battle, April 9, 1917, and suffered wounds to his back, thigh and wrist. Many of the stretcher bearers were conscientious objectors and "enormously brave." They were loaded that day and forced to leave him behind but promised to return at first light. He lay in a trench all night immobile and afraid the rain would cave the sides in on him. Others had died that way. At dawn, footsteps sounded through the mist and true to their word they carried him to a field hospital. He refused to have his hand amputated and proceeded through a series of operations at several hospitals, in time returning to Canada to convalesce.

At the start of the war, Phyllida Bridgewater had abandoned her studies at the Slade School of Art in London to become a masseuse (physiotherapist). She came to Canada to work in the convalescent home where Joseph recuperated. He claimed to have fallen the moment he saw her. They were married for fifty-one years and had six children, eventually arriving at a devoted old age. His dream of living in Canada was left to his children. My aunt wrote, "Mother said she thought all young men who had been in the trenches were damaged, not just physically."

From Our Listeners: Gordon Robertson Writes Home

Told by Joan MacKay, Prince George
Canadians were regarded as a force to be reckoned with by their enemies after the military success at Vimy. It also boosted the spirits of the Canadian troops. Joan MacKay tells us her father Gordon Stuart Struan Robertson wrote about a rising optimism just two days after the Vimy Ridge victory:

"By now I suppose you will know with what success the drive started and the Canadians help start it. The whole affair was a walk-over and why old Fritz doesn't quit is more than I can make out." April 30: "We are by now in support of a detachment of Canadians who went over the top a few days ago. Needless to say, it was a success—as it generally is when the Canadians attempt it. Some of our boys were talking to a Frenchman not long ago and the talk was as follows:

Canadian: 'What do you think of our advance?'

F.M.: 'Tres bon, French take Vimy, no keep it. Germans take it back. English take Vimy, no keep it, Germans take it back. Canadians take Vimy, Germans no get back.'"

From Our Listeners: Graffiti in the Tunnels

By David Tickner, Abbotsford
My grandfather, John Cameron, was born on March 24, 1886, in Aberdeen, Scotland. For reasons long lost, he and a sister were sent as children to Manchester, where they were brought up by an aunt. He apprenticed as a moulder, married, had two children, and in 1910 emigrated to Canada, settling in Brandon, Manitoba, where he worked for the Brandon Machine Works.

On September 22, 1915, John enlisted in the Queen's Own Cameron

Highlanders of Canada, a unit of the 16th Canadian Scottish Battalion. He was twenty-nine years old.

On June 28, 1916, the battalion arrived in France just in time to participate in the calamitous fighting in the Somme River valley through the summer and fall of 1916, particularly near Thiepval Ridge and Courcelette (Regina Trench). On the December 14, 1916, John was promoted to lance corporal.

At the end of March 1917, the 16th Scottish moved to the Vimy Ridge sector and was billeted at the Maison Blanche farm—or, to be more precise, billeted in the souterrain—the caves and tunnels dug forty to sixty feet into the chalk under Maison Blanche. These caves, some of which date from medieval times, were a base and staging area for Canadian soldiers.

While waiting and resting at Maison Blanche in the days and hours before battle, soldiers carved hundreds of pieces of graffiti into the cave and tunnel walls. The graffiti includes names and dates, images of people and animals, hearts ("Bill loves Mary"), a post office box carved into the chalk and used during the war, and complex and detailed battalion crests and symbols. A few years ago, a television documentary, *Vimy Underground,* was produced, which tells the story of these caves and of some of the men who carved this graffiti.

These men carved such images on the cave and tunnel walls knowing that within hours or days they might be wounded or dead. In the face of possible death, they were actively and creatively remembering. Remembering was an embrace of life, a vital act. Their graffiti became their memorial—"Remember me—I was here."

One of the images featured in the documentary was the crest of the 16th Canadian Scottish with the name "J. Cameron" carved beneath. A set of words appears on the television screen: "John Cameron. Age 31. Moulder. From Manchester. Survived the war." John Cameron—my grandfather.

In the early morning hours of April 9, 1917, Easter Monday, the men of the battalion moved forward from Maison Blanche and followed their comrades already moving through the Bentata Subway, one of the many tunnels that gave protection to the soldiers before they emerged and engaged in the fighting at Vimy Ridge.

I have tried to imagine that morning as these young men picked up their packs and weapons and walked single file down the narrow subway tunnel, walking toward that moment when they would break out into the open and move toward their attack on the German lines.

I think about my grandfather. He emerged from the Bentata Subway that morning and as he walked toward the enemy, head down into a storm of flying metal, one of the millions of pieces whirling through the air hit and knocked him down.

He was struck in the neck by a piece of shrapnel. On April 12 he was evacuated to a hospital in England. The records indicate that he remained in a Reserve Unit in England until December 21, 1918. He was struck off strength on February 8, 1919, and presumably returned to Canada with the 16th Scottish when the battalion returned to Canada on HMTS *Empress of Britain* in April 1919.

John spent the rest of his life in Brandon. After the war, he had two more

War graffiti. David Tickner's grandfather John Cameron carved his initials in chalk while waiting for battle in underground caves near Vimy Ridge.
Courtesy of David Tickner

children, one of whom was my mother, Jean, who has lived in Abbotsford, BC, for almost thirty years.

According to my mother, John was a strict but caring father. He was active in the Anglican Church and was the kind of man who would quietly and unobtrusively do a good deed or provide a hand or word of encouragement to someone in need without wanting to be seen to be doing so. In his "stiff upper lip" English manner, he preferred to demonstrate his care in subtle and behind-the-scenes ways. The unemployed men of the 1930s Great Depression travelling back and forth across the country always seemed to find some food or work for food if they came to the back door of the Cameron house; not just from John, but also in equal measure from his wife, Florence.

As I look back and recall him through a child's eyes, I see a quiet, good-humoured and generous man. One thing I remember is the disdain and disgust in his voice when speaking of bully beef—he wouldn't go near it. I liked tinned bully beef, a cheap and easy meal on our table in the 1950s. I realize now how much bully beef must have reminded him of life in the trenches during the war.

John died in 1964.

In the years after World War I, the 16th Canadian Scottish evolved into what is now the Canadian Scottish Regiment (Princess Mary's) based in Victoria and other locations on Vancouver Island. Many 16th Battalion artifacts and memorabilia from World War I are found in the Regimental Museum in Victoria.

From Our Listeners: James Lennox Dugan, Missing in Action

By Alison Patch, Burns Lake

My great-uncle James Lennox Dugan served with the Royal Highlanders (Black Watch) in the 78th Battalion. He was killed in action on March 1, 1917, just before the major offensive started. His name is on the Vimy Memorial. Three people from two sides of my family all served together in the same battalion before the links of

the family were forged. James Lennox Dugan is my maternal great-uncle and was an enlisted man. Two officers in the same battalion were my paternal grandfather, Howard Henderson Patch, and his brother-in-law, Henry Morgan. In a strange coincidence, my grandfather was injured on the same day that James was killed.

From Our Listeners: Remembering George James Waters

By Lois Williams, Port McNeil

My mother Grace died at age seventy-eight in 1992, never knowing her father, George James Waters. He was killed April 9, 1917, at Vimy when she was just three years old. Her mother, Lily-Maude, passed away when my mother was twelve. Mom was an orphan who always regretted never having known her father.

In 1995 I went on a journey in my mother's honour to visit Vimy and my grandfather's resting place at the Givenchy Cemetery. In the Vimy area I visited a second-hand shop. A bugle in pristine condition sitting high up on a shelf caught my eye. When the merchant brought it down for me to look at, I almost fainted. The bugle was from my grandfather's Central Ontario Regiment! I had felt many times that it was more than good fortune that was guiding me in my journey to know my grandfather. I almost felt his hand upon my shoulder many times on this journey.

In the Vimy battle, he was chosen to be a gunner because of his good marksmanship. He was born in Great Yarmouth, England, and immigrated to Vancouver with his new bride around or before 1912. My grandfather worked as a carpenter for Viner Construction in Vancouver. As a young man in Norfolk England he liked to play rugby.

Before I left his grave in Vimy I wanted to leave a part of me with him, and a memory of Canada. The only thing I had besides the flowers were a few Canadian coins in my pocket. I buried them in the dirt at the foot of his headstone. I hope he knows he is loved and remembered for who he was and his sacrifice to his new country.

From Our Listeners: Postcard from the Front

By Rod McNairnay

After searching for a number of years for information on my great-uncle Hugh McDonald's World War I service history, I was finally rewarded when I discovered his regimental number and an old postcard he sent home as they were preparing for the battle to take Vimy Ridge.

I was given this photograph, Uncle Hughie's service decorations, his badge and one collar dog by some strange twist of fate. I feel very privileged to have them. I hope that you might print my photo. Someone might recognize the other two lads that drove along with him.

From his regimental number I was able to get a copy of his service file from Ottawa, then track him around France and Belgium for three and a half years through the war diaries of his brigade, the 4th Canadian Field Artillery. He participated in the Battle of the Somme, Vimy, Paaschendaele, Amiens and Valenciennes. He took up his former occupation in Winnipeg as a driver for T. Eaton Co., which he did for forty-six years. He died on April 24, 1983—ninety-one years less a day.

Courtesy of Rod McNairnay

Lessons of Vimy

Dianne Rabel is a teacher-librarian at Charles Hays Secondary School in Prince Rupert. She makes Canada's war history and its impact on people real by leading her students on battlefield tours—to Vimy and beyond.

By Dianne Rabel, Prince Rupert

When I started teaching twentieth-century Canadian history a few years ago, it didn't take long to realize that there was something missing: I had never been to the battlefields. Worse still, I taught an exchange student whose excellent German education and exposure to significant sites gave him a depth of understanding I lacked.

So the next summer I went on a battlefields tour. Another summer, another tour. I was hooked! I knew that students would benefit just as I had, so the following year I took forty-two students to Vimy Ridge.

Participants were required to do several things, the most important of which was a soldier study. A few of them chose a relative, but most chose one of the names on the local cenotaph. It didn't matter so much who they studied; the goal was that each person make an emotional connection to one of these men.

The students worked hard to piece together their soldiers' stories. They found information online, looked at both primary and secondary documents, read through soldier files we ordered from Ottawa, combed through newspaper archives, interviewed family members and even pored over war diaries. In the end each student wrote an account that paid tribute to one man's sacrifice.

Unfortunately none of our fallen were buried in cemeteries we planned to visit, so we did another study. This time each student took a Canadian who died at Vimy Ridge on April 9, 1917, and was buried in the beautiful Cabaret-Rouge Cemetery nearby. When we visited the cemetery, each student found the appropriate grave, planted a flag, lit a candle and shared the soldier's story. It was a deeply moving ceremony.

We were able to fit many meaningful visits into our days in Belgium and France. In Ypres we stopped at the Cloth Hall, we found the names of more than a dozen local men on the magnificent Menin Gate, and then visited the Brooding Soldier monument at St. Julien where so many British Columbians fell in the first gas attack. The highlight of the day, especially for the boys, was a private museum at Hill 62 where a portion of a British trench system has been left untouched since 1915. Students explored the trenches, tunnels and shell holes, knowing that men from our own city fought and died on that very ground.

On the anniversary of the battle we were on the hill. We marvelled at the beauty of the monument. We walked where the 102nd Battalion, Northern British Columbians, fought and died. But it was a stormy day and thousands were there, so parts of the site were closed. I encouraged students to visit again if they ever had another chance. The monument is amazing to see on a sunny day, and I knew they

Students from Charles Hays Secondary from Prince Rupert at the Vimy Monument.
Courtesy of Dianne Rabel

would love to explore the tunnels where soldiers waited underground the night before the attack.

Before we moved on to Juno Beach and the German casemates that overlook the Allied landing sites of World War II, we did one more thing that isn't on most student itineraries. Very close to Cabaret-Rouge is another cemetery for soldiers who died the same day as the men we honoured. The cemetery is Neuville–St. Vaast, and the fallen are German. Some of us even found our own surnames there. We were immensely moved as we walked between the crosses and the memorial stones of German Jews, recognizing the common humanity.

The tour held many unforgettable moments, and no one came home unchanged.

Dianne Rabel's students have a deep appreciation for and understanding of what those young warriors must have experienced. The compelling profiles that follow were researched and written by the Prince Rupert students. We appreciate their contribution.

Lieutenant Adair Carss, 102nd Battalion, CEF (1891–1916)

By Devin Harris, Prince Rupert

His name: Adair Carss. Like many others he died for his country, but in his case he didn't have to. Adair was born in Rapid City, Manitoba and grew up in Victoria, BC. When he was a young man his family moved to Prince Rupert where his father set up a law practice. Adair wanted to follow in his father's footsteps so he studied law at UBC, with the goal of becoming his father's partner.

Adair's life leading up to enlistment was studded with athletic and dramatic accomplishments, glamorous parties and academic studies. He eventually achieved his goal of joining his father, Alfred, at the bar and joined Carss & Carss in Prince Rupert. Adair's life was wonderful. He had an excellent career, working side by side with his father, attending all the upscale parties as one of Prince Rupert's most eligible bachelors and participating in every possible athletic activity. But like thousands of others, he felt the need to serve his country. On May 5, 1916, in Victoria, at the age of twenty-five, he became a lieutenant in the Canadian Expeditionary Force.

The war was already very much under way when Adair enlisted. The supply of soldiers was dwindling and by 1916 soldiers were shipped overseas quickly and spent less time than earlier men had in preparation. Because of his education and leadership ability he became an officer immediately. Appointed to the 102nd Battalion Northern British Columbians, Adair saw action within a few short months. After disembarkation in France he became an early casualty. On July 24, 1916, he was wounded but was soon cleared and able to rejoin the battlefield.

Adair met his demise on September 23, 1916, at the Battle of the Ancre Heights (Regina Trench) and his death occurred in an unusual way. Soldiers form bonds with one another; they make friendships which make their job so much harder; no one would want to see a friend die and would likely, if given the opportunity, try to save him and do anything in his power to help. But Adair did not die for a friend. He went to assist a mortally wounded German soldier. It takes great character to stay by a friend who is dying; it takes even more to stand by your enemy, to be the last reassuring voice this person hears, someone whom you may have just been trying to kill. The German soldier had a concealed grenade and hurled it at Adair when Adair went to his aid. Adair showed great bravery and compassion but was not shown the same. He died later that day of his wounds. A popular and influential citizen had passed away, and his death seemed particularly cruel and unjust.

Adair's father, who was appointed a judge during the war years, was devastated. Alfred Adair did not last long after his son's death. He was ill, and in hopes that expert treatment would restore him to health, he sought treatment in Rochester, New York. But it was too late and Alfred Carss died on April 14, 1919. Adair's mother, Annie, and his younger sister were alone.

Adair Carss may not have left behind a wife and child, but he did leave behind a legacy of loyalty, success and bravery. It takes great character to leave an exciting life for one in the trenches, with torrential rain, rats, lice, danger and fear your daily companions. Adair showed great character and sadly paid the ultimate price. He is buried in Albert Communal Cemetery in northern France. Adair Carss is a name that should always be remembered. Rest in peace.

Captain Donald Mackenzie Moore, 16th Battalion, CEF (1877–1915)

By Kenny Ree-Hembling, Prince Rupert

Donald Mackenzie Moore was born in 1877 in Hopewell Hill, New Brunswick. His religion was Wesleyan. Moore stood at five feet ten inches and he had grey eyes. He had a brother named C. Archie Moore and his mother's name was Ann Rogers Moore.

Near the turn of the century Donald Moore moved to the West Coast as did his cousin, Cyrus Peck. Cyrus was six years older and Donald's best friend. The men settled into life on the north coast and fully participated in the business and social activities of the new city of Prince Rupert. On Moore's attestation paper he called himself a cannery man living in Prince Rupert, BC; however, this tells only a small part of the story. Cyrus Peck and Donald Moore were partners in business and had holdings in newspapers, insurance, sawmills, canneries and so forth. They were incorporated as Peck, Moore & Co. Together they built the Cassiar Cannery and Donald oversaw the operations. The *Prince Rupert Directory* of 1910 lists Donald as president of Georgetown Sawmills. Donald and Cyrus were two very busy entrepreneurs, well respected and a vital part of life in this city when the Great War broke out.

In addition to pursuing all of these business interests, Donald Moore was active in the community. He was a member of the prestigious Prince Rupert Club, whose members included the most influential and powerful people in the city.

Captain Donald Mackenzie Moore.
Courtesy of Kevin Moore

Like his cousin, Donald was active in the local militia, the 68th Regiment Earl Grey's Own Rifles. This experience, his age, his leadership ability and his standing in the community meant he was obvious officer material. Following the declaration of war, he and Cyrus wasted no time in going south to enlist. On November 6, 1914, he boarded SS *Prince George* en route to Victoria. Donald enlisted on November 9, 1914, at the age of thirty-seven. He was assigned to the 30th Battalion initially, a nominal role. Later both he and Cyrus were transferred to the 16th Battalion, the famous Canadian Scottish, as officers.

Donald Mackenzie Moore was not in the war for very long. He was reported wounded and missing in the Battle of Festubert on May 24, 1915. Festubert was a bloodbath, and at least three more men from Prince Rupert died in a stretch of five days during the ten-day battle. The bodies of three of those four men were never found. One was Lionel Crippen of the 7th Battalion, well known for his salted herring business at Dodge Cove and for his employment as city clerk in Prince Rupert. The other two were Private Harold Christie Medcalf, a farmer, also with the 16th Battalion, and Sergeant Colin Milburn, a clerk, with the 19th Battalion. When the battle at Festubert was over, Canadians had gained nine hundred metres of ground with a loss of 661 Canadian lives. Citizens of Prince Rupert were horrified at the deaths of so many prominent local men.

Cyrus Peck refused to believe that his cousin could have died, and he denied in the press for months that it could be so. Often families would cling to the hope that their loved one had been taken prisoner. Much later, when no evidence of a body or prisoner status had been found, Donald was presumed to have died on May 22, 1915, in battle. His name can be found on the Vimy Memorial on the north wall, section 3, as well as on the Prince Rupert cenotaph. His name was also inscribed on a brass plaque dedicated to the fallen members of the Prince Rupert Club. The present whereabouts of this plaque are unknown.

Donald Moore was paid for ninety-two days of service, earning a total of $451.10.

Like thousands of others, he answered the call to come to the aid of the motherland, and paid the ultimate price within months on the killing fields of France.

Private Frederick Farran Bradshaw Darley, PPCLI (1891–1916)

By Seamus McConville, Prince Rupert

Frederick Darley had an interesting history; while living in Prince Rupert only a short time, he became a local war hero. Darley was born in Carrick-on-Shannon, County Leitrim, Ireland, on September 13, 1891. His parents were Henry S. Darley, a captain in the Imperial Army, and Charlotte E. Darley. He studied at Mountjoy School in Dublin and at Dublin University.

Fred and several of his brothers emigrated to Canada at a time when young men were flocking to the Canadian West from the British Isles. He arrived in Halifax on April 8, 1913, and entered the service of the Canadian Bank of Commerce three days later. He was sent to Prince Rupert, a young city, incorporated only three years before.

Fred was a popular young man about town and was seen at local dances and social occasions. He stayed with the bank for about eighteen months. He joined the 68th Regiment Prince Rupert Light Infantry. But on February 9, 1915, Fred went south to Victoria to enlist with the Canadian Expeditionary Force. It appears he was in great health when he enlisted. He was six foot one, which was quite tall for the time, and declared fit for battle. Fred and five older brothers signed up, all with different Canadian battalions in six different cities.

Fred was attached to the Princess Patricia Canadian Light Infantry (PPCLI) as a private in February 1915 and shipped off to Europe. He was immediately put into battle in the Ypres area and soon suffered an injury. The war diaries state that the brigade was under constant heavy shelling from German artillery and lost a few men to that. A day before his injury, a lieutenant and captain were wounded in the Polygon Wood, which is where the PPCLI was holding the trench. The next day, an unceremonious entry in the war diary of April 26 reads, "Still hold same trenches (Casualties 9 men wounded)." Fred Darley was one of those injured. He was hit in the head by shrapnel and rendered unconscious for close to four days.

From *The Daily News*, Prince Rupert, July 16, 1915

As it turns out, this battle was the infamous Second Battle of Ypres, where German forces, against the Geneva Convention, attacked the Canadian positions with chlorine gas. This battle ended with two thousand Canadian soldiers dead and countless others injured. The head injury was tragic because at this time Canadian soldiers fought without helmets. According to the medical report, Fred remained semi-conscious for about five weeks. He underwent an operation in Boulogne, France, for one of the fractures in his skull. The doctors also reported "a piece of brain about the size of a small orange was fungating"—in other words, the portion of brain protruding from the skull was necrotizing: the tissue was dying. The good news was it disappeared after a few weeks. He was in the hospital in Leeds, England, for close to nine weeks, and then Northern General Hospital for three weeks. He was struck off strength from the PPCLI on May 3, 1915.

After the initial injuries he suffered, Fred recovered remarkably well. On the medical paper dated August 3, 1915, it says he was "in fair physical shape." It did note, however, that he still suffered some of the effects of the injury, such as when bending down his blood throbbed in his head, and he had a loss of hearing in his left ear and some memory problems, such as becoming confused when two people talked at the same time. A very positive development was that he had no headaches and his memory was "fair." He also had a few scars, such as one just above his eye where the skull was depressed, at which the medical examiner stated that the "pulsing of the brain can be seen from the depression." There was also a smaller scar at his hairline.

On November 18, 1915, he was discharged from the army, fourteen months after he had begun his service. The Pensions and Claims Board finally approved his pension on September 29, 1916. He was to receive $384 a year. The *Prince Rupert Daily News* published a photograph of him in his hospital bed with the report that he was getting better and would be returning to Rupert soon. Sadly, his return to Prince Rupert never materialized because on November 22, 1916, Fred Darley died at the age of twenty-five because of complications from the injuries he suffered at Ypres. He is buried at Hanwell Cemetery in the United Kingdom, and his sacrifice, along with that of many others from Prince Rupert, is commemorated on the Prince Rupert Cenotaph.

Four of the brothers survived the war, but three weeks after Fred's injury, his brother Cecil was killed in action at Festubert. This Irish-Canadian family paid a cruel price.

From Our Listeners: A Canadian Pilgrimage

By Wendy Kerry, Port Alberni
Half a million people pay homage at the Vimy Monument each year. As Wendy Kerry can attest, experiencing the National Historic Site can have the power to change lives.

Visiting Vimy Ridge had a profound effect on me and the emerging direction of my life. On reflection it was possibly a life-changing experience for me. I had not fully comprehended that a relatively small, yet committed army cobbled together from an emerging and diverse community called Canada could change the direction of a horrific war where so many more powerful nations had tragically failed over the course of many years. During and after my visit I became increasingly convinced that the Vimy victory marked the true "Birth of Our Nation." Beyond any shadow of a doubt, the Vimy experience greatly enhanced my inner desire to do something about those "Vimy Ridges" that confront us almost a hundred years later and gave me the courage to be an unapologetic and proud CANADIAN.

Wendy Kerry at the Vimy Ridge National Historic Site of Canada.
Courtesy of Wendy Kerr

Victor Gordon Tupper, MC: His Biography and Letters

From Reginald H. Tupper's Victor Gordon Tupper: A Brother's Tribute
This privately published account of his brother's wartime experiences includes letters and excerpts from letters written by Gordon to their mother, Lady Janet Tupper.

Victor Gordon Tupper was the fourth son and youngest of six children born to Sir Charles Hibbert, and Lady Janet Tupper. Born February 4, 1896, in Ottawa, his Godmother was Lady Aberdeen, wife of Lord Aberdeen, Canada's then Governor General; he was named Gordon after the Aberdeen family name.

His father was the Justice Minister and Solicitor General in a succession of Tory governments including the brief period his grandfather, Sir Charles Tupper, was Prime Minister.

(His first name, Victor, was given to commemorate the fact that his grandfather was returned to parliament on the day of his birth.)

After the defeat of the Conservative Party in 1896, his family moved to BC and eventually settled in Vancouver.

He was educated at University School in Victoria and at Highland in Hamilton. He was a dynamic, adventurous young man whose interests were mainly in the outdoors: hiking and fishing; at school he excelled in football (rugby) and marksmanship.

As his brother, Reggie, put it in his tribute: "His happiness lay in action, and wherever daring entered the contest, he was pre-eminent."

He volunteered for service immediately war was declared, August 1914, and enlisted in the Seaforth Highlanders of Canada, No. 3 Company, as a private.

The Seaforths with other regiments were later drafted together into the 16th Battalion, Scottish.

His Company Commander was his brother-in-law, Captain Cecil M. Merritt, who was killed in action at Ypres, early on in the war, and whose own son (Gordon's nephew), Colonel C.C.I. Merritt, was awarded the VC for his action in the Dieppe raid of 1943.

In 1915 he received his commission and rose to the rank of Captain in 1917.

He saw action first as a Transport Officer (logistics and re-supply), and later he was put in command of a Communications unit where he was awarded the Military Cross for his heroic work in maintaining communication lines between HQ and the front lines, as well as between artillery "spotters" and their guns.

The award appeared in the *London Gazette* dated Nov. 14, 1916: "For conspicuous gallantry in action. He kept signal communications under heavy fire. Later, he personally supervised the repair of wires that had been severed, displaying great courage and determination. He has previously done fine work."

He was killed in action at Vimy Ridge in April 1917.

Letters:

June 21, 1916: Battle of Sanctuary Wood (Mont Sorel). I will now do my best to tell you about our big show, which came off on the 13th. It is the first letter I have tried to write since the action. To begin with, the Third Division lost about 1,500 yards of trenches, of 500 yards depth…It was quite light when we got into position and so only two battalions (the 14th and the 15th) charged; and we supported them. Without any artillery help the thing was impossible. They were mowed down by machine-gun and shrapnel…You can't imagine what a modern barrage is like. Hell is not strong enough…all the time it was raining hard; the trenches (ditches of course) were worse than they were last winter; and we were all in summer clothes…

The 16th (Battalion) came quickly into action, and we sent those Huns flying in great shape. Lots of prisoners, but hundreds killed…

I had two close shaves—stunned twice. Once by a piece of casing, hitting my steel helmet; and again by a chunk, cutting through the padding of my overcoat and glancing off the side of my neck. My Sam Brown belt was cut in two. I was in the act of shooting a Hun at the time; but when I got to my feet, the swine was standing by, with his rifle and equipment on the ground. So I took him prisoner…You can't imagine how cowardly the Huns were. One officer put his arms around my neck, and cried on my breast when he found that I wasn't going to kill him…Those of us who got out alive were certainly born to die in our beds! They say that April 22, 1915 [the second Battle of Ypres, with the first use of gas primarily against Canadian troops] was merely play compared with this.

June 23, 1916: It makes it much easier when we think that the show was a huge success; and we did more than was expected of us. Really I never enjoyed two hours more in my life than when we were attacking. Wonderful excitement! But "holding on" the next day and being pounded by heavy "crumps" was no fun!

July 1, 1916: I'm afraid I have been terribly bad about writing this last month, but the papers I suppose explained the reason. We have been very busy on this front. In fact it has been the hardest month we have ever put in; and the few of us remaining consider ourselves lucky (or unlucky) for not having a nice wound and being safely in hospital. Personally, I have no desire to get away from; I want to see the thing through.

August 26, 1916: You seem to have an idea that one over here lives under a continual strain. Get that idea out of your dear head, right away. Taking it all round, life in this part of the world is quite amusing and not bad at all. Will you believe me when I say that I have enjoyed the last two years more than any others in my life? Of course, we are under great strain sometimes, but never for long, and we make up for all of that when we are out of the line. One could not find such healthy excitement as we have here in any part of the world. Please don't worry about me. I never do; and I hate to think that I make you uneasy, even for a minute.

Final letter, on the eve of the action at Vimy Ridge, April 1917: My Dear Father, I am writing one of those "in case" letters for the third time, and of course I hope you will never have to read it. If you are reading it now, you will know that your youngest son "went under" as proud as Punch on the most glorious day of his life. I am taking my company over the top for a mile, in the biggest push that has ever been launched in the world, and I trust that it is going to be the greatest factor towards peace.

Dad—you can't imagine the wonderful feeling—a man thinks something like this: "Well, if I am going to die, this is worth it a thousand times."

I have been over two or three times before, but never with a company of my own.

Think of it! A hundred and fifty officers and men who will follow you to hell if need be!

I don't want any of you dear people to be sorry for me, altho' of course you will in a way. You will miss me, but you will be proud of me. Mind you, I know what I am up against, and that the odds are against me. I am not going in the way I did the first time, just for the sheer devilment and curiosity. I have seen this game for two years and I still like it, and feel my place is here.

So much for that.

I want to thank you from the bottom of my heart for all your loving kindness to me. This war has done wonders for me, and makes me realize lots of things which I would not have done otherwise. I could write a book about it, but you know what I mean.

Goodbye, dear Father, Mother, and all of you. Again I say that I am proud to be where I am now.

Gordie

Tributes from Officers and Peers:

The attack was launched on Easter Monday—with what result the whole world knows. A witness saw Gordon was struck on the hip by a shell fragment as he reached the German barbed-wire defenses, and must have died within a few seconds. "His expression was one of surprise, the faint flicker of a smile spreading from his half-opened lips…We were able to bury Gordon with military honours. The Pipers played that wonderful lament, "The Flowers of the Forest." He is buried in the British Military Cemetery at Ecoivres, a tiny place…

He was the very best type of a clean, brave, and good soldier, cheery as could be at all times, ready to go anywhere, and he'd always go himself into any dangerous place where he had to send his men. Everyone thought the world of Gordie Tupper. I can't believe he has gone: "With a cheery smile and a wave of the hand, / He has wandered into an unknown land."

He was a topping sportsman of the first class, and had done awfully well. He was a wonderful soldier, and every officer and man in the battalion had the greatest respect and admiration for him

His colonel wrote: "He was a brave boy, cool in action, and the men were devoted to him. He was eager to take part in the assault which he knew was to take place shortly. His death will be a great loss to the regiment."

Another colonel said: "I held your son's character and abilities in the very highest estimation; I cannot exaggerate them. I regarded him as one of the most promising young officers in the army. He was endowed with great courage and judgement, and had tact and insight into human character far beyond his years. Although many of his officers and men were older than he, they followed him with loyalty and enthusiasm."

A brigadier-general wrote: "I know how brave he was, and felt that his devotion to duty and disregard of personal danger might cost him his life."

His divisional commander wrote: "He was an officer of whom I was proud, and in whom I had the greatest confidence in all circumstances. I trusted him implicitly; and the measure of an officer's efficiency is the amount of confidence you can put in him. To be a success, an officer must be an instructor as well as a leader. Your son was a brilliant trainer of the men under his command, and was their true leader always."

The Vimy Foundation

The Vimy site will be enhanced by a permanent visitor centre, expected to be built by April 2017. The Vimy Foundation is raising donations to add to the Government of Canada's five-million-dollar contribution. For further information, visit vimyfoundation.ca.

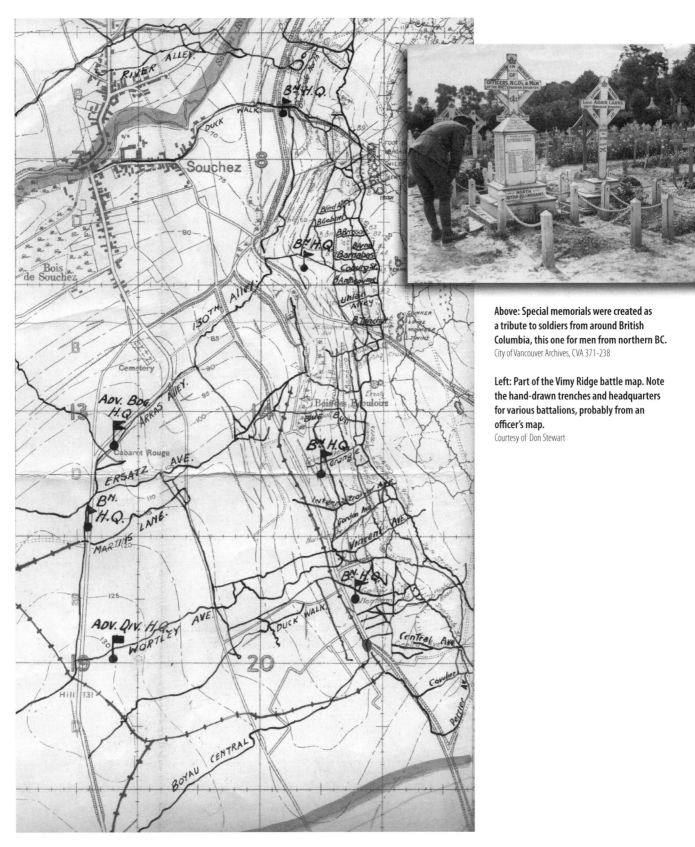

Above: Special memorials were created as a tribute to soldiers from around British Columbia, this one for men from northern BC.
City of Vancouver Archives, CVA 371-238

Left: Part of the Vimy Ridge battle map. Note the hand-drawn trenches and headquarters for various battalions, probably from an officer's map.
Courtesy of Don Stewart

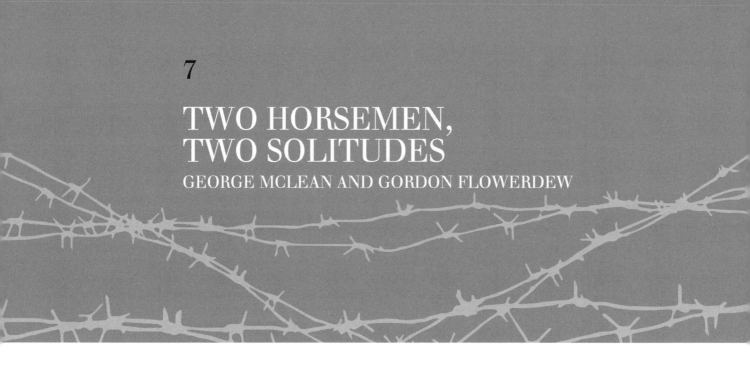

7

TWO HORSEMEN, TWO SOLITUDES

GEORGE MCLEAN AND GORDON FLOWERDEW

Before the war broke out, riding horses was a way of life for most men in the Thompson–Nicola country. The Model T didn't start to change that until the war was over. The hills near Kamloops were full of cowboys, Indian cowboys and remittance men who wanted to be cowboys. And many of them ended up in the Canadian Expeditionary Force.

Front page of *Kamloops Telegram*, Oct.11, 1917.
From the *Kamloops Telegram*, Oct. 11, 1917

First Nations War Hero

When George McLean came back to British Columbia from the front in October 1917, the headline in the *Kamloops Telegram* read, "'German killer' returns home." Private McLean was a hero. He had been awarded the DCM for bravery at Vimy Ridge earlier that year. A crowd of 250 local citizens came out to see him. A military band serenaded him. Red Cross girls were there to give McLean and his comrades cigarettes.

"There were two machine guns playing on us and one of our officers got hit," he told the crowd. "I pulled him out of the mess, and at the time I was close to the Germans' dugouts. I knew there were about sixty of the enemy there, and I got hold of my bombs. Just as I was in the act of pulling the pin, my partner, who was close to me, got it in the head. Then I bombed them, and I bombed them again and again. They ran like rabbits into their dugouts."

McLean was not a kid when he enlisted in Vernon in October 1916. He was forty-one and had previously served with the 2nd Canadian Mounted Rifles to fight in the Boer War. Horses were a big part of his life as a cowboy in Douglas Lake. And he went back to that life as soon as the war was over.

The *Kamloops Telegram* story said his father was a Scottish pioneer and his mother an Indian. But that wasn't quite right. He had First Nations heritage but the story was a lot more interesting than the paper let on. But more on that later.

What McLean had done at Vimy was truly astounding. He was credited with single-handedly killing nineteen of the enemy and capturing forty others.

"After they ran into the dugout," McLean told the crowd, "I kept bombing them until their sergeant major threw up his hands shouting, 'Don't throw the bomb' and I didn't. He came out of the hole and handed me his automatic pistol and asked how many there were of us and I told them 150."

In fact, there was just George. He marched them back to Canadian lines. McLean told the *Telegram* that they were disgusted at having been fooled. It was quite a day for the cowboy from Douglas Lake.

The British Immigrant

George McLean wasn't the only hero from the Kamloops area. Victoria Cross winner Gordon Flowerdew lived not far away at the British fruit farming enclave of Walhachin. Their lives couldn't have been more different.

Flowerdew was educated at Framlingham College, a private school in Suffolk, England. He came to Canada before the war to ranch and farm and ended up living among other members of the English gentry on benchland above the Thompson River. Walhachin was one of many BC real estate schemes designed to lure second sons and remittance men interested in an easy life of fruit farming and lawn tennis in the wilderness. On June 20, 1914, the front page of the *Ashcroft Journal* proclaimed, "Rosy Future for Walhachin":

> The London office claims that the name of our little town is getting well known in investment and emigration circles now, and that a big rush will be on before long. Lord Islington and the Marquis [of Anglesey] would have made a trip out here this spring but for unsettled conditions at home.

Gordon Flowerdew (right) on horseback with Paddy Cameron (see Chapter 1) in France, March 1916.

Courtesy of Lorraine Cameron

Settlers had already built an elaborate irrigation system to bring water from the hills above and make the sagebrush bench bloom with apples and other crops. The idea was noble, but like the war to come, it wouldn't turn out the way people expected.

Flowerdew ran some shops in town, but he had bigger dreams. He joined the local militia and drilled on horse in desert. When war broke out, he enlisted almost immediately, serving with a unit of the BC Horse and then Lord Strathcona's Horse.

As a son of empire, Flowerdew was immersed in the glories of imperialism. He wanted glory too but told a fellow officer the highest honour, the Victoria Cross, was probably an unattainable goal. "I shall never be brave enough to win it. Valour has reached such a standard that you have to be dead before you win the VC."

By 1918, Flowerdew was given command of his own unit. Being in the cavalry was a bit of a letdown. For most of the war, trenches made the cavalry almost useless. Without open ground, there was no place for men on horseback to break through. Then in the last year of the war, there were some stunning offensives that overran the trenches. In March 1918, Flowerdew got his chance. At Moreuil Wood, he led a daring cavalry charge into enemy lines.

Flowerdew died in that "last great cavalry charge" of the war. But his gallant gesture won him the cherished Victoria Cross. His citation read:

For most conspicuous bravery and dash when in command of a squadron detailed for special services of a very important nature. On reaching his first objective, Lieutenant Flowerdew saw two lines of enemy, each about sixty strong, with machine guns in the centre and flanks; one line being about two hundred yards behind the other. Realizing the critical nature of the operation and how much depended on it, Lieut. Flowerdew ordered a troop under Lieut. Harvey, VC, to dismount and carry out a special movement, while he led the remaining three troops to the charge. The squadron (less one troop) passed over both lines, killing many of the enemy with the sword; and wheeling about galloping on them again. Although the squadron had then lost about 70 per cent of its members, killed and wounded from rifle and machine gun fire directed on it from the front and both flanks, the enemy broke and retired. The survivors of the squadron then established themselves in a position where they were joined, after much hand-to-hand fighting, by Lieut. Harvey's part. Lieut. Flowerdew was dangerously wounded through both thighs during the operation, but continued to cheer his men. There can be no doubt that this officer's great valour was the prime factor in the capture of the position.

They buried Flowerdew in France not far from the battleground.

Back in Walhachin, they could have used him. While the men were away, the irrigation system was washed out and there was no one to fix it. The dream in the desert collapsed shortly after the war, and a lot of buildings were dismantled and carted away. The hotel, once an exclusive enclave of English respectability, disappeared. It was never meant for cowboys and other regular folks.

Above: Gordon Flowerdew's VC is held at the Imperial War Museum in London.
Courtesy of Framlingham College, Suffolk, England

Right: Flowerdew's famous cavalry charge was the subject of a painting by war artist Alfred Munnings.
Alfred Munnings, *Charge of Flowerdew's Squadron*, CWM 19710261-0443, Beaverbrook Collection of War Art, © Canadian War Museum

The Rest of the McLean Story

When the war was over, George McLean made it home alive. He was happiest in the hills around Douglas Lake and he was the best kind of hero, a survivor. But there was more to his story than cowboying and capturing prisoners.

That newspaper said George's father was a Scottish pioneer and his mother an Indian. In actual fact, George was the son of Allan McLean, one of the notorious Wild McLean Boys. It was Allan's father who was Scottish, a well-known Hudson's Bay chief trader. Allan's mother, Sophia, was First Nations. Allan and his brothers came to a bad end after a murderous rampage through the Thompson–Nicola country. They were hanged for murder in the 1870s.

Mel Rothenburger, the former mayor and newspaperman in Kamloops, is a descendant. "I do know that George was very sensitive about that connection to the Wild McLean Gang," Mel told us. "He did not like to talk about it, and it was just not a subject that you brought up. It was obviously very sensitive as it was with other members of the family."

The life he loved best—George McLean (far right) with fellow Douglas Lake cowboys before the war.
Courtesy of Mel Rothenburger

"Whether or not he was intentionally trying to make some amends for the acts of his father and his father's brothers," says Rothenburger, "we don't know, but certainly he was seen to have done that. So if that was his objective, he succeeded because it did restore some sense of self-respect among members of the family. When George is mentioned, the connection to the Wild McLean Gang is mentioned in the same context, and notation made that he was one of the good guys in a family."

George McLean died in September 1934 and is buried somewhere on the Nicola Reserve. There was some thought of giving him a military funeral at the time, but his friends took him back to the hills he loved and buried him in a simple grave. To mark the anniversary of the war, Mel Rothenburger is working with the Nicola Band to locate that grave and provide a headstone more suitable for a war hero.

"Well, I think he was a true hero," he says. "From what we do know about him, he was one of these guys who did some amazing things, under incredibly trying circumstances, but he wasn't a braggart, didn't go around talking about it. He came home and just quietly returned to his love of horses and ranching. He went back to what he was doing before. I guess you could call it an ordinary life, like the rest of us."

Another Commemoration

In England, Gordon Flowerdew's old school at Framlingham is also working to keep his name alive. The Society of Old Framlinghamians have made trips to his grave in France and the Imperial War Museum in London holds his Victoria Cross for safekeeping. In Walhachin, now a small retirement community, the local museum keeps his memory alive as well. Like George McLean, he'll be remembered in the sagebrush hills of the Thompson–Nicola country.

Walhachin: A Gentlemanly Occupation

By Michael Kluckner

Few BC communities changed as much as Walhachin during World War I. All of the optimism that had created it a few years earlier was swept away. The kind of people who founded it and were, to put it bluntly, sucked in by it, emerged into a completely different world in 1918.

Situated in an arid, sagebrush-studded valley along the Thompson River east of Ashcroft, Walhachin appeared to be an ideal spot for the kind of British-flavoured orchard community that had been established in the Okanagan Valley in the first years of the twentieth century. Growing fruit was a "gentlemanly occupation," requiring some considerable capital to begin but, it was said, allowing for a leisurely lifestyle once the trees became established.

As with the Okanagan Valley, Walhachin's small "fruit ranches" were marketed in England and attracted people of "education and refinement." In fact, most were the kind of second sons who stood no chance of inheriting property at home—a mix of men who usually had achieved little in school, the military or the civil service.

On the surface so genteel, the community became "a catch-all for rejects" in the words of Bertram Footner (1880–1972), the itinerant, "lower-born" English engineer who designed and built most of the Walhachin bungalows with high-hipped roofs and wide, spreading verandahs in the style of Britain's hot-climate colonies in Africa, where he had previously wandered in search of work. The population peaked at about 150, supplemented by about fifty Chinese workers and servants plus seasonal labourers.

All but one of the unmarried Englishmen decamped in August 1914, forming the Walhachin Squadron of the 31st British Columbia Horse. As the war progressed, more of the older and married men also enlisted, leaving a population of only about fifty by 1918. However, very few of Walhachin's soldiers died in combat and most returned after the war, staying only briefly before moving on to more practical opportunities.

The war had wrecked fortunes and land had little value. As financier Rex Mottram remarked in Evelyn Waugh's *Brideshead Revisited,* "Everyone of that sort is poorer than they were in 1914."

Walhachin itself turned out to be a badly planned, poorly located community, a combination of poor soils, sharp frosts and a substandard irrigation system making sustainable orcharding impossible. By 1922 all of the original British settlers had abandoned their holdings.

Bert Footner and his wife, Norah, stayed in Walhachin during the war years, maintaining buildings and attempting to manage the orchards while they started a family. Footner's impatience with his well-born neighbours was matched by Norah's dislike of rural BC life, for she had grown up in England in comfortable circumstances. They leased property a few miles farther west on the CPR mainline but failed as farmers. He picked up work as a builder elsewhere in BC before moving to California. But, son Vern recalled, as they didn't want their children to receive an American education they returned to Canada, eventually settling in Victoria where the pre-war British dream survived mostly intact.

A few historic buildings survive today in Walhachin, home to a handful of people. The tiny community hangs on to its memories, while the former orchard lands on the bench below grow fine crops of alfalfa, easy to irrigate with modern pumps.

Walhachin—an unlikely Eden.
Courtesy of the Clarke family

Gordon Flowerdew's horse.
Courtesy of the Clarke family

Remembering Walhachin

An interview with former MP Nelson Riis

Mark Forsythe: How did Walhachin become established and why was it there?

Nelson Riis: It was basically set up as a land development company by some very entrepreneurial individuals from the United Kingdom. They had all sorts of lovely brochures extolling the virtues of this part of British Columbia, most of which was untrue or photographs of other places. Nevertheless, they did attract a number of people from England to journey out and buy estates and set up large apple orchards and other fruits, including tobacco. I guess we'd call them gentlemen farmers; they didn't do much of the actual work themselves but they hired Chinese labourers as well as other labourers from the surrounding communities and ranches. They carried on a very genteel lifestyle.

Mark: Some of them were remittance men?

Nelson: They were sort of two categories. Older men, who for whatever reason had decided to seek their fortunes in this part of Canada. And then a large number of young men in their twenties who had gotten into different kinds of difficulties back home and their families decided it would be better for their family to have them leave England and go out to the colonies—in this case Canada—and maybe run their landed estate in the Walhachin area. So they were really almost forced to be there, and receiving an allowance from home.

Mark: We've heard stories that some of the regular folk weren't allowed in the hotel bar. How much was the British class system alive?

Nelson: I don't know if it was ever formal policy, but the settlers that settled at Walhachin weren't much interested in the surrounding countryside. They weren't interested in mixing with the ranchers; they were certainly friendly, but they had their own parties and balls and their own newspaper. They had their own lifestyle that had very little to do with the surrounding community but more to do with the communities back in England.

Mark: Something like the Raj?

Nelson: Very much like the Raj and people viewed them as kind of curiosities. Many stories in the local newspapers would refer to them as the "unusual group of people," and they spent a lot of their time dressed up. For the men, a great part of their time was taken up with sports and military exercises.

Mark: Then World War I comes along and what happens?

Nelson: Things happen very quickly. As soon as war was declared, of course, the call went out to the colonies to support England in the venture and, immediately, I think virtually every single male in the community signed up and returned to fight for England. Some women stayed behind, some of the workers stayed behind, but for the duration of the war there were no original men there. And then afterward, a few trickled back, but they didn't stay very long.

Mark: Why was that?

Nelson: Many went off to various parts of the empire, taking up different positions—a police chief in the Sudan, another person a plantation manager in Jamaica. They had gone on to other pursuits, perhaps more appropriate to their status in England. The ones that did come back stayed two or three years and then realized the folly of this Walhachin settlement as a viable agricultural endeavour. It was never set up properly; it just had too many things going against it; and of course mainly the people there weren't committed agriculturalists to start with. It was too late for them to get back into that mode of lifestyle.

Mark: So it was a genteel idea, but Walhachin didn't have the right soil conditions or water supply?

Nelson: Always a major concern was the water supply; it's a very arid part of the country. Very little rainfall or snowfall. It was pretty well doomed to failure from the beginning. The romantic explanation is of course the men enthusiastically volunteered to go back to England to fight for the country, which of course was true, but I suspect that they were more interested in leaving Walhachin behind as a bad dream. It failed for many, many reasons. The soil problems, the agricultural potential for various types of fruit never suited to the area, water was a major issue, markets were an issue, expertise—and also they had a lot of bad luck. Bad engineering in various irrigation works and they never worked properly. It was a logistical, economic nightmare. Walhachin was basically a fraudulent land scheme from the very beginning, designed to make money for the shareholders of the English company primarily, but it was never set up to be a successful agricultural settlement—like so many land schemes.

Nelson Riis wrote his master's thesis on Walhachin.

The latest technology at Walhachin.
Courtesy of the Clarke family

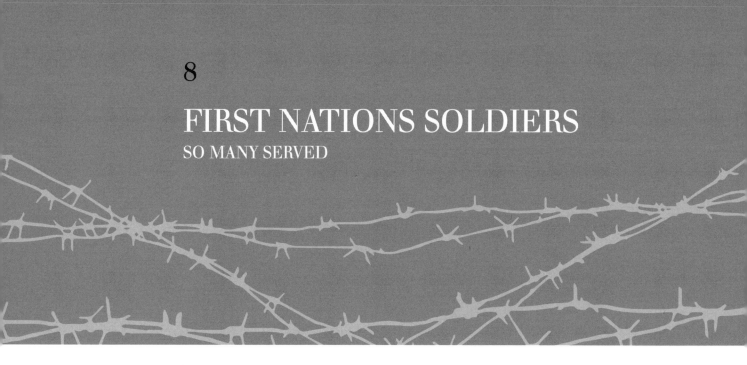

8

FIRST NATIONS SOLDIERS
SO MANY SERVED

They were denied land, rights as citizens and lived in poverty. Their children were forced into residential schools where the objective was to "kill the Indian in the child." But when the war began, BC's aboriginal people stepped forward in remarkable numbers, even after being told they were not wanted. Approximately six thousand aboriginal soldiers served from across the country; by the end of the war 35 percent of the eligible population had enlisted. A partial honour roll at the end of this chapter reveals that aboriginal men signed up from most regions of BC. Canada cannot forget them.

Above and Beyond: The Indigenous War Effort

By Katherine Palmer Gordon

From the very beginning of World War I, Indigenous volunteers enlisted in droves. Like thousands of other young men in Canada, they were motivated by a strong desire to protect the territories on which—in their case—their ancestors had walked for millennia. In total, more than four thousand Indigenous men fought for Canada. Three hundred would never return home.

These young men, all of eligible military age—between twenty and thirty-five years—accounted for more than one-third of the eligible male population at the time holding registered Indian status under the *Indian Act*. That is the only Indigenous demographic for which records exist; those numbers do not include non-status First Nations men, nor do they account for the Métis or Inuit people who fought for Canada. The proportion of the Indigenous population who enlisted was as high as (and in some local cases far higher than) the average enlistment rate for non-Indigenous men.

In British Columbia, as news of the war spread, First Nations communities across the province were emptied of their young fathers, uncles, brothers and sons. Many volunteers lived in remote areas, spoke little or no English or French and had never left their home territories to travel to another region, let alone a foreign country. That didn't stop them. One man named John Campbell travelled thousands of kilometres by foot, canoe and steamer to reach Vancouver to sign up. Every eligible male from the Okanagan Head of the Lake Band enlisted, including Private George McLean, who single-handedly captured nineteen prisoners at Vimy Ridge in 1917.

McLean earned himself a Distinguished Conduct Medal, one of more than fifty medals for acts of bravery that were awarded to Indigenous soldiers. But the men were not the only ones who deserved recognition for their dedication to the war effort. Their wives, mothers, aunts and sisters in turn provided overwhelming support for the troops. Indeed, Indigenous communities raised so much money for the war effort that the federal government eventually ran a poster campaign encouraging non-Indigenous communities to follow their lead.

In other words, Indigenous men and women in Canada proved themselves patriots of the first order—despite the fact that their country had treated them so poorly since the earliest days of Confederation. It might have been more understandable if every one of them instead had refused to help. In 1914 status Indians were not permitted to be citizens (and would not gain that right for another forty-six years). They could not vote in federal or provincial elections. They were also deprived of many other fundamental human rights, including freedom of association and the right to raise their children in their traditional ways.

Indigenous men also faced barriers in enlisting that non-Indigenous volunteers did not. When Canada first entered the war, the government attempted to prohibit status Indians from enlisting on the basis that European nations might consider them "savages" and treat them inhumanely if captured (no such treatment was ever recorded). The attempt at prohibition proved fruitless, however. Most recruiters simply didn't know about it or ignored it, recognizing the harsh reality that Canada needed as many soldiers as it could get. Indigenous volunteers were happy to oblige.

Sadly, the veterans who returned learned they had fought for a country that would take a very long time to thank them. Those who did come home faced continuing discrimination and disrespect. Assistance provided under the *War Veterans Allowance Act* (such as education subsidies, government employment and land grants) were not made available to status Indian veterans who returned to reserve communities. They remained disenfranchised until 1960, and continued to be constrained from exercising many rights that Canadian citizens enjoyed. Recalling the relative freedom of their existence overseas where they were able to mingle freely with their fellow soldiers as equals, some re-enlisted in the military.

National Aboriginal Veterans Day is celebrated on November 8 each year but is not officially recognized by the government. It was inaugurated in 1992 by Indigenous veterans' groups from British Columbia and Manitoba to protest against the fact that at the time Indigenous veterans were not allowed to march or to lay wreaths in national Remembrance Day ceremonies as an officially recognized group.

By 1995 that finally changed. That year, Indigenous veterans were officially given the recognition they have always deserved in Canada for the enormous contribution they made—not only in World War I, but in every subsequent conflict in which Canada has been engaged.

Katherine Palmer Gordon lives on Gabriola Island and has written extensively on treaty issues. Her most recent book is We Are Born with the Songs Inside Us*.*

Fighting for an Uncertain Future

As Katherine has written, First Nations soldiers were at the forefront of the war effort. They were under the same economic pressures as the general population, and they probably understood

Recruiting offices, like this 242nd Battalion Foresters Receiving Centre, were kept busy signing up soldiers. Many First Nations men ended up in the Foresters' Battalion.
Dominion Photo Co. photo, Vancouver Public Library 20195

Johnny Harris (seated on the left) and a friend as ranch-hands.
Courtesy of Vernon Museum and Archives, Photo No. 3613

the privations of military life much better. They were patient in hardship, accustomed to working in the elements and eating substandard food at irregular intervals. And they could shoot straight. In other words, they made perfect recruits.

Private Johnny Harris of Armstrong was typical. His father was a farmer and local Native leader. His mother was a daughter of local rancher Cornelius O'Keefe. Harris was married and had two children, both born in the earlier years of the war. He was a rancher and in his mid-twenties when he enlisted on January 22, 1917.

Harris was shipped overseas in the summer of 1917 and served with the 47th Battalion (now the Westminster Regiment). He saw some desperate fighting at Passchendaele and Amiens and was part of the now famous Hundred Days campaign, the Canadian Corps' dash to victory.

"It was unquestionably the most decisive campaign ever fought by Canadian troops," historian Jack Granatstein wrote in the *Globe and Mail.* "The cost in lives and wounded was terrible—45,000 casualties, 20 per cent of all Canadian losses in the war."

One day stood out. General Erich Ludendorff called August 8, 1918, the Black Day of the German Army. Germany reported about thirty thousand casualties on that day alone. Over twelve thousand surrendered. The German high command knew that the end was near. But the fighting was fierce.

Johnny Harris would not see his wife and children again. Harris took a gunshot to the head during the height of the fighting. He died of his wounds on August 15 and is now buried at St. Sever Cemetery, near Rouen.

Men like Harris served and died without the right to vote or many of the other benefits of Canadian citizenship. They considered themselves loyal British subjects and enlisted willingly. But their deaths would take a terrible toll on First Nations communities back home.

With assistance from Leonard Gamble in Armstrong, author of So Far from Home.

From Our Listeners: My Grandfather, Peter Christopher (1896–1970)

By Louise Alphonse, editor of the Secwepemc News, *Shuswap*

Peter served his country in two world wars. In the first, he was in active duty in the infantry, and in the second, he was in the Army Reserves and based in northern England. Like many other veterans, Peter was forever scarred by what he witnessed at war with all its tragedies.

When he was in the Army Reserves, he served as a support for his fellow community veterans, who counted on him in their leave time. His presence kept them grounded and he gave them comfort in the absence of family and home.

He returned home and spent time on the land—more than likely as part of his own healing. He left numerous memories with friends and family of the land he loved. He was a big game guide, hunter, trapper, rancher and carpenter. Peter married Marie Abel Jules from Simpcw First Nation and had twelve children.

Peter's son Roy wrote:

In the early 1930s, Peter and Louie Emile (who also served in World War I) both played hockey with the Alkali Lake Braves, a team of First Nations players from the Northern Shuswap communities. The team was renowned for their skill and stamina and were perennial champions of the Cariboo Hockey League. They had to travel to Williams Lake by horse and sleigh, camp in tents and eat outside as they were not allowed in hotels or to eat in restaurants. In 1932 they were invited by Chief Andy Paul to play in Vancouver against an All Star team. They played two games and lost by one goal. Louie Emile scored the only goal for the team. It was the first time they had played on artificial ice; they had only nine players on the ice and still drew four thousand fans to each game.

When my dad was in World War II, my mother was responsible for raising the family and ensuring the family had food, shelter and other necessities of life. *My mom hunted moose, deer, bear and other animals to feed the family, and trapped in winter. I am very proud of my dad and mother.*

As we remember Peter Christopher, we also cherish our freedom because of the sacrifices he made.

Peter Christopher (left) and a friend during World War II in London. Christopher served in two world wars.
Courtesy of Roy Christopher

Conscription—Enslavement?

On November 17, 1917, the Allied Indian Tribes of British Columbia sent a telegram to Prime Minister Borden:

> The Prime Minister of Canada, Ottawa
> We, chairman and secretary Committee Allied Tribes of British Columbia consider we should inform you [that] recently announced view [of] Canadian Government [of] Indians within Military Service Act has caused serious unrest among Indians of this Province, who, while loyal British subjects, yet on account [of] land question not settled and citizenship withheld have long thought rights of men denied them and now having no voice in Canadian affairs, regard enforced military service as enslavement. We are sure any attempted enforcement of Act against Indians would be forcibly resisted and probably cause bloodshed. We ask you [to] specially consider that oppression of any weak race would violate principles for upholding which Britain and Dominions are in war, and further fact that on account of Irish question [being] unsettled, Irish people [are] excluded from British Conscription Act. We hope you will accept this warning as sent in helpful spirit and take prompt action required by state of affairs.
> P.R. Kelly, Chairman, J.A. Teit, Secretary

This telegram appeared in the Victoria *Daily Colonist* on November 20. On December 11, the Victoria *Daily Times* published an article headlined, "Indians Not against Conscription Plan." The paper's Duncan correspondent wrote that "great indignation was felt by the Indians

John Davidson and J.A. Teit in camp at Botanie Valley near Skwoach Mountain, 1914.

John Davidson photo, City of Vancouver Archives, CVA 660-891

where the [Allied Tribes] telegram appeared in the papers...The Chiefs would like it made known that while they do not wish to go to fight, the idea of bloodshed never entered their minds, as they enter only the kindliest feeling for the white people."

Teit responded a few days later:

Your correspondent's article is headed, "Indians Not against Conscription Plan," but the article itself fails to prove this is the case. I believe it is well known that the same Indians whose names your correspondent mentions...had already protested against conscription before Mr. Kelly and I sent our telegram.

Teit continued:

I can unhesitatingly aver that the Indians of BC are against conscription. I have not yet met a single Indian in favor of it. The Indians are not, however, against the volunteer system and they raise no objections to individuals of their tribes enlisting...The fact that we have told the Government of this conscription trouble among the Indians is no proof that we created it. The trouble was here already and others are responsible for it—not we.

An election was under way and the Allied Tribes found themselves in the middle of it as some papers lined up with Borden's government and others with the anti-conscription movement. The protests of Teit, Kelly and the Allied Tribes did eventually achieve their aim. In January 1918, a regulation passed by order-in-council exempted Indians from conscription.

James Teit continued to fight for the Native cause after the war ended but died of cancer in 1922. He was not yet forty. In 1927, the *Indian Act* was amended to prohibit First Nations from raising funds to pursue claims without the approval of the federal government. The Allied Tribes collapsed.

Aboriginal Soldiers from the North Coast

By Dianne Rabel, Prince Rupert

An ornately decorated memorial graces a wall in the Metlakatla band office. On it are inscribed the names of four young aboriginal men who went to France in 1915 and 1916 and never returned: James Newell Leighton, Andrew O'Rielly, Dan Pearson and John Edward Rudland.

Metlakatla is an aboriginal village on an island in Prince Rupert's harbour. Although the rate of enlistment was higher in other parts of the country, there were still many young aboriginal men on the north coast who answered the call to arms. They came from Prince Rupert, Metlakatla, Port Simpson and the salmon canneries that lined the Skeena and dotted the coast. They came from Haida Gwaii, the Nass and villages farther inland. Many were fishermen, but as soldiers, quite a few of them were assigned to pioneer, forestry and railway battalions. These troops did hard physical labour in addition to combat: digging and repairing trenches, lumbering, laying track, building roads and bridges, and disposing of ordnance.

The casualty rate was high. More of them than one would expect succumbed to tuberculosis or pneumonia, a few were killed in action and others died of wounds. Some were evacuated home due to illness or injury. From Port Simpson, Walter Ryan was killed in action in 1916 and Gordon Anderson died of wounds in 1917.

The Beynons were an interesting family. Originally from Port Simpson but living in Victoria when war broke out, three sons were eager to do their part. George, age twenty, signed up in 1915. A few months later, his two younger brothers went to enlist. Richard was accepted but John, the youngest of the three, falsified his birthdate and was turned away. He was only fifteen. Fortunately for him, by the time the recruiters were prepared to accept him the war was over. Both George and Richard are buried in France.

Two northern aboriginal soldiers were awarded the Military Medal. One was from Metlakatla, Dan Pearson, and he received his decoration for actions at Hill 70 in August 1917. Two months later he died of pneumonia. The second soldier, David Faithful, came from Port Simpson, and he survived the war. David's citation read:

This scout in front of Valenciennes on November 1, 1918, rendered invaluable assistance to his company in the advance by going well forward and sniping and putting out of action several enemy riflemen and machine guns, who were troubling our men.

When the final objectives had been reached a party of the enemy were seen attempting to prevent our consolidation. Although the enemy artillery fire was extremely heavy, Private Faithful climbed to the top of the chimney and dispersed the company by rifle fire.

His great daring under extremely heavy fire and his skill and gallantry were of invaluable assistance to the success of the operation.

In Memory of Julian Boyce (1899–1976)

By Louise Alphonse, editor of Secwepemc News, Shuswap

Julian was born in 1899 to Sicwemtkwe. He was a self-provider, hunting and trapping to make a living. He worked as a ranch hand for the 105 Mile Ranch and the Buffalo Lake Ranch. Because of his experience, he was able to provide support and advice to early non-Native settlers who came to the area.

He served his country on two occasions, in World War I in active duty, and in World War II in Army Reserves back east. He received medals and was recognized for his courage and bravery. It has been said that even though he returned from a violent environment overseas, he remained a kind and gentle person and treated everyone with respect.

During that turbulent time in his life, in the midst of the war, he befriended a soldier from a neighbouring community. They supported each other and survived the return home. During their time of crisis they had made a promise, and upon returning home, Julian kept that promise.

He rode to Chu Chua. They were married and raised, not only their own sons and daughters, but many grandchildren.

We cherish our freedom today, and cherish the memory of Julian Boyce, and all he stood for.

The Honour List of World War I Aboriginal Veterans

Indigenous people from across British Columbia signed up for service. What follows is a partial list of aboriginal people who served, their home First Nation community and, in some cases, when they died.

From these slim details we're still able to see how some people served and the ultimate sacrifice that many aboriginal soldiers made.

Gordon Anderson, Port Simpson (Tsimshian) / 47th Bn, #463009, DOW / Buried France

Tommy Andrew, Little Shuswap Lake Band (Secwepemc) / Pte. Canadian Forestry Corp (CFC) Reg. #688014 / Died October 1918

Thomas Armstrong, Okanagan Band, Vernon (Okanagan)

Alex Joseph Arnouse, Adams Lake Band (Secwepemc)

Keome Basil, Tache Band (Dakelh) / Forestry Reg. #2388302

Wilfred Bennett, Kamloops Band (Secwepemc)

David Bernardan, Oweekayno, Rivers Inlet (Wuikinuxv) / Commanded Motor Transport vessel

George Philip Beynon, Port Simpson (Tsimshian) / 102nd Bn, #102219 / Buried in France

Richard Arthur Beynon, Port Simpson (Tsimshian) / Pte. 103rd Bn Reg. #706601 / Died December 22, 1918

William Brewer, Okanagan Band, Vernon (Okanagan)/ Pte. 30th Regt. BC Horse (to 47th Bn) Reg. #2142307 / Died January 9, 1918

Eugene Bull, Tache (Dakelh)/ Forestry Reg. #2388303

Frank Charlie, Quesnel (Carrier-Tsilhqot'in) / Forestry Reg. #2388316

Joseph Charlie, Ashcroft Band (Nlaka'pamux) / 131st Bn Reg. #790936, 104th Regiment Militia

Thomas Charters, Aspen Grove (Nlaka'pamux) / Pte. 54th Bn Reg. #443593/ Died October 1916

David Chase, Chase (Secwepemc) / Reg. #107160

Edwin Victor Cook (Cooke), Nimpkish Band, Alert Bay (Namgis) / Pte. (DCM) 102nd to (7th Bn) Reg. #703323 / Died August 1918

Roy Cromarty (a.k.a. Sam Roy Garner) Chilliwack (Sto:lo) / Pte. 47th Bn Reg. #790949 / Died December 18, 1917

Samuel Cromarty Chilliwack (Sto:lo) / 131st Westminster Bn #790920, 104th Reg. Militia

Edward Dix, Masset Band (Haida) / Pte 197th Bn (to C.F.C.) Reg. #913628

Louie Emile, Canim Lake (Secwepemc)

Alexander Eneas, Kamloops Band (Secwepemc) / 172nd Bn Reg. #687717

David Faithful, Port Simpson (Tsimshian) / Pte. 143rd Bn to 47th Bn (MM) Reg. #826587

Abel Francois, Chase (Secwepemc) / 172nd Bn Reg. #688160 / Attested Kamloops, 1916

Charlie Andrew Gabriel, Kamloops Band (Secwepemc) / 2nd Bn CMR

Alexander George, Kamloops Band (Secwepemc) / Pte. Reg. #2137304 102nd Rocky Mountain Rangers

Eddie Gott, Big Bar (Upper Stl'atl'imc) / Reg. #2138875

Francis (Frank) Gott, Lillooet (Upper Stl'atl'imc) / 102nd Bn Sniper Reg. #703706

Henry Gott, Big Bar (Upper Stl'atl'imc) / Reg. #2023157

Nelson Gott, Lillooet (Upper Stl'atl'imc) / Pte. 172nd Bn Reg. #687089, prev. 102 RMR / Died August 11, 1917

(Jimmy) James Guy, Alexandria BC (Secwepemc) / Pte. 54th Bn "Kootenay" Reg. #443773 / Died March 1, 1917

Donald Grant Macpherson Haldane, Chase (Secwepemc) / Tpr. Lord Strathcona's Horse (Royal Canadians) RCAC / Died March 30, 1918

Whitefield Haldane, Chase (Secwepemc) / Pte. 27th Bn Reg. #2619 / Attested Valcartier, September 1914 / Died June 4, 1918

Pete Harry, Kamloops Band (Secwepemc) / Reg. #687180

Peter Harry, Kamloops Band (Secwepemc) / Boer War, 224th Canadian Forestry Bn Reg. #1013116

Maurice Joseph Isaacs, Akiaqnuk, Columbia Lake Band (Ktunaxa) / Pte. Canadian Forestry Corp Reg. #2208369

Joseph James, Skookumchuck Band (Lower Stl'atl'imc) / Pte. 143rd to (47th Bn) / Attested Sidney, 1916 / Died August 22, 1917

Harry Jimmy, North Bend First Nation (Nlaka'pamux) / 143rd Bn Reg. #826960

Edward Joe, Kamloops Band (Secwepemc) / 172nd Bn Reg. #687686

Eli LaRue Jr., Kamloops Band (Secwepemc) / 242nd Bn Reg. #1048376

Allan Lavigeur, Kamloops Band (Secwepemc) / 172nd Rocky Mountain Rangers Reg. #687092

George Laviguer, Kamloops Band (Secwepemc) / 172nd Bn Reg. #687639

James Newell Leighton, Metlakatla (Tsimshian) / Pte. 11th Bn CMR to (29th Bn) #116966 / Died August 27, 1917

Joe A.S. Leonard Sr., Kamloops Band (Secwepemc)

William Thomas Louie (Bill), Deadman's Creek (Secwepemc) / Reg. #3206975

James Manuel (Jim) Kamloops Band (Secwepemc) / 47th Bn / Reg. #687608

Robert Matheson, Metlakatka (Tsimshian) / 143rd Bn BC Bantams' Reg. #826487

George McLean, Upper Nicola Band (Okanagan) / Boer War (CMR), World War I 54th Bn Reg. #688302 (DCM)

Frank Moody, Nass River (Nisga'a) / Pte. 1st Canadian Pioneer Bn Reg. #154323 / Died October 8, 1916

Andrew Mowatt, Hazelton (Gitksan) / Reg. #826553

Charles Mowatt, Hazleton (Gitksan) / 143rd Bn Reg. #826550

David Mowatt, Hazelton (Gitksan) / 143rd Bn Reg. #826552

Andrew Natrall, Squamish FN, North Vancouver (Skwxwu7mesh) / Gnr./Sniper Reg. #826846

Charles Newman, Squamish FN, North Vancouver (Skwxwu7mesh) / 131st Bn to (37th Bn) Reg. #790989, 104th Regt. Militia

George Newman, Squamish FN, North Vancouver (Skwxwu7mesh) / Mach. Gnr. Reg. #3790759 / Four years in France and Germany

Andrew O'Reilly, Metlakatla (Tsimshian) / 29th Bn Reg. #116985 / Died July 23, 1917 / Buried in the UK

Albert Pearce, Metlakatla (Tsimshian) / Attested September 1915 #154336 / Served in France / Died November 17, 1918, in Vancouver

Daniel Pearson, Metlakatla (Tsimshian) / Pte. 143rd Bn to 47th Bn (MM) Reg. #826488 / Died October 15, 1917

Francois Pierrish, Neskonlith Band (Secwepemc), CFC

William Pierrish, Neskonlith Band, (Secwepemc) / Reg. #687994 / Attested 1916 Salmon Arm

Frederick Prince, Fort St. James, Necoslie (Nak'azdli) / Forestry Corp (Vancouver Reinforcement Draft) Reg. #2388305

Charles Ryan, Port Simpson (Lax Kw'alaams) / 1st Can Pioneers 154322 / Attested October 1915 Vancouver

Walter Ryan, Port Simpson (Lax Kw'alaams) and Victoria / Pte. 1st Pioneer Bn #154332 / Attested September 1915 Prince Rupert / Died July 7, 1916

Abel Sampolio, Adams Lake (Sexqueltqin), Chase (Secwepemc)

Frank Baptiste Samplio, Adams Lake (Sexqueltqin), Chase (Secwepemc)

James Alvin Scott, New Westminster / Pte. 29th Bn Reg. #790216 104th Regt. / Died June 9, 1917

Noel Seymour, Seabird Island band (Cheam Reserve) Sto:lo / Pte. 42nd Coy Canadian Forestry Corp / Attested Vancouver / Died June 10, 1918

Alexis Song, Fort St. James (Carrier—Sekani) / Forestry Corp Reg. #2388306

August Soule Sr., Adams Lake (Sexqueltqin) Chase

Bernard Sutherland, Fort St. James (Carrier—Sekani) / Forestry Corp Reg. #2388307

Cillesta Thomas, Nadleh Whu'ten, Fort Fraser (Carrier—Sekani) / Forestry Corp Reg. #2388304

Jonas Thomas, Nadleh Whu'ten, Fort Fraser (Carrier—Sekani) / Forestry Corp Reg. #2388308

George Todd, Fort St. James (Stuart Lake) (Carrier—Sekani) / Forestry Corp Reg. #2388309

Alex George Tomma, Kamloops Band (Tk'emlups) / 102nd Battalion

Harry Tronson, Okanagan Band, Vernon / 30th Regt. BC Horse Reg. #2142320

James Tronson, Okanagan Band, Vernon / Pte. 47th Bn Reg. #2142318 / Died October 26, 1917

Isaac Willard, Kamloops Band (Tk'emlups) / Pte. 11th Bn, BC Horse (Vernon) / Attested Victoria 1916

Peter Wilson, Hazelton (Gitksan) / 143rd Bn Reg. #826551

More information on aboriginal veterans is posted at www.vcn.bc.ca/~jeffrey1/ tribute.htm.

From Our Listeners: Sapper Major Angus W. Davis

By Paulette Cave

My father started as a mucker at the Virginia Mine near Rossland. Angus Davis prospected, staked claims and managed mines in the Slocan, Boundary country, the environs of Nelson and the East Kootenays. He played on the 1907 Sandon hockey team.

In 1914, the thirty-four-year-old father returned to Nelson from a business trip. During the train journey, he made a decision about the recent outbreak of war. "Let the young fellas go first. If fighting lasts more than a couple of years, I will get involved."

"Davis, we've enlisted you," said his pals as he stepped off the train. What could he do? They headed to the Allan Hotel to celebrate.

In due course, the gang was in Vancouver, boarding the CPR train to Valcartier, Quebec. They stretched their legs at Winnipeg, a rumpled, unshaven crew. My father overheard an elegant female onlooker sniff, "The dregs of Vancouver."

The first Sunday at Valcartier, recruits were sorted, denominationally, for church parade. My father, craving quiet with a good book, joined the "no affiliation" group. After a morning mucking out the stables, he smartly converted back to Anglicanism.

The war memories Dad shared with his children were stripped of the horror:

He and his men were playing cards in a field when someone spotted a yellow cloud rising in the distance. It was the first gas attack.

A German plane crashed, killing the pilot. The men rushed to go through his pockets.

My father and his men bivouacked in a burned-out church.

While tunnelling toward enemy lines, the Canadian Sappers could hear Germans talking in their own tunnel.

During inspection of the troops by an exalted personage, our uncle Guy Davis dropped his rifle. It clanged on the cobblestones. First there was "hell to pay," then, after a session in the bar, all was smoothed over.

My father needed a light for his cigarette. A hand shot through the dark and a cultured English voice said, "Here you are, sir." It belonged to the Duke of Connaught.

He came "this close" to being bayonetted by a Ghurka soldier, as he walked at night in no man's land. The Canadian accent saved the day.

Of the eight comrades who left Nelson, three would be killed: Sapper G. Ravel, Lieutenant W.G. McFarlane and Lieutenant A.J.L. (Alfie) Evans.

A Piper Visits France

By SFU student Kevin McLean

It's easy to think of the hundreds of thousands who gave the ultimate sacrifice during the Great War as simply a large number symbolizing mechanized warfare and the carnage that the war brought. When I first saw a cemetery in France that held the fallen soldiers of the Great War, I was reminded of the massive numbers I read in the history books. The hundreds of markers before me were just part of the masses of dead that seemed so far removed from my life.

But then I found the grave of a very famous Canadian and Victoria Cross recipient—Piper James Cleland Richardson of the Seaforth Highlanders of Canada. Like me, he was a piper. He was just twenty years old when he died—that would have been me two years ago.

I also found the grave of my great-uncle William McLean who died during the Hundred Day Offensive in 1918. He was thirty-three years old when he died and left behind two very young children and a wife of seven years. Those children would grow up without a father and his wife would continue without a husband.

Because I was probably the first and only person to ever make a point of finding William's grave, I wanted to do something unique in his honour so I played a piobaireachd—the traditional music of the bagpipes. I played "The Fingerlock," which was the traditional tune of the McLean clan in Scotland. As I was playing, I realized that most of the other graves around me had probably never been visited individually yet those people too had a unique story about the sacrifice they made and the people they left behind. At that moment the numbers I read in the history books all changed. It was no longer tens of thousands of soldiers who died, but rather tens of thousands of individual Canadians just like me.

I realized that each of the soldiers who died had a family, friends, liked music or sports or reading, told jokes and was truly proud to call themselves Canadian. They were the young and compassionate teenager who lived across the street or who sat beside you in math class. They were your son, your grandson, your brother, your father. They were the stars of the sports teams, the class clown, the first person to ask you to dance in high school. They had just gotten married to their high school sweetheart. They had two young kids who were barely old enough to walk and they had just been hired to their first real job. They were all individuals.

I now understand that remembering the Great War is not about studying politics or memorizing dates and numbers—it's about the individuals who gave up everything they had for their country. I often hear that Canada lacks the history of Great Britain or the patriotism of the United States of America, but the individual sacrifices made during the Great War in the name of Canada make me proud to call myself a Canadian. I am proud to be a part of the same country that these individuals knew was special enough to die for.

Above: Laying down corduroy road. Many men served behind the lines, building roads and bringing in supplies where there wasn't much opportunity for valour. But they were still vulnerable to artillery and gas attacks.
CWM 19920085-220, George Metcalf Archival Collection, © Canadian War Museum

Left: SFU piper Kevin McLean plays at James Richardson's grave in France.
Mariane St-Maurice photo, True Patriot Love Foundation

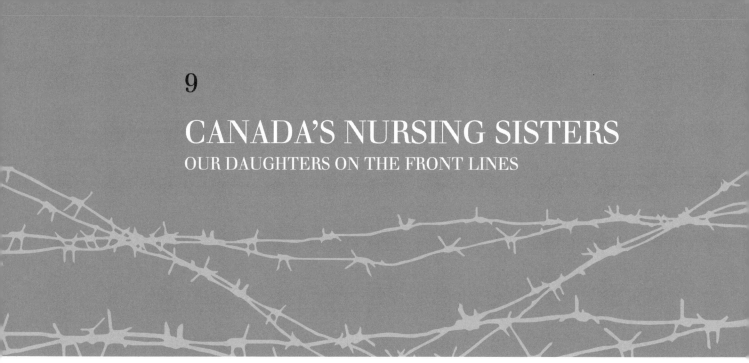

9

CANADA'S NURSING SISTERS
OUR DAUGHTERS ON THE FRONT LINES

British Columbia and the other western provinces produced some tough fighting men, accustomed to the outdoors and hardships. It also produced a tough breed of nurses, sometimes horrified by the carnage, yet resigned to endure under incredible difficulties. Some were raised to be proper Victorian ladies, but that propriety was put aside on the front lines.

Victoria author Maureen Duffus wrote a book about it, *Battlefront Nurses of World War I.* Maureen was inspired by the life of her aunt, Nursing Sister Mary Ethel Morrison, who made a precious photo album documenting her experiences.

"I knew that my aunt was in the Nursing Sisters Corps," Maureen told us. "And I knew from family members that she was decorated and was a very brave person. She had a Royal Red Cross—and I had no idea at the time this was such a tremendous award, the prime award for Nursing Sisters."

British Columbia women enlisted in large numbers to care for the wounded.
Stuart Thomson photo, Vancouver Public Library 17800

Morrison and fellow nursing sister Elsie Dorothy Collis joined the Canadian Army Medical Corps in Victoria in the summer of 1915, as soon as the British Columbia medical unit was formed. Both went on to the Mediterranean Front in Salonika in 1916 with No. 5 Canadian General Hospital. Both were in France near the front lines when German aircraft bombed Canadian hospitals in the Boulogne area in 1918.

"These were ladies born in Victorian days and very gently brought up," says Maureen. "They decided to train as nurses, and when the war came along I don't think they realized they would be in such ghastly conditions."

They trained in tents and then were sent over to England as a group, where they were divided into different hospitals for their training. But they were all in Salonika together. Later in France, they could be assigned to any hospital in need.

"It was particularly dangerous when they got to France and very close to the front line. The trains came in daily with more and more wounded, and by then they were so used to it they would just say, 'more femurs.' It was mentioned very matter-of-factly."

For her distinguished service, Nurse Morrison was called to Buckingham Palace in 1917 to meet with the Queen Mother, who presented her with the Royal Red Cross Medal.

The award was made to fully trained nurses of the official nursing service who had "shown exceptional devotion and competency in the performance of actual nursing duties, over a continuous and long period, or who performed some very exceptional act of bravery and devotion at her post of duty."

In 1938, Nursing Sister Morrison told the *Canadian Nurse* publication, "Month in and month out, a constant stream of gassed and wounded patients were cared for with a complete turnover every three weeks. Day duty, night duty followed one another until at last came the eleventh day of November, 1918. At the eleventh hour, surrounded by our wounded patients, we realized that the order to 'cease fire' had gone into effect. The War was ended."

Maureen Duffus was inspired by the story of her aunt, Nursing Sister Mary Ethel Morrison, pictured here in uniform.
Courtesy of the Duffus Family

Nursing Sister Robina Stewart served in Salonika, Greece, where she was reunited with Kamloops doctor Howard Burris.
Courtesy of the Burris Family

From Our Listeners: A Wartime Romance

As told by Stewart Burris, Kamloops
We received many stories of parents and grandparents who served in field hospitals. Ross, Doug and Bruce Dickson remembered their grandmother in Kamloops, Ruby Burris, who served in Salonika. Ruby's son Stewart Burris, a retired doctor still living in Kamloops, found some of the pictures shown here. He helped tell the story of his mother and father, who served together in the Medical Corps.

My father, Dr. Howard (H.L.) Burris, first became interested in joining the army with the Rocky Mountain Rangers in Kamloops. He trained as a medical officer with the local militia starting in 1911. Just before the war broke out, he was over in Vienna doing postgraduate study.

"I did not realize how lucky I was to get away from the Continent before World War I broke," he wrote in his memoirs.

H.L. returned home to Kamloops and before long joined up with the 5th Canadian General Hospital.

"When I arrived home in late August, the war situation was serious. The French and British armies were in full retreat. Recruiting was brisk everywhere and nearly every available man joined up; town and country were being depleted of young men, and it was natural that, being the unmarried member of our clinic, I felt I must soon enlist."

At about the same time, Robina Stewart, a nurse from Selkirk, Manitoba, who had graduated from Winnipeg General Hospital, took a nursing position in Trail where a sister was already working. Robina moved to Kamloops in 1914 where she briefly met H.L. before joining the nursing service of the Canadian Army Medical Corps. In no time she too was over in London with the No. 5 Canadian General Hospital Unit.

Active service took them both to Salonika and Cyprus where the No. 5 Canadian General Hospital Unit was stationed to handle casualties. The unit was in Salonika at the request of the British Army medical director during a desperate shortage of medical units for the Eastern Front.

They even withstood Zeppelin attacks. H.L .Burris remembered them in his memoirs:

Late in February 1916, the Red Cross ship carrying our nursing sisters from Egypt anchored in the [Salonika] harbour and was bombed at night by a Zeppelin and considerable damage was done to one side of the ship. Fortunately, all nurses were on the other side and suffered no injury or casualties. On February 27, 1916 another Zeppelin, the LZ85, accompanied by a fleet of airplanes, destroyed a large part of the ammunition dump at the harbour's end and inflicted a moderate number of casualties in the City. Our hospitals escaped injury and the Zeppelin was brought down by gun fire, though in its fall it travelled about ten miles and fell into a marsh across the harbour.

While they faced considerable danger during the Salonika posting, Howard and Robina also had time to get to know each other better. Stewart remembers his father talking about that:

> Howard had a chest illness for three or four months and had to return to Cyprus where he became a medical patient. But their romance was already well underway. Howard was now a Major under the Commanding Officer, Dr. E.C. Hart. He would soon be a Lieutenant-Colonel. Robina was a senior nurse putting off the many medical officers especially while my father was ill in Cyprus. When they were finally reposted to London and Liverpool in 1917, they were able to enjoy some dancing and theatre.

Stewart also remembers that his mother's favourite musical from the time in England was *Chu Chin Chow*. This musical comedy served as a welcome diversion for the war weary, premiered in London in August 1916 and ran for five years and a total of 2,238 performances, a record that stood for nearly forty years. *Chu Chin Chow* was a favourite with soldiers on leave and nearly three million people saw the show.

Finally the Great War was ending. Howard and Robina were married In Liverpool on May 3, 1919, in Reverend Ian McLaren's church in Sefton Park. One week later, after a short honeymoon, Robina received her army nurse discharge and sailed on the *Aquitania* for Canada. Howard, unable to travel with her because of crowded ship space, followed three weeks later on the *Mauretania*. After a visit with Robina's parents in Selkirk, Manitoba (her father owned and ran the *Selkirk Record*,

Robina Stewart and Howard Burris sightseeing in Egypt.
Courtesy of the Burris Family

a well-respected Manitoba newspaper), they were on their way to Kamloops. The doctors back home had been busy too with the outbreak of influenza that hit after the war.

"I was met by a very tired team of doctors," H.L. wrote in his memoirs.

Robina and H.L. raised two sons and three daughters in Kamloops. Howard passed on in 1972 and Robina in 1980. Son Stewart and his son Alan were both doctors at the Burris Clinic in Kamloops and retired before the clinic closed in 2013, after serving Kamloops for 110 years.

For many nurses and soldiers heading off to war, it was the first opportunity to experience life outside Canada. Maureen Duffus says Robina and H.L. took every opportunity to explore when they weren't working: "I really admired the fact they were so keen on sightseeing. Nothing would stop them. They were in Egypt waiting for their Salonika camp to be ready and they saw everything. They just went everywhere: on picnics, up the Nile and got becalmed, their sightseeing was a marvel. There are dozens of pictures of nurses on camels."

From Our Listeners: The Eyes of an Angel

Harlan Tucker Goodwin shared the following story about his father, Clive Merritt Goodwin, and Annie Tucker, the nurse who looked after him. Thanks to Harlan's son Doug Goodwin for assisting.

By Harlan Tucker Goodwin, Burnaby

Unlike many veterans, my father was not reluctant to talk about the Great War. Like them, though, he was very selective in the stories he would tell. I never heard about the hard times, the friends lost, the frightening nights. He liked to talk about training in England, the horses he cared for, the camaraderie.

His favourite story was how he opened his eyes one day and saw an angel.

Clive Merritt Goodwin was from New Westminster, BC, but had made his way to Halifax with his box of tools to start his life as an electrician. It was there that he enlisted with the Canadian Expeditionary Force. Leaving his tools in the home of his landlady, Clive went overseas, obtained the rank of corporal and ended up in the horse-drawn artillery. Like so many other Canadians he found himself at Vimy

Ridge, preparing for the battle that was soon to come.

Although he was often behind the front lines because of his work with the artillery horses, Clive was not immune to danger. One of his stories was about the day he was slogging through the trenches when the soldier behind him tapped him on the shoulder, handed him a piece of shrapnel, and said, "You might want to keep this. It just hit your backpack. If it didn't you would not be here right now."

While at Vimy, Clive was diagnosed with appendicitis. On April 7, 1917, just two days before Canadian troops attacked and captured the ridge, Clive was evacuated and shipped back to England. I often wonder whether the unwanted appendicitis saved his life.

It is at this point in the story that my father took most delight. Recovering in his Cliveden hospital bed, he woke one morning and looked up...right into the eyes of an angel. It took a moment to notice the angel wore the uniform of a nursing sister, the woman who would one day become my mother.

Annie Tucker from Winnipeg had enlisted with the Canadian Medical Corps in 1917, one of over three thousand Canadian nurses who served during that war. Like the other nurses, Annie was given the rank of lieutenant. More affectionately, they were nicknamed "bluebirds" because of their distinctive blue dresses and white veils.

Since corporals could not fraternize with officers like Annie, getting to know each other was difficult. Somehow they managed. How much of a future together they planned at that time I do not know. When Clive discovered after being discharged that his electrician's tools had all been destroyed in the Great Halifax Explosion of 1917, he decided to start anew and seek Annie out. He eventually found her nursing in Los Angeles, and in 1920 they were married and moved to BC.

I wish this story could have been told from Annie's point of view as well but I never heard it—she died suddenly on my fourteenth birthday, long before I was interested in such ancient parental history.

Harlan added this postscript: In 2011 a highlight of my life happened when I, my son and his son stood together at midnight at that magnificent Vimy Ridge Memorial. I wore my parents' medals proudly on my chest and held their memory

Nursing Sister Annie Tucker, wearing one of the elaborate nurse's coifs.
Courtesy of the Goodwin Family

in my heart, in that place where the boundaries between living and dying, past and present, life and death, are so clearly fragile.

Thomas Pidgeon

In his mother's papers, Harlan Goodwin found her autograph book. This small book contains names, drawings and poems from soldiers she nursed. On January 1, 1918, Thomas Pidgeon, a twenty-year-old soldier from Prince Edward Island wrote the one shown here.

We wondered who T.D. Pidgeon was and what happened to him. Here is a bit of that story. Searching through attestation papers from World War I, we found Thomas Dewey Pidgeon, a farm boy from Wheatley River, PEI, who joined the 8th Canadian PEI Siege Battery, one of the PEI units that stayed together through the war.

The Siege Battery was the target of a gas attack in July of 1917. Thomas and his fellow soldiers were temporarily blinded by the gas and shipped back to England—where Nurse Tucker encountered some of them at the Taplow Hospital at Clivenden.

Many soldiers survived gas attacks and were sent back to the front after months of recovery. Thomas was not so lucky. He was shipped back to Canada aboard a hospital ship.

From Nurse Tucker's autograph book—a tribute poem from a recovering soldier.
Courtesy of the Goodwin Family

Thomas ended up in Nova Scotia and married a local nurse but never fully recovered from the injuries to his lungs. He died at the Vernon Jubilee Hospital in 1920. His body was sent back to Nova Scotia where he is buried.

From Our Listeners: War Crimes—The *Llandovery Castle*

By David Griffiths
Our next story comes from David Griffiths, a Vancouver Island maritime historian.

Christina Campbell was born in 1877 at Inverness, Scotland. She was just sixteen in 1893 when she travelled out alone to Victoria to join her older brother Angus and his family.

When not helping out in her brother's clothing shop on Government Street, Christina took nursing courses at Royal Jubilee Hospital and graduated from there in 1897. In 1915 she enlisted in the Canadian Army Medical Corps (CAMC), with the Canadian Expeditionary Force.

Twenty-five hundred CAMC Nursing Sisters served overseas during World War I and forty-six would never return home. Christina would be one of those.

After completing her basic, military and medical training at Esquimalt, Nursing Sister Campbell sailed for England for further training and was first deployed to a field hospital in France in October of 1915.

After two weeks of orientation at a one-thousand-bed tent hospital, she was transferred to the No. 5 Canadian General Hospital in Egypt, where she joined the Medical Evacuation Force and was employed in accompanying the wounded back to hospitals in England.

In June of 1916 Christina was reassigned to a five-month posting in Salonika, where the relentless pace, the heat and the horror finally took its toll. After two solid months of night shifts, she was invalided back to England, suffering from nervous exhaustion and chronic insomnia.

After regaining her strength at a Canadian Red Cross hospital in London, she returned to her casualty transportation work with No. 5 CGH, after which she was reposted to serve for eight months at a hospital in England.

In March of 1918 Nursing Sister Campbell was assigned to transport duty aboard the Canadian hospital ship *Llandovery Castle,* responsible for the care of servicemen returning home to Canada. The brand new 517-foot, 11,423-ton *Llandovery Castle* had entered the service of the Union Castle Line in 1914 on the East Africa run and had been commissioned as a hospital ship in July of 1916.

In peacetime the liner would have accommodated 216 first class passengers, 116 second class, and 100 third, serviced by a crew of 250. In wartime she was converted to 622 hospital beds, with a medical staff of 102, plus crew.

On the night of June 27, 1918, HMHS *Llandovery Castle* was seventy miles off the Irish Coast, on the last leg of a voyage from Halifax, Nova Scotia, to Liverpool. On board were 164 crew members and 94 medical staff, including fourteen nursing sisters, Christina Campbell among them.

According to the Hague Convention, of which both Germany and the Allies were signatories, hospital ships were required to be clearly identified as such and were to be allowed to safely make their passage "without let, hindrance, or molestation."

On the night of June 27 all lights were burning aboard the *Llandovery Castle.* A huge electric cross burned over the bridge, strings of green and white lights were strung along both rails of the ship and the red crosses on her hull were illuminated by electric lights.

To First Lieutenant Patzig, the commander of the German submarine *U-86,* which had been tailing the hospital ship for some hours, there could have been no doubt of his would-be victim's identity. Despite this, at 9 p.m. Patzig ordered a single torpedo to be fired at the *Llandovery Castle.* It struck amidships on the port side, just aft of the engine room.

The ship immediately lost all electrical power; the lights went out and the Marconi radio set was made inoperable. No distress signal was ever sent. Most of the engine-room crew were either dead or wounded, and consequently did not respond to signals from the bridge. The *Llandovery Castle* continued making forward headway, increasing the rate of water entering her hull and making it difficult to launch the lifeboats safely.

The lifeboat containing Christina Campbell, her thirteen fellow nurses and a boat's crew of nine men became entangled in the launching ropes and was dragged along the ship's side. As the *Llandovery Castle*'s stern sank, the suction flipped the lifeboat, throwing everyone into the water.

An eyewitness would later report that all the sisters had lifejackets on.

A number of lifeboats were successfully launched, including the last to leave the ship, containing her master, Captain R.A. Sylvester.

Within ten minutes of the torpedo striking her the *Llandovery Castle* was gone. The boats began picking through the floating debris in search of survivors until *U-86* motored onto the scene and ordered Captain Sylvester's lifeboat alongside.

The U-boat commander, Patzig, accused Sylvester of carrying American flying officers and munitions aboard the *Llandovery Castle*—both accusations he denied. Two Canadian medical officers were dragged aboard the submarine and roughly interrogated, before being returned to the lifeboat.

U-86 commenced to zigzag at high speed through the field of wreckage, ramming the lifeboats as she went; Sylvester's boat narrowly missed such a fate and drifted out into the darkness. Revolver and cannon fire replaced the screams and shouts of survivors in the water, as Patzig attempted to destroy forever any trace of his action.

Soon, all was silence. Captain Sylvester and his twenty-three companions were the only survivors of the *Llandovery Castle*'s 258 souls. They were picked up a day and a half after the sinking by a British patrol boat.

After the war the *Llandovery Castle* massacre was the first British war trial to be held at Leipzig, but Patzig eluded prosecution by fleeing the country, and although two of his officers were sentenced to four years each, they were soon released when it was deemed that Patzig himself was solely responsible for the incident.

Inscribed on Halifax's Cross of Sacrifice, Christina Campbell's name is one of three thousand names of those Canadian women and men lost at sea during the two world wars. "Their graves are unknown, but their memory endures."

Above: Red Cross volunteers pose with a French lieutenant for a funds campaign.
Stuart Thomson photo, City of Vancouver Archives, Gr War P14

Left: An obituary card for Nursing Sister Christina Campbell, killed when *Llandovery Castle* was torpedoed by a German U-boat.
Courtesy of David Griffiths

Far left: A popular fund-raising poster used the U-boat attack to sell Victory Bonds.
Courtesy of David Griffiths

Nursing Sister Marjorie Beatrice Moberly

Some nursing sisters never made it overseas. Marjorie Beatrice Moberly graduated from the Nursing School of the Royal Jubilee Hospital in Vernon.

In October 1918 she died of influenza at the Coquitlam Military Hospital. The obituary in the *Vancouver Province* read:

> The death occurred at the Coquitlam Military Hospital on Saturday of Nursing Sister Marjorie Beatrice Moberly, aged 23. She had applied for overseas' service eighteen months ago, but was not called on until the influenza outbreak, when she immediately went to Coquitlam. After a few days she contracted the disease. She was the first military nurse to die from the epidemic. She was the daughter of Major Moberly of the Board of Pension Commissioners.

Before She Was a Rattenbury, She Was a Heroic Nurse

Alma Clarke grew up in Kamloops. She was born in 1895, the stepdaughter of a prominent local newspaperman. Alma excelled at music, composition and performance. She attracted many admirers and just before the war, she married a dashing Irishman, Caledon Robert John Radcliffe Dolling. Dolling was a realtor in Vancouver, but when war broke out, he soon joined

From Our Listeners: Tell Them to Carry on—The Bombing at Etaples

By Rosamond Norbury, Maple Ridge
Rosamond Norbury sent us this story about her grandmother's sister, Gladys Wake, who was killed in a notorious hospital bombing.

British Columbia contributed its share of nurses to the war effort, several of whom did not return. Nursing Sister Gladys Maude Wake—known as "Bob"—was born in Esquimalt, British Columbia, on December 13, 1883. She was a tiny woman—five feet one inch tall, weighing 112 pounds. Her family lived in British Columbia for many years, but she was residing in England when World War I broke out. A trained nurse, "Bob" volunteered her services and in 1916 was appointed a nursing sister in the Canadian Expeditionary Force. It is interesting to note that even though Gladys Wake had British parents and was living in England when World War I broke out, she chose to serve in the Canadian Armed Forces. She served in several hospitals over the next two years: at the Duchess of Connaught's Canadian Red Cross Hospital, No. 1 Canadian Stationary Hospital in Salonika, No. 4 Canadian General Hospital in Etaples, and in England, No. 11 Canadian General Hospital. In October 1917, she joined No. 1 Canadian General Hospital in Etaples.

This excerpt is from Nurse Elsie Dorothy Collis's journal. She and Gladys Wake graduated from the Royal Jubilee Hospital School of Nursing in Victoria.

May 19, 1918: Had a terrible air raid from 10:30 p.m to 12:30 a.m. Was a beautiful night—as light as day...Before I left for supper I heard distant guns and thought nothing of it. Had just got to the kitchen door when bombs began to drop. There were several in the mess quarters and that set the rows of huts on fire. Two dropped outside the club, another outside our new quarters, the whole place was wrecked—poor little "Bob" was buried, she had a fractured femur, a huge wound in the other leg and several smaller ones. Miss McDonald was killed. She had a small wound but it must have severed the femoral artery as she died of haemorrhage almost immediately. Wounded were taken to G ward. Several

bombs dropped on the officers lines. One on top of Hill 60. Killed one M.O. who was standing up and several others. There were about six of us in the kitchen on the floor. It was dreadful. We could see the fires through the window, hear the men shouting and calling. Hear bombs dropping, the guns would all stop until the machines came within range. All one could hear was their continual buzzing—then the guns again, then the bombs. The windows all fell in, dishes kept breaking, the plaster walls fell in in places. We were sure the next one would hit us. When there was a lull, we hurried back to the wards. One badly hurt man was brought to hut X dying. Three planes returned, one dropped several bombs then left us alone, several of the hill wards were hit, one destroyed. Where the men slept a number where killed and nearly as many wounded. The O.R. was very busy the rest of the night. Private Wilson was killed.

May 21. Miss McDonald was buried this a.m. A number of us went, also No. 7, all our men. Capt. Hughes was also buried. These funerals are dreadfully trying. Saw "Bob" this morning, she looked terribly ill—has the most dreadful wounds, gangrene, I'm sure from the odour. Miss Saunders came while I was there. Miss Wilson brought her from Le Treport. She was on a case so glad she got here. Poor little "Bob" died at three o'clock. Saw Miss Wilson for a few minutes.

May 22, "Bob" buried at 9:30. We all went to the funeral, it was dreadfully trying. 46 of the boys were all buried together in one long grave.

"Bob" was one of three Canadian nurses who were mortally wounded on May 19, 1918. That night, fifteen German planes attacked Etaples. During a hellish two hours, 116 bombs were dropped over the hospital complex. The nurses' quarters of No. 1 Canadian General sustained a direct hit, scattering debris and setting it on fire. Witnesses say that during the extended raid, one bomber used the bright moonlight and the flames from the rubble to spot both patients and medical staff in the hospital debris, and fired on them repeatedly. Throughout the ordeal, up. The couple moved briefly to Prince Rupert where they were the talk of the town.

Dolling became a captain in the Royal Welsh Fusiliers. Despite bad eyesight, he went overseas and received the Military Cross for bravery in February 1916. A few months later, he was killed by shell fire at Mametz Wood during the Somme offensive.

Alma was desolate but anxious to get to the front to do her part. She joined the Scottish Women's Hospital Organization, which was then working with the French Red Cross at Royaumont, an abbey that had been turned into a military hospital. Alma experienced the worst of it, bombardments, dreadful wounds and amputations. She herself was wounded in action and received the Croix de Guerre from the French government for her bravery.

The rest of the story is better known. Alma remarried but fled that disastrous second marriage and moved back to Victoria where she met architect Francis Rattenbury. Rattenbury left his wife for Alma and the ensuing scandal forced them to leave Victoria for England. In 1935, Rattenbury was murdered by his chauffeur, who was said to be Alma's lover. The chauffeur was found guilty of the crime. Alma was cleared. Despondent and worn down by one of the most widely covered trials in British history, she committed suicide just a few days later. A tragic end for a brave nurse.

Alma Clarke Dolling Rattenbury (lower left). She was awarded the Croix de Guerre from the French government for her bravery while serving as a nurse.
Courtesy of Anthony Barrett

The funeral for Nurse Wake at Etaples.
William Rider-Rider / Department of National Defence / Library and Archives Canada / PA-002562

nurses and attendants continued to scurry to the aid of the wounded. Wake was among those in the nurses' quarters when it was hit. As flames crackled around her, recognizing that she was unlikely to survive, Wake begged black-faced stretcher bearers to leave her and save themselves. Despite her protests, they pulled her from the burning hut. Above them, German planes flew low, sending a spray of machine-gun fire among the rescuers. Wake eventually died of extensive damage to her legs and a fractured femur.

Eighty years later, in 1998, through the efforts of an Esquimalt historian, Sherri Robinson, a mountain located at the northeast junction of Meager Creek and the Lillooet River was named in Glady's honour. Mount Wake was named under a BC Ministry of Environment, Lands and Parks program that names previously unidentified geographical features in honour of those who gave their lives serving Canada during times of war. Gladys is also remembered with a plaque in St. Paul's Anglican Church in Esquimalt, the church her family attended while living there.

A truly courageous woman, her last message to her family and on her gravestone was "Tell them not to be sorry, but glad, and tell them to carry on."

A Letter Home from a Victoria Nursing Sister

A vivid description of what it was like to serve in those field hospitals in the last year of the war is contained in a letter from a nursing sister published by the Victoria Daily Colonist *in early August 1918. Phyllis Green wrote to her mother:*

Since June 5 we have had an awful time. Three thousand wounded Americans have passed through our hands, and the past three weeks seemed like a nightmare. The US Marines went into action and got pretty well blown to cinders, and our ambulance was the nearest one from the front for the gravest cases needing urgent attention. The park is full of tents of wounded. Even the village church has been turned into a temporary ward, sixteen operating tables going at once, night and day.

I shall never in all my life forget the first two nights after the arrival of the first detachment of these poor wounded. The stretchers came up the stair in one perpetual stream, the clothes of the men were cut off them, and in turn they went on the tables and had their operations. They then were replaced on the stretchers and taken back to the ambulances (as soon as they were out of ether), and shipped on to Paris: only the amputations and severe shock cases were put into bed. We gave morphine to every man upon arrival, so there was not much suffering from discomfort as one would imagine. Some of the stretchers when we uncovered them had carried men already dead. It has been terrible.

I have been in charge of the Shock Ward and believe me, if it had not been for a good, kind YMCA clergyman who sat with the dying continually, I don't know what I should have done. What with cutting the clothes off the dying, so as to get them into the operating room, and giving them hypos as quickly as I could shoot, I had not a moment for the poor dying boys. But this good YMCA clergyman is the best, or rather one of the best, men I have ever known—sincere and quiet. . .

But the sad and dreadful sights of this month of June. We have evacuated as many as possible today as there is an American drive now without pause night and day. We expect the wounded in an avalanche any hour, and there is at the present moment a raid going on. The Germans are overhead, and every cannon within ten miles is firing. We have had this raid affair for the last four nights. Last night was the worst. The noise was tremendous! But they did not reach Paris, only the environs.

For the moment, good bye, dearest mother. We will have a good time together yet. Don't worry.

Your loving Phyllis

From Our Listeners: My Uncle Donald Rose

By Ron Rose, Vancouver

I never knew my uncle Donald Rose. He was killed fighting in France during World War I three years before I was born.

Private Rose, #71303, 27th Battalion, Manitoba Regiment of the Canadian Expeditionary Force, joined up in Winnipeg October 25, 1914, soon after the war broke out. Private Rose escaped an early brush with death. His record shows that he was invalided to England with a gunshot wound, treated, rehabilitated and returned to the front line. Less than two years after his enlistment, he was missing, presumed killed, on the first day of the Battle of Flers-Courcelette. He was one day short of his twenty-eighth birthday at the time of his death.

The Canadians, along with British and New Zealand troops, were part of a historic surge on the Somme front, led by tanks for the first time in warfare. There were high hopes for a breakthrough, but many of the cumbersome tanks broke down and the Germans, well dug in, resisted desperately. The Canadians took Courcelette but became bogged down amid heavy casualties.

British war dispatches reported the disaster of the Flers-Courcelette offensive, which began September 15, 1916, and was finally called off September 25. The twenty-eight-ton tanks, lumbering across no man's land at half a mile an hour shedding rifle fire and machine-gun rounds, panicked the enemy into an early retreat and the British press hailed a tremendous victory. However, only fifteen of forty-nine tanks made it across the front, and the terrible toll of fallen soldiers multiplied as the days wore on. Among the Allied casualties was Raymond Asquith, the son of the British prime minister, Herbert Asquith.

The Canadians, on the left flank of the offensive, captured the village of Courcelette under machine-gun fire from rapidly built positions behind the front that escaped the artillery, tank and infantry assault.

A fellow soldier who survived the Flers-Courcelette offensive wrote Donald's parents in Ontario saying he believed the body was found and buried in a Canadian war cemetery at nearby Contalmaison, but the Commonwealth War Graves Commission found this was not so, and Private Rose's name was later carved with 11,284 other missing heroes in the limestone grandeur of the Vimy Memorial.

(Young Donald had moved from the small town of Orillia, Ontario, to Winnipeg for a job in what was then the gateway to the west. He boarded in the family home of a young woman, Ethel Little, who would become my mother because Donald introduced her to his brother Alexander, who also came west for a job. Alexander G. Rose and Ethel May Little married some time later, and they brought me to the West Coast when I was three. The 1921 census reported us all living at the house with Ethel's widowed mother, Elizabeth. My father was the only one who had an income. He made twenty-six hundred dollars as a newspaper editor in the preceding year, a comfortable wage in those days. I was told later that he bought one of the newfangled Model T Fords the day I was born.)

10

BC WOMEN AND THE GREAT WAR
BREAKING BARRIERS

W hile some women headed overseas as nursing sisters, many remained on the home front, where they had to make do under difficult circumstances. Whether it was keeping a farm going, or raising children alone, or working in a factory, the challenges were sometimes overwhelming. In too many cases, fathers, brothers and husbands never returned. In other cases, they returned as changed men, strangers who brought their traumas and sometimes an unwelcome violence back with them. The war also changed some things for the better and brought the vote for most, though not all, women. Here are some stories that illuminate that difficult time.

Getting the Vote during the Great War

By Jean Barman

Among the many changes in British Columbian life prompted by the Great War was women's gaining the right to vote alongside their menfolk. The campaign was already under way, but it took the war to break the stalemate.

The assumption that only men could make decisions in the public realm was passed down from Britain's common law tradition to its North American colonies and then into section 41 of the *British North America Act* that brought Canada into being in 1867. Since BC joined Canada in 1871, the women of British Columbia had been determined to secure equal rights at the ballot box. Later in that same year the leading American proponent, Susan B. Anthony, argued for women's suffrage, the right to vote, to an enthusiastic audience in the new provincial capital of Victoria. Eight months later the first of numerous unsuccessful suffrage bills was introduced in the provincial legislature. Support came from middle-class reformers and from moderate elements within the labour movement but it was not enough. Women did gain the right to vote for local school boards, an area of public life considered within their realm of expertise as mothers. A turn-of-the-century bill giving women the franchise was supported

Right: A working class reformer—Helena Gutteridge.
Courtesy of the Royal BC Museum, BC Archives Image C-07954

Far right: Activist Helen Gregory MacGill fought for women's suffrage. The war finally broke the stalemate in the battle for the vote.
R.H. Marlowe photo, City of Vancouver Archives, Port P1140.2

Below: Campaigns for War Savings Certificates urged Canadians to support the war effort—whether in the kitchen or through one's paycheque.
Courtesy of Don Stewart

Below right: Wartime demanded a new passion for basic foods like the time-tested potato.
Courtesy of Don Stewart

by a petition signed by some twenty thousand British Columbian men and women and nearly, but not quite, received legislative consent.

The suffrage campaign was notable for cutting across the class lines that sometimes divide British Columbians. Among the activists were Helen Gregory MacGill, a genteel wife and mother, and Helena Gutteridge, a strident working-class reformer making her own way in the world. Despite their different emphases in reform, they were joined in perceiving the legal status of women as, in MacGill's words, "outmoded, harsh and morally repugnant." The organizing efforts of the two women and their supporters kept the issue alive, as did opposition Liberal Party support as of 1912.

The Great War turned the tide. Across Canada patriotism was perceived on the home front as a fight to eradicate the ills of society, including women's prohibition from voting. The national stalemate was broken when in 1915 Manitoba gave women the vote, followed in short order by Alberta and Saskatchewan. Backed by a broad coalition of reform groups, British Columbian Liberals made suffrage part of its successful 1916 election campaign, which included a referendum on the issue. Suffrage was approved and the resulting April 1917 act gave women the right both to vote and to be elected to the legislature. Nationally women received the franchise in two stages: war nurses and immediate relatives of military men in 1917, followed by all women the next year.

The Great War's aftermath would see a consolidation of the gains that had been signalled by female suffrage, cutting across gender, social class and, over time, skin tones. As summed up by MacGill's daughter Elsie, "The drive for social legislation was now so steady and continuing a force that it and the other benefits due to the women's voting potential were accepted as natural features of the social landscape." British Columbia would be a leader in enacting a spate of legislation so doing.

The Bert family on a stone boat used to haul water on their Galiano farm.
Courtesy of Diana Best

From Our Listeners: The Women Left Behind

By Diana Best

There are no medals for the women who are left behind to carry on alone when men heed the clarion call of war. In 1914 all the able-bodied men of the Gulf Islands left for a war that was supposed to be over by Christmas.

Victor and Winifred Best had a small farm at Sturdies Bay on Galiano Island. Winifred, at the age of thirty, was left to carry on alone to manage the farm with four boys under the age of seven and another baby on the way. There was also the additional worry of her husband fighting in France and her two brothers killed on the same day at the battle of Ypres. Family and friends were left far behind in England.

Winifred had graduated as a teacher and had little knowledge of farming. The farmhouse had no running water, electricity or phone. She had to learn to use all the tools of farming, to milk the cows, shear her own sheep, even to fell trees and cut wood with a crosscut saw for the ever-hungry fires. Water was carried on a stoneboat from the pump with the help of a horse and the boys. Much was spilled along the way. Her only help was Prudencia, a young woman from Colombia who spoke very little English.

Adding to these problems, the winter of 1916 brought "The Big Snow," six feet on the level for six weeks. During this time neither food nor mail reached the farm. The roofs of the barn, stable and woodshed collapsed under the weight of snow. The only water had to come from melted snow. It was a time for pioneer improvisation and Winifred Best met every challenge.

Winifred Best, née Thompson, was the daughter of a strict Baptist minister; so strict, in fact, that he barred Winifred's sister Muriel from the house for attending a dance at the age of sixteen! Winifred graduated from the University of Edinburgh as a teacher at a time when it was unusual for a woman to even attend university.

In the early 1900s she had sailed for India to teach and work as a Baptist missionary, but on the way out she met Victor Best, young son of a brewing family on his way to run an Indian brewery. They were such a handsome couple, but Baptists and beer were not allowed, so Winifred wrote to her sister and explained that Victor was on his way to improve beer for the Indians, a somewhat different mission. They were married in Quetta, where soon afterward she nearly died of typhoid fever.

They returned to England where their first son, Vincent, was born, followed by Gordon; then they emigrated to Chicago where Victor took courses in veterinary medicine and where their third son, Alan, was born in 1910. Not liking life in the US, they moved to Calgary where Norman was born. The children did not fare well in that climate and they moved to the coast where they rented a small farm at Sturdies Bay on Galiano Island.

From Our Listeners: The Family William Morris Left Behind

By Katey Wright, New Westminster

My grandmother, Mary Morris, was two years old when she and her family immigrated to Canada from England in 1906. The Morris family—at that time Mary, elder sister Edie, and parents Martha and William—settled in Vancouver and moved a number of times, ending up in the Collingwood neighbourhood, where Mary and Edie attended the little Carleton School. By the autumn of 1914 the family had increased to seven children, with number eight on the way. William Morris, my great-grandfather, immediately enlisted in the British Armed Forces. The family doctor told William that with so many children and another one soon to arrive, he must not go overseas to war, but William was resolute. So rather than returning to school in September 1914, my grandmother Mary and her sister Edie, then ten and twelve, stayed at home to help their mother with the children. Mary never returned to school and for the rest of her long life she felt keenly her lack of education, despite being one of the wisest people I ever knew.

When World War I ended in 1918, William returned to Vancouver and resumed his place as head of the family. Soon after his return, my grandmother Mary (who was fourteen by this time) was cleaning up after a meal, finishing by wiping the table. William was not satisfied with the job she had done. He cuffed her on the side of the head, causing her to stumble onto the floor, and said, "Now get back here and do that properly." He had always been a rather hard man but this kind of violence, it seemed, was something new. Martha, my great-grandmother, a gentle and submissive woman in her married life thus far, strode into the room. "Willie," she said firmly, "I've done without you for four years. I can do without you again."

I've always thought that it was a very emancipated thing to say. World War I brought out incredible things in all those who lived through it, whether at home or abroad.

The war put new strains on marriages when the men came home. William and Martha Morris in Vancouver around 1910.
Courtesy of Katey Wright

From Our Listeners: An Ambulance Driver with the Voluntary Aid Detachment

With source material from Diana Filer

"Their faces glowed ruddily in the frosty air. Their whole appearance suggested sturdiness and pluck," said the *Daily Province* newspaper.

Women on the home front stepped up by the thousands to do men's work—from farms to factories. Some volunteered overseas as nurses; others, like Grace Evelyn MacPherson, got close to the front lines behind the wheel of an ambulance.

The young secretary at Pennington Typewriter Company in Vancouver was feisty, had lots of friends and was one of the first women to buy her own car. With the onset of war, Grace joined twenty-five thousand other people at the rail yards to watch the 72nd Battalion head off, her older brother Alex among them. She later read a telegram delivering news of his fatal wound at Gallipoli. Grace was determined to serve and sent a letter to both the Canadian War Office and the British Red Cross asking to become an ambulance driver. She was flatly rejected. Grace sailed to England, landed a job at the Canadian Pay Office and continued her solitary campaign.

The nineteen-year-old managed to arrange a face-to-face meeting with Sam Hughes, Canadian minister of militia. Her diary describes his reaction. "Said France was no place for me, but I might do good work in England and would give me a letter to Colonel Hodgetts of the Red Cross." Hughes said he would stop her "or any other girl from going to France." Carnage at the Somme changed everything. Men driving ambulances were now in high demand at the front lines, creating an opportunity for Grace and other women to reinforce the ambulance convoy. She crossed the channel to Boulogne two days before the Vimy attack and was soon helping transport the wounded from this seminal Canadian battle to hospitals at Etaples.

Grace was one of only three Canadians among the hundred British women; facing their class system was a rude awakening for the young working-class woman. However, she proved herself to be one of the best drivers, carrying the wounded from train to hospital along muddy, bombed-out roads. The volunteer ambulance drivers (VAD) were also tasked with repairing and maintaining their own ambulances; Grace was an ace at fixing and replacing tires on her Canadian-made McLaughlin Buick. It's clear from her pocket diary that she relished the adventure. "It was glorious to think that at last I was actually driving an ambulance. It was a dream hatched out and means more to me than anything has meant to me yet."

Grace cut quite a figure in her aviator helmet, goggles and black leather trenchcoat. The demands on the VAD were exhausting: twelve-hour shifts were the norm. Sometimes when the "show" was on, shifts were stretched to thirty-six or forty-eight hours. Her pay was a paltry fourteen shillings a week. And don't get caught dancing in your spare time or you were shipped home within twenty-four hours.

By the spring of 1918 the Germans were becoming desperate and began attacking hospitals and ambulance trains from the air. Following her return from France, Grace provided this chilling account in *The Gold Stripe*, a local tribute to Great War veterans:

It was a beautiful moonlit night. No warning was given. There were sixty machines in the raid, coming over in relays of 20 each. The men's quarters of the staff of No. 1 Canadian General Hospital were the first to be hit, suffering about 115 casualties, seventy or more killed, among them was Sgt. Brown, a charming Vancouver boy. The nurses' quarters suffered as well: three nurses killed instantly, and many severely wounded. Many of the other camps also had hundreds of casualties, the total list approximately 750. The Huns dropped aerial torpedoes, man killing and incendiary bombs, and while the huts were in

First published in 1918 for the British Columbia Amputees Club, *The Gold Stripe* featured art, poetry and prose. It was dedicated to "BC men killed, crippled and wounded in the Great War." Courtesy of Don Stewart

flames, they swept down and peppered the dead and wounded with machine gun bullets. . .and when there was a lull of a few minutes, thirty of the drivers were ordered out, and then the last squadron came over, and we drove and faced the music. There were ghastly-gruesome sights indeed, but it was much nicer to be driving than sitting idle in our huts.

Grace was noted by peers and superiors for staying calm under pressure. An entire chapter is devoted to her in Sandra Gwyn's *Tapestry of War:*

A letter in the Vancouver Province that survives among her papers tells us that she performed with great courage and resourcefulness during that terrible night. "She is a very gritty woman," wrote Captain Donald Martyn, MC and Bar. "She was the first on the scene with her machine and she worked all night without a quiver and let me say, there were not a few men panic stricken on that awful night of horror...In the estimation of officers here and of her own corps, Miss MacPherson is described as 'the bravest of them all,' to quote one high official's words."

On her return to Vancouver, Grace married Major David Livingston and raised two children. She died in 1979.

Diana Filer holds a photo of her mother, Red Cross ambulance driver Grace MacPherson. Courtesy of Mark Forsythe

From Our Listeners: Socks for the Troops

By Sally Dzus, Port Alberni

My great-grandparents Mary Ann and Alfred Deardon were members of the Salvation Army from the time the Salvation Army "opened office" in Victoria in 1887. My great-grandmother and my grandmother were members of the Home League, the women's group of the Salvation Army. During World War I the ladies of the Home League knit socks to send overseas to the troops. The young ladies of the Salvation Army would put their name and address on a slip of paper and put it in the toe of a sock hoping for a letter or note from a soldier serving overseas. As the Home League was active in every corps of the Salvation Army in Canada, I have often wondered if any romances developed from this practice.

From Our Listeners: My Mother's War

By Victoria Drybrough, Port Alberni

My mother, Kathleen Stewart Dodd, was born in 1903 to an upper middle class family in England. When she was seven, her mother, father and brother moved to Vernon, BC. My grandparents didn't consider the "wilds" of Canada to be an appropriate place to raise a daughter, so they left her in England in the care of her aunt and uncle. She lived a privileged life, learned all the things an Edwardian girl should learn, from needlework to music. She was very close to her cousins and the family accepted her as one of their own. The children were educated by governesses until the age of twelve, when she and her cousin, Kit, were sent to Harvington College in London.

On February 19, 1916, at the age of thirty-nine, my grandfather enlisted in the Canadian Expeditionary Force and was shipped overseas. As we know, the war continued to escalate and some of the worst fighting came near the end. My mother told me her father claimed he was worried for her safety in England and turned up one day at her school in 1917 and told her that she would be leaving for Canada in a few days' time. She barely had time to gather some clothes and a few of her things before she was whisked away to board the *Olympic,* sister ship to the *Titanic,* now a troop carrier. She was placed in the care of a stranger—a woman whom none of her family knew—and sailed off into the stormy waters of the Atlantic Ocean. She was only fourteen years old.

From Halifax the lady rode the train with her as far as Montreal, where she disembarked and left my mother to continue her journey alone. She thought she was travelling to the ends of the earth and longed for her family back in England.

In Vernon she was met by her mother and brother, both of whom she barely knew and hadn't seen since she was a little girl. Her new home was a small wooden house with an outhouse behind and farmland all around. It was the opposite of everything she had ever known. To make ends meet, her mother used to play the piano for the silent movies at the local theatre. She also did dressmaking, with my mother's help. Later that year my grandfather was injured at Ypres and returned home with his lungs badly damaged from mustard gas. My mother quit school and went to work at the Hudson's Bay Company to help support the family. In December 1918 her brother fell through the ice at a skating party and drowned. Her parents were devastated and all hope of a decent income to support the family was lost. My mother got a job at the Vernon telephone office and became the head breadwinner for the family for several years until her father opened a real estate office. Any hopes she ever had of returning to England disappeared.

In 1921 she met and fell in love with Horace Foote, whose family owned the hardware store. When my grandfather learned about the relationship, he put a stop to it, saying she would be marrying beneath her. Once again he had ruined her hopes for a happy life.

She married my father, Harry Kendall Cross, in December 1927 and they were married for sixty-two years. He was not a bad man, but he carried baggage from the war and they were certainly not suited. I often wonder what kind of life she would have had if the war had not intervened and she had remained in England with the family who loved and supported her.

Kathleen Dodd with her father.
Courtesy of Victoria Drybrough

EVERYWOMAN'S WORLD

Miss Victoria

FROM PAINTING BY
K. MUNN

CONFEDERATION NUMBER
More than 130,000 Circulation

JULY
1917

Continental Publishing Co., Limited, Toronto, Canada

Trade Mark Registered 1913, Department of Agriculture, at Ottawa, by
Continental Publishing Co., Limited, Toronto, Canada.

FIFTEEN
CENTS

This was the most widely read magazine in Canada during World War I.
Courtesy of Don Stewart

From Our Listeners: A Love Story—W.J. Johnston's Postcards and Letters

By Gail Simpson, Victoria

Our grandfather, W.J. Johnston, was a native Victorian. His mother came to Victoria in 1862 or 1863 at the age of nine from Scotland on *Norman Morrison*.

He worked in Dawson City as a printer. When he returned to Victoria and married our grandmother, he had a hard time finding a good job. In 1916, "Dos" (his nickname because of his connection with Dawson) decided to enlist even though he was well over forty, because by then he and Granny had two girls of their own as well as the seven children she had brought to their marriage.

The military promised she would get a monthly stipend and he'd get a modest allowance for every month he served. He was part of the Pioneers group, sappers who dug trenches.

We grandchildren find the letters very touching, and the greeting cards too. I was surprised to see the postcards of Belgian cities blown to bits. A military historian told me they might have been the property of German soldiers, originally meant as propaganda, to incite further energy from the soldiers to do more damage. He suggested the Canadians might have come by them from captured Germans. I don't know about that; I was just shocked that someone could have been in those terrible streets taking postcard pictures. I love the greeting cards and his loving notes to his daughters and wife.

In 1917, in France, he was injured in the leg and transported to a military hospital in England. After several months, he died of infection. My mother was only three when he left so she didn't really remember him. But because of Granny's devotion, his letters and her stories about their father, he was a very real presence in his daughters' lives for the next seven decades.

Gail Simpson forwarded her family's collection of letters, postcards and other images to the Canadian Letters and Images Project, where they have been digitally scanned and are now part of this online archive. The collection spans all conflicts Canada has been involved in. If you have materials to share, visit www.canadianletters.ca.

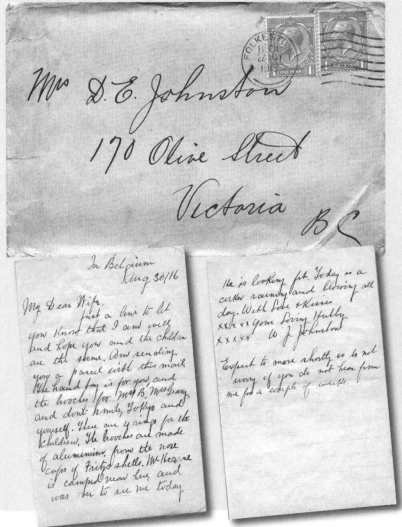

Dear Mabel:
Here is a Souvenir
card from Belgium.
I hope you are having
a good time during
the holidays.
Be a good girl & help
Ma. With love & kisses
from your loving Daddy
xx   W. J. Johnston

Miss Mabel Johnston
170 Olive St
Victoria
BC

LITTLE GREY HOME IN THE WEST (3).
There are hands that will welcome me in,
There are lips I am burning to kiss—
There are two eyes that shine just because
they are mine,
And a thousand things other men miss.

WORDS BY D. EARDLEY-WILMOT.   BY PERMISSION OF CHAPPELL & CO., LTD., THE PUBLISHERS OF THIS SONG.
MUSIC BY HERMANN LOHR.   BAMFORTH COPYRIGHT.

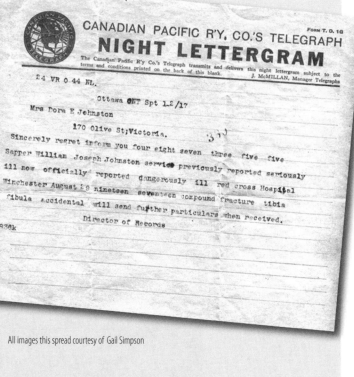

CANADIAN PACIFIC R'Y. CO.'S TELEGRAPH
NIGHT LETTERGRAM
FORM T. D. 1G
The Canadian Pacific R'y Co.'s Telegraph transmits and delivers this night lettergram subject to the
terms and conditions printed on the back of this blank.
J. McMILLAN, Manager Telegraphs

24 VR O 44 NL.

Ottawa ONT Spt 12/17

Mrs Dora E Johnston

170 Olive St;Victoria.

Sincerely regret inform you four eight seven three five five
Sapper William Joseph Johnston service previously reported seriously
ill now officially reported dangerously ill red cross Hospital
Winchester August 18 nineteen seventeen compound fracture tibia
fibula accidental will send further particulars when received.
Director of Records

936k

All images this spread courtesy of Gail Simpson

11
TALES THE CENOTAPHS TELL
SACRIFICE, REMEMBRANCE AND COMMEMORATION

Just about everywhere you go in British Columbia, you'll find cenotaphs. They are often the centre point in a community, a visual reminder of the people who gave their lives for us. Sometimes the people who built these monuments got the names wrong or didn't have all the names of those who were killed. But behind every name on those monuments there is a story. Our listeners helped us tell some of them.

When the cenotaphs were built just after the war, the names were familiar. Then, with the passing of years, the details were lost, buried in old newspapers and not easy to track down. Today, with the power of the internet, we can stand in front of a cenotaph, power up

A community affair—constructing the cenotaph at Ingram Flat near Rock Creek in the 1920s.
Courtesy of Pat McCutcheon

Lunchtime for the Kettle Valley cenotaph crew.
Courtesy of Pat McCutcheon

a cellphone and google a name. Attestation papers pop up; family stories and photographs appear. We can see a face, piece together a story. One hundred years after the cataclysm, we can reimagine what it was like for those who went overseas and never came home.

The Story of One Cenotaph

The Kettle Valley Cenotaph east of Osoyoos sits beside Highway 3 along the Kettle River. It serves as a monument for the whole Boundary country, from Bridesville in the west to Greenwood and Phoenix in the east. In the 1920s after the war was over, community members came up with a pyramid design, brought in horse teams with local rock and started to build. Picnic food was laid out and the job got done.

The cenotaph still stands not far from a grove of Ponderosa pines. It's a good place for a walk. Even in winter, you can stop and brush off the snow and look at the names.

The first thing you may notice is that some last names appear twice or even three times. There are three Olivers, two Glossops, two Caves. The war took an enormous toll on some families.

The Kettle Valley Cenotaph. Each name has a story.
Courtesy of Greg Dickson

The Olivers: Father and Son Killed on the Same Day

It seems unimaginable. Receiving a telegram that a son has died in battle. One day in the early summer of 1915, Sophia Oliver received a wire informing her that her husband, Sidney Oliver, and son William were both killed on the same day at Ypres: April 24, 1915. The shock of losing both a husband and a son at the same time must have been inconceivable.

Sidney was a forty-four-year-old miner when he signed up in September 1914, one of the first from the district to go overseas. His son William was twenty-one years old, a rancher by trade. They joined the 7th Battalion; their service numbers are consecutive so they must have signed up at the same time. The war was going to be over by Christmas, and Sidney, whose parents were in Buxton, might have thought the war was a good opportunity to see the folks at home. He had served with a unit of the Dragoon Guards in England so military practice was familiar and he entered service as a lance corporal. But Ypres was a bloodbath, a finger in the

Western Front that was exposed to enemy fire on three sides. When Sidney and William were killed, word spread fast through the small town of Greenwood.

Sophia later moved to Trail. Another son, James, enlisted in June 1916 after the death of his father and brother. He was a horseman by trade and was just nineteen when he was killed at Vimy Ridge on April 9, 1917.

The Glossop Cousins: Sons of Empire

TOLD WITH HELP FROM SUE DAHLO AND LORRI HARPUR FROM THE BOUNDARY COUNTRY

Major Walter Herbert Newland Glossop was one of many retired imperial army and navy officers who came to British Columbia in the early 1900s and attached themselves to real estate and investment schemes intended to lure more English investment to the province.

After a stint with the Indian Army, Major Glossop emigrated to Rock Creek in 1905 and was one of the prominent men behind the Kettle Valley Irrigated Fruit Lands Company. Ted Gane of Kaleden wrote a lot about the venture. The company got a lot of ink in 1906 and 1907 and was capitalized at about a hundred thousand dollars. Two thousand acres were purchased, and flumes and ditches were built. But because the soil and climate was unfavourable for fruit growing, the project was abandoned after the Great War. By that time, Glossop and his cousin, Naval Commander Henry Anthony Pownall Glossop, were both dead.

Major Glossop was active in military organizing in the Boundary country and was in command of the 102nd Rocky Mountain Rangers. He married locally and started a family in mid-life. But in April 1916, he made the abrupt decision to re-enlist with the 225th Battalion. Perhaps the fruit land scheme was collapsing or perhaps he was drawn by the desperate situation on the Western Front.

Not much is known about the Glossop cousins' wartime service. But both men died in England in 1918 and their deaths may have been war related. Herbert's son, who never really knew his father, was killed in World War II.

At least one other name on the cenotaph seems to be related to the Glossops. Thomas Cave was an English-born law student living in Grand Forks when he enlisted in January 1916. He drilled with the Independent Rifle Company there. The *Grand Forks Sun* reported that he was killed in France while rescuing an officer in late 1916.

One of Walter Glossop's brothers had married a Cave—in fact, a sister of Lord Cave, Prime Minister Lloyd George's home secretary. Thomas Cave was a nephew and so he may have been attracted to the Boundary country by the Glossop connection. The other Cave on the cenotaph does not seem to be related.

Top: Major Herbert Glossop—Indian Army and Rock Creek.
From *Grand Forks Sun*

Above: Margaret (Daisy) Harriott Glossop with the children.
From *Grand Forks Sun*

Captain Jack Tuzo: Killed in East Africa

There's a Tuzo Creek along the Kettle Valley Railway cycling trail. Captain Jack Tuzo was the only son of Dr. Henry Tuzo, who first came to British Columbia in 1853 and served with Governor James Douglas. His sister Henrietta was a charter member of the Alpine Club of Canada. Jack Tuzo was educated in England, where he studied engineering and worked for railway companies. He came to the Boundary country to be assistant chief engineer on the construction of the Kettle Valley Railway. On completion of the section between Midway and

Penticton, he returned to England and enlisted with the Royal Sussex Regiment. He was stationed for a time in Bangalore, India, and then posted to East Africa, to help reconstruct railways destroyed there by the Germans.

Captain Jack Tuzo worked on the Kettle Valley Railroad and died fixing rail lines in German East Africa. Photo from his Engineering Institute death notice.
Courtesy of the Engineering Institute of Canada

Diseases were as much of a threat as attacks from the enemy in those parts and Tuzo contracted blackwater fever and died in a military hospital in Dar es Salaam in April 1918.

An obituary in the *Journal of the Engineering Institute of Canada* said: "Captain Tuzo was keenly interested in the development of southern British Columbia and was one of the pioneers in that district. He was a strong believer in the future and had many interests there. His sad death, occurring so soon after the opening of the railway through that section will be a great loss."

Tuzo's nephew, John Tuzo Wilson, became a renowned Canadian geophysicist who achieved acclaim for his contributions to the theory of plate tectonics. Tuzo's son, born in India in 1917, went on to command forces in Northern Ireland during the troubles.

From Our Listeners: The Story of Edward Greenwood Christensen

By Susan Dahlo, Rock Creek

Eddy Christensen's story is the unique tale of an ordinary young man from a typical family in a Western Canadian town—Greenwood. His story is representative of thousands of stories of the forty-three thousand British Columbia men who served overseas in the Great War. In fact, half of the Canadian infantry in World War I came from west of Ontario, an area that contained only a quarter of the population of Canada.

British Columbia had experienced a huge boom of immigration from the 1890s onward. The government of Canada had sold Canada to the world with the slogan "Free Homes for Millions" and many people moved in. The population of BC at the 1901 census was 190,000 and by 1914 the population stood at 435,000.

The Christensen family had immigrated to the United States from Denmark in the 1880s. On hearing of the great mining activity in the Boundary area, they moved their family up into Canada in 1895. Edward Greenwood Christensen was born in Greenwood on April 8, 1896, one of the first children born in the town.

The Christensens had totally adopted their new country. They always spoke English and kept no old-world customs. They wanted to ensure that their children had all the benefits possible in a land of English-speaking Canadians. The family moved so that the father, Mark, could work in the newly built Boundary Falls smelter. Edward went to school in the little one-room schoolhouse in Boundary Falls.

In 1903, Mark was a trustee of this little school with ten pupils. Eddy grew up in a large family of nine children and, like all pioneer children, had to be tough, daring and self-reliant to survive. These attributes were later absolutely necessary to survive the horrible conditions in the mud and mire of France.

Eddy, like the boys of his generation, had a British education. The history of Britain was the stuff of the textbooks used in Canadian schools. British culture was dominant. When the British Empire was threatened, a strong patriotism

Eddy Christensen when he signed up in Phoenix in June 1916.
Courtesy of Susan Dahlo

came out in the Canadian people. When Robert Borden spoke in the House, "We stand shoulder to shoulder with the British Dominions in this quarrel," everyone murmured approval. When Eddy signed up on May 30, 1916, in Phoenix, he felt this patriotism for his country, but also the sense of adventure and duty ("I will do my best to do my duty to God, the King and my country"). By 1916, the stories and photos coming back from the front showed some terrible things.

Who can explain why these men continued to sign up in droves? Certainly from our perspective today, we cannot understand how these men could volunteer to be "cannon fodder" on the foreign soil of Europe. On his attestation papers, it states that Eddy was five feet nine inches and had a chest measurement of thirty-five inches with a range of expansion of three inches. This is very scrawny by today's standards but for those days he was quite tall and wiry.

Initially, Eddy and the other new recruits from the Boundary area took their basic training in Grand Forks. The training grounds were at the fairgrounds along the river just south of the city. Then on Saturday, July 8, 1916, they boarded a special thirteen-car train along with seven hundred officers (including Colonel J. MacKay, the commander) and men from the Kootenays for a trip up to the army camp in Vernon for further training. From Fernie came 312 men, Cranbrook 122, Nelson 178 and Grand Forks 55. To give them a send-off, hundreds of local citizens waited from midnight to almost 4 a.m. for the train departure. They de-trained at the wharf in Penticton, where again throngs of people turned out to send off their "khaki clad" boys. In fact, as reported in the *Penticton Herald,* "It seems as if the entire population of the town had turned out to see the soldiers."

They immediately boarded the sternwheeler SS *Sicamous* for passage up Okanagan Lake. At Vernon, they joined other volunteers, so that when the Duke of Connaught visited the camp later that summer, he reviewed four thousand troops.

In the fall of 1916, the battalion was moved to New Westminster in final preparation for the overseas journey. They entrained there and travelled for five days across the great expanse of Canada in the cold January of 1917. If things were the same for the 225th ("two-two-bits") as for the 54th Battalion, which had made the trip in November of 1915, every day they were given a march. Embarkation for England took place on January 26, 1917, from Halifax on SS *Grampian*. They arrived at Plymouth, England, on February 6, 1917, and immediately entrained and arrived at the camp in Seaford, Sussex, the following day.

Canada had planned to send over a 5th and 6th Division to her army in France but because of the devastating slaughter at the Somme, the 225th Battalion and all the other battalions were to be absorbed into the ranks of the existing four divisions. Eddy was forthwith assigned to the 16th Reserve Battalion. Strenuous training was the order of the day.

On April 9, the 54th Kootenay Battalion, of which Eddy was later to become a member, participated in the Battle of Vimy Ridge. The battalion was part of the 4th Canadian Division, the division that was to assault the highest point of the Vimy Ridge, which was, for this reason, the most strongly fortified and formidable part of the entire position. They suffered significant casualties but Canadians really proved their worth and courage in the battle; it was the first of the great assaults of 1917 in which the Canadians took part and it was the first exclusively Canadian victory. The Canadian achievement in capturing Vimy Ridge owed its success to sound planning and thorough preparation, but above all to the splendid fighting qualities and devotion to duty displayed by officers and men on the battlefield. Historians agree that this victory in battle marked a decisive turning point in Canada's long march to nationhood. The imperial ties were forever loosened. Canada entered the war as a junior partner of Great Britain and emerged as an equal—with a vote at the League of Nations.

On May 3, 1917, Eddy was proud to be posted to the 54th Battalion. He entrained bound for Southampton and embarked to Le Havre on May 4, left for his unit on May 7 and joined the unit in the field on May 21. This was the day on which Lieutenant-Colonel Carey, DSO, reported to the battalion to take over command.

Training again commenced and was carried on daily. Sports were also freely indulged in, and on May 27, brigade sports were held in which the 54th easily carried off the honours, both in football and in track events.

The Canadians continued operations in the Arras area. The 54th alternated between holding the front line and being relieved and moving back to the Château de la Haie. Toward the end of June, the corps commander, Lieutenant-General Sir Arthur Currie, paid the 11th Brigade a visit and inspected the 54th Battalion in training. On July 11, His Majesty King George V drove through the area and all ranks had an opportunity to see him.

At the end of July, the 54th moved into the Vimy Salient near the town of Lievin in preparation for the taking of the town of Lens. Eddy and his battalion were exposed here to German gas, 5.9-inch shells and flying bricks. On the fateful day of August 13, Eddy was killed in an explosion. His body was never found. The most feared and dreaded telegram, edged in black, reached his parents in Boundary Falls. The family went into deep mourning for their son and brother who had just turned twenty-one. His memory still burns brightly in the Christensen family and he will be forever young. As with all the war dead, we wonder what would be now if these young men had lived, and still we cannot make sense of it.

Eddy's name is among the 11,285 names of Canada's soldiers on the Vimy Memorial in France. These are the names of those known to be dead, but whose graves cannot be found. His name is among the thirty-one names on the cenotaph at Ingram Bridge, erected in 1924. These were men from the Greenwood district who gave their lives for king and country. His name is also in the First World War Book of Remembrance in the Peace Tower in Ottawa. Eddy was one of the 6,224 men from British Columbia who were killed overseas in this war. The Christensen family applied to the Ministry of Environment, Lands and Parks of BC to have a geographical feature in southern BC named for our beloved uncle, Edward Greenwood Christensen. On Remembrance Day, November 11, 1998, the province of BC and the Canadian Permanent Committee on Geographical Names named Christensen Creek, thirteen kilometres north of Greenwood, in remembrance of Eddy. Lest we forget.

The Phoenix Cenotaph

The Kettle Valley Cenotaph also includes the names of the men listed on the Phoenix Cenotaph, at the old mining camp of Phoenix, high in the mountains between Greenwood and Grand Forks. The Phoenix Cenotaph is about all that is left of the once-booming mountain city. But it can be hard to get to on November 11 because of the weather, so a plaque was added to combine the ceremonies at Ingram Flat.

Nelson journalist Greg Nesteroff told us that nearly fifty Phoenix men volunteered after the war broke out. The names of fifteen men who were killed are on the cenotaph. Over twenty more were wounded.

When the war ended, the city began considering a memorial to its fallen sons. But before anything was decided, the Granby Company pulled out of Phoenix, spelling doom for the town. Many buildings were sold for salvage, including the city's skating and curling rink. The Phoenix Rink Company, which owned the arena, met with stockholders and decided proceeds from the sale would be put toward a war memorial that would outlast the town.

The rink's sale raised twelve hundred dollars, enough to pay for the war monument, with four hundred dollars left over to donate to the Royal Canadian Legion in Grand Forks to ensure its care (more on the famous Phoenix Hockey team in Chapter 15).

The inscription on the cenotaph includes a line from the Roman poet Horace: *Dulce et decorum est pro patria mori,* which roughly translates as "It is sweet and right to die for your country."

Grand Forks and the Hendersons

With help from John Henderson

When we spotted three Hendersons on the Grand Forks Cenotaph, we wondered if our CBC Vancouver colleague John Henderson might know more. It turned out he was related to the brothers who were killed. Here they are, three Henderson brothers who went to France and never came home.

Arthur
1883 – 1916

Harold
1892 – 1917

John Jr.
1889 – 1918

Far left: The Grand Forks Cenotaph, lists three Hendersons killed on the Western Front.
Courtesy of Mike Elliott

Left: The three Henderson brothers—Arthur (top), Harold (middle) and John Jr. (bottom)—never made it home.
Courtesy of John Henderson

Captain Hendy Henderson—a cousin who was also killed in action.

Courtesy of John Henderson

The first to be killed was Arthur, who died at the Regina Trench on November 18, 1916. He was the oldest son. Arthur left behind his wife, Elizabeth, and a growing family.

Harold died a year after Arthur, on November 6, 1917. He went overseas with the 29th Battalion, the famous Tobin's Tigers. He served as a scout and died after he was hit in the head by shrapnel.

John Jr., or Jack, was killed at Amiens on August 17, 1918. He was a prospector by trade and his middle name was Baptist. He was the last brother to die. On August 30, the *Grand Forks Sun* reported:

> On Monday, news reached this city that Jack Henderson, son of J.B. Henderson, had been killed in action in France. Deceased was raised in this city but he enlisted at Calgary. The casualty list has dealt severely with the Henderson family. Two other of Henderson's sons, Arthur and Harold, were killed in action some time ago. A nephew, Arthur Henderson of Chilliwack, and son-in-law Chris Coughlan, have also fallen on the battlefield. Mr. Henderson's only living son, Herwood, is now in service in England.

Herwood, or Herb as he was known, survived the war and moved to Powell River. He worked for BC Hydro and lived until 1968.

The other cousin, Captain Richard "Hendy" Henderson from Chilliwack, was killed by a shell on April 11, 1917. Hendy enlisted at age forty and went overseas with the Canadian Engineers. He was consolidating the ground at Vimy Ridge when he was hit.

A Great War Time Capsule in Nelson

By Greg Nesteroff, Nelson

In the fall of 2011, a time capsule was removed from the cornerstone of Nelson's Anglican church hall, ahead of the building's sale. One of the most intriguing items in the tin box, entombed in 1922, was an honour roll listing 222 church members who enlisted in World War I.

Nelson historian Greg Scott holds a list of 222 Anglican church members who fought in World War I. The list was among the items in a time capsule opened in 2011.

Courtesy of Greg Nesteroff

Entitled "Whose Debtors We Are," the small card gives surnames and first initials, along with red crosses next to those who were killed, and notations for those who received military medals and crosses. Church historian Greg Scott sent the names to Sylvia Crooks, chronicler of Nelson's wartime history, who created mini-biographies of each. Although she came up blank on twenty-eight of them, she found at least basic information on the rest. In 2005, Crooks published *Homefront and Battlefront: Nelson BC in World War II*, which profiled every local man killed in that war. For the local archives she also compiled two loose-leaf binders detailing those who died in World War I—in all, some four hundred pages—and referred to that information.

"Some of it I had at my fingertips," she says. "Certainly any of the men who were killed in the war, because I'd already done those volumes for the archives. Some of the others I didn't go as far afield."

The list of 222 Anglican Church members that was among the unique items in the time capsule opened in 2011 included:

- Captain Cyril E. (Buster) Armbrister, who received the Military Medal for "conspicuous gallantry and devotion to duty in operations." Just before the war ended, "with the greatest courage [he] rushed across the front in full view of the enemy guns, [and] gained a small bank from which he bombed the enemy's only means of escape." After the war, he became a Hollywood radio and film writer and director.

- Private Percival Charles Bland of the 27th Battalion CEF, an accountant at the Hudson's Bay Company, who was reported missing at the Somme in 1916. His commanding officer wrote: "He was loved by all the officers of his platoon, and all men thought so much of him throughout his regiment."

- Captain William Garland Foster, former editor and manager of the Nelson Daily News. He already had military training in Ottawa and went overseas as quartermaster of the 54th Battalion. Shortly before the war ended, he was injured in the Battle of Cambrai and later died, age thirty-nine. His wife, Annie Garland Foster, served overseas as a nurse but had returned to Canada by the time of his death.

- James Hurst, a Boer War veteran who worked as a deckhand and purser on the Kootenay Lake sternwheelers. Captured after a gas attack at Ypres in 1915, he spent the rest of the war in a German prison camp. He returned home to Crawford Bay and his job on the steamers. He was also an organist and choirmaster for the church, leading Christmas carollers around town.

- Three nursing sisters, including Jessie Robina Gilchrist, who enlisted with the army medical corps in 1917.

Lots of prominent Kootenay family names are also on the list, including Attree, Grizzelle, Horswill and Mawdsley.

Crooks says she gathered the information simply because she thought the church might like a more detailed record of the people and stories attached to each name.

"I got interested in some of the men who were in the war but survived," she says. "I thought I'd like to try to get a picture of all those who went off, not just the ones who were killed."

The card itself is now in the Touchstones Nelson archives.

From Our Listeners: William Philip of the Canadian Engineers

By Marianna Harris, Vancouver

My great-grandparents immigrated to BC from Scotland in 1891 when my grandfather William Philip was four years old. In 1910 he was involved in forming an artillery unit in North Vancouver. A petition was circulated to obtain fifty recruits, but instead of an artillery unit, an engineers unit was formed.

In 1913 (several months after his mother's sudden death) he married Annie Edythe Teale in North Vancouver. In 1915, Annie Edythe's brother, Harry, died in World War I while serving as an English soldier. And yet her husband enlisted and left her at home with two very small daughters. Nancy was just two years old and Flora only two months old. His family was living with his father in North Vancouver, and while he was gone, his wife and daughters suffered from the Spanish influenza and survived, though the youngest had to learn to walk again.

In March 1916 William was with the 6th Field Company militia; he enlisted March 8, 1916, and embarked on May 15, 1916. He was twenty-nine years old. On March 20, 1916, he was accepted for the Canadian Expeditionary Force, arriving in England on May 29. It appears that he left from Bramshott for France on October 17, 1916. On May 29, 1918, he was appointed as warrant rank class II with the 12th Battalion Canadian Engineers. He was still overseas July 19, 1918, returned to Toronto June 6, 1919, and was discharged June 20, 1919.

In 1919 when his family met him at the CPR station in Vancouver, the children were five and three years old and this man was a stranger. He put the younger one, Flora, on his shoulders to carry her home. She offered him a red rose a neighbour had given her before she left home.

He was granted twenty acres at the corner of Old Yale and Coghlan Roads in Aldergrove from the Soldier Settlement Board and in 1920 took his family away from their grandfather in North Vancouver to this farm. Toward the end of his life he suffered severe confusion and memory loss and ended up living in George Derby Home for Veterans in Burnaby. It was never clear whether his incapacity was due to his service overseas. I was very saddened by the last years of my beloved grandfather's life.

William Philip. Courtesy of Marianna Harris

From Our Listeners: Prince Rupert and the Peters Boys

By Sam McBride, great-nephew now living in the Kootenays
Here is the story of one family that made an incredible sacrifice.

At the outbreak of war in August 1914 there were four sons of former Prince Edward Island premier Frederick Peters and Bertha Gray in British Columbia. Born in Charlottetown, they moved with the family to Oak Bay, BC, in 1898, and then Prince Rupert in 1911.

John Francklyn "Jack" Peters, twenty-one, and nineteen-year-old fraternal twins Gerald Hamilton Peters and Noel Quintan Peters lived at the family home in Prince Rupert. Frederic Thornton "Fritz" Peters, twenty-four, recently retired from the Royal Navy as a lieutenant after eight years of service, was in the Okanagan working as a CPR engineer. Jack and Gerald both worked as bank clerks, but Noel was unable to find employment due to a moderate, but noticeable, mental disability. All three of the younger brothers trained with the Earl Grey's Own Rifles militia but, unlike Fritz, would not have chosen a military career in normal circumstances.

Fritz, who received his nickname because of his German-like obsession with toy soldiers and marching as a youngster, rushed to England to rejoin the Royal Navy as first officer on the destroyer HMS *Meteor*. His three brothers dutifully went to enlist in the Canadian Army, but only Jack passed the physical. Noel's rejection because of perceived disability was not a surprise, but Gerald failing because of a narrow chest was a devastating blow to his pride and an embarrassment for the family.

Jack joined the 7th British Columbia Battalion in the First Contingent, which trained at soggy Salisbury Plain in England before arriving in France on February 15, 1915.

Anticipating censorship of his letters home, Jack suggested the following code in a letter sent in early February 1915: "If I begin my letter 'My Dearest Mother' it means that I am billeted in South France. 'Mother' (alone) means that I am at the base. 'Dear Mother' means that I am going to the front right away."

Gerald undertook an exercise program recommended by Fritz and then, ensuring that he would be assessed by different examiners, travelled to Montreal where he successfully enlisted and joined the 24th Battalion (Victoria Rifles) in February 1915.

Private Jack Peters (1892–1915)

In a letter to Gerald Peters dated March 11, 1915, Jack wrote:

> You remember Boggs who used to command the High School cadets. He was killed by a sniper a few weeks ago. He was a lieutenant in E Company. Pretty hard luck so early in the war.
>
> I'm writing this letter in the actual firing trench. Shells whistle over me every minute and now and again a bullet hits the parapet above. Sounds exciting but it isn't. Just a little monotonous. We go out for a rest tonight to our billets, which are generally barns. We get plenty of freedom and can go to the villages to buy what we can—which isn't much because they only give us three francs a month. I've got nearly $50 to my credit now which I cannot draw. If I were you I'd have some pay assigned because it's so easy to fritter it away in England.
>
> I suppose you know about Fritz winning the DSO and being mentioned in dispatches. Won't Father and Mother be tickled to death!

(Lieutenant Herbert Boggs of Victoria, BC, died February 26, 1915, in the Ypres Salient. He was the first BC boy, and one of the first Canadian officers, to die in the war.)

Above: Jack Peters. His remains were never found.
Courtesy of Sam McBride

Left: A Prince Rupert art class in front of the local cenotaph.
Courtesy of Dianne Rabel

Fritz had received the Distinguished Service Order medal, second in rank only to the Victoria Cross, for valour in the Battle of Dogger Bank on January 24, 1915, in the war's first confrontation between the British and German fleets in the North Sea. After the *Meteor's* engine room was hit by a German shell, Fritz coolly braved flames and scalding water to save the lives of two ratings and prevent further explosions.

Jack was an easygoing, happy-go-lucky fellow who was content to leave the heroics to older brother Fritz. To ease his mother's anxiety, he said in a letter to her dated January 27, 1915, "You needn't worry about me because I don't intend to put my head up above the trench to shoot the Germans. Me for where the earth is thickest and highest." Hearing that his mother planned to travel to England, Jack wrote, "I hope you'll be able to make it in the summer. Just about the time when I am invalided back to England."

However, in the chaos of the Second Battle of Ypres on April 24, 1915, when Germans used poison chlorine gas for the first time in an offensive against Canadian troops, Jack, serving with the 4th Company of the 7th Battalion, disappeared in the vicinity of the village of St. Julien. With no other protection against the gas, Jack may have been one of the Canadians who famously held urine-soaked handkerchiefs against their nose and mouth to keep functioning. The stout defence by the courageous Canadians that day prevented a German breakthrough at Ypres that would have had dire consequences for the Allies. Jack was officially listed as "missing," but his family believed a rumour that he was at German prison camp in Hanover.

In a letter to his mother dated April 20, 1916, a year after the Ypres battle, Fritz said, "I think it is now quite certain that the end of the war will see Jack on his way home." However, a month later, in late May 1916, the Red Cross confirmed that Jack was not among the prisoners of war, so Canadian authorities declared he had died "on or after April 24, 1915," with no identified remains.

Lieutenant Gerald Peters (1894–1916)

Longing to be close to her boys serving in the war—particularly her favourite child, Gerald— Bertha Gray Peters arrived in England in June 1915 and stayed there with relatives or in rented quarters for the next year and a half. Gerald and his mother were best friends and soulmates who shared a love of literature and theatre.

Gerald arrived in France in September 1915 with the Victoria Rifles and was in trench action in the Ypres Salient through the fall and early winter. In early 1916 he was thrilled to be called back to England for officer training. Writing to sister Helen in a letter dated February 16, 1916, Gerald said:

The favourite son—Gerald Peters was killed in 1916.
Courtesy of Sam McBride

No doubt Mother has told you already about my amazing luck. The right amount of pull has succeeded in getting me a commission and I am back in dear old England and out of that Blasted Bloody Belgium. You can't imagine how glorious it is to be back. It was simply miserable over there, no glamour or glory of war, just unending work and nothing to do if you did get any spare time. It isn't hard to look back on, but at the time there was little fun in lying in ditches while their horrible machine guns swept over you, pattering everywhere…I had a periscope shot to pieces in my hand a few days back. It gave me a horrible shock and nearly knocked me down. The same instant a fellow near me had his brains blown out by the same machine gun. I left Belgium without any sorrow…

Mother came down yesterday, and joined me here…I do hope she will be able to take a little cottage near here while I am training, it would be so lovely for both of us

I rather dread going back as an officer. It is a real responsibility—even a junior officer—as he has control of a platoon, about 50 men, and perhaps a big extent of trench. Fancy having to take out wiring parties to within 40 yards of the Germans and work for three hours in the open. It's bad enough to be on these parties, let alone commanding them. However, it will be better in most ways, and I will have a glorious time in England first. If you ever hear a man say he wants to get back to the firing line again, you can tell him he is a darned liar.

Gerald transferred to the 7th Battalion as a lieutenant. Writing to Bertha on May 24, 1916, he was caught up with the enthusiasm among the Canadian soldiers preparing for a massive summer offensive to defeat the Germans:

I can't tell you how splendid this battalion is. The spirit of all the officers and men is wonderful. The C.O. seems to be thought the world of by everyone. He is right there every time, keeps the battalion on the go…Harris seemed really delighted I had come, and introduced me to the others as one of his "oldest chums." Rather decent of him. He talked a lot of poor old Jack. He said he had never met a man so cheerful and optimistic always. He often saw him at Salisbury, and Jack was one of the ones who never kicked then. You can't think how glad I am to have him. I know he will help me a lot when he comes back next week.

It will reassure you to hear that we are going in to a pretty civilized part of the line. The method in the battalion is to give the Germans complete hell the first time in a trench, and then secure the upper hand at once. The men seem to be beyond compare.

On June 2, 1916, the Germans surprised the Allies by capturing Mount Sorrel, about ten kilometres southeast of St. Julien in the Ypres Salient. Standard practice in the war was to immediately launch a counteroffensive, before the enemy could establish themselves in the captured territory. The following morning, on June 3, 1916, Gerald and his unit (No. 3 Company of No. 11 Platoon, 7th Battalion) were sent out on a charge that lacked coordination and had no chance of success.

Writing to Gerald's father, Frederick Peters, from a London hospital in August 1916, Sergeant Major Dawson said:

I have just got your address, and I thought I should like to let you know your son died just like a hero…

We got orders to advance from our present front line, which was really our old support line, as the Huns were occupying our front trench. Well, Sir, we had about 700 yards to go, and the rain of machine gun bullets was just like hail stones, but the boys just went over to their death with a mighty cheer. I saw Gerald drop, and the last words I heard him say were "Keep on boys, right after them." I shall always remember him, he was the coolest boy I think I have ever seen, and he seemed so young. He dropped just about 60 yards outside our parapet, and that is the last I saw of him…

I know how it must have upset you all, over Gerald's death, but I am glad I can console you a little with the story of how he died, as game as a lion and as gentle as a lamb. His life was short but, by God, he was a man. It quite upset me when I heard he was killed.

Gerald was listed as missing until his death was confirmed in early July. Writing her sister Margaret on July 5, 1916, Bertha said, "It has crushed my soul. I cannot write about it." She begged Fritz to go to Ypres to investigate Gerald's death, and what was being done with his remains. Fritz learned that Gerald crawled into a shell hole for safety after being hit by bullets, and later was found dead at a different spot. Gerald was buried in a nearby cemetery which was destroyed by shelling later in the war, so Gerald joined Jack among the thousands of Canadian dead at Ypres with no identified remains. Both their names are on the Menin Gate Memorial.

Private Noel Peters (1894–1964)

Unable to serve in the army, Noel suffered a serious nervous breakdown in the spring of 1915 because of relentless bullying and harassment from gangs and individuals who assumed he was shirking his duty. In May 1917 he was finally accepted for service in the Canadian Forestry Corps and went overseas for logging work in Allied countries. He survived the war but was estranged from his mother, who resented that he was alive and Gerald wasn't. Noel lived on the fringes of society in Vancouver and died at Shaughnessy Veterans Hospital in 1964.

Capt. Fritz Peters, VC, survived the Great War but was killed in an accident in the Second World War.
Courtesy of Sam McBride

Captain Fritz Peters, VC, DSO, DSC and Bar, DSC (US), RN (1889–1942)

Fritz received another medal for valour, the Distinguished Service Cross (DSC), in March 1918 for his attacks on enemy U-boats. Retiring from the navy in 1920, he returned at age fifty in 1939 to serve in World War II. In July 1940 he was awarded a Bar to his DSC after a trawler force under his command sank two U-boats. He earned the Victoria Cross and the US Distinguished Service Cross for valour in the attack on the harbour of Oran, Algeria, on November 8, 1942, in the Allied invasion of North Africa. Tragically, Fritz died five days later when the flying boat transporting him back to England crashed into Plymouth Sound.

Years later, Helen Peters Dewdney, who died in Trail in 1976 at age eighty-nine, was often asked about her brother Fritz who won all the medals. While she was proud of Fritz's accomplishments, she could not reflect on him without also talking about brothers Jack and Gerald, who died with scant recognition early in the Great War.

From Our Listeners: A Cool Head in the Trenches

As told by granddaughter Dalcy Gripich, Cranbrook

William Robertson was born in 1886 and came to Cranbrook from Kelso, Scotland, in 1908. He worked as a CPR lineman and married his sweetheart, Violet, and started a family. In 1915 he headed off with other local men to train at the Vernon Camp with the 54th Kootenay Battalion.

The 54th reached England in late November 1915 and continued training at Bramshott. Billy showed leadership abilities and was made a sergeant.

In August 1916, the 54th was on its way to the front, stationed in the Ypres Salient, a notoriously exposed section of the front in Belgium. One of his fellow soldiers, Private Johnnie Kelly, wrote to a friend in Cranbrook about the experience:

The mud and the rain is the worst we have to contend with and is certainly hell. There isn't much to write about from here, and we can't say anything about the country. We are out for a rest now and we sure need it. It will take a week to scrape the mud off our clothes.

Kelly was with Sergeant Robertson the day he was killed.

I suppose you will have heard that Bill Robertson got killed. We had just finished dinner and Bill was going behind the parapet (the front of the trench). I think it was a sniper got him. The bullet entered under the arm and lodged beside his heart. He only lived about half an hour and was unconscious all the time.

Sergeant Fred Pye, in another letter home, thought the injury might have been caused by flying metal:

W. Robertson who was a sergeant in my platoon was killed by shrapnel a few days ago. He died very peacefully and quickly. A cooler head and a better NCO you couldn't wish for in the trenches, and everybody feels his loss very much.

Sergeant Robertson is buried at Reninghelst New Military Cemetery near Poperinge in Belgium. Three other brothers from Scotland were also killed in the war, an incredible sacrifice.

Grandaughter Dalcy Gripich visited her grandfather's gravesite in 2006 with other family members. She feels it's important for the family to know more about the sacrifice Sergeant Robertson and his brothers made:

I have been taking the family to war memorials and graveyards for many years so we can all get to know the man in the photograph in some small way. We've been to Ottawa and the War Memorial at Edinburgh Castle where we had his name added to the books.

Sergeant Robertson is one of over 110 names on the Cranbrook Cenotaph and is listed on Cranbrook's Wall of Honour.

A memorial to the Cranbrook boys who died. Over 100 never made it home.
Courtesy of Dalcy Gripich

Remembrance at Fort Langley Cemetery

The green canopy of chestnut trees billows high above Glover Road, named after veteran and former chief of police Frank Wesley Glover. Creamy white blossoms push forth on these eighteen trees each spring, and by autumn we hear and feel the crunch of chestnuts underfoot. The trees run parallel to a wrought iron fence that separates Fort Langley's main street from the village's cemetery and were planted to honour local men who left to fight the Great War, but never returned.

A stone cenotaph with Celtic cross sits atop a knoll near five tall cedar trees. It was built after the Great War from public donations, an initiative led by two returned soldiers, Captain Dr. Benjamin B. Marr and Major Archibald Payne. Directly behind the trees is the veterans' section. Each year, small Canadian flags mark their individual plots. Many of these graves belong to men who returned from war, but soon died from their wounds. Some, like William "Billy" Allard, enjoyed a longer life after seeing action at the Somme, Vimy and Passchendaele. His brother Eugene was killed at Passchendaele—Allard Crescent was named in his memory. Another brother died six years after being gassed.

About fifteen years ago the local tradition of visiting the cenotaph had fallen away and only two residents appeared at the war memorial for Remembrance Day—veteran Gordie Gillard and local merchant Brenda Alberts. With the support of local clergy, they spearheaded a revival of the ceremonies that now attract some thirty-five hundred people each year. Canada's recent commitments in Afghanistan may be part of the explanation. Veterans march down Glover Road in the shadow of the chestnuts, a lone piper leading them into the cemetery. Parents speak quietly with young children; RCMP, ambulance, fire and military personnel, cadets, Scouts and Girl Guides all stand silently. Elderly vets stay warm and dry beneath blankets and tents. All pay attention to the ritual of Remembrance—the poetry, prayers, song and hollow trumpet sounds of the Last Post. We also hear the words. "Never, never forget the debt of gratitude we owe them."

The Celtic cross of the Fort Langley war memorial.
Courtesy of Mark Forsythe

Charlie's Tree: A Veteran's Remembrance

Most people zoom past without a second glance. Charlie Perkins's Tree stands at a slight bend in Highway 1 where Surrey and Langley meet. The tree is now an old stump, wrapped with ivy and faded Canadian flags. A white cross is nailed above a sign reading: 1919. Charlie and four friends used to swim in a hole near what was then a towering Douglas fir on the Perkins's family farm in the years before the Great War.

All these young men went off to fight, but only Charlie returned home alive after serving as an instructor for the Royal Flying Corps at Camp Borden and Fort Worth, Texas. Two of his brothers also served and survived. In 1919 Charlie planted ivy at the base of what his family called the "Big Tree," a fitting tribute to his friends and others killed in training flights or while serving overseas. Many years later the Trans-Canada Highway was being surveyed through Surrey, and here historian Chuck Davis picks up the story:

> Then, in 1960, Highway 1 began to be built through Surrey. Its proposed route would put it right through the little glade Charlie had cleared. The memorial tree would have to go. Charlie, now a senior citizen, protested, and friends and neighbours joined him in that protest. They were heard by Highways Minister Phil Gaglardi, and the highway engineers curved the road to go around the tree. This is perhaps the only instance in Canadian history where a major highway was diverted to avoid harming a tree. You can see the bend in the road to the right of the eastbound lanes of the Trans-Canada between the 176th Street and 200th Street exits.
>
> Charlie's tree was set on fire by vandals and consequently was topped at twelve metres. Each Remembrance Day a wreath is placed there by members of the Whalley Branch of the Royal Canadian Legion. Travel just a little farther east, almost to the 264th Street exit, and you'll see a new sign marking the Highway of Heroes, a tribute to Canadians killed in Afghanistan.

Charlie's tree, a landmark on the TransCanada Highway.
Courtesy of Mark Forsythe

From Our Listeners: Quesnel, the Centre of Sacrifice in the Central Interior

By Brian Milthorp, Penticton
On August 29, 1914, this letter appeared in the *Cariboo Observer*:

> *Where Does Quesnel Stand?*
> *To the editor of the Observer:*
> *Sir, not long ago England was roused by a speech from the King the gist of which was "Wake up, England." Where are our leading citizens, to strike the note of help which a town of our size at any rate can offer? Are the people of Quesnel content to sit back and do nothing, when the Empire is engaged in a life and death struggle? Has the magnitude of this fight not dawned on our citizens?*
> *Faithfully yours, Englishman*

Several men left town to make their individual contributions. British-born A.J. Pickup and Captain Geoffrey Watson had left for England to accept commissions in their old regiments as soon as the war broke out. Sam Scobie had joined the 101st Edmonton Fusiliers and by September 19 was at Valcartier training with the first contingent. Joseph Callanan, only son of Barkerville physician and Conservative MLA for the Cariboo Dr. Michael Callanan, had enlisted in the 29th Vancouver Battalion. Henry Stoner, resident engineer PGE Railway, left for Fort George, presumably to join the "Legion," and Carl Beatty had followed young Callanan's lead and enlisted in one of the Vancouver battalions.

But it was not until May of 1915 that there was any organized recruitment in the interior of the province. Until then, men who wished to enlist had to travel to Vancouver or Victoria as there were no military units operating outside the major centres. By May 8, twenty-seven men were awaiting placement as there were no vacancies in the established British Columbia battalions.

That changed when the 54th Kootenay Battalion based in Nelson was authorized to recruit in Quesnel by the Militia Department, and by May 28 recruiting officers Lieutenant Archer and Sergeant Major Edwards had arrived in town and had signed up forty successful candidates.

On September 25, 1915, Private John Craig became the first Quesnel resident to be reported "killed in action." Craig was born in Quesnel and had been living in Vancouver when the war began. He had enlisted in the 47th New Westminster Battalion but had been transferred to the 7th to replace the dreadful casualties suffered by the First Contingent during the poison-gas attack at the Second Battle of Ypres in April of that year.

In 1916, a new battalion was authorized for central British Columbia: "The Cariboo Battalion." Recruitment proceeded quickly for this new battalion officially designated as the 172nd Battalion Cariboo Rangers, CEF. By the end of February, over seven hundred men from the Boundary country in the south to the new settlements on the line of the Grand Trunk Pacific Railway in the north had poured in and were assembling at the regimental headquarters in Kamloops. By the end of March, sixteen men from Quesnel and the Barkerville area had left and there would be many more to follow.

The *Cariboo Observer* wrote in January 1916:

The historic name "Cariboo" is to figure in the final chapter of the story which is now being written in letters in blood and fire on the fields of Flanders and France...and its reward will be won on the blood-red fields of battle. The volunteers of 1916 will face unknown dangers and surmount...difficulties to add another page to the record of an Empire's glory. Every man of military age, and physically able to pass the medical should offer himself without delay, and thus help to prove that the spirit of '62 still thrives and abides in the district. Friends will be able to remain together from the time of attestation...and when the period of probation is over will be comrades in the trenches, and shoulder to shoulder in the wild rush of the iron game.

Over sixty local men are listed on the Quesnel Cenotaph. More than ten men were missed. Among the dead, three from the little community of Soda Creek, all from the 54th Battalion, are listed as killed in action on January 12, 1916: Private Richard Davis, Private Arthur Duckworth and Private Alexander Hendry.

Brian Milthorp has written extensively on the war effort in Quesnel and the Central Interior.

Boys from the Cariboo at Willows Camp in Victoria, holding a Quesnel pennant. They joined the 67th Western Scots.
Quesnel and District Museum and Archives 1958.277.1

From Our Listeners: My Grandfather Alfred James Nash (1893–1988)

By Charlie Nash, Cawston

He was born in Borstal, England (a small village up the hill from Rochester). His father was from the Whitechapel area of London. The family were butchers. His mother was from the Faversham area. Her father was a master mariner for the Medway River area.

Alf's father went to the Boer War after the Black Week in 1899 and did not return. Alf's grandmother, who lived with them and was a significant caregiver to the family, passed in 1902. Alf's oldest brother died in 1905 and his mother died in 1908. Alf's older brother, Phil, had been given a one-way ticket to Saskatchewan in 1907. After the mum died, Alf at fifteen was also given a one-way ticket to Saskatchewan. He left the train at Portage and Main and found work.

He enlisted at Birtle, Manitoba, in 1915 and joined the 44th Battalion in March, with basic training in Sewell, Manitoba. He landed in Plymouth, England, and trained in Folkstone. Drafted to go to France in July and was transferred to the 1st Canadian Mounted Rifles. Was moved immediately to the front in the Ypres Salient. First action was at Hooge. It was ten days in the line, ten days in support and ten days in reserve. In June of 1916 the troops moved to the Somme. In one battle 803 went in and forty-two came out. Only eighteen were not wounded. Alf was grazed in several places by bullets and shrapnel but was otherwise OK. In the vicinity of Corcellette several runners were killed moving information from headquarters to the front. Alf volunteered to run. On one mission he passed the information to the commander and he said he had a Nash in his group. Alf met his youngest brother, Ted. Alf did not know he had enlisted. His words for Ted were: "What the hell are you doing here?" On his third job he was hit by a sniper's bullet that cut the artery in his leg. In the medical area he was left as dead. A Scottish doctor saw him twitch and ordered the attendants to move Alf to another area. Eventually he got to England and was able to recover. He met a childhood friend, Kitty, while in the hospital and asked her to marry him. She declined as she would not leave her mum nor England.

Once he returned to Canada he met several vets in Vancouver. They set up a shake-making business near the town of Hope. A few years later he married a local girl, took over her family's farm and had four kids. His brother Ted, who also got a one-way ticket to Canada in the 1910s, returned from war, married, had two kids, and settled in Victoria, BC. He worked for BC Tel and lived to a hundred years old. Alf's older brother Phil also went to World War I and found front-line action. After the war he returned to Saskatchewan, married and had eight kids.

I knew my grandfather, Alf, for over thirty years. We stayed at his place on weekends in the early 1960s developing the farm. My dad took over the family farm in 1965 and Alf lived on adjacent land. Alf loved the land and loved farming. He had a wonderful orchard. Alf told me to keep going to school as "It does not cost you anything to pack around education."

Alfred Nash was wounded and left for dead.
Courtesy of Charlie Nash

From Our Listeners: Albert Leslie Knight

By Merlin Brunt, Chilliwack

One of my great-uncles was Albert Leslie Knight, though he went by Leslie for his first name. He was the younger brother of my grandmother, Irene Bunt (née Knight). Leslie was born in Popcum (the original spelling) on September 30, 1898, and he and the family moved to downtown Chilliwack (on Spadina Avenue) in 1902.

In June of 1916 Leslie graduated from Chilliwack High School on Yale Road East. One year later, at age eighteen, Leslie enlisted in the Canadian Army and he soon shipped overseas to the World War I European theatre. He served with the Canadian Motor Machine Gun Brigade.

On Sunday, March 24, 1918 (less than eight months before the war ended), Great-uncle Leslie was killed in action during the German offensive near Nestle, France, at the age of just nineteen years.

Nestle had been held by the Germans during the early part of the war, and occupied by French and British cavalry on March 18, 1917. On March 25, 1918, it was again taken by the Germans, after severe fighting with French and British troops. It was recaptured by the French on the following August 28. Leslie's parents were initially informed that their son was reported wounded and missing in action.

On April 9, 1923, the City of Chilliwack unveiled a memorial that honoured its

World War I casualties. The cenotaph monument is located immediately behind the original city hall on Spadina and the names on the honour roll include Albert Leslie Knight.

On July 26, 1936, the Canadian National Vimy Memorial was unveiled near Vimy, Pas-de-Calais, France. It is dedicated to the memory of Canadian Forces members killed during World War I. The monument is the centrepiece of a 250-acre preserved battlefield park that encompasses a portion of the grounds over which the Canadian Corps made their assault during the Battle of Vimy Ridge. There are 11,169 names on the monument, one of which is Albert Leslie Knight.

Recently my brother discovered a framed proclamation issued from Buckingham Palace by the King of England in 1918 commemorating the death of our great-uncle Leslie Knight in World War I. Unbeknownst to us, this document had been left to us by our grandmother back in the 1980s.

Literally thousands of brave Canadians have perished in the various wars of the past century, and this is a brief profile of one such soul who is not only from my hometown of Chilliwack, but also from my family.

From Our Listeners: He Never Knew His Father

By Greg Scott, Nelson

In 2004, I connected with my then eighty-nine-year-old cousin, Jack Andrew, and because of my previous family research I was able to provide him with information about his father who died in World War I, when Jack was only one and a half years old. He knew little of his father other than possessing a few pictures, as little information was ever passed down. This proved to be a moving experience for all involved.

In August 1914, at the outbreak of World War I, John Andrew and his brother Lees, my grandfather, were both motormen, driving streetcars for BC Electric Railway. They had emigrated from Manchester, England, in 1908 with their parents and siblings. In June 1914 John married local girl Catherine Travis and in May 1915 their son Jack was born.

What possessed twenty-eight-year-old John to enlist in 1916 is unknown as he would have been exempt as a married man until at least the Military Service Act of 1917. Enlisting in the 62nd Battalion at the Drill Hall in Vancouver, John signed his attestation papers at Camp Vernon on September 28, 1915, underwent training and was shipped to England on April 1, 1916, aboard SS *Baltic*. After further training, he was drafted to the 2nd Canadian Mounted Rifles (CMR) and after landing in France, he reported to the unit in the field on May 31, 1916, in the Ypres sector of Flanders as one of 160 replacements.

Between June 3 and 16, the CMR Battalion was devastated in the Battle of Mount Sorrel, where they lost 50 percent of their fighting strength, but as a new replacement, Jack would have probably been held back as a reserve. During the following month, his duties would have consisted of further training, fatigue duties and taking his place in the line as dictated by normal unit revolvement. However, on July 25, 1916, at Maple Copse on Observatory Ridge, John was severely wounded by a German artillery barrage. This was during a German counterattack for a trench raid led by then Lieutenant George R. Pearkes, later Victoria Cross winner and Lieutenant-Governor of BC.

It was German policy in World War I to always counterattack, called a "hate" in the trenches. This raid was not only well documented in the supplement to the 2nd CMR war diary but also in Pearkes's biography, as well as that of another future VC winner, Prince Rupert's John MacGregor, who was Pearkes's sergeant on the raid.

On August 5, 1916, the raid was noted in a wire service story in the *Nelson Daily News*, which also reported John's death in its lengthy casualty lists. It was not normal to record names of "other ranks" in the war diary except for the awarding of medals; therefore, the record of John's demise simply reads "Enemy shelled our front & support lines causing twelve casualties (one man killed)." John was one of the wounded and was transported through the normal dressing station and field hospital system, eventually ending up at General Hospital No. 13, a British hospital at Boulogne, France.

There he died of his wounds on August 1, 1916, the cause recorded as "GSW to right arm, right leg and right face." The term GSW (gunshot wounds) covered not only gunshot but shrapnel and other types of projectile wounds. John's time in France was brief, totalling just over two months, and his early death was quite common for new arrivals. John is buried in Boulogne Eastern War Cemetery and is one of forty BC Electric employees to give their lives during World War I.

John's wife, Catherine, was awarded a payment of $180 and a widow's pension and like many widows of the time had no choice but to take her young son and go home to live with her parents. She never remarried and died in 1974 at the age of eighty. Son Jack, who stated that he "was on pension till he was twenty-one," went on to work for BC Hydro, the successor to BC Electric, and passed away on March 7, 2005, just short of his ninetieth birthday.

I have since had the occasion to recount this story to fellow Nelsonite Tim Pearkes, grandson of George. In typical lawyer fashion, he jokingly pointed out the "statute of limitations" in connection with any family responsibility with John's death. How things do go around!

The Cenotaphs of Hedley, Penticton, Prince George, and Nanaimo

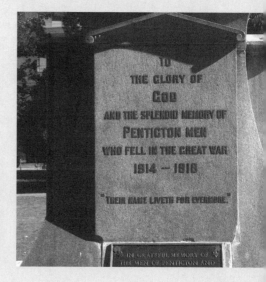

Above: The cenotaph in the old mining town of Hedley in the Similkameen.
Courtesy of Greg Dickson

Above right: Our Glorious Dead—a long list of Nanaimo and District men killed in action.
Courtesy of Greg Dickson

Right: Prince George's new cenotaph was unveiled in Veteran's Plaza in 2009. It is designed to echo the two pillars of the Vimy Ridge monument.
Courtesy of Mark Forsythe

Far right: Penticton's cenotaph—to the Glory of God.
Courtesy of Greg Dickson

Above: Under construction—a memorial to the men of the Canadian Artillery who fell during the Vimy advance.
CWM 19920085-790, George Metcalf Archival Collection, © Canadian War Museum

Left: Wounded at Passchendaele—the bodies of British Columbians killed at the front never made it home. Many were buried where they fell.
Carrying wounded at Passchendaele, CWM 19930013-477, George Metcalf Archival Collection, © Canadian War Museum

12

THEY FOUGHT FOR CANADA
BUT THEY COULDN'T VOTE

In 1914, British Columbia went to war with its anti-Asian prejudices intact. That meant excluding those who were trying to settle in Canada and marginalizing those who were already here. The policy was systematic, denying Asian immigrants the vote and blocking their enlistment in West Coast regiments. The government used HMCS *Rainbow* to turn back South Asian immigrants aboard the *Komagata Maru*. And it quarantined Chinese labourers crossing Canada for the front and returning to China. Incarcerating may be a better word, and if quarantining for health reasons was the motivation, some experts now believe that policy was a miserable failure.

Japanese Canadians

Japanese Canadians had been coming to BC since the 1870s and were active in the fishing industry on both the south coast and the north coast. Going into the war, Japan was allied with Great Britain, and the Japanese Navy helped defend our coast. But that alliance seemed to be lost on many British Columbians. The Japanese could not vote, and there was little public support for their efforts to win the franchise.

One man, a Vancouver newspaper editor, made it his mission to help Japanese who wanted to be part of the war effort and build support for the franchise. Yasushi Yamazaki was publisher of the *Tairiku Nippo*. He avidly followed the progress of the war in the English-language media, and he could see that the war was not going well. By 1915, troops were bogged down in trench warfare, and the casualties were alarming. Soon, every able-bodied man would be welcome, regardless of height, weight or skin colour. So Yamazaki set about organizing the Japanese Volunteer Corps in the city. Japanese Canadians would prove their loyalty and win the vote.

There were problems from the start. A cynical rival newspaper editor ridiculed Yamazaki's efforts and sowed doubt in the minds of recruits. Military authorities dismissed the unit as too small even when enlistments topped two hundred. After months of training, it looked like the Japanese Volunteer Corps would be forced to disband. Yamazaki was stymied, his dream

of a Japanese corps from British Columbia dashed. To make matters worse, British Columbia regiments would not allow the Japanese to enlist with them.

Yamazaki wired the minister of the militia:

> We hereby offer you one full battalion of naturalized Japanese, all British subjects. Please wire if our offer is likely to be accepted and if not please explain reasons as much high feeling of disappointment will come to our colony. One company has drilled at our expense three thousand dollars per month for nearly three months. We are all British subjects and ask no conditions except to be treated as citizens.

Yamazaki travelled personally to Ottawa and tried to see the prime minister. Then he asked to see Minister of Militia Sam Hughes, but was not able to speak with him. A Vancouver member of parliament did meet with Yamakazi, but he was openly hostile to Japanese serving in the army.

In Britain, a wire from the Cabinet War Policy Committee was much more supportive:

> It is considered desirable to utilize the services of Canada's Japanese British subjects if willing and Canadian authorities have no objection. [British] Army Council…inquire whether Canadian government could include proposed battalion in those selected for fourth division…and will be very glad to accept the offer if this can be done.

They wanted to do their part—the Canadian Japanese Volunteer Corps pose with organizer Yasushi Yamazaki.
Nikkei National Museum 2012-10-1-2-41

But Major General Willoughby Gwatkin of the Canadian War Office said the Japanese were not ready and declined the offer. Then something unusual happened. Word started to spread that units in Alberta did not share the racism of the officials in BC. They were prepared to welcome the Japanese. Alberta was having a hard time filling the ranks and the provincial regiments started to reach out to the Japanese in British Columbia. The 191st and 192nd Battalions sent recruiters directly to Vancouver. Suddenly, competition for the trained Japanese recruits was brisk. Some men from as far away as the Skeena and Nass Rivers were soon enlisted. They trained and received their Canadian uniforms in Alberta and were on their way to England and France. There, they served with distinction and many were decorated for bravery. Yamazaki's work was done, but winning the franchise would be much harder.

From Our Listeners: Sergeant Major Masumi Mitsui, MM—Hero of the 10th Battalion

Told by David Mitsui, his grandson

While I was growing up in Hamilton, my grandpa never spoke of being wounded in action on April 28, 1917, or being awarded the Military Medal for Bravery for his "conspicuous bravery and distinguished conduct in action" on August 16, 1917. He also didn't speak of his family's experience of having his Port Coquitlam farm being confiscated, or of being interned during World War I. In fact, he never spoke to the grandchildren about this part of his life at all.

At the age of twenty-one, Masumi Mitsui, of samurai ancestry, emigrated from Japan in 1908 and began his new life in Victoria, BC, as a dishwasher, waiter and chauffeur.

When World War I commenced, a group of Issei in Vancouver, wanting to show their patriotism to Canada, tried to enlist in the Canadian Expeditionary Forces. However, the government of British Columbia refused to allow them to enlist because of the prejudicial and racist attitudes against Orientals at that time. The government especially did not want to give them the right to vote.

Undaunted by this discriminatory policy, 222 Japanese Canadians from British Columbia travelled to Calgary, Alberta, where they were permitted to enlist. Masumi Mitsui voluntarily enlisted on September 1, 1916, with the 192nd Overseas Battalion, Calgary, and was posted with the 9th Reserve Battalion and then proceeded to France for active duty with the 10th Battalion, 2nd Infantry Brigade, 1st Canadian Division, on March 5, 1917. After the Battle of Vimy Ridge, both Masumi Mitsui and Tokutaro Iwamoto were awarded the Military Medal for Bravery on Hill 70.

In September 2003, I was fortunate to visit many World War I battle sites in northern France, including Vimy Ridge, Passchendaele and Ypres. I walked up Hill 70, following the 10th Battalion's advance. On Hill 70, the German concrete machine-gun bunkers are still there. From the chalky soil, I picked up British and German bullet casings, shards of barbed wire, and an intact shell casing from a British eighteen-pounder. It was a moving experience walking on the chalky ground that was once a major battlefield and knowing that my grandfather, as part of the 10th Battalion, played a role in overtaking Vimy Ridge and Hill 70.

I recall my dad telling me about my grandfather's war experience. I certainly cannot imagine the horror of war, the smell of death and sulphur and blood, the endless mud and water-filled trenches and shell holes, the gunfire and bomb blasts and gas attacks. During the mustard gas attacks, the soldiers were told to remove their underwear, urinate into it and breathe through it, hoping that the uric acid would neutralize the gas. And finally the tremendous loss of watching their comrades die and so many get injured. It was through these unimaginable conditions that my grandfather led his thirty-five men into battle and found a way to keep his men moving forward in spite of the tremendous casualties and unrelenting gunfire. Whenever they found shelter in a farmhouse or village, he would look for whatever alcohol he could find and fill his canteens. After a successful attack or gaining some ground, he would lift their spirits with a drink from his canteen. It was during the battle of Hill 70 that he was awarded the Military Medal of Bravery as he "showed marked ability and efficiency in leading 35 Japanese Canadians in the battle…he salvaged the Lewis gun when his gun crew became casualties and then caused the enemy many casualties…and afterwards, he did excellent work in mopping up and assisting the wounded."

Like so many other Canadian soldiers, the Japanese Canadian soldiers demonstrated their courage through difficult battles and their bravery many times over in the face of a difficult foe. In spite of the anti-Asian prejudices of other soldiers and the field commanders' perceptions that they were unfit for battle, the Japanese Canadian soldiers demonstrated their fortitude throughout the campaign. For their courageous efforts during combat, they, like all other Canadian soldiers, received the British War Medal and the Victory Medal. My grandfather was honourably discharged on April 23, 1919.

After the war, the Japanese Canadian community in BC raised money for, constructed and dedicated the Japanese Canadian War Memorial in April 1920 in Stanley Park. It has become the centrepiece for remembrance and commemoration of the Japanese Canadian soldiers who fought for our freedom. The memorial includes a Japanese lantern at the top with an eternal flame.

In 1931, Masumi Mitsui was president of the newly formed Canadian Legion Branch No. 9. The contingent, including Corporal Saisonuke Kobuta, businessman Saburo Shinbone, Naburo Murakami, Rikuzo Hoita, Nobuhei Watanabe and Legion Provincial Secretary Robert Macnicol, travelled to Victoria to lobby the BC legislature in an effort for all persons of Japanese ancestry to win the right to vote. By a single vote, their efforts were partially successful: only the Japanese Canadian veterans of World War I were given the right to vote in British Columbia.

Far left: Decorated for valour at Hill 70—Masumi Mitsui (centre) with comrades.
Courtesy of David Mitsui

Left: A lasting memorial— the Japanese Canadian cenotaph in Stanley Park.
Courtesy of Greg Dickson

After the vote and upon their return to Vancouver, they did not immediately celebrate their accomplishment. Their thoughts were with their fellow soldiers as they gathered at the memorial in Stanley Park to honour their fallen comrades.

After the Japanese attack on Pearl Harbor on December 7, 1941, the Canadian federal government determined that all persons of Japanese ancestry were enemy aliens and the entire Japanese Canadian community living along coastal BC was a security risk. Nisei (born in Canada) and Issei (a new immigrant) alike were to be sent to an internment camp in the BC Interior, or they could choose to be put on a boat to Japan, even if they were Canadian born.

My grandfather, a decorated World War I Canadian soldier, was told to report to Hastings Park. So outraged was he by the government's actions, he threw down his medals on the floor with disgust and exclaimed, "What good are these?"

At some point in 1942, the eternal flame in the lantern atop the Japanese Canadian War Memorial in Stanley Park was extinguished. Some thought it was extinguished because of the blackouts resulting from air raid threats.

The Mitsui family was interned in the Greenwood Internment Camp and my mother's family, Kawamura, was interned in New Denver, the current site of the Nikkei Internment Memorial Centre National Historic Site of Canada.

The prejudicial policies and decisions, the confiscation and loss of property, the internment, the separation of families and the relocation of families after the war ended were recognized on August 2, 1985. From the very beginning, my grandfather participated in the redress effort to lobby the federal government to make a public apology and for financial compensation.

It took the effort of many leaders in the Japanese Canadian community and the National Association of Japanese Canadians (NAJC), led by Art Miki, and specifically the formation of the National Coalition for Japanese Canadian Redress, for the federal government and specifically the Honourable Brian Mulroney to finally initiate discussions for redress with the NAJC for the injustices experienced during and after World War II.

As part of this acknowledgement, my grandfather, one of the last surviving Japanese Canadian soldiers of World War I in Canada, at the age of ninety-six, was invited to Vancouver to participate in the rededication ceremony and to relight the eternal flame atop the Japanese Canadian War Memorial in Stanley Park. He remarked, "I've done my last duty to my comrades. They are gone but not forgotten."

My grandfather was a very proud veteran. Growing up, I recall that every Remembrance Day, he would put on his uniform, his Legion beret and his World War I medals. My dad told me that when I was about five years old, while visiting him on Remembrance Day, I asked my grandfather for his shiny medals. He said that one day I would receive them. Upon his death, I received them in his will.

My grandfather did not attend a public Remembrance Day service after World War I until November 11, 1983. He felt honoured to serve with his comrades in Europe and he continued to have great respect for the military throughout his entire life. However, he never forgave the government for its decision to intern the Japanese Canadians during World War II and for what it did to his family. He died in April 22, 1987, six months before his hundredth birthday and a year before the federal government announced the signing of the redress agreement. It would make financial compensation of twenty-one thousand dollars to those who were interned, but only to those who were still alive.

Unfortunately, the internment of the Japanese Canadians during World War II and the participation of Canadians of Japanese ancestry during both world wars and the Korean War continue to be an unfamiliar part of Canadian history for many Canadians.

The exhibit highlighting the role of the 10th Battalion in the Calgary Military Museum (formerly the Museum of Regiments) and the display on the internment of the Japanese Canadians during World War II in the Canadian War Museum goes a long way in recognizing this piece of Canadian history for the education of future generations.

As a lasting legacy to the Japanese Canadian veterans of World War I, the Honourable Peter Kent wrote me a letter, dated July 21, 2011, saying that he approved my proposal to declare the "Japanese Canadian Soldiers of World War I Winning the Right to Vote" as a national historic event, as the first persons of Asian ancestry to gain the right to vote in BC and Canada. However, it was not until 1949 that all Canadians of Japanese ancestry were given the right to vote in Canada. A process is now in place to create a plaque recognizing this event. The plaque will be installed at the site of the Japanese Canadian War Memorial Cenotaph in Stanley Park, Vancouver.

David Mitsui would like to recognize the assistance of authors Barry Broadfoot, Ken Adachi, Roy Ito and Lyle Dick (retired national park historian), who took a personal and professional interest in his family's history. As well, his father, George, and his sisters, Amy Kuwabara and Lucy Ishii, shared stories.

Masumi Mitsui posed with his medals when he was 97 years old.
Courtesy of David Mitsui

Greenwood's Japanese World War I Veterans

BY CHUCK TASAKA, WHO GREW UP IN GREENWOOD

I was born in 1945 and by the time I was seven or eight, I looked forward to the Japanese war veterans coming to our house to visit my parents regularly. The one person who really stood out in my memory was Iidon, as he was called by my parents. Years later, I asked what his last name was, and my mother said something like "Yuyama."

Iidon was a Russo-Japanese war veteran, but by the time he was in Greenwood he was an elderly man. Mind you, for a young child every adult was old! Being a single man and living alone in a small one-room suite, he must have enjoyed coming to our place because the Tasaka family had so many children and it was lively. Whenever it was bedtime, I always asked Iidon to tell me war stories. Even in my youth, I thought of him as quite small in stature, but he was enthusiastic and youthful in his speech. I remember Iidon sitting on a wooden chair against the wall nearest to my bed. I would see him standing at attention and reminiscing about what he did during the war. He talked (in Japanese) so proudly of his duty and accomplishments. Oh, how I became so interested in war history from a child's point of view. (I never missed a John Wayne or Audie Murphy war movie.) Iidon was a cherished guest at our house.

Toichi Nitsui and Yonesaburo Kuroda

The World War I veterans who came to our house regularly were Mr. Nitsui and Mr. Kuroda. Toichi Nitsui was Mom's cousin so he was a frequent visitor. The first thing I asked, along with my brothers and sisters, was to see his machine-gun wound. Mr. Nitsui was proud to lift up his pant leg and show us the brown scar on the calf. He was actually too young to enlist, so he lied about his age and got in anyway. After the war, Toichi drove a taxi in Vancouver, but in the thirties he worked in Ucluelet on Vancouver Island. Several of his daughters were born in places like Port Alberni and Deep Bay. It was fun listening to him because he embellished his stories to make them extremely exciting. Mr. Nitsui was a type of person who took no guff from anyone. If there was a fight, he'd be the first one to help out.

Toichi and his wife, Katsuko, remained in Greenwood and he died in the Grand Forks Hospital in 1976. He was buried in Oceanview Cemetery in Vancouver. The Nitsui family had five children: Miyoko, Chiyo and Judy. Joyce and Ken passed away.

Mr. Yonesaburo Kuroda, on the other hand, was a distinguished city slicker. He was always dressed to the hilt with a fedora hat, woollen long coat, slacks and leather gloves. His posture was so upright that it gave Mr. Kuroda the appearance of a very proud soldier. He too was wounded in battle. Again, the children looked forward to seeing his machine-gun wound. His brown scar went from one end of the calf to the other side. Mr. Kuroda wouldn't hesitate to show the children his battle scars. He never brought up the gory side of war himself, but whenever I asked him how his fellow soldiers died, he would tell me. Mr. Kuroda told me that he saw his comrades fall on the ground decapitated or blown to pieces by shell bursts.

Mr. Kuroda lived in No. 3 Building (Gulley Block/McArthur Centre) and he was a watchmaker. He died May 16, 1962, at the Trail Hospital and was buried at the Greenwood Cemetery.

Kiyoji Iizuka

Mr. Kiyoji Iizuka was born January 27, 1887, and he was a stowaway to Honolulu, Hawaii. His first trip to Canada was November 2, 1910. He enlisted in the Canadian Army and was wounded in action May 7, 1917. He rejoined his unit after recovering but was injured in a transport accident on March 28, 1918. Again, he rejoined his unit only to get wounded once more on September 4, 1918. Kiyoji was repatriated to Canada, December 24, 1918, earning a Military Medal, British War and Victory Medals. He went back to Japan in 1923 to bring his wife and daughter to Canada.

Kiyoji Iizuka was wounded in action in the Great War and interned during World War II.
Courtesy of the Greenwood Military Aviation Museum

Mr. Iizuka worked as a fisherman and painter while living on Powell Street. He was sent to Greenwood in October of 1942. Mr. Iizuka was a tough hombre and I'm sure no one messed around with him. He lived in Greenwood for a long time tending to his beautiful vegetable garden across the creek until he finally returned to his roots and lived on Powell Street in East Vancouver in 1969. He died December 23, 1979, and is survived by his daughter, Hidi Nishi, in Vancouver and his son, Fumio, with his wife, Hiromi, in Greenwood.

Yasuo Takashima

Mr. Yasuo Takashima was another war hero who was awarded the Military Medal. He was a private person who kept to himself. Katsuyoshi Morita wrote a chapter about Yasuo in his book, *Powell Street Monogatari*. Mr. Morita got acquainted with Mr. Takashima in 1942 when they arrived in Greenwood. As time passed, Yasuo started to open up and gave more information about himself. Mr. Takashima came from Kumamoto, Kyushu, and at eighteen fought in the Russo-Japanese War of 1904–5. Being single and adventurous, his journey took him to Hawaii and finally to British Columbia. In 1907, Yasuo lived and worked in the Nass Valley, near the Alaska Panhandle. When Yasuo returned to Vancouver, he bought a samurai sword with a white scabbard to patrol the streets around Powell and Cordova for any anti-Asian riots.

In 1914, Yasuo enlisted in the Canadian Army. It wasn't in his plan to be a war hero as he was given a "coolie" job in the trenches. When there were so many casualties, Yasuo was given a gun and asked to attack. He ran and darted until he got behind the enemy line and captured a German machine-gun nest. Yasuo didn't think he did anything extraordinary, but he was awarded a medal personally by the Duke of Connaught.

After the war, Yasuo wandered and tried to settle down, but circumstances in the Okanagan killed his ambition to farm. An angry mob destroyed all his plants. Yasuo planned to go back to Japan, but again misfortune befell him. His "friends" borrowed and took the money that he had saved to go to Japan. The so-called friends apparently lost his money in a gambling game. By this time, the Pacific war had begun and he was asked to go to Greenwood. All he packed was his war medal, sword and a rosary given to him in France by a daughter of a woman he helped and befriended. Yasuo stayed in Greenwood until after the war, but he became ill and was taken to the veterans' hospital in Vancouver where he died. No one seems to know to where his cherished possessions disappeared.

Tsunekichi Kitagawa

Tsunekichi Kitagawa was asked to guard internees in 1942 because he was a veteran.
Courtesy of Midori Kitagawa

Tsunekichi Kitagawa was born March 28, 1887. He was a fisherman in the Queensborough area of New Westminster in the early 1900s. Mr. Kitagawa enlisted in the Canadian Army and was wounded in battle. In 1942, Tsunekichi was asked to be a gate guard at Hastings Park because he was an army veteran. Ironically, his family was confined inside the park. He decided with four other Japanese veterans, one being Mr. Kuroda, to go to Greenwood to look for housing. Initially, his family had to share a place with two other families. Later, the Kitagawa family lived in a house on their own in Anaconda and finally across from Greenwood Park. Mr. Kitagawa worked for the CPR and later he was a night watchman at Boundary Sawmill in Midway. Tsunekichi returned to Steveston and died in 1969 at the age of eighty-two. Mr. Kitagawa had seven children.

With information given by Midori Kitagawa.

Masumi Mitsui

Masumi Mitsui's story has been well documented by his grandson (see the story on page 160). Masumi was of samurai stock and began his life in Victoria as a dishwasher, waiter and chauffeur. After he enlisted in the Canadian Army, he fought at the Battle of Vimy Ridge. He and Tokutaro Iwamoto were awarded the Military Medal for bravery. By war's end they were awarded the British War and Victory Medals.

Hirokichi Isomura

Hirokichi Isomura from Nagoya fished during the summer and ran a shoe repair shop on Hastings in Vancouver in the off-season. He never set foot in Greenwood because he protested that army veterans should not be treated as "enemy aliens" and be exiled. As a result, he and his eldest son were sent to a POW camp in Angler, Ontario. Sadly, Mr. Isomura never had a chance to see his family in Greenwood. His wife and children were sent to Greenwood and they lived in No. 10 Building (Frazee Block) and several other buildings, but the separation took its toll. Mrs. Isomura died, leaving her children in the hands of the communal neighbours. The children were moved frequently around Greenwood by the BC Security Commission. Eventually, the children were reunited with their older brother and father in Moose Jaw, Saskatchewan.

Mr. Isomura was quite badly wounded at Vimy Ridge so he moved his family to Vancouver to receive frequent care at St. Vincent's Hospital, Shaughnessy Hospital and George Derby. He took his family each year to the Remembrance Day ceremony in Stanley Park. Mr. Isomura was buried in Forest Lawn Cemetery in the veterans' section in 1957.

With research by Linda Kawamoto-Reid.

Others Interned at Greenwood

According to Mr. Morita's book, there were other war veterans in Greenwood but they did not stay too long as they moved along elsewhere during the war years.

Nuinosuke Okawa was born July 24, 1884. He was a carpenter and served in the Russo-Japanese War for three years. Mr. Okawa enlisted in Calgary in 1916 and was wounded in battle. He was sent to Greenwood but later moved to Hamilton and York, Ontario.

Tsunejiro or "Thomas" Kuroda sailed from Yokohama to Honolulu on November 29, 1905, at age nineteen. He was a farm labourer in Hawaii. Thomas was a bachelor and good friend of Mr. Kitagawa. From Greenwood, he moved to Slocan and finally to New Denver to be placed in an old age home.

Kichiji Shimizu was born December 10, 1887. He came from Hawaii to BC in August 1907 as a labourer. Mr. Shimizu enlisted June 2, 1916, in Calgary. He died June 29, 1953. In an interview with Kiyoshi (Harry) Imai, he told me that Mr. Shimizu gave him his cherished German Luger pistol and war rifle that he brought back from the front. They were both living in Steveston in the late thirties. Harry didn't know his first name at the time. It was always "Mr. Shimizu" to a young teen. Harry had to leave most of his possessions behind when the internment of the Japanese began in 1942. Mr. Shimizu moved up to Prince Rupert and he passed away June 29, 1953.

Yoshimatsu Fukaye was born in Yamaguchi-ken in 1883. Mr. Fukaye came to Canada as a labourer and watchman, and he enlisted in the army August 8, 1916. Yoshimatsu was interned in Greenwood and was on the voters list in 1945. Between 1949 and 1962, he was on the voters list in New Denver. Very little is known about him in Greenwood.

The Japanese who volunteered in World War I included men who came from samurai stock and veterans of the Russo-Japanese War, but mostly they were just tough, able-bodied, blue-collar workers. They fought with the samurai fighting spirit, but more importantly they fought to bring honour to their families and community. Most fathers would give their sons the advice that they were not fighting for their own glory. The advice might go something like this: "No bring shame to the family. Mo' betta come home in a coffin."

These men had to enlist in Alberta because British Columbia wouldn't take them. By enlisting, these soldiers were led to believe they would automatically be granted the franchise and the right to vote. Unfortunately it took until 1931, but even then only these soldiers were allowed vote. In 1949, the Canadian government officially granted all Japanese the franchise and the freedom to move back to the West Coast.

These proud soldiers not only fought the enemy, but they had to fight for the right to vote, receive equal job opportunities and eliminate discriminatory practice against all Japanese living in BC:

50th Battalion (175th Overseas Battalion)
Kiyoji Iizuka 697032 Tokyo / wounded / Military Medal
Hirokichi Isomura 697033 Aichi-ken / wounded
Yonesaburo Kuroda 697079 Shiga-ken / wounded

10th Battalion (192nd Overseas Battalion)
Tsunekichi Kitagawa 898557 Kumamoto-ken / wounded
Masumi Mitsui 898559 Fukuoka-ken / wounded / Military Medal
Tsunejiro Kuroda 898533 Kumamoto-ken
Nuinosuke Okawa 898336 Shizuoka-ken / wounded
Yoshimatsu Fukaye 898545 Yamguchi-ken

191st Overseas Battalion (Served with 10th and 50th)
Toichi Nitsui 895424 Wakayama-ken / wounded
 Yasuo Takashima 895539 Kumamoto-ken / Military Medal

52nd Battalion (13th Canadian Mounted Rifles)
Kichiji Shimizu 228439 Aichi-ken

Chuck Tasaka is a retired teacher living in Nanaimo. He's working on a book titled Family History of Greenwood–Midway—My Hometown, My Furusato.

Saving Vancouver's Japanese Canadian War Memorial

By the Japanese Canadian War Memorial Committee
It is an iconic part of Stanley Park. But after over ninety years, the Japanese Canadian Cenotaph is in need of some special maintenance. The Japanese Canadian War Memorial Committee is raising the funds needed to ensure the cenotaph will continue to serve as a memorial to Japanese Canadians who served and died for their country.

Over 220 Japanese Canadian volunteers served in World War I. When Japanese volunteers from British Columbia were turned away in this province, many travelled to Alberta to enlist. There, they were welcomed by Alberta regiments and served with distinction on the Western Front. Fifty-four of them made the ultimate sacrifice and never made it home. It was for these men that the Canadian Japanese Association erected the monument on April 9, 1920.

The cenotaph itself is a work of art. The pillar is carved Haddington limestone. The base features carved granite petals embedded with names of the battles where Japanese veterans fought. And the marble and terracotta Japanese-style lantern atop the monument was lit until Pearl Harbor was bombed. It was re-lit in a ceremony by one of the last surviving World War I vets, Sergeant Masumi Mitsui in 1985.

During World War II, Japanese Canadians were declared enemy aliens and not accepted for enlistment. But toward the end of the war in 1945, 156 Japanese Canadians were recruited to serve as much-needed interpreters, interrogators and translators, and two lost their lives. Over a hundred were trained in the S-20 Canadian Army Language School Pacific Command in Vancouver to serve in military intelligence. When the Korean War broke out, Japanese Canadians again stepped up to serve Canada. Nineteen enlisted and one soldier lost his life. Some thirty former Japanese Canadians, deported to Japan in 1946, enlisted in Japan to fight for Canada and headed for Korea in 1950.

To mark the hundredth anniversary of World War I, the Japanese Canadian War Memorial Committee together with the Nikkei Place Foundation hopes to raise fifteen thousand dollars to restore the cenotaph, reproduce the Japanese Canadian Legion No. 9 flag and replace the plaque that dedicates the monument.

The committee continues to organize Remembrance Day ceremonies annually at the cenotaph and they hope British Columbians will help to preserve this important monument in honour of the sacrifices made on our behalf.

The "They Went to War Campaign" will run until September 2014, but donations will be welcome throughout the Great War anniversary years. Contributions can be made to the Nikkei Place Foundation for the "They Went to War Campaign."

From Our Listeners: Two Chinese Brothers Determined to Serve

By Judy Lam Maxwell, Vancouver

When World War I broke out, two brothers Wee Hong Louie (born 1894) and Wee Tan Louie (born 1897) from Shuswap wanted to enlist but most BC regiments refused all recruits of Chinese descent. Nevertheless, Wee Hong was able to sign up with the Forestry Draft in Kamloops in 1917, while Wee Tan went to Calgary to enlist in February 1918 and ended up reinforcing the 10th Canadian Infantry Battalion. Both brothers were proudly part of the Canadian Expeditionary Force in Europe.

Wee Hong served as a gunner in France with the 102nd Rocky Mountain Rangers Regiment. He was later transferred to communications to serve as a wireless operator. Wee Tan, on the other hand, was noted for his quickness and small stature and served as a runner in France, Holland and Belgium. Wee Tan was wounded in action, sustaining hearing loss from shelling. Each of the Louie brothers received the British War Medal and the Victory Medal.

After the war, Wee Hong attended the University of Chicago and graduated as an electrical engineer. He decided to settle in eastern Canada—in Orillia, Ontario—to establish a career. Wee Hong purchased the West End Radio Shop and applied for a business licence, but he was refused. When he complained to the prime minister's office about this, the refusal was confirmed. Insulted and in protest, Wee Hong packed his World War I army uniform and medals and sent them to Prime Minister Mackenzie King, notifying him that he did not risk his life for a country that would treat veterans so poorly. Realizing their ignorance and inability to dispute his loyalty to Canada, the government returned the items to Wee Hong with a letter of apology and a business licence. Wee Hong Louie operated the shop until he retired in 1976.

Judy Lam Maxwell is a Vancouver historian.

Wee Tan Louie. Courtesy of Wayne Louie

More about Wee Tan Louie

An interview with Chris Brown

CBC National reporter Chris Brown was able to track down more on Wee Tan Louie for a special Remembrance Day story. He spoke with Mark on *BC Almanac*.

Mark Forsythe: Tell us more.

Chris Brown: He was born on a homestead near Kamloops in 1894 to parents who'd come here to work in the gold fields and later build the railway. When war broke out in 1914 he had been working as a ranch hand on the Douglas Lake Ranch near Merritt. There were a lot of obstacles, but he made a decision to try to enlist. What is remarkable about this story is his determination to fight for his country when it was clear it didn't want him because of the colour of his skin.

Mark: So what happened in 1914 when war broke out?

Chris: A lot of young Canadian men signed up but Chinese Canadians were effectively banned by the army. Throughout the whole war, in an army of six hundred thousand, only a couple of dozen would ever be allowed in the ranks. But young Wee Tan was more determined than most. He bought a horse and he rode from the Kamloops area over the Rocky Mountains in the dead of winter. According to his family, that was a three-month journey. Wee Tan was trying to enlist in an Alberta regiment. And unlike BC, Alberta regiments were accepting Asian recruits. He was off to the war, and in the spring of 1918 he was on the front lines as a machine gunner and a chauffeur for the officers. I talked to his youngest son, Wayne Louie, who is in his seventies and lives in Kamloops: "I think it's unbelievable what he did. I mean how many people would do that? How many people would go and fight for your country when you weren't wanted. I mean, he was very patriotic to Canada. He wanted to make this his home. And he wanted us to grow up proud, not only being Chinese but being Canadian."

Mark: Given all the racism of the time, why did Wee Tan do it?

Chris: Well, he died in 1970 so we can't ask him directly, of course, and his kids didn't before he died. But this is Wayne Louie's best guess: "That was his dream, to fight for his country. This is his country. He was born and raised in BC, and I guess he just wanted to be as good as the next person, in reference to white people."

There really didn't seem to be much to gain for Wee Tan, or any of the other few dozen Chinese Canadian vets. They came back to a country that still didn't want them; where it would take another thirty years to get the right to vote. And yet, he had this burning patriotism, to take this incredible trip over the mountains. He eventually settled in Ashcroft and had a successful trucking company and raised a family.

Mark: You met his wife?

Chris: That's another incredible twist to this story. Wee Tan's wife, Lilly, was fifteen years younger than him, and after he died she continued living in their bungalow, and she's still alive on this 2013 Remembrance Day. Lilly Louie is 102, born in 1911. I visited her and she told me her husband never spoke about the war:

"Never, never, never. And he never talked to the children about it. And they never asked him about it. He was gentle. He looked after his family and was good to the children."

Over forty years after he died, his wife's memories of Wee Tan are dimming. But she is a living link to the Great War, a widow of one of Canada's very first Chinese Canadian soldiers—a young man who went to war, with seemingly nothing to gain and everything to lose, and thereby made a very powerful statement about his loyalty to his country.

The Chinese Labour Corps

An interview with Peter Johnson

While British Columbia regiments were reluctant to enlist Chinese soldiers, the British War Office was more than happy to transport labourers directly from China to the Western Front to help in the war effort. Peter Johnson is the author of *Quarantined: Life and Death at William Head Station, 1872–1959*. He has researched the use of Chinese labourers for the war effort, and their quarantine at William Head near Victoria.

Mark Forsythe: What role does William Head play in this story?

Peter Johnson: The site of the William Head Penitentiary, out on William Head Peninsula, was a quarantine station, but it closed in 1959. The World Health Organization said, "Right, the fight of infectious diseases is over." Besides we needed the place for prisoners.

Mark: Was it also used as a tool for exclusion?

Peter: No question. The politics of privilege and the economics of indifference kept Ottawa from taking on its responsibility. Part of the contract of joining Confederation was that the federal government would provide British Columbia

The Chinese labour corps were technically a non-combatant force, but saw plenty of action in their work near the front.
From *The Graphic Magazine*, Mar. 16, 1918

with quarantine services. Well, it never did. In 1871 when BC joined Canada there wasn't even a federal quarantine office here. It took almost another twenty years for Ottawa to get its act together—they were shamed into it by a little white girl who died without access to any kind of station whatsoever. Certainly the politics of indifference played a role and also the history of racial prejudice. The Chinese were clobbered with a head tax, and in 1903 it doubled to five hundred dollars. Often quarantine legislation was used to support policies of deportation or policies of racism. That's a common theme that runs throughout the book.

Mark: As you traced the history of quarantine in BC, you also tell us about the Chinese Labour Corps. Who were these people and what was their role in World War I?

Peter: It's such a sad episode. It was mutually beneficial for China to send labourers to the European theatre of war and for Britain, who needed these labourers. There had been precedents for organized movement of indentured Chinese labourers all throughout the nineteenth century. The California gold rush needed Chinese miners; the CPR hired indentured Chinese labourers; the Boer War required them; the war in the Balkans needed Chinese labourers.

China was beginning to be overrun by foreign influences; the British were there, the French were there, the Russians and Germans were in China, as were the Japanese. At the turn of the twentieth century the Boxer Rebellion wanted all of these foreigners out. The Germans had occupied part of the northern province of China called Shandong and the Chinese also wanted them out. But the Japanese invaded Shandong and decided it would be a good jumping-off spot for their attack on Manchuria. Russia was involved in Inner Mongolia.

So there were reasons China wanted to ship out labourers. The new Chinese government believed if they were chucked out and they helped Europe with their war, then perhaps Europe would help rid them of the Japanese. Of course, it never happened.

And, of course, in Europe, there was the horror of the Somme in 1915, with fifty thousand dead the first day, half a million dead in six months. There were German submarine bases along the Belgian frontier that were destroying a million tons of British ships every month. All those working for the Allies along the front lines were required as regular members of the army, so they needed some kind of reinforcement corps.

Mark: What were the jobs of the Chinese Labour Corps?

Peter: They did everything from repairing tanks to working in steel and chemical plants, loading and unloading ships at port, shoring up the trenches, building huts, sandbagging, railway lines, the Chinese Labour Corps—ninety-six thousand of them we believe—really enabled the front lines to keep going. It took a year to organize and the Brits didn't tell the Chinese what they were doing because China was neutral. China didn't enter World War I until August of 1917, so all of this is happening two years before that.

Mark: They were put into extremely dangerous situations, weren't they?

Peter: It was actually horrific. They landed at Dunkirk and were fired upon. They were gassed as they moved along the line from the Somme to Ypres and were involved in whatever front-line attacks were going on. They were a non-combatant force. They were called the Chinese Labour Corps, and that was Churchill's idea. He believed that if he recruited men in the regular army from the hinterlands of the Chinese Mongolian frontier that would break Chinese neutrality. So let's pretend they are a volunteer force and call them a labour corps.

Mark: The cover story was that they were just providing a service?

Peter: Providing a service, and we paid them thirty cents a day, whereas a regular soldier would make $1.30 a day. I have to hand it to the British War office as they really organized this fast movement. Think of it, little Chinese villages on the northern frontier. They wouldn't be interested in fighting in Europe. Europe was a war-mad continent as far as the Chinese peasants were concerned, but somehow they would recruit thousands of Chinese peasants, many of them illiterate.

Mark: When they arrived on BC shores, some were quarantined, and essentially quarantined again as they travelled across the country in sealed railway cars?

Peter: That's how the prime minister waived the head tax. If we keep them in sealed trains there won't have to be a head tax. The other reason was not to let the Chinese community across the country know what they were doing, because the Chinese communities, still embittered by the CPR not living up to the agreement of paying them properly after the building of the railway, would notify the Chinese Labour Corps on the trains and get them the hell out. And take them to North Battleford, Saskatchewan—or wherever else across the country that had labourers who worked on the CPR. They were also afraid that the Germans might catch on to this.

And so they came by ship. Fifty to sixty days from China. Another ten days waiting in a sealed part of William Head Quarantine Station. But there were too many of them. A quarantine station was constructed to handle a thousand people and many of those would be in tents. Suddenly by August of 1917 there were thirty thousand Chinese labourers at William Head. It was a horror story. They filed out into the community of Metchosin and stole doors and fence posts to lie on, to keep out of the rain, and raided the gardens for food. There were food riots.

Mark: How many of these labourers transited through Canada and came back?

Peter: Numbers vary. I would say a minimum of eighty-four thousand went across Canada; probably forty thousand of those came back to William Head, and they got rid of them as fast as they could. I think the official position was "Let's get this over as fast as we can." It became a terrible footnote to the enormity and pity of World War I.

Mark: It's important to acknowledge this now.

Peter: Especially for the Chinese community in BC and Canada. They for the longest time suffered the brunt of racist policies both in the administration of quarantine and in general racist policies. The Chinese community wants the rest of Canada to know that many Chinese labourers worked on behalf of the Allies, and supported what was a horrific losing battle on the Western Front. And they are as much Canadians by virtue of that and other acts in Canada as any other immigrant group. So it's in a way an attempt to manifest some sort of great levelling. We are you. You are us. We are all the same. I think immigration history is about that. And it's very interesting because of the *Komagata Maru* incident in Vancouver in 1914. The Indians are holding a memorial to that. So it's really important that immigrant races tell their story. We're all immigrants.

The final resting place for members of the Chinese Labour Corps—Sain-en-Gohelle near Lens on the Western Front.
Courtesy of Mark Forsythe

Sikhs Also Served

The memories of the *Komagata Maru* incident and its blunt rejection of Sikh immigrants were fresh in the memories of the Sikh community when war was declared. But there were still some Canadian Sikhs who decided to serve. At least a thousand Sikhs from India enlisted, and ten Sikhs in Canada also signed up. Five had served previously in the Indian Army. Not much is known about these men, though the Sikh community has attempted to commemorate their service in recent years. Canadian filmmaker and historian David R. Gray discovered the Sikh story while working on another project. His film *Canadian Soldier Sikhs: A Little Story in a Big War* was the result.

"The story was an unknown aspect of early Canadian Sikh history," says Gray. "It was also something of a puzzle. Why had these men enlisted for Canada when clearly they were not welcomed in this country? The telling of this story also became a challenge. Could I find enough information on ten men in an army of thousands? Would there be photographs of them? Would there be personal stories to cover the sparse military records?"

Gray turned up some precious letters and while finding photos that could be properly identified proved challenging, the story he was able to tell was a compelling one. These are the men who served. At least six had BC connections:

- John Baboo: signed up in Winnipeg, came to BC after the war and died in Saanich in 1948
- Sunta Gougersingh: signed up in Montreal, killed in action in Belgium in October 1915
- Buckam Singh: signed up in Ontario, wounded twice in 1916, died August 1919 of war-related injuries
- Hari Singh: signed up in Toronto, survived the war and died in 1953 in Toronto
- Harnom Singh, a.k.a. Harry Robson: signed up in Vancouver in October 1916, wounded in 1918, returned to farming in Chilliwack, date of death unknown

- John Singh: signed up in Winnipeg, survived the war, next of kin in Fraser Mills, BC, died in 1971
- Lashman Singh: signed up in Ontario in 1915, court-martialled for striking a superior officer, returned to duty in August 1918, killed in action in France, October 1918
- Ram Singh: signed up in Vancouver, December 1917, served with the BC Regiment, last known address after the war, Grand Forks, details of death unknown
- Sewa Singh: signed up in Vancouver, June 1918, died in 1957
- Waryam Singh: signed up in May 1915 and served in Bermuda and France, wounded in April 1917, discharged in March 1918, ended up in Vancouver, details of death unknown

The letters of Waryam Singh, sent back to India, are particularly precious. On November 18, 1916, he wrote:

I believe this war will soon be decided. You know that there is frost in this part of Europe. What can I say? The frost or rain falls every day and the mud is beyond description and the war is terrible. The Germans are war weary and I could write a lot about their bad condition but time will not allow. On the 13th and 14th of November, 3,000 to 4,000 prisoners were brought into the trenches…The treacherous German is however very hard to convince that he is beaten. I am hopeful that he will soon be crushed.

On November 23, he wrote his father:

On the 4th of November there was a big fight and much hand to hand fighting took place and many prisoners were taken. Shells and bullets were falling like rain and one's body trembled to see what was going on. But when the order came to advance and take the enemy's trench, it

Despite discrimination in Canada and across the British empire, Indian recruits served loyally on the western front.
From *The Graphic Magazine*, Jan. 8, 1916

was wonderful how we all forgot the danger and were filled with extraordinary resolution. We went over like men walking in a procession at a fair and shouting. We seized the trench and took the enemy prisoners. When we took the trenches, some of the enemy escaped and some were taken. The dead were countless. The bravery we showed that day was the admiration of the British soldiers. After the fight they asked how it was that I was so utterly regardless of danger.

A few months later he was wounded and then got trench fever and pneumonia. His illness probably explains his discharge before the end of the war. He disembarked in Victoria in March 1918. Not much more is known about what happened to him after that.

Nothing much changed for the men who came back to Canada. Their families could still not join them and they could not vote. The search continues for more about the lives of these men, but Gray's film goes a long way toward opening up a dialogue and recognizing their service.

"With the help of Sikh temples and communities across Canada," says David Gray, "we have made some progress in solving some of the mysteries of this little story in a big war."

From Our Listeners: My Grandfather Herbert Arthur Armishaw

By Susie Armishaw, Procter

Private Herbert Arthur Armishaw was born in Walsall, Staffordshire, in December 1889. He immigrated to Canada at the age of twenty-four in 1912, along with his parents and a multitude of siblings. That same year he married Lucy. He was foreman of the crew that paved Hastings Street, later moving to Vancouver Island where he worked as a coal miner in Cumberland. According to his attestation papers, he enlisted in the Canadian Infantry in April 1916 and saw action overseas as a member of the 102nd Battalion, Regiment 506704. I am told his unit was responsible for digging tunnels toward German lines to blow up enemy fortifications. That's about all I know about his war experience as he wasn't one to talk about it. (His younger brother, Sergeant Major Robert Armishaw, was wounded in action.)

Herb returned to Canada in 1919 to homestead in Cedar on the east coast of Vancouver Island. He cleared land with horses, began farming near Akenhead Road beside the Nanaimo River and raised a family and had two dairy farms—the second one on Gordon Road, close to Harmac, was run by my father, George. Herb started the first dairy in Nanaimo, named Baby's Own Dairy. He was actively involved in the farms operations until his death at ninety-three.

After his death, the government appropriated his house for the Duke Point project, razing it and building the highway where it once stood. My grandfather would roll over in his grave if he knew, and he would have fought them tooth and nail. His second farm (where I was raised) is still there. Everyone driving off the Tsawwassen–Duke Point ferry drives through the intersected fields. He was a pioneer.

Herbert and Lucy Armishaw. Courtesy of Susie Armishaw

13

THEY CHOSE NOT TO FIGHT
SOCIALISTS, PACIFISTS AND DESERTERS

For those facing unemployment or a difficult life in the backwoods of British Columbia, the army meant a steady paycheque and regular meals. But for some socialists and pacifists it was better to face hardship than to betray one's convictions. Sometimes it took as much courage to endure the taunts and disdain and stay out of the fighting. When conscription was introduced in 1917, that choice became even more difficult. Enlistment posters reminded men who chose not to fight that they were out of step with the mood of the country.

The Socialists Oppose the War

The platform of the Socialist Party of Canada was published in every issue of its official newspaper, the *Western Clarion:*

> The irrepressible conflict of interest between the capitalist and the worker is rapidly culminating in a struggle for possession of the reins of government—the capitalist to hold, the worker to secure it by political action. This is the class struggle.

The *Western Clarion* was published in Vancouver, even then a hotbed for utopian ideas. The paper followed national affairs before the war and warned its readers to be wary of growing militarism. In March 1913, commentator John Amos "Jack" McDonald wrote that Prime Minister Borden's plan to give the Imperial Navy a gift of warships was imperialism at its worst:

> Borden has launched his naval policy in a lengthy address in which he reviewed the reasons for making an emergency contribution of three great battleships of the dreadnought type, to be used in defending the shores of "our glorious empire"...It must appear humorous indeed to all class-conscious workers, who are neither the owners of property or the possessors of steady jobs, to be told over and over again by Cabinet aspirants and ministers of the Crown that "those dreadful Germans" are watching every opportunity to land on the soil of Britain, and that we must be ready to risk our lives to protect those shores with a strong military and naval force.

Join the fight. A typical enlistment poster.
Library and Archives Canada, C-029484

The provincial election of 1916 provided a bigger soapbox for the Socialist Party. Jack McDonald ran as a candidate and wrote about the prospects for success in the *Clarion*:

Once again, the workers of British Columbia are given an opportunity to decide whether they want a continuation of capitalist rule. One would be inclined to think that the workers of this province have experienced enough misery and starvation to cause them to wake up and decide on taking a line of action in accord with their own interests at the present time. But again, will they? I think not!

The party ran McDonald in Fernie and union organizer Ginger Goodwin in Ymir. Both men were opposed to the war and made no bones about it. The election was held on September 14 and McDonald's prediction proved true. Every Socialist was defeated. The voters were more concerned about booting out the once-mighty Conservative Party of Richard McBride (now in disgrace and unsalvageable even under a new leader). But McDonald thought the Socialist Party had done pretty well:

In the Ymir riding a clean and vigorous fight was put up by Comrade Goodwin who, for the first time, entered a campaign as a representative of the Socialist Party of Canada...Much credit is due to Com. Goodwin for the manner in which he conducted the fight.

Conscription and Crackdown

Freedom of speech was great. But with more and more BC boys on the front lines, anti-war sentiments weren't going to be popular. In May 1917, Prime Minister Borden introduced the *Military Service Act*—conscription. The days of publicly challenging the war effort were coming to an end for McDonald, Goodwin and other conscientious objectors.

In labour circles, Goodwin became a bit of a star after his election campaign. He got a job as a full-time secretary of the Mill and Smeltermen's Union in Trail. Then in 1917, he was elected a vice-president of the BC Federation of Labour. The *Military Service Act* became law in late August, but Goodwin was given an exemption for health reasons. He was a poor physical specimen because of bad teeth and lung disease, and anybody who looked at him could see that.

Goodwin's health issues did not slow down his labour organizing. In November 1917 he led a strike by smeltermen that lasted five weeks and put Kootenay miners out of work as well. Goodwin was earning a reputation as a troublemaker and a lot of people wanted him out of the way. In late November, the local conscription review board decided to revisit his exemption on health grounds and in a surprising reversal found him fit for service. Goodwin filed an appeal and just to be safe, headed for the coast.

In April, the Central Appeal Tribunal turned down his bid for exemption from military service. In May he was ordered to appear for duty in Victoria. He never showed.

Instead, Ginger Goodwin headed for the backwoods around Cumberland, where a fugitive could count on labour support and protection. He was camped out in the bush near Comox Lake on July 27, 1918, when a police search party looking for evaders caught up with him. It is unclear exactly what happened, but Goodwin had a rifle and when Constable Daniel Campbell of the Dominion Police spotted him, Campbell opened fire. Goodwin was hit in the neck and killed. Campbell claimed he shot in self-defence and there was talk of manslaughter charges. But a grand jury decided not to commit him for trial.

Labour leader Jack Kavanagh told the *Vancouver Province* that trade unionists didn't believe Campbell's claim that he killed Goodwin to save himself. "Goodwin saw fit to evade the draft," said Kavanagh. "The question is, was it a killing in self-defense, or was it murder? We think it was murder."

Goodwin's funeral was held on August 2 in Cumberland and his death triggered mass demonstrations. In Vancouver on the same day, trade unionists called British Columbia's first general strike.

The Vancouver newspapers condemned the walkout. Under the headline "British or German—Which?" the *Vancouver Sun* declared:

> Every man who desires to be considered a good citizen will continue to work today. Every man who lays off in obedience to the infamous recommendations of extremists without honor or conscience will stain himself with something that can hardly be distinguished from deliberate treason.

The *Vancouver Province* agreed:

> Hundreds of union labor men from British Columbia have died bravely fighting for empire in France and Flanders. For none of these have organized workers been asked to pay such honor as they have been called upon to offer to the man who was killed with a rifle in his hand resisting the law of the country.

There was a strike, but it lasted only ten hours. Returning soldiers attacked union offices and the *Vancouver Province* reported that some strike leaders were forced to kiss the flag. Under the heading, "Yesterday's Lesson," the *Province* concluded:

> No Canadian city has given an exhibition so shocking to loyal sentiment as that which was forced upon the community by order of the authorities of the Labor Temple...It is time now for the union workers to consider their relations to the community and decide whether they can afford to remain any longer subject to the present direction and control.

Socialist writer Jack McDonald outside his bookstore.
Courtesy of Greg Dickson

Conscription also put newspaperman Jack McDonald on the run. He headed first for Seattle. But on June 5, 1917, all men between the ages of twenty-one and thirty-one were ordered to register for the US draft. Jack complied but quickly headed back to Canada. In October, he was called for a medical examination under the *Military Service Act* and placed in category A—fit for service. He managed to keep a low profile for the rest of the war and the authorities tried various measures like amnesties to get more voluntary compliance. Maybe as a writer, McDonald was not considered a serious threat to the public peace.

McDonald ended up in the United States after the war and ran a socialist bookstore in San Francisco for many years. He was killed in a car accident in 1968. His daughter Mary came back to Canada and was active in the bookstore business and the Raging Grannies.

The Goodwin Grave in Cumberland—Labour Place of Pilgrimage

Ginger Goodwin's grave at the Cumberland Cemetery is still an important landmark for the labour movement. Trade unionists and politicians looking for the labour vote still visit. NDP leader Jack Layton laid a wreath there in 2003. He told the crowd:

> It sends a chill up your spine. You feel like you're in the presence of some great tap root of resistance in the struggle for justice and equality. And I find myself thinking of Ginger Goodwin in the hills being hunted down in our country because he refused to go off and take up weapons...to

Goodwin's grave in the Cumberland Cemetery.
Courtesy of Greg Dickson

shoot down other working people in a far off land. What a lonely moment that must have been for him and what a struggle that must have been.

The headstone is rather unusual, displaying a hammer and sickle, a bit of artistic licence that Goodwin would not necessarily have chosen. But it is impressive and there is now a stop of interest and commemorative historical plaque along the cemetery road as well.

The Doukhobors—Toil and the Peaceful Life

The Doukhobors came to Canada in the late 1800s to escape religious persecution in Russia. They were settled first in Saskatchewan (then the Northwest Territories) where they were granted land. When the new provincial government tried to break up their communal holdings, about five thousand under direction from leader Peter the Lordly Verigin moved to British Columbia, mostly to communities in the west Kootenay and Boundary country.

It was always understood that the sect was pacifist. This was one of the key reasons they left Russia. An extract from a Minute of Canada's Privy Council on December 6, 1898, read:

> The Minister is of the opinion that it is expedient to give them the fullest assurance of absolute immunity from Military Service in the event of their settling in this country. The Minister recommends that under the power vested in Your Excellency in council by the above provision, the Doukhobors, settling permanently in Canada, be exempted unconditionally from service in the Militia upon the production from the proper authorities of their community.

So when the war broke out, Doukhobors again sought assurances they would be free from military service and that was given. But their farming neighbours who sent their own boys to war resented the exemption given to the Doukhobors that allowed them to continue to farm and prosper as they had done before the war.

Peter Verigin sensed there was trouble and took steps to show his people were prepared to support the war effort in other ways. In December 1916, he announced that the Doukhobors would donate cash and a carload of their famous jam to the local Patriotic Fund. The *Grand Forks Sun* reported:

> Mr. Verigin agreed to give, commencing on the 1st of January next, $100 per month during the coming year. In addition to this cash subscription, he stated the Society would ship a carload of jam, valued at $5,000 to the military authorities at the coast.

Things calmed for a time. But in May 1918, when the war was at its hottest, local farmers met again and demanded conscription of Doukhobors into a farm labour force. The *Sun* reported that a resolution to that effect was unanimously passed by the delegates:

> Whereas the Doukhobors made a compact with the former government releasing them from all combatant service, and owing to the above condition, all our young able-bodied men have been taken away from our farms and necessary industries for the successful carrying on of the war, and the Doukhobors and other aliens are taking advantage of the scarcity of labor and are retarding the work of the country by holding out for exorbitant wages, be it resolved that this meeting request the provincial government to urge the federal government the necessity of immediately conscripting all Doukhobors of military age...and to set wages for different industries, the government to take all wages over $1.10 a day and board, the same as our men at the front are receiving.

Peter "Lordly" Verigin.
Image B-03945 Courtesy of the Royal BC Museum, BC Archives

In April 1919 when the war was over, there was more agitation, this time for the government to purchase the Doukhobor lands, close the colony and set up a settlement for returning soldiers in its place.

Nothing came of that, but the communal way of life was collapsing due to internal conflicts and other pressures. On October 29, 1924, somebody blew up the train car Peter Verigin was travelling in, killing him and eight others. The crime has never been solved.

Some Did Serve

While pacifism was the official doctrine of the Doukhobors, there are some indications that leader Peter Verigin advised the federal government in 1914 that Independent Doukhobors who left the communal way of life did not deserve the military service exemption. Some did end up serving, including two men from the community of Thrums near Castlegar.

John Nevacshonoff enlisted in June 1916 and served with the 232nd Battalion in France. He later told his children he was just fifteen when he signed up to fight the Germans. It was a bitter experience that he later came to regret. A family obituary quoted him as saying he "had given three years of his life to the devil by participating in the First World War."

Another Thrums man, Demitri Kolesnikoff, is also listed among those who served. His military records indicate he was thirty-six years old when he was conscripted in June of 1918 into the 1st Depot Battalion at Calgary. His military records indicate that he initially failed to appear under the Military Service Act. Because he was conscripted late in the war, it is not clear whether he ever went overseas.

In December 1919 there was a general amnesty for all those who avoided conscription. For those who did serve and deserted, the stakes were even higher.

From Our Listeners: Ghost in the Barn

By Joe Harrison, Garden Bay

Officially, my mother's brother, Private William Henry Wallington, with the Canadian 101st Battalion, died at Vimy Ridge in France on October 9, 1916, a week after his nineteenth birthday. This third son of William Henry Wallington of Wainwright, Alberta, enlisted in Winnipeg on January 6, 1916, and was dead ten months later.

My mother only learned the truth in 1953. My aunt Lena's husband, James Ackley, told us how Henry had returned from the dead to the family homestead in March 1917 with his horrific story.

As Private Wallington climbed to the ridge from the field kitchen with dinner that evening in 1916, a great "whumf" and flash erupted, creating a massive hole where his machine-gun emplacement comrades were alive seconds before. Opening his eyes and flat on the ground, he could only stare in horror. For months the Germans had used miners to tunnel and place explosives metres under the Canadian position. After such an explosion, all units had been instructed to assume the worst with a stern warning to expect a second booby-trap explosion if anyone came near.

As the fog rolled in, Henry limped down toward Arras. By dawn he had slipped inside one of many bunkhouses of New Zealand miners recruited to sink tunnels from the Wellington Quarry under the front to counter the German mining strategy. Henry collapsed on a bed where he sank into a stupor. It seemed just moments later when he remembered sitting bolt upright, elated and exuberant. He suddenly realized that nobody would be looking for him. "You never saw a man so happy to be dead," he later told Jim Ackley.

Doffing his remnants of uniform and scrounging bits of clothing here and there, his army duds were smouldering in an incinerator as he casually mixed with the miners going for dinner. Later he joined another noisy group boarding the train down to Calais on leave.

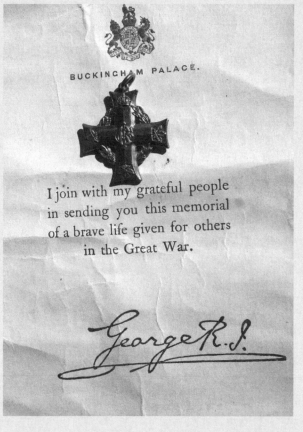

BUCKINGHAM PALACE.

I join with my grateful people in sending you this memorial of a brave life given for others in the Great War.

George R.I.

Within a week he joined the crew of a Yank freighter as a new man. "Harry Wellington from South Dakota" sailed to Halifax, and was sleeping in Jim's barn by March 1917. Soon reunited with his father in Wainwright, they were only too aware that deserters faced the death penalty. "Let's get the hell out of here!" Henry's father said as Jim hitched up the team.

My mother was never told the secret until Uncle Jim's visit in 1953. She had just received a letter of notification from an estate administrator in Pierre, South Dakota, stating that her father had died, leaving her a sum of money. Remarkably, he also said he had two affidavits stating that her supposedly dead brother was not only alive, but had a son in San Francisco.

Both William Henry Wallingtons, my mother's father and brother, had fled from Canada, fittingly changed their surnames to "Wellington," blended their identities and married women named "Mary" and "Mary K." American census records document the complex ruse.

My mother was born both deaf and silent. Raised by her sister Lena and her husband, Jim, she never spoke a word until, as an eight-year-old, she saw "the ghost in the barn." At supper that night she said her first word, "Goat," pointing to the barn.

My mother had spotted someone sleeping in the loft wrapped in a white sheet and horse blanket. "Goat," she repeated. "We don't have a goat, Violet. No goat." Lena mouthed the words. Then my mother drew a little picture of a ghost in the condensation on the window. When Lena and Jim took the coal oil lamp out to the barn, there was good old William Henry, leaning on one elbow and grinning. This image still comes alive for me every Remembrance Day.

The medal and note that William Wallington's family received upon his "death."
Courtesy of Joe Harrison

Shot at Dawn

Desertion could result in execution, and in most cases, these executions resulted from ongoing disciplinary issues. During the Great War, over twenty Canadian soldiers were executed for military offences between 1916 and 1918. Two served with BC regiments.

Private Thomas Moles was from Somerset but served with the 54th Kootenay Battalion. He was absent without leave on at least four occasions and was also disciplined for drunkenness.

In October 1917, he was charged with desertion. At 05:30 on October 22, 1917, Moles was executed by firing squad. His remains are located in Ypres Reservoir Cemetery.

Private Henry Hesey Kerr was from Montreal but served with the 7th British Columbia Battalion in France. He was disciplined for being absent without leave on at least two occasions. In November 1916 he was charged with desertion after failing to report during the Somme offensive. At 06:45 on November 21, 1916, Kerr was executed by firing squad. Private Kerr's remains are now located in Quatre-Vents Military Cemetery.

The government of Canada has offered an apology and formally announced its regret for these executions. On December 11, 2001, Minister of Veterans Affairs Dr. Ron Duhamel rose in the House of Commons and read into the parliamentary record the names of twenty-three Canadians who were executed, and then announced their names would be written into Parliament Hill's Book of Remembrance.

The Nominal Roll and Casualty Book of the BC Regiment. Kerr's execution, confirmed by General Douglas Haig, was written in the right column.
Courtesy of Greg Dickson

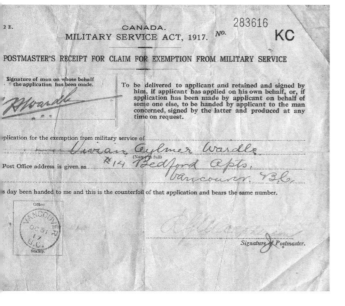

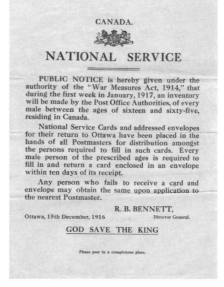

Far left: Claims for exemption from service were made on religious, moral or ethical grounds. Just a few thousand were accepted. Many conscientious objectors played non-combatant roles.
Courtesy of Don Stewart

Left: Canada was running out of volunteers for the war effort, so for the first time introduced the controversial practice of conscription.
Courtesy of Don Stewart

14

BC'S INTERNMENT CAMPS
BEHIND THE BARBED WIRE

The internment of so-called enemy aliens during the Great War was one of British Columbia's darker chapters. Compared to the Japanese internments of World War II it has been almost forgotten. But through the work of the Canadian First World War Internment Recognition Fund, the Ukrainian Canadian community and members of the Croatian, Serbian, Polish, Hungarian and German communities, what happened in camps around British Columbia is becoming better known. (In Ontario, subjects of the Ottoman Empire were also interned.)

As the war broke out in 1914, Prime Minister Borden promised that all loyal Canadians would be protected from persecution. "We have no quarrel with the German people," Borden told the House of Commons in mid-August, after war had been declared. "Nearly half a million of the very best citizens of Canada are of German origin, and I am sure that no one would for one moment desire to utter any word or use any expression in debate which would wound the self-respect or hurt the feelings of our fellow citizens of German descent."

The same respect, said Borden, applied to those with ties to the Austro-Hungarian Empire:

We have declared by Order in Council and by proclamation under the authority of His Royal Highness the Governor General that those people who were born in Germany or in Austria-Hungary and have come to Canada as adopted citizens of this country, whether they have become naturalized or not, are entitled to the protection of the law in Canada and shall receive it, that they shall not be molested or interfered with, unless any among them should desire to aid or abet the enemy or leave this country for the purpose of fighting against Great Britain and her allies. If any of them should be so minded we shall be obliged to follow the laws and usages of war in that regard with all the humanity that may be possible. But up to the present, we have seen no disposition among these people to do anything of the kind. They are pursuing their usual avocations and behaving themselves as good citizens of Canada. We honour and respect them for it, and have every confidence that they will pursue that course throughout this crisis, however long it may continue.

So things started out with good intentions. But that didn't last for long. When it became clear that the war was not going to end overnight, moves were quickly under way to intern not only potential combatants, but also working people and their families.

"All subjects of enemy states were designated enemy aliens regardless of ethnicity," says Ukrainian heritage professor Bohdan Kordan. "But there is a unique BC story to internment that is neither widely understood nor told."

That history includes the grim truth that the province was in the depths of a depression

This mural in Vernon commemorates the local internment camp, which is now a school playing field.
Courtesy of Greg Dickson

in 1914. Jobs were scarce, and recent immigrants were resented. including hard-working Ukrainians and Croatians, who were considered subjects of the Austro-Hungarian Empire even though the links were tenuous.

"Anti-immigrant sentiment was very strong within both the court of public opinion and the political leadership in British Columbia," says Professor Kordan.

Over five thousand Ukrainians were interned, not because they were a threat to the security of the province, but because they were considered a threat to the economic prosperity of more established workers. The thinking was that by removing them from the mines, mills and logging camps of the province, there would be more and better paying jobs for others.

But having removed these men from the general workforce, the province of British Columbia then decided that it would save some money by putting them to work on some rather dubious mountain road projects.

"Use of prisoners as a source of labour was routine practice," says Professor Kordan. "The principle was simple. There was work that needed doing and cheap prisoner labour, which was suddenly available and seen as an opportunity, would be utilized."

In 1915 a businessman wrote to Premier McBride: "Regarding my interview today on the subject of employment of alien prisoners at Vernon...There now appears to be an opportunity to link up the Okanagan with the Kootenays at little or no expense to the province. Surely this is an opportunity that should be made use of."

BC Minister of Public Works Thomas Taylor read the letter and advised the premier: "Regarding the employment of alien prisoners interned at Vernon on the Edgewood–Vernon road. May I say that the proposal contained in [the] letter meets with my strongest approval."

And so it turned out. Internees were pushed hard, paid twenty-five cents a day, and deprived of food when they didn't co-operate. They lived in a shadow world where there didn't seem to be any established rules governing how they would be treated. The use of force to get prisoners to work was supposed to be prohibited by international law. But despite protests, the practice continued.

The Vernon Internment Camp with fence line.
Courtesy of Vernon Museum and Archives

Camps were dispersed around the province: Vernon, Nanaimo, Edgewood, Monashee–Mara Lake, Revelstoke, Field–Otter and Fernie–Morrissey. One camp in Montreal opened on August 13, even before Prime Minister Borden delivered his speech on tolerance to the House of Commons. Camps at Vernon and Nanaimo opened in September 1914. Vernon was the second-last of the twenty-four internment camps to close in February 1920.

The camps were something families did not want to talk about. Not only were men interned, but wives and children were also put behind barbed wire. Escapes were not uncommon. Escapees in Canada were shot at and at least one was killed.

With assistance from Professor Bohdan Kordan, director of the Prairie Centre for the Study of Ukrainian Heritage, St. Thomas More College / University of Saskatchewan, and Andrea Malysh in Vernon, program manager for the Canadian First World War Internment Recognition Fund.

Sharing Internment Stories for Future Generations

FROM A VISIT WITH ANDREA MALYSH, PROGRAM MANAGER, CANADIAN FIRST WORLD WAR INTERNMENT RECOGNITION FUND

Canada's World War I "concentration camps" were not something that families who were interned talked about. For most, it was a painful memory, better forgotten. But now that the internment is widely seen as an injustice, many families are learning about what happened to their parents and grandparents and why.

Andrea Malysh of Vernon is of Ukrainian descent and has been working on the First World War Internment Recognition issue since 1997. She went to school in Vernon but did not learn until much later that the playing fields at her school were actually the site of one of BC's largest prison camps.

The Kohse family at the Vernon Internment Camp—a typically staged photograph in their Sunday best.
Courtesy of Andrea Malysh

Today, a small Ukrainian Orthodox Church sits across the street and there is a memorial plaque beside the playing field so that people can understand a bit better what happened there between 1914 and 1920.

"I never could have imagined that Ukrainian and others of Eastern European descent were held here," says Andrea. "This is where the government sent families, and some were still behind barbed wire here in 1920 when the camp was finally closed."

In June of 1997, when the memorial plaque was unveiled, one of those internees was able to attend the ceremony. Fred Kohse was just a child when he entered the camp with his parents. He spent six years there.

"The Kohse story is quite amazing," says Andrea. "Fred's father was German (Prussian) and his mother was English. When his father was interned at Nanaimo, his English mother put her baby into a rowboat and rowed up the gorge to the detaining centre where her husband was held and asked to be with him."

At first the authorities told her the camp was no place for an Englishwoman. But she told them she had nowhere else to go as the government had confiscated their property and wealth. So she eventually joined her husband behind the barbed wire.

"The Kohses were first sent to Nanaimo internment camp until the government decided that Vernon would be the facility that would house men, women and children," says Andrea. "But the war dragged on for years, and Mrs. Kohse realized she had to find a way out."

At first, she appealed to the camp staff. She wrote letters and made appeals based on her English ancestry.

"Camp authorities left her with little doubt that her request to be released would be ignored," says Andrea. "They tore up her letters right in front of her."

Gradually she befriended an Englishwoman who lived on the other side of the camp fence

Below: Fred Kohse and his cousin Victor Heiny at the Vernon Internment Camp— Fred would return to the site many years later.
Courtesy of Andrea Malysh

Below right: Fred Kohse (middle) on his return to the Vernon Camp in 1997 to unveil a memorial plaque.
Courtesy of Andrea Malysh

and who agreed to smuggle out a letter. It was sent to the House of Lords in England, who took their time in processing the request. When they finally did act, the war had been over for almost two years.

Fred Kohse (internee #5019) and his mother and father were finally free. The family later moved to northern Vancouver Island and settled near Kelsey Bay, where Fred learned farming and logging. Fred became a fisherman and captain of trollers. He spent sixty years in the fishing industry before he passed on in July 2001.

"If Fred had not come forward, his story would have been lost," says Andrea. "It was a special moment for me when he came to Vernon to be part of our ceremony. He told me that so much had changed, but he still remembered the dry hills around the camp from the days when he was interned there."

Today, finding stories like this one is a big part of Andrea's work. So it was a big surprise just last year when her sister was searching through some family papers and found their grandfather's old passport and some other documents.

"It turned out to be the Austro-Hungarian passport that he entered Canada with," says Andrea. "That was really the beginning of his problems when the war broke out. He was Ukrainian but he came from the part of the Ukraine that was under the Austro-Hungarian Empire and that made him an enemy alien."

The other papers included registration cards for both him and his wife that had to be presented every month to the local authorities. A lot of Ukrainian farmers were allowed to stay on the land to provide food for the war effort. But if they stepped out of line and didn't present their documents, they could quickly join those behind the barbed wire.

"The strange part of this story is that I had been telling people since 1997 to hunt through their family papers to find out if their parents were subject to internment," says Andrea. "When

Andrea Malysh stands beside the memorial plaque on the site of the Vernon Internment Camp.
Courtesy of Greg Dickson

Andrea Malysh holds her grandfather's Austro-Hungarian passport—where his problems began.
Courtesy of Greg Dickson

my sister found these papers, it was the first time I realized that my own grandparents were caught up in the internment too. After further searching through Library and Archives Canada, I found my great-grandfather, Wasyl Luchak, listed as being interned in Spirit Lake, Quebec, POW #864. Now this was a shock to our family."

Many documents like these have disappeared. Government archival records of the camps were systematically destroyed in the 1950s, making it difficult for historians to piece together all the details. But as more personal stories are found, the true history is gradually emerging.

"Most people now know about what happened to Japanese Canadians during World War II," says Andrea. "But educating people about internment during the Great War is even tougher because the survivors are all gone. They came to this country to escape tyranny in Europe and ended up victims of that same tyranny right here in Canada."

Scorned at Home—Serving Canada at the Front

Despite this harsh treatment, Ukrainian men who were still at liberty and others who were considered enemy aliens attempted to sign up to fight for Canada.

"As enemy aliens, they were prevented from enlisting. Naturalized citizens, however, could enlist and many did so," says Professor Bohdan Kordan. "The reason for their enlistment differed very little from the general population. Military service offered them relief from the difficult employment situation in the country."

Some changed their names or enlisted as Russian subjects. And, yes, it was not unusual to find individuals who were serving overseas but whose relations were interned back in Canada.

The story of Sergeant Filip Konowal stands out as an illustration of service in the face of discrimination. Konowal was born in the Ukraine in 1888 and served in the Russian Imperial Army. It's believed he came to Canada around 1913 and joined up with the 77th Battalion in July 1915, listing his place of birth as Russia. A declaration of his Ukrainian heritage might have had a different result. His wife and daughter were still in the old country.

Konowal transferred to the 47th Battalion (New Westminster) in the summer of 1916 and was made a lance corporal. In August 1917 near Lens, France, he was wounded in the neck and face while attacking and capturing a series of German machine-gun posts. Konowal was deadly with a bayonet and killed at least sixteen of the enemy. He kept fighting even after he was wounded and that caught the attention of his superiors. After he was evacuated back to Britain for medical care, he received a Victoria Cross from the King for "one of the most daring and heroic [exploits] in the history of the army."

Konowal was made a military attaché at the Russian Embassy and promoted to sergeant. He returned to Canada briefly in late 1918 but his military service was not yet over. He was assigned to the Canadian Siberian Expeditionary Force and left Vancouver for Vladivostok. In June 1919 he returned to Canada and was finally discharged.

The postwar years were difficult for Konowal. He suffered from what we now know as

Another photo of the Vernon camp.
Courtesy of Vernon Museum and Archives, Photo No. 3698

post-traumatic stress disorder. His wife and daughter were lost in the Stalinist purges that followed the revolution. During the Depression, Konowal found work as a junior caretaker in the House of Commons after another VC recipient came to his aid. Prime Minister Mackenzie King discovered that he was washing floors and made him a special custodian in his office.

Speaking of his experiences, Konowal once told a newspaperman, "I mopped up overseas with a rifle, and here I must mop up with a mop." But there were bright spots. When the royal family visited Ottawa in 1939, Konowal was again honoured at the National War Memorial. He tried to enlist in World War II but was too old. Then in 1956, he went overseas again with other VC winners to meet with Prime Minister Anthony Eden and the Queen. He died in 1959.

(See Chapter 3 for more about Victoria Cross recipient Filip Konowal.)

How the Newspapers Reported the Internment Camps

WITH THANKS TO LORNE ADAMSON AT THE VERNON MUSEUM ARCHIVES FOR TRANSCRIPTIONS
Here is some of the reporting from the Vernon News *during the war years. The editorial position of the paper was that internees were much better treated than those held in German prisons.*

There is some evidence that a class system developed at the Vernon camp. Aristocratic German civilians, who were members of the pre-war German immigrant elite of Vancouver, were treated differently. They were granted special favours ostensibly in order to observe the Hague Regulations, which called for a better quartering and subsistence for those of the officer class or its equivalent.

The Germans brought maids and hired cooks. They had concerts and tended gardens. The Austro-Hungarian (Ukrainian and Croatian) prisoners could expect hard labour on work crews in the bush and in the national parks.

September 17, 1914. Will Bring War Prisoners to Vernon for Safe Keeping

German prisoners of war are likely to be brought to Vernon in the near future, the military authorities having taken over the large building fronting on Lorne Street, just west of Mara Avenue, to be used as a military prison.

The building, which was originally a provincial jail, but until last autumn was used as a

Men who didn't serve overseas were sometimes pressed into service to guard internees.
Courtesy of Vernon Museum and Archives, Photo No. 16123

branch of the Provincial Hospital for the Insane, is well suited to the purposes for which it will be used.

A force of men is already at work, making alterations and repairs, but as yet it is not known when the prisoners of war will reach Vernon, nor how many will be kept here.

January 7, 1915

There are now 57 German and Austrian prisoners in the Vernon Internment prison…We are asked to mention the fact that a skating rink which has been formed on the grounds is not for the use of the general public as some seem to imagine, but is reserved for prisoners and members of the BC Horse who are acting as guards.

June 6, 1915

A special train on Sunday brought in eighty more alien prisoners from the coast for the local internment camp. This brings the number now interned here up to about four hundred and thirty. It is expected that about 200 of these will leave shortly for Monashee to engage in work on the road to Edgewood.

April 6, 1916

A German prisoner named Forseller was "found missing" when the roll was called at the Internment Camp on Sunday night, and is still at large, though every effort is being made to locate him. This man is said to be a particularly dangerous alien and served for some time last year in the 54th Battalion, where he had enlisted as a Belgian. Suspicion was aroused and he was arrested as a spy, and found to be a German. It is not known how he affected his escape and apparently there is no clue as to his present whereabouts.

April 13, 1916. Editorial: Interned Prisoners

Perhaps we in Canada err just a little in the treatment accorded to interned aliens. It seems just possible that in our desire to give these imprisoned enemies a "square deal" that we lean too much to the side of clemency. At any rate, nobody acquainted with conditions in the Vernon Internment Camp will accuse the local authorities of undue severity. That kindness and consideration are by no means appreciated by the Germans held in durance here was made amply plain last week when it was found necessary to remove half a dozen of these men who had been guilty of rank insubordination, from the camp to the city jail. Their removal was the signal for a volley of abuse from their compatriots in the camp, who hurled all manner of foul insults at the officers and police, while they loudly cheered the departing prisoners.

We make no comment upon this incident, as the Censor does not encourage criticism of this nature, and we agree in the wisdom of his restrictions. It is permitted, however, to indicate how British prisoners are treated in Germany, and by way of contrast to the manner in which we handle our foes in this country we need do no more than call attention to the following press dispatch. We do not for a moment advocate reprisals in kind. Indeed it would be impossible to conceive of British or Canadian authorities acting in such a manner no matter how sore might be the provocation. But when we have the horrible plight of our countrymen in German prisons brought so forcibly to our notice it is hard to keep one's feelings under control.

September 7, 1916. Prisoners Escape From Internment Camp: Sensational Get-away of Twelve Aliens on Saturday Night

By digging a tunnel nearly one hundred feet in length which started under the kitchen in the Internment Camp and came out on the premises of a nearby German resident named

Frank Scherle, twelve alien prisoners at the Vernon Camp of Detention made their escape on Saturday night.

The work has evidently been carried on for some time as the tunnel was carefully prepared and must have taken a long time in getting it through.

The 30th BC Horse has had parties out scouring the country for the fugitives since Sunday morning, but so far without locating any of them.

Scherle was arrested on Tuesday by Chief Clerke, of the city police, who has been active in this investigation. We do not know what punishment may be given him if he is found guilty, but it will hardly, we imagine, be as severe as that accorded to Nurse Cavell who was shot on the charge of assisting prisoners to escape from German clutches in Belgium.

The tunnel through which the prisoners escaped was not discovered until a large bread box was moved in the kitchen, when the opening beneath it was disclosed. The earth was distributed under the floor of the kitchen which stands some height from the ground.

September 21, 1916

Three of the twelve alien prisoners who escaped from the Internment Camp were captured last week by details of the 30th BC Horse and the 172nd Battalion, and were brought in on Monday. They had worked their way down Kalamalka Lake and across the divide back of Kelowna, to a point near Midway where they were rounded up. The other nine are still at large, though search parties are scouring the country in all directions. It is said that three other men answering the description of the escaped prisoners were recently seen near the Indian reserve at the head of Okanagan Lake, and parties of the 30th BC Horse are now on their trail. The three men brought in say that the escape was made by different parties of prisoners at intervals between 11 o'clock and 3 o'clock, and that they separated as they left the tunnel. No great degree of reliance is placed upon their statements, but it seems evident that they did not hang together after leaving the camp, and it is thought that one party took the direction of the Nicola district.

March 28, 1918

A prisoner escaped from the Alien Internment Camp on Tuesday night. He appears to have climbed the fence between nine and ten o'clock and made his getaway. One is at a loss to know why any German should wish to change the salubrious atmosphere of our model camp for the hostile and unsympathetic environment outside its kindly walls. It appears, however, that even the ties of love fail sometimes to bind the erratic temperament of some of those whose liberty it has been found necessary to curtail.

The Conservative Party Speaks Out

A Conservative prime minister and a Conservative British Columbia premier were among those behind the internment of Ukrainians and other Canadians in 1914. But in 2005, Conservative leader Stephen Harper rose in the House of Commons to call for restitution for those who were interned:

Between 1914 and 1920 Canada witnessed its first internment operations under the *War Measures Act.* Thousands of loyal Canadians were systematically arrested and interned in 24 camps throughout the country simply because of their national origin. Nearly 9,000 Canadians were interned, the vast majority of Ukrainian origin.

At the outset of the First World War, western Ukraine was occupied by the Austro-Hungarian Empire and Canada was of course at war with Austria-Hungary. In the midst of wartime hysteria, everyone with a connection to Austria-Hungary was deemed a threat to our country. Often of course this was simply incorrect. Ironically, in this case many thousands of Ukrainian Canadians had actually fled the occupying power in their homeland. A knowledgeable assessment of the situation could have led to only one conclusion: these refugees of Canada's wartime enemy were not enemies of Canada. They were new, loyal British subjects and allies of our wartime cause.

In fact, in 1915, I should mention that the British foreign office twice instructed Ottawa to grant Ukrainians "preferential treatment," arguing that they were to be considered "friendly aliens" rather than "enemy aliens." Yet the federal government of the time simply would not listen and would not change course.

Throughout the internment operation the civilian internees were transported to Canada's frontier hinterlands where they were forced to perform hard labour under trying circumstances. Some sites that we all know well today, including Banff and Jasper national parks and the experimental farms at Kapuskasing, were first developed by this pool of forced labour. Again ironically, as Ukrainian Canadians were being interned for having been unfortunate enough to enter this country with Austro-Hungarian passports, other Ukrainian Canadians who had entered Canada on different foreign documents were serving Canada loyally in overseas battle.

Let us not forget Ukrainian-Canadian war veteran Philip Konowal, who was awarded the Victoria Cross by King George V for his brave wartime service. He was a Ukrainian Canadian honoured, while at the very same time his fellow neighbours and descendants of Ukraine were wondering why they had chosen Canada to be their new home while they were being interned.

The Spy Scare—Truth or Fiction?

British Columbia was a pretty attractive place to invest in before the recession hit in 1913. British money fuelled the province's expansion in hydro power, railways and mines. Belgian money helped develop the fruit lands in the north Okanagan. And German aristocrats were attracted by the potential to get rich here too.

One former Prussian officer, Constantin Alvo von Alvensleben, helped found the Vancouver Stock Exchange, built a fortune in real estate and was president of some prominent mining and resource companies. He cut a dashing figure and had a full-page profile in the 1913 edition of *Who's Who and Why,* listing his military and business credentials.

When von Alvensleben arrived in Vancouver in 1904, he was almost penniless. But he made the best of the then booming economy. Family connections with the Kaiser helped, and he became influential and wealthy as more and more German aristocrats were drawn to the Alvensleben magic. By 1913 he was widely believed to be a millionaire.

But the recession and then war broke him. When the real estate market collapsed, so did Alvensleben's good luck. German capital started to dry up and Alvensleben couldn't convince his influential friends that good times would soon return. When war was declared in 1914, his German connections turned into a liability.

It didn't help that rivals spread rumours that if the Germans won the war,

Alvensleben would become the "governor" of British Columbia. As a former army officer and an enemy alien, his assets could be seized, and they were while he was travelling outside the country.

Afraid of arrest, Alvensleben and his family fled to the United States, which was still neutral. But when the Americans declared war in 1917, he came under suspicion there and was interned until 1920. After the war, he returned to the business world he loved, trying to rebuild his fortune on both sides of the border. But he never fully recovered financially. He died in Seattle in 1965.

Alvo von Alvensleben—a German spy or just an unlucky businessman.
George T. Wadds photo, City of Vancouver Archives, Port P1082

The Spy at the Baron's Manor

Ask patrons at the Baron's Manor Pub in Port Kells about the building's history and there's no shortage of stories—including a ghost in the attic. Its walls are covered with reproduced photographs from a hundred years ago, and the man who built the once-elegant sixteen-room home figures prominently among them. Carl von Mackensen, a former Prussian cavalry captain emigrated from Germany and built the house in 1910. Locals dubbed it "The Castle" because it had a turret on top and suits of armour in the hallways. The baron farmed chickens and appears to have been a popular member of the community, noted for hosting lavish Christmas parties. When war broke out, everything changed.

In the fall of 1914 the atmosphere was tense with rumours that the German light cruiser *Leipzig* was heading for BC waters after sinking a British freighter; newspapers reported a German flag flying in the interior community of Phoenix; and there were whispers that spies were at work among the population. In 1915 von Mackensen made the mistake of flying the German flag from his rooftop. Locals threatened to shoot it down, and soon he was shipped off to an internment camp in Vernon where he would spend the next four and a half years.

Stories about the baron persisted: a radio room in the turret had been used by the baron to send coded messages to the German Navy, he helped smuggle German nationals across the line into a neutral USA, and one report said he had secret plans to give property to favoured Germans after the war was won. All of von Mackensen's assets were taken from him, and after the war he was deported back to Germany where he died in 1967.

The evidence used against him was lost in an office fire in the sixties, but the stories about the Port Kells spy won't go away. As for that ghost…

Use of Cameras in Canada Under War Conditions

The people of Canada are happy to welcome to their country all those whom they believe to be their friends and wish to do everything possible to make their visits pleasant and free from restrictions.

Baron's Pub in Port Kells. Once the home of Baron von Mackensen—another German accused of being a spy who was sent to internment in Vernon and later deported back to Germany. Courtesy of Mark Forsythe

This pamphlet provided a not-so-subtle warning about just what people could photograph.
Courtesy of Don Stewart

From Our Listeners: Dr. T.B.R. Westgate, POW

By Vic Leach, New Westminster

My maternal grandfather, Dr. T.B.R. Westgate, was a prisoner of war from July 1914 to January 1916 in Kongwa, Tanganyika, which, along with Zanzibar, was part of German East Africa. In 1902, he was employed by the Church Mission Society out of London, United Kingdom, and was sent to Tanganyika where he founded Huron College in 1903 (based on Huron College at his alma mater, Western University in London, Ontario). He had returned to England in 1912 and was asked to go back to Kongwa in 1913 for a short term.

Three hundred and twenty-three kilometres is not a long distance by today's standards to go from Dar Es Salaam to Kongwa, or to the nearest railroad station at Morogoro, which was 194 kilometres from Kongwa. But in those days it was a great trek with people carrying luggage, and it would take a four or five days or so to go this distance. The short stay ended up to be much longer than anticipated as war travel restrictions began in the summer of 1914. His wife and three children—aged ten, nine and four—were left to find their own living in England.

Though he lost a lung because of his incarceration, having it removed in 1918–19, he managed to travel across Western Canada and the North by canoe, snowshoe, train, horse and buggy, and with bush pilots and later by car from as far east as Hudson Bay to Aklavik and western Vancouver Island.

From Our Listeners: Wilderness to the Trenches

By Lori Williams, West Vancouver

My grandfather Rupert Williams, like many other Canadian World War I veterans, was reluctant to talk about his wartime experience. We have reconstructed his service from the few stories he told and his service records.

Rupert Norman Williams was born to a successful green grocer in Greenwich, England, on April 24, 1887. He had three older brothers who had moved to Canada to seek their fortune. His head was full of their stories. Despite his father's reservations, Rupert left Greenwich and travelled to Canada as a young man of eighteen. He made his way across the country to what is now Alberta, where he had adventures that young men in England could only dream about, working as a cowboy, a prospector and miner, a rancher and a curious explorer. He was good with his hands and willing to take on just about any job he was asked to do.

In late 1914, Rupert's boss asked him to travel to the junction of the Finlay and the Parsnip Rivers to do some prospecting. While there, he encountered a Frenchman who told him that England was at war. His loyalty to England was such that he immediately set off to sign up as a soldier. This journey required him to travel by dugout canoe on the Peace River with its many portages. He then walked to Edmonton and made his way to Red Deer to enlist. He joined the Canadian Expeditionary Force as a private serving with the 2nd Canadian Mounted Regiment.

After travelling to England and receiving his training, Rupert landed in France on January 30, 1916. To the best of our knowledge he was transferred to the fighting at Ypres in Belgium in February 1916. Rupert was not a tall man at five feet six and a half inches. While this might have bothered him before the war, in the trenches, he was able to stand up to his full height with his head still below the surface while most other soldiers had to stoop. His small size made him a perfect candidate for digging and crawling through tunnels under the battlefields to intercept German intelligence. This was a necessary task but one he did not relish.

On June 2, 1916, his luck ran out when he was hit by shrapnel in his right forearm and thigh. His arm was broken and badly damaged. He was transported first to Boulogne and then to England for operations and further treatment. He spent months in recovery. He was not very good at sitting still, however, and made himself useful while in hospital until his discharge in February 1917. His medical records contain this note from one of his physicians: "This patient has proven himself a valuable man in this hospital being in charge of the preparations for operations for two months. We would like to have him attached here with us in this capacity."

After his discharge from the hospital, Rupert was unable to return to active duty due to the weakness in his right arm. He was kept busy working for the Canadian Forces as a clerk and later in an assistant nurse role on Canadian hospital ship *Araguaya*, which made twenty voyages during the war and transported 15,324 patients.

When he returned to Canada, Rupert made his way back to Alberta. He later married my grandmother in Calgary and during the Depression they moved to Comox, British Columbia, where they lived and raised their children. Rupert died at ninety-one in 1978 in West Vancouver.

Rupert Norman Williams.
Courtesy of Lori Williams

15

THE WAR'S LASTING LEGACY
INSPIRING ARTS, CULTURE AND SPORT

For most men and women, the Great War was a struggle for survival. For a special few, it would become an inspiration for their creative lives, or an opportunity to put in place the teamwork and discipline they were learning on the sports fields and on the hockey rinks that dotted the young province. Sometimes, athletic heroes became war heroes, and for artists and writers, the horrors of the front lines compelled them to put down in words what their experiences were really like. For the generations to come, the war and its aftermath provided fertile ground for novels, plays and works of history.

Telling the Great War Story in Song, Verse and Novel

> And we're all praying, "Please God, don't let the fighting be over before I can get over there and take part"—*from John Gray's play* Billy Bishop Goes to War

When John Gray and Eric Peterson stepped onto the stage at the Vancouver East Cultural Centre just before Remembrance Day 1978, they didn't realize they had a hit on their hands. *Billy Bishop Goes to War* had all the ingredients for success: catchy tunes, sometimes morbid humour, imaginary dogfights in the sky. But a newspaper strike and a postal strike were also under way, not the best conditions to premiere a new play.

From humble beginnings in Vancouver, *Billy Bishop* went on to play in Toronto, Washington, New York City and Great Britain. Almost forty years later it is often still playing somewhere in the world, a testament to the enduring theme of the little guy caught up in a great war.

That is the legacy of the war, that an event of a hundred years ago still has the power to inspire writers, poets, musicians, artists and photographers. The men in the trenches certainly appreciated the written word. Whether it was a psalm from the Bible or a suspenseful thriller, soldiers at the front ate up whatever they could get their hands on. Books arrived in packages from home and they were a welcome respite from the tedium and terror of the trenches.

The Thirty-Nine Steps by future Canadian Governor General John Buchan came out in 1915, and it was passed from soldier to soldier. An admiring officer wrote to the author:

The "shocker" arrived just before dinner-time, and though, with our early rising, sleep is very precious to us, I lay awake in my dug-out till I had finished the last page. This, I take it, is the supreme test of a "shocker": one should never be able to lay it down. It is just the kind of fiction for here. Long novels I cannot manage in the trenches. One wants something to engross the attention without tiring the mind, in doses not too large to be assimilated in very brief intervals of spare time. The story is greatly appreciated in the midst of mud and rain and shells, and all that could make trench life depressing.

Frederick Niven

Poets tried to put the story of the war in words that would have meaning not only in the trenches, but also on the home front. While John McCrae's "In Flanders Fields" is probably the best known of these, in British Columbia, one of our first successful writers, Frederick Niven, penned a tribute to the famous Christmas Truce of 1914.

In Flanders on the Christmas morn
The trenched foemen lay,
the German and the Briton born,
And it was Christmas Day.

The red sun rose on fields accurst,
The gray fog fled away;
But neither cared to fire the first,
For it was Christmas Day!

They called from each to each across
The hideous disarray,
For terrible has been their loss:
"Oh, this is Christmas Day!"

Their rifles all they set aside,
One impulse to obey;
'Twas just the men on either side,
Just men—and Christmas Day.

They dug the graves for all their dead
And over them did pray:
And Englishmen and Germans said:
"How strange a Christmas Day!"

Between the trenches then they met,
Shook hands, and e'en did play
At games on which their hearts were set
On happy Christmas Day.

Not all the emperors and kings,
Financiers and they
Who rule us could prevent these things—
For it was Christmas Day.

Oh ye who read this truthful rime
From Flanders, kneel and say:
God speed the time when every day
Shall be as Christmas Day.

A heavy howitzer on the Somme—while there was a Christmas truce in 1914, the spirit of goodwill was short-lived.
CWM 19920085-021, George Metcalf Archival Collection, © Canadian War Museum

Alan Twigg of *BC BookWorld* says Niven was "British Columbia's first professional man of letters and the first significant literary figure of the Kootenays. He lived by his wits, as an independent writer, mainly on the outskirts of Nelson, from 1920 until 1944." Niven first came to BC in 1898, and although he was rejected for military service for medical reasons, he wrote for the British Ministry of Information during the war, a job also held by John Buchan.

Hubert Evans

Of the early BC novelists, Frederick Niven was considered one of the best. Hubert Evans was the next generation, a newspaperman who wanted to write serious stuff. Evans spent a few months writing for the *Nelson Daily News* before enlisting with the 54th Kootenay Battalion in 1915. He moved to the Signal Corps in 1916 and was wounded at Ypres. By the end of the war, he was a lieutenant.

Evans managed to keep a pen close by through his wartime experiences. He wrote some very entertaining dispatches back to the Nelson paper from training camp in Vernon:

> Everyone in camp attended church parade on Sunday, including that loyal old reprobate, Casey Jones, our battle-scarred veteran bull dog, who disgraced himself by becoming involved in a fight. No, that is hardly fair to the old boy. Two collies started it, and so shocked Casey's sense of Sabbath sobriety that he sailed in and well nigh did for one of the belligerents. He dragged him over the ground and hung to the young upstart until he howled for help. His part of the service ended, Casey fell asleep among the men of the number 2 platoon.

The front didn't provide much inspiration for humour. Evans' biographer Alan Twigg says of that experience, "in response to the horrors he witnessed in the trenches as a soldier in WWI, Evans wrote an autobiographical novel, *The New Front Line* (1927), about a soldier named Hugh Henderson who migrates from older societies to the 'new front line' of idealism in the wilds of BC."

The insatiable desire for something to read.
E.T. Sampson photo, City of Vancouver Archives, Gr War P33

The New Front Line isn't one of Evans's best books and is long out of print, but it does capture the mood of returned soldiers seeking some kind of solace out on the land. Much more successful was Evans's *Mist on the River* (1954), a novel that inspired many other Canadian writers and earned him the title of "elder of the tribe."

Peregrine Acland

Hubert Evans wasn't the only newspaperman from BC to join up and then write about his experiences. Peregrine Acland was editing the *Prince Rupert Daily News* but enlisted in September 1914 when the war was just getting under way.

On his way to England, Acland wrote a rather idealistic war poem called "The Reveille of Romance":

Peregrine Acland was a newspaperman in Prince Rupert before writing a Great War novel.
48th Highlanders Museum

> All come to that gay festival of rifle, lance, and sword
> Where toasts are pledged in hot heart's blood and Death sits at the board;
> For laughing love dreams its delight on lawns of asphodel,
> But when the world makes holiday it seeks the courts of Hell.
>
> Now Cossack, Briton, Gaul and Serb clash with the Goth and Hun
> Upon grim fields where whoso yields Romance at least has won:
> For, amidst all the dying there, the battle-flame and thunder
> Herald rebirth of Joy-in-Life, the Renaissance of Wonder.
>
> Though warriors fall like frosted leaves before October winds
> They only lose what all must love, but find what none else finds
> Save those proud souls that strive to soar beyond their mortal bars
> And brooding on Olympian heights are fellows to the stars.

The poem continues on—a little flowery for contemporary readers—and closes with these words:

> Who sighs then for the Golden Age? Romance has raised her head
> And in the sad and sombre days walks proudly o'er the dead,
> —But had we served her loyally through all the vanished years
> We might have had the cup of joy without the price of tears.

This kind of writing was common in the opening year of the war. Rudyard Kipling, who was to lose his own son on the Western Front, wrote in similarly idealistic terms in September 1914:

> For all we have and are,
> For all our children's fate,
> Stand up and meet the war.
> The Hun is at the gate!
> Our world has passed away
> In wantonness o'erthrown.
> There is nothing left to-day
> But steel and fire and stone.

Peregrine Acland was seriously wounded at the Somme and wrote about his experiences in the 1929 novel *All Else Is Folly,* one of the classic books about the Great War. Ford Maddox Ford thought the book was pretty good and wrote the preface. "It will be little less than a scandal if this book is not read enormously widely," he wrote on the dust jacket. *All Else Is Folly* is now back in print.

Robert Service was a bank clerk in Victoria and Kamloops and later wrote a book of poetry about his Red Cross service.
Library and Archives Canada / PA-110158

Robert Service

Robert Service spent time as a bank clerk in Victoria and Kamloops before he was transferred to the Klondike. He became known as the "Canadian Kipling." Poetry made him rich and in 1912, he left the Klondike for good. He was forty-one when the war broke out and tried to enlist. His varicose veins kept him out of the fight. But he worked for a time as a stretcher bearer and ambulance driver for the American Red Cross until health problems forced him back to Paris, where he wrote *Rhymes of a Red Cross Man* (1916). The book is dedicated to the memory of his brother, "Lieutenant Albert Service, Canadian Infantry, Killed in Action, France, August 1916."

High and low, all must go:
Hark to the shout of War!
Leave to the women the harvest yield;
Gird ye, men, for the sinister field;
A sabre instead of a scythe to wield:
War! Red War!

Rich and poor, lord and boor,
Hark to the blast of War!
Tinker and tailor and millionaire,
Actor in triumph and priest in prayer,
Comrades now in the hell out there,
Sweep to the fire of War!

Sachimaro Moro-oka

A unique perspective on the front-line fighting can be found in Sachimaro Moro-oka's book, *On to the Arras Front.* Japanese Canadians had a difficult time enlisting with BC regiments because of racism. As mentioned earlier, they had a much easier time enlisting in Alberta, where regiments didn't have a race bar.

Moro-oka arrived in Canada in 1906 and worked as a fisherman on the Skeena River. He enlisted with 175th Battalion (based in Medicine Hat) along with over fifty other Japanese British Columbians. When he left Alberta for the front, hundreds of people lined the streets and actually shouted, "Hooray for the Japanese." Moro-oka was wounded at Vimy. Roy Ito, in his book on Japanese war experiences, *We Went to War,* captures some of Moro-oka's memories.

A shell exploded among a group of men and created a terrible mixture of blood, flesh and mud. We looked on in horror. There were bodies with no heads. One poor soul was blinded, blood pouring from his eyes. We crawled over the parapet. We were already cold and wet as we slid into a water-filled shell hole to escape the bullets flying over our heads. We encountered dead men, Germans and Canadians. Stretcher bearers were out searching for the wounded. I wondered how men could possibly survive such conditions.

Moro-oka wrote a haiku that Roy Ito translated:

Hei o yaru
Rhine no kawa ya
Yuk ke mizu.

Soldiers advancing to the Rhine
disappear like snow
falling into water.

Moro-oka was wounded and sent to a hospital in England and when King George and Queen Mary visited, the King seemed fascinated by Moro-oka. "Are you Japanese? Can you speak English? How is your wound? When did you join the Canadian Army?"

Stage and Song

An interview with John Gray

The story of flying ace Billy Bishop as told and performed by John Gray and Eric Peterson brought this Canadian hero to a new generation. *Billy Bishop Goes to War* was launched at the Vancouver East Cultural Centre in 1978. Here's Mark's conversation with John Gray.

Mark Forsythe: How did you immerse yourself in the Billy Bishop story?

John Gray: Way back then, we were interested in Canadian heroes because we hadn't really heard of a lot of them. They weren't being taught in school, nobody knew about them, and there was this general assumption that they weren't very interesting. And so, the actor Eric Peterson came across this book that Bishop wrote himself between his two tours of duty, and we thought either this guy was a homicidal maniac or there is something about Canadians that we don't really explore very much. Of the top ten air aces, six of them were Canadian. The Canadian contribution to that war effort was so far beyond anything that our population would have justified, the whole idea of Canadians as a sort of pacific people that don't fight was certainly belied by these guys.

Mark: If you could go back to the seat at the Vancouver East Cultural Centre, what was it like to roll Billy Bishop out for the first time?

John: We were totally unconfident that anyone would be the least bit interested because he was unknown by then. I think Pierre Berton did some things on television on him, but just little snippets of his statistics. We had no confidence whatsoever that the people in British Columbia would give a damn.

Mark: And what was the initial reaction to it?

John: The initial reaction was just a slow buildup. We had a simultaneous newspaper strike and a post office strike. It wasn't ideal to get the word out! We blamed it on that when we would start with 40 percent houses, and after two weeks we were selling out like crazy. But that became the rule as we toured all over Canada: the first or second performance would be 40 percent houses, and then by the end it would be packed out. It just seemed to catch on by word of mouth.

Mark: This was after the anti-war movement of the sixties and early seventies. Who did you notice in the audience?

John: There were lots of First World War vets alive then. Don MacLaren—another BC ace from North Vancouver—he came. He was pretty deaf but he was that fighter-pilot size, a bantam size that most of them seemed to have. And we would get a lot of World War II guys as well. One of the things that we felt very strongly was the anti-war movement, when it spread over to the notion that not only is war a bad thing, which is a little like saying cancer's a bad thing. But to go on and say that the guys that fought then were deluded or stupid, that kind of characterization was really wrong. Second World War vets were kind of grateful that somebody actually bothered to get the details right, what it was like to be there. Not knowing how it was going to turn out.

We tend to treat both world wars as though they were scheduled to be over in 1918 or 1945. They weren't. As far as people were concerned at the time, that was life—that was the rest of their lives, and for many of them it was. And so we'd go backstage after the show and these guys who are vice-presidents of oil companies or transportation companies, they'd be coming in and telling us their own stories with their arms stretched out like kids behind them as though they were planes. It was really kind of touching.

Mark: And as a performer, what was it like playing to someone who had experienced the front—what are you thinking as you're going through your performance?

John: For the first while we felt a little embarrassed. Here we were portraying something, and the biggest danger that we faced was that we might not get sufficient applause. So we felt a bit shallow. But their generosity was unbelievable. Even years later, when we were doing the show in remounts, we'd have people who flew jet fighters in Korea who'd come back. That was almost the best part of it. Sometimes it would be guys who were in the trenches. One guy claimed to have seen him [Bishop]; he was at Passchendaele and he got into the RAF as a mechanic because as he put it "I got tired of the mud." They're very good at understatement, and he claimed to have seen one of Bishop's victories.

Mark: It strikes me as an authentic connection with an audience that doesn't happen very often.

John: No, it doesn't. The wonderful thing is we did it again at the age of sixty-two, the age Bishop was when he died. We had to play him as an old man because we were old men. People came who had brought their parents to the show, and now they were bringing their kids to the show.

Mark: Here we are one hundred years later, is it still important to acknowledge what happened at that time?

John: Unless we really get our heads around what that war was like for Canada, we will never have any sense of how we got where we are now. That was the signal event of the last one hundred years. Before that, the assumption was that in all ways our superior civilization, European civilization which Canada was a part of, was getting better and better. And then suddenly this superior civilization found itself in a bloodbath that was the worst thing that had ever happened in the history of the world. That in itself turns the whole twentieth century into an addendum to the First World War. Plus, before the First World War, Canadians were a bunch of colonial hicks. That's what we were looked at as by the British and the French—but suddenly they realized that it was a good thing to be strong, to have a high pain threshold, to handle machinery, to be able to ride horses and to be able to deflect when you're shooting ducks so that the target will run into your bullet. All of these skills that suddenly became so important in the First World War were things that Canadians had. And they realized what they had in common...and that had more to do with building the country than anything else.

Broken Ground

AN INTERVIEW WITH JACK HODGINS

Novelist and short story writer Jack Hodgins lives on southern Vancouver Island. He was raised in the small rural community of Merville in the Comox Valley. Jack's fiction has won the Governor General's Award. He is the 2006 recipient of the Terasen Lifetime Achievement Award "for an outstanding literary career in British Columbia" and the Lieutenant-Governor's Award for Literary Excellence. In 2010 the Governor General appointed him to the Order of Canada. His 1999 novel, *Broken Ground,* is an exploration of the dark, brooding presence of World War I in the lives of the inhabitants of a "soldier's settlement" on Vancouver Island. It won the Ethel Wilson Fiction Prize. Mark spoke with him about Merville and his World War I research.

Mark Forsythe: Who named Merville?

Jack Hodgins: It was the veterans of the First World War who populated this place, which was nothing but wilderness before. The BC government had some arrangement for these plots of land to be available to returned soldiers. So when I came along several years later, I was surrounded by these adults who had fought in the First World War and had great stories to tell if you could get them to tell.

One of them gave me the impression he had actually dug the Panama Canal himself! They had this very interesting past, which took me most of my life to actually dig out of people, or read about them when a number of members of the community decided some of their memories should be recorded. A little book was made and put together on the history of Merville, where different families contributed their own stories. It was like the second or third generation writing down the tales that their parents or grandparents or great-grandparents had told. There's a record of them meeting and deciding on a name for the place and so they went through all kinds of possibilities that sounded more like modern real-estate developments—very romantic sounding.

But eventually they decided on Merville because it was the name of a little community in France where many of them had fought.

This really intrigued me, of course. I was dying to see the original Merville and a number of years ago, the cultural minister of France invited a number of Canadian writers to come over for a special festival. I was chosen to be one of the ten people, from right across the country. Having met a number of the photographers and moviemakers they sent ahead of time to film us in our own territory, I got friendly with one of them, and was asking about the location of this original Merville. It turned out to be Merville-au-Bois, a not-too-long drive from Paris. This fellow offered to drive me up there, so I spent a day in the original Merville, was introduced to the mayor of this little place, who told me tales of its past, walked me around and showed me the remains of one of the trenches that still hadn't been completely filled in. It's actually a village of no more than two blocks long sitting out in the middle of farmland, and not very far from a number of war memorials in the area.

Mark: Were you able to think why these soldiers who returned might have wanted to honour this place this way?

Jack: He showed me one photograph—in fact he gave it to me—it was a postcard type of photograph of a number of soldiers who looked as if they were camped out in a local barn or very large building of some kind. He gave me the impression that they probably stayed in that village for quite a long time before moving on to some other part of the battlefield.

I got the impression it seemed to be a fairly central part of a central battle at a certain time. So he was very happy to talk about what he knew, or what he was told by his parents about the battle, and we had a nice dinner in his home.

Before I left he said, "I have something to give you." He went outside and came back in and had this ten-inch-high shell casing. It's about two-and-a-half inches wide and ten inches long. He'd taken it outside and he filled it up with dirt and he said, "Here, you can take this memory of the war and this soil from the original Merville and take it to your Merville to scatter it on the ground." So I was absolutely thrilled with this as you can imagine—this is a wonderful thing to be taking home. But you know I got back in my hotel in Paris and started to worry that I would not be allowed on the plane with French soil in my suitcase. It broke my heart, but I had to empty the shell...so I dumped the soil out into the wastepaper basket in the Paris hotel, and clutched the shell casing to myself and brought it home.

Mark: Where does it sit now?

Jack: It sits on the windowsill at the back of my desk so that whenever I'm working it's just there, between me and the trees outside.

Mark: This all happened as you were thinking about and researching your novel Broken Ground, which is kind of the story of Merville. Did it help you?

John: It did very much. I had long been thinking I should be doing something with this. Nobody else has written a piece of fiction based on the people who settled here or on this piece of land. Maybe I have a responsibility to do it, and I had always been fascinated with the First World War, partly because of having grown up among these people. After I got home and started writing, an opportunity came for me to go back to France to a conference and I went back to Merville-au-Bois, just to renew my memory and to say hello to the mayor and his wife who had been so good to me. But all of it sort of accumulated, and I practically memorized the book of memoirs by the settlers of Merville and acknowledged that in the back of the novel *Broken Ground.*

[Jack talks about visiting the Vimy Monument to take part in a ceremony.]

I was driven there by a young French couple who claimed to not really understand why I cared about it, but nevertheless were very kind and took me out there. It was the day of the ceremony itself, so there were a lot of people gathered. A brutally cold day. The literally white monument standing up against the sky made my whole self go cold to see it. There was something so powerful in it...and I had the time to walk through some of the tunnels that had been preserved and showed how the Canadian soldiers had been hiding and waiting for the chance to take the attack that was eventually successful—and not so successful in others. A great place, a great moment. There was a moment when we were all gathered together beneath the monument to sing "O Canada." It wasn't a very large crowd, but it was very moving indeed. I hadn't anticipated the reaction that I had. So much of what Canada is now has its roots in that Vimy battle, the sense of identifying with this country, even while fighting alongside the other countries, I think it must have made a huge difference to the way people felt when they came back to their homes. It really was home...and opportunities to create new homes as they settled new parts of the country. Personally I think it's one of the most important things that we can remember—most important moments, most important events, most important place maybe.

Three Victoria Soldiers' Poems

By Robert Taylor, Victoria

Selected from Victoria newspapers and one regimental magazine, these three poems express something of the education, values and mortal concerns of many Canadian soldiers in the Great War. The first expresses the idealism and romanticism of some recruits; the second reveals the fear and necessary courage of the soldier under fire; the third, with bitter humour, suggests a soldier's sense of alienation from some civilians and their misguided concerns. Victoria's soldiers shared these attributes with their compatriots, but tended to be more literate and to feel more deeply "British" than was the case with servicemen elsewhere in the Dominion.

Born in 1887, Edward M.B. Vaughan trained with the Victoria Fusiliers at the Willows Camp. He was killed in May 1917.

The First Canadian Expeditionary Force

They rose at honor's bidding
To save the land from shame.
Their names shall live forever
On Britain's roll of fame.
Their limbs were torn and shattered
By German shot and shell.

Yet still their spirit triumphs
Though strewn in heaps they fell.
For every fallen hero
A hundred bayonets shine,
To guard our red cross banner
On many a hard fought line.
The crimson banners swelling
On every wind that blows
Hold firm the cause of Freedom
Against unnumbered foes.

Hail to the deathless heroes!
The first to draw the blade;
Their lives and homes and loved ones
On Freedom's altars laid.
They rose at honor's bidding
To save the land from shame.
Their names shall live forever
On Britain's roll of fame.

Daily Times, August 4, 1917

As did many of Victoria's soldier poets, Vaughan retained a romantic view of modern combat, imagining "banners swelling" and referring to the enemy with archaic words such as "foes." He believed that he was fighting for "honor" and "freedom." Typical of many of Victoria's soldier-poets was Vaughan's loyalty to Britain and its Empire, not to Canada.

Kenneth George Halley of Salt Spring Island, born in 1879, served with the First Canadian Pioneer Battalion at the Battle of Courcelette in 1916, which cost Canada 24,029 casualties.

Afterwards

The battle's over now. The regiments stand
Shattered and worn upon the ridge they've won.
Staring with weary eyes o'er "No Man's Land,"
Clouded in smoke which masks the morning sun,
Praying a quick relief may come before
Endurance dies, and they can fight no more.

A silence settles down o'er the battle ground.
The brazen voices of the guns are still
Tho' every breach contains a waiting round
Eager to scream across the captured hill,
To headlong hurl the hostile legions back
And crumble to the dust their fierce attack.

The battle's over now, the joy bells peal,
And all thro' Britain's Empire hand clasps hand;
The platform speakers praise our wall of steel;
Hysteric crowds cheer madly thro' the land.
But could they see the ground that we have won,
They'd cease their cheering e'er they well begun.

Blackened and scarred, scorched by a poisoned breath,
Stand remnants of a forest dead and still.
Nothing could live before the hand of death
Which fell with dread precision on the hill
And other forms in grey and khaki dressed
Lie 'neath the trees in never-ending rest.

Crater joins crater where the great shells came,
Amid the tangled wire and liquid mud,
Where ruined villages still smoke and flame,
And streamlets turn to pools of slime and blood.
While here and there, its day of warfare done,
Half hid in earth there lies a shattered gun.

Look near the forts that drown the captured hill,
Mixed with the clay and trampled in the mire,
Small grim-faced heaps are lying stiff and still,
Caught by the blast of dread machine gun fire;
They fell a ripened harvest to the gun,
And every man is some poor mother's son.

But watch the ridge: a sudden movement there;
A hushed expectancy that one can feel
As tho' some mighty voice had cried "Beware!"

See from the hostile trench a gleam of steel,
Then high above a brilliant rocket soars,
And down between the lines the barrage roars.

Gone is the silence—nerve destroying screams
Herald the shells which hurtle thro' the air;
Columns of mud spout up in fan-shaped streams,
Splinters of steel are shrieking everywhere,
While powder smoke, a reeking, dusky pall,
Falls like a great drop curtain over all.

Thro' the dense fog the rifle bullets whine;
Rattling machine guns hurl their leaden rain:
Wave after wave breaks on the thinning line,
Rolling away to form and charge again,
While thro' this hellish music loudly runs
The never ending thunder of the guns.

Crowded and close the wavering advance
Crouches to bursts of shrapnel overhead.
Down thro' their ranks the high explosives dance.
Hell's imps and outcasts dancing for the dead,
All wreathed in smoke that ghoulish ballet there,
Mocks these poor wrecks who lie too still to care.

Grumbling and slow the thunder dies away
Like some gorged beast by slaughter satisfied.
Slowly the smoke lifts and the light of day
Floods to the ridge where countless men have died.
Look, you of England, see them lying there,
Stout, stalwart sons your Empire ill could spare…

Daily Colonist, March 13, 1918

Like Vaughan, Halley could not avoid using archaic romantic words such as "legions" but he also described realistically the nature of combat in the Great War. The poem comes closer than almost any other piece of verse published in Victoria during the war to giving a real sense of a modern battlefield.

Moreover, he expresses a sense of identity with the enemy which was not uncommon among Canadian servicemen; that is, "forms in gray [the colour of the German uniforms] and khaki."

Like Vaughan, he was proud to be "British" and identified with the British Empire.

An untitled poem by Private John Mynott suggests that, while perhaps fighting for "honor" and "freedom," many a Victoria soldier had more mundane concerns. Like most Canadian soldiers, he did not support the prohibition of alcohol sales. Training at the Willows Camp in Victoria, thirty-year-old Mynott proposed a pithy toast:

Here's to a temperance supper
With water in glasses tall,
And coffee and tea to end with—
And me not there at all.

Western Scot, January 26, 1916

The Canucks' daily tot of rum gave him warmth in damp cold trenches, a temporary sense of well-being and a brief surge of courage before going "over the top."

These and other poems can be found in Robert Ratcliffe Taylor's book, The Ones Who Have to Pay: The Soldiers-Poets of Victoria BC in the Great War.

From Our Listeners: "Joe in 1916"

By Scott Gould, Vancouver

A song I wrote tells a story that was told to me many times by my grandfather about his brother Joe, who was machine-gunned in World War I. He was crossing a footbridge and got it all down one side of his body. He was brought back to England and placed in a convalescent hospital in a converted Chivers Jam factory in Kent.

My grandfather, then in his twenties and not having seen any family since he ran away from home at thirteen, went to see Joe and took him out exploring in a wicker wheelchair. They spied some tasty-looking apples over an orchard wall, so my grandfather climbed over to get some and the keeper chased them down the street, apples flying everywhere.

Joe eventually died of his injuries, I believe, and I don't know if my grandfather ever laid eyes on another member of his immediate family. But afterward he called all young men (and the occasional young woman) "Joe." We were all called Joe, all the time. I guess he just wanted a chance to say the name.

Being of fairly diminutive stature, he was always amazed at the height attained by his sons and grandsons, and was often heard to remark to my grandmother, "Gee, Joe is growing tall. Eh?"

My grandfather was one of the more amazing gardeners in a family full of green thumbs (on both sides). That gift did not come to me, however, though I do have a very clear memory of Grandad showing my father and me how to graft apples onto root stock.

Here's my song.

Joe in 1916

If I hold really still
I can hear you, Joe,
in the creaking of this wicker chair, you know.
And I still see those apples hanging over the wall, long ago.
It must have been fall, Joe.

Remember us laughing and the wheels of the chair?
The tumbling apples on the cobblestone stair,
and the keeper was calling
to bring back the ones that I stole
for you long ago, Joe.

Everywhere I go, I see you go.
Every seed I sow, I sow two.

One is for you.
Every gun seems like the one that got you
in the setting sun, everyone saw it but you.
Slim chance you'd pull through, Joe.

It's for apples we fought
and decidedly not
for sixteen more months
in this hospital cot.
Mr. Chivers you gave him so much, gave a lot—
Thanks for the thought.

Every gun seems like the one that got you.
In the setting sun, everyone saw it but you,
on the bridge at Verdun.

If I hold really still
I still see you, Joe,
in the orchard and down by the sea, and so
when I look at these apples hanging over my wall,
in the fall
and my sons growing tall,

Everywhere I go, you go too.
Every seed I sow, I see you
sowing for two.
Every son seems like the one you should see
if the sun at Verdun had been shining for me.
It wasn't to be, Joe.

Now the blossoms are over the wall, you see
and my grandsons are growing as tall as the tree,
and the keeper is calling
to bring back the one that I stole
when all along it was you, Joe.

Words and music by Scott Gould, March 23, 2013
To listen to the song, go to http://cherriesinthedish.com/2013/05/30/joe-in-1916-words-music-by-scott-gould/.

From Our Listeners: The War Diary of Corporal Kempling

Contributed by Chris Kempling, Salt Spring Island

Almost a hundred years ago, a twenty-two-year old carpenter from St. Catharines, Ontario, landed in northern France as a soldier in the Battle of the Somme. His name was Corporal George Kempling, and he was my grandfather. He kept a daily diary of his three months in the field, from June 29 to October 7, 1916. The Battle of the Somme lasted from July to November that year and cost over 1.2 million casualties. My grandfather was one of them, but he was one of the lucky ones, because he survived. These are excerpts from the war diary of Corporal Kempling, 5th Platoon, "B" Company, 26th Battalion, 5th Brigade, 2nd Canadian Division.

Wednesday, July 12, 1916: At last we have had notice to leave for the front line, or, as the boys say in careless way, "up the line." On the troop transport we were crowded on top of each other like a bunch of pups in a basket. We docked at Le Havre at 5:30 a.m. and marched 5 miles to our first camp. On the way we came by a big job of filling in a ravine done by German prisoners. They were a pretty glum looking lot. At the camp we took up advanced instruction in shooting, bayonet work, charging from trench to trench and other stunts. About 14 men a day are hurt, mostly by jumping in and out of trenches with rifles and fixed bayonets. One man landed on his bayonet and buried it up to the hilt in his right side.

Wednesday, July 19: About 1:30 this morning a German aeroplane, flying low dropped three bombs on our officers' quarters, but none of them went off. We brought down four planes with our anti-aircraft fire that night. Life for a man who don't gamble is a bit slow, for it is nothing but pitching pennies, playing Crown and Anchor and poker. They are a nice bunch of fellows, though so many get drunk every night. If a man don't drink, chew, smoke or gamble, he is out of a lot, but I promised Gussie I wouldn't.

Monday, July 24, Flanders, Belgium: Sunday seems to be as good a fighting day as any other. We have 150 rounds of ammunition and two gas helmets each. The gas used by the Germans is usually chlorine gas…Everybody hopes the war will be over in six weeks, but it looks like another winter to us.

Tuesday, July 25: Three men were killed by snipers in the trenches not far from us. One dugout was blown in, killing seven men in it by a bursting Fritzie rum-jug, as the heavy shells are called.

Thursday, July 27: I feel a little sick at the stomach at the prospect of a hand to hand fight; and excited too, but I was really hankering for a mix-up. I guess it is the old John Bull in a fellow.

Saturday, August 5: Fritzie has our railway line marked, for bunches of machine gun bullets whistled close over my head, and an occasional sniper's bullet passed right through where I had taken my head down from between the ties just a second before. The work party in front of us had one of their men shot twice in the neck. His neck and face was covered with blood and our stretcher bearer thought he was dead…Went to Renningheist for a bath and a change today. Three miles there, three miles back. Whew! Long walk for a bath.

Monday, August 14: Today King George and Sir Douglas Haig visited the camp and our little hut was the only one he visited. We intend putting up the Royal coat of arms and a notice saying "Patronized by Royalty."

Monday, August 21: I have fired my first shot at Fritzie. He sent over a whiz bang which burst just on top of the parapet. Three of us were thrown flat by the force of the explosion and half buried in dirt. That is about as near death as I have come yet.

Friday, Sept. 15: A wonderful new machine was used for the first time today, in the history of the world. It is a sort of armoured car, armed with two 4-inch Hotchkiss guns and eight machine guns. The machine is like a flattened out square and has no wheels, just a continuous track. When the Germans saw fifteen of these machines on our Canadian front, heading our charge it scared them so stiff our boys walked right through them.

Sunday, Oct. 1: At last, Fritzie got a direct hit on the roof of our bunker. Owing to it being an extra heavily timbered roof the shell did not burst inside. But it bashed the roof in and drove a beam down on my head, forced my front teeth out and splintered the rest. After I had recovered, I ran to a nearby dugout trying to eat something, I collapsed and cried like a baby. Two days and a night with nothing to eat, fighting or working continuously, with no sleep and at last, this crack on the head did me in. So I went out with three other walking cases.

Saturday, Oct, 7: I'm at the Casualty Clearing Station and expect to move out any moment. Every time I think of the front line experience I had, I turn violently sick at the stomach. God grant that I may get to England for a while as my nerve is gone.

My grandfather was suffering from shell shock, or post-traumatic stress syndrome as it's called now. For years afterward he would go to pieces at a loud unexpected sound, and became deaf for most of his adult life. On Remembrance Day, I wear the poppy and remember that my grandfather put his life at risk in the fields of Flanders so his grandchildren could enjoy the peace we now have.

Corporal George H. Kempling, 26th Battalion.
Courtesy of Chris Kempling

From Our Listeners: A Boy Soldier's Diary

By Victoria Drybrough, Port Alberni

My father, Harry Kendall Cross, was born in 1899, the youngest of five boys. His eldest brother was much older and lived in the US, and two other brothers were medically unfit for service. But Fred, seven years older than my father, was the dynamic, fun-loving brother who kept the family's spirits up through good times and bad. He enlisted on March 23, 1915, at the age of twenty-two. Desperate to be with his brother, my father enlisted on December 14, 1915, lying about his age to qualify. Believing him to be staying with relatives and working in England, my grandmother didn't realize what he had done until June 1917, when she wrote to the overseas Military Forces of Canada and told them what had happened.

I have the letter from the Canadian Record Office, Old Bailey, London, dated September 1, 1917, informing her that my father had been located and returned to England where he would be "retained" until he turned nineteen.

On October 8, 1918, Fred—a corporal in the 3rd Battalion, Canadian Machine Gun Corps—died in the military hospital at Etaples from gunshot wounds. My father's diary began on January 1, 1919, when he is already in France with "C" Battery, 1st Canadian Machine Gun Battalion.

Etaples, France, New Year's Day, 1919: I have learned that Fred was wounded twice. Once on Oct. 1, 1918. He refused to go to D.S. and was fatally wounded on Oct. 5, 1918.

January 7, 1919: I am very anxious for my mother who is seriously ill over Fred's death.

January 23: I went down to visit Fred's grave. I wish I had enough money to buy a wreath.

On January 31, he left Etaples for the Canadian Embarkation Camp at Le Havre. On February 1 he wrote:

I am sick and weary of this damned box car. There is 1/2 inch of coal dust on the floor and 33 of us in the car. We are all about frozen. If we only had a bottle of rum or whisky we could sleep.

There seem to have been few comforts, even in England.

February 9, 1919: We are all lousy, broke, and have had no leave. If they don't do something by tonight we are going to riot. We want our leave.

And the following day:

The riot started at six p.m. last night. The infantry turned out with fixed bayonets but were driven off. We raided all the NACB canteens and all YMCAs. Also Tin Town. Things are very serious and a number of casualties are reported. They have brought up some reinforcements, but it's no use. They can't stop it. Some have been bayonetted.

On March 7, he reported another riot at Kimmel Park, Rhyll, North Wales. Five were killed, including a VC major, and forty were wounded. After two months in England, he finally set sail from Liverpool of April 1, 1919, aboard the White Star liner *Megantic*. I noticed he wrote about the rousing welcome the troops received in Halifax and cities in Eastern Canada. The farther west they came, the less welcome they received.

My father was just nineteen years old when he arrived home in Hastings Park, Vancouver, on April 15, 1919. "I wish poor old Fred was coming home too," he wrote. My grandmother never regained her health after the loss of her son.

Harry Kendall Cross (far right) and Fred Cross (third from right) with relatives in England.
Courtesy of Victoria Drybrough

British Columbia's Athletes Go to War

Young men (and women) in pre-war British Columbia were as "sports mad" as they are today. Amateur leagues for baseball, lacrosse, curling and canoeing were incredibly popular. And hockey was on the rise as covered arenas started to spring up on the West Coast. And it wasn't just a big city sport. All through the Boundary and Kootenay in mining and smelter towns you could see high-calibre hockey games with professional players. The mountain mining community of Phoenix had an outstanding team and would have challenged for the Stanley Cup in 1911—but their letter arrived too late. The story of the 1915 Stanley Cup had a happier ending for British Columbia

The men from this province who went to war were champions in many games of skill. Two men competed internationally in marksmanship. In the Okanagan, recruits cut their teeth racing eighteen-foot war canoes. And others excelled at track and field and mountaineering.

The love of sport continued at the front. British soldiers went over the top kicking footballs in front of them to steel their nerves. And at Christmas 1914, along the Western Front, British and German troops played football during an improvised truce.

Men in search of something to remind themselves of the normal life back home embraced their love of the game. And the endurance, discipline and teamwork they developed through play proved invaluable in the trenches, where instinct and a cool head could mean the difference between survival and death.

Some didn't make it home. In the Okanagan, that spelled the end of the war canoe league for over a decade. But stories like the ones we found still have the power to inspire.

Hockey Was Big during the War Years

As Canadians entered the trenches at Flanders in March 1915 news from the front was grim, and daily casualty reports were a must-read in local newspapers. But Vancouver's hockey fans did have something to cheer. Frank Patrick's Vancouver Millionaires claimed the Stanley Cup in convincing fashion—the first team from the fledgling Pacific Coast Hockey Association (PCHA) to do so.

The One and Only Vancouver Stanley Cup

Brothers Frank and Lester Patrick were professional hockey players who came west to work in their father's logging and sawmill operation at Nelson. After Joe Patrick sold the business in 1911 they combined a love for the game with entrepreneurship to create a new hockey league on the West Coast. The Patricks built the country's first artificial ice arena at the corner of Georgia and Denman Streets, with enough seating for 10,500 spectators. A brick exterior prompted locals to dub the new arena "The Pile." The Patricks wanted to keep fans in the seats and that meant bringing in stars from the east and opening up the game by allowing forward passes, a blue line and penalty shots. Goalies were also allowed to move around. Spectators watching that 1915 Stanley Cup series against the Ottawa Senators were witnessing the future of the game, as these innovations were later adopted by the NHL. Frank Patrick was responsible for twenty-two rule changes that stand to this day. His brother Lester ran the PCHA team in Victoria, where his Cougars won the cup in 1915.

Frank wore multiple hats: owner, manager, coach and player. Frederick "Cyclone" Taylor was a true star lured from the east who led the team with six goals as they swept the eastern champions three games to none (6–2, 8–3 and 12–3). Twenty thousand fans watched the three playoff games, some travelling into the city from Chilliwack and other Fraser Valley communities via the BC Electric line. They paid anywhere from fifty cents for cheap seats to fourteen dollars for box seats—a small fortune when the average day's pay was about two dollars. Craig Bowlsby described the Millionaires' Stanley Cup victory in his book, *Empire of Ice:* "The Vancouver dressing room was a mass of celebration. Ottawa's haughty reserve broke down, and the Senators crowded into the Millionaires' sanctum to give their congratulations. They readily admitted that they had been beaten by the better team."

Millionaires star Fred "Cyclone" Taylor.
Stuart Thomson photo, City of Vancouver Archives, CVA 99-778

Art Duncan, Flying Ace

William James Arthur "Art" Duncan played with the team in the 1915–16 season, then enlisted with the CEF. Before going overseas he suited up with the 228th Battalion hockey club of the National Hockey Association in Toronto. He would soon trade a hockey stick for the control stick of an aeroplane, scoring eleven victories with the Royal Flying Corps. Duncan was awarded a Military Cross, and later a Bar to his Military Cross:

> For conspicuous gallantry and devotion to duty. This officer sighted fifteen enemy scouts attacking eight of ours and immediately joined in, destroying one enemy aeroplane, which fell with a wing off. He then attacked and drove down three other machines, maintaining the fight until the eight had got back to their lines. He has also, with another officer, destroyed an Albatross scout, which he followed down to a height of 200 feet, in spite of heavy machine-gun fire from the ground.

On his return from the Great War, Captain Duncan rejoined the Millionaires and played professional hockey and coached until his final season with the Toronto Maple Leafs in 1931.

Art Duncan.
Stuart Thomson photo, Vancouver Public Library 17979

The War's Lasting Legacy

Essential for Morale

When he wasn't playing hockey or lacrosse, Cyclone Taylor worked for the British Columbia Department of Immigration and volunteered two weeks into the war. But immigration officials were considered too important, and Taylor was made exempt from service. So was team owner Frank Patrick, who wanted to establish a Sportsmen's Battalion like those being raised in the east, but his professional hockey team was deemed essential for morale on the home front. Other professional hockey players enlisted, including Allan "Scotty" Davidson, a fast skating star who captained his Toronto Blueshirts to a Stanley Cup in 1914. He was killed while fighting in Belgium in June 1915 at the age of twenty-three.

The Vancouver Millionaires won the PCHA championship five more times and went to the Stanley Cup final three more times. In 2014 the Vancouver Canucks and Ottawa Senators met again at the NHL Heritage Classic; this time the Senators prevailed in front of fifty thousand frustrated fans at BC Place Stadium. These days some hockey faithful can be seen wearing the famous Millionaire "V." The glory days of 1915 can still fire the imagination and hopes of Vancouver's long-suffering hockey fans.

The Fighting McWhas—Five Brothers Who Served and Survived

With help from Chad Walters, a descendant

The McWhas came from New Brunswick but most of them ended up somewhere in Western Canada in the years before the war. Back in New Brunswick, Percy and his brothers Fred and Arthur (Cappy) curled and played hockey and rugby. And they were good. Arthur's rink won the Ganong Cup and later represented New Brunswick at the Briar. Clifford was a pretty good baseball player as well.

When he came west, Percy McWha became a star hockey player with the Phoenix Club, a mountain mining city near Greenwood that disappeared after the war when the market for copper collapsed.

The Boundary mining district around Greenwood, Grand Forks and Phoenix was booming in the early 1900s. Boundary and Kootenay mines and smelters were a big part of the BC boom and they produced some impressive hockey clubs as well.

The boys from Phoenix stood out. In 1911, the team was a force to be reckoned with in Western Canada and the northwest US. With the provincial title sewed up and an international cup in their display case, team management decided it was time to challenge for the Stanley Cup, and they sent off a wire to Ottawa. Unfortunately, the team was too late to qualify.

For history fans, it is a fantasy hockey story that has enough fact to keep the dream alive. The Phoenix legend lives on in the hearts of many Boundary hockey fans.

When the war put an end to hockey in Phoenix, Percy McWha signed up in June 1916. He listed his occupation as electrician. He featured in some of the dispatches from friends at the front. This letter appeared in the *Grand Forks Sun* on January 18, 1918, one of many letters from soldiers sent to friends at home:

> Your letter reached me in a muddy little village in France. I have been up in Belgium for awhile and that part of the world is worse than France. My chum was killed there last trip…There are a number of Grand Forks in this battalion. Rooke was wounded and McWha has been transferred to another battalion and has a bombproof job.

By 1918, a lot of men were looking for bombproof jobs, jobs that might keep them out of the line of fire and provide a safe return home to friends and family. To die with only a few

British Columbians and the Great War | 209

Top: Percy McWha, back row, centre, 1911.
Courtesy of the Greenwood Military Aviation Museum

Above: Clifford McWha in NH uniform, centre, 1913.
Courtesy of Chad Walters

Above right: Five of the McWha brothers—who all survived the Great War—from top left: Arthur, Clifford, Percy, Frederick and Godfrey (Jake).
Courtesy of Chad Walters

months of fighting left seemed even more pointless than it did in the early years of the war. Percy McWha's new job, whatever it was, did prove to be bombproof. He and all his brothers who served survived, one of the happy stories of the war years.

Percy's brother Clifford (who was known as Duce) played baseball in New Hazelton while working on the *Yukon Telegraph*. Descendant Chad Walters says Duce became a friend of poet Robert Service while he was in the north. And the Great War wasn't the only scrape he was involved in. Before that, he was a cable operator in Bamfield when the *Valencia* went down in 1906. Clifford was one of the first on the scene to rescue survivors. Over a hundred died, including all the women and children. Chad's mother once said that Clifford "was involved with some kind of sea rescue in very bad weather."

The Seaton Boys and War Canoes in Peachland

With help from grandson Don Seaton in Vernon

The war changed communities in some unexpected ways. The community of Peachland in the central Okanagan had a vibrant sporting life before events in Europe interfered. The pride of Peachland was its war canoe team. There were men's teams, women's teams and mixed teams—all racing beautiful thirty-foot wood canoes. It is believed that Peachland hosted and won its first war canoe race in September of 1909. The last Peachland Regatta was in August of 1913. The next August, British Columbia was at war and members of the team were enlisting. Some never returned.

Alec and John "Jack" Seaton were members of one of those championship teams. They were farming and ranching around Peachland before the war. Donald Alexander "Alec" was the oldest, born in 1895 and the first to enlist in May 1915. In June he took the steamer *Sicamous* to Vernon Camp and wrote home:

Private Donald Alexander Seaton.
Courtesy of Don Seaton

> They paid our way to Camp and also dinner on the *Sicamous* and it was some dinner—spring lamb, green peas, cocoanut pudding and ice cream. We came to Vernon on the passenger train. There are tents innumerable—cook tents, supply tents, as well as tables and wash stands. All the Peachland bunch are together. We get paid $5.00 per week and will be docked $10 dollars for our uniform.
>
> Aug. 21, Shorncliffe, England—Last Monday we had a review before the Duchess of Teck, Queen Mary's mother, and Sammie Hughes (the Minister of the Militia) with about 10,000 men on the field. It looked swell to see the bayonets shining in the sun, to hear the six bands, and the pipes. It sure makes a person hold his head up. Expect King Geordie any time. Working 18 hours a day, with 500 of us digging trenches along the coast opposite the big French seaport town, Calais. If Germany gets the upper hand in France, they will immediately bombard the British coast. Just my old trade, handling a shovel. Better eat a few peaches for me. They sell fruit here, but if some BC fruit was here, a person would have a gold mine...
>
> Nov. 21—I will be in Flanders by the early part of December. It's all foolishness going to the front—they say it is dangerous over there.
>
> Dec. 3—(somewhere in Belgium) Your humble servant is lying on a pile of straw in an old barn at a farmhouse. The firing is six miles away and the large guns are plainly heard, the rockets plainly seen. Soaked through. Quite a bit of sport on now—2 football games on the 1st and tomorrow a bunch of running races and more football. I am not getting cold feet yet, but it seems rotten shooting a human being. However, that is what we are here for.
>
> Dec. 7—Our pack now weights at least 90 pounds—150 rounds of ammunition, a rifle, entrenching outfit, bayonet, water bottle, haversack, ground sheet, one double blanket, overcoat, 2 extra pairs of socks, washing and shaving outfits, as well as other dope we use. So it sure weighs, but we are equal to it any day.
>
> Feb. 3, 1916—I heard from John [his brother] to-night. I am sorry he didn't tell me he was going to enlist or I would have told him not to. By the time he is here, we may be in Berlin.
>
> April 2, 1916—There are not very many out here who will be sorry when the war is over, believe me. It's no good and four months is plenty for yours truly. You asked me if I "really liked the life out here." Well it's got to be done and we might as well smile as cry. The one thing that bothers me the most is seeing fellows laid out and no possible means of avenging their deaths. Archie [his brother] speaks of several more Peachland boys thinking out enlisting. I hope they don't have to come out here.

On April 29, Private Donald Alexander Seaton's mother received a telegram advising her that her son was killed in action on April 14, just a few days after he sent his last letter. The *Vernon News* ran a story under the headline "A Peachland Hero" that said "it was a great shock to all when we heard a Teutonic shot had found its home in his manly breast."

Above: Sergeants Whyte, Sanderson and Jack Seaton. A note on the back of the photograph reads: "Sidehill Gougers" at Amherst, April 1917.
Courtesy of Don Seaton

Above right: Peter Ord of the Penticton Museum with one of the partially restored war canoes.
Courtesy of Mike Elliott

His captain in the 7th Battalion wrote:

He and the balance of his bombing party were having a game of their own with a German who was firing flares. As he fired each flare, they all loosed their rifles at the flash. This caused the German to stop and commence to fire back at them. One of those bullets hit your son and killed him. He was laughing at the time because of the way in which they had bothered the enemy.

Brother John was wounded twice at the front but survived the war and settled in Winfield. Archie signed up in November 1916 and was killed near Vimy Ridge. Another brother, Bill, was too young to serve but had a distinguished career as a teacher and educator. A Vernon school is named after him.

The War Canoe

The Penticton Museum and the SS *Sicamous* Inland Marine Museum are in the process of restoring some of the vintage Okanagan war canoes. Races are being held again to commemorate the golden age of canoe competitions before the war.

The War Canoe
By F.M.B.
[part of a tribute poem that appeared in the *Kelowna Record* in 1918]

A blearied sun, in a smoky sky,
The lake with a little chop,
A pavilion hung with bunting gay,
And a grandstand packed to the top.
A band had played, the people cheered
And applauded with much ado,
When the starter announced through a megaphone:
"The race for the War Canoe."

The classic race—the day's event—
Was the silver cup and shield,
And the Okanagan championship,
On a fair and open field.
So Peachland brought the best she had,
And a valiant showing made;
Fifteen men wore green and white,
To compete with the Fire Brigade

Peachland's Tragic Loss in World War I

By LOCAL HISTORIAN RICHARD SMITH

Peachland gave a greater sacrifice to Canada per capita than any other town in the Dominion. As in many towns in the Canadian West, immigrants were encouraged to start a new life in this new country. Many of those early pioneers, many single men, came from the British Isles. They were looking for land, gold and prosperity for their future. When World War I broke out, these same young men were still loyal to the country of their birth and signed up in great numbers to defend the "old country." Such was certainly the case in the town of Peachland and not limited to single men either. They waved their families and friends goodbye as they boarded the great steam sternwheeler SS *Sicamous*, which took them to the Canadian Pacific Railway troop train at Vernon, BC, for training in Eastern Canada. Having signed up so early in the war, their chances of becoming a casualty were greatly increased.

Certainly through the war the CPR telegraphs arrived with terrible news for the local population and at the same time letters home were arriving at the little post office. Slowly as the war progressed some of the wounded returned home to tell tales of trench horror, and some to say nothing, as the experience was best put out of the mind.

To honour their citizens who made the supreme sacrifice, a cenotaph on a boulevard was created, duly engraved. The mayor planted a memorial maple tree at the intersection of the two main roads in town. In 1919 the Governor General of Canada arrived to honour the veterans and open the local fall fair. Two other Governors General would come in 1948 and 1951 to do the same, Alexander of Tunis and Vincent Massey. In recent years the cenotaph was moved and rededicated, and the maple tree was cut down, not to be replaced.

In August 2013, a memorial Paddle Festival honoured our war canoe team members who put their paddles down in 1914 and took up arms instead, never to paddle again.

Local citizens do turn out in very large numbers for the annual November Remembrance Day ceremony, as they always have since World War I.

Peachland Cenotaph.
Courtesy of Greg Dickson

From Our Listeners: Sports Star to Trench Runner to Mayor

Told by Evelyn Sangster Benson

J. Lewis Sangster was one of five brothers living in New Westminster who formed a basketball team, then went on to become regional champions. Lewis also won Minto Cups with the New Westminster Salmonbellies and was a talented sprinter. The eldest brother, Walker, was killed going over the top, and soon Lewis and his twin, Philip, had enlisted in different regiments with the hope of sparing their mother another tragic telegram. Both survived the war, and Lewis served as mayor of New Westminster in 1949–50. His daughter Evelyn Sangster Benson tells the family story in A Century in a Small Town *(Westminster Publishing). Here are excerpts describing some her father's wartime experiences.*

During the fighting in France, the twins tried to keep track of each other's regiments. During a lull in the fighting, Dad heard that Philip's group was just down the road. Carefully slipping away, he located one of Philip's sergeants and inquired of his whereabouts. The sergeant stepped to the entryway of a nearby bunker and yelled, "PRIVATE SANGSTER...REPORT!" No answer, so Dad stuck his head into the bunker and yelled. "ILIP-PHAY!" Immediately he heard a voice reply. "EWIS-LAY!" Their childhood use of Pig Latin brought the brothers together in a bear hug. It was October 30, 1916—their twenty-fifth birthday!

Later in the war, Dad got word that Philip had been wounded in a nearby battlefield...It was later confirmed that Philip had been wounded, taken captive, operated on without anaesthetic and eventually "exchanged" along with other Canadian prisoners for German prisoners, Uncle Phil was left with a permanent limp.

Dad's talents as an athlete and outstanding sprinter were the reason he was recruited as a battalion scout. There were no walkie-talkies in that war, and messages were sent and replies received by runner. This was a dangerous job, and enemy snipers were on the alert for lone soldiers travelling with speed. Sensitive messages were memorized in case of capture. Dad was young and confident and often took shortcuts through enemy territory if his message was urgent...Dad didn't carry a weapon if he could help it. The weight slowed him down. Speed was of the essence!

The best night's sleep he ever had overseas was when he and his buddy were allowed to sleep in a barn. The grain harvest had just finished and a whole bin in the barn was full of bran. The two young soldiers snuggled down into the bran, pulling it over them like a blanket. The bran seemed to contain its own warmth, and the dryness of the bran sucked every bit of dampness out of their clothing.

Being continually wet was one of the worst tortures of trench warfare. Their socks rotted on their feet. They were constantly berated to keep their feet dry but it was an impossibility. On one of the first days Lewie Sangster bedded down inside a pillbox, soaking wet to his skin, a British sergeant entered with the daily "tot of rum"—the traditional right of all British servicemen, not just sailors. He filled each man's tin mug and when he came to Lewie, my father said, "No thank you, Sergeant, I promised my mother I would never touch alcohol and I signed a pledge." (Dad was a good Baptist boy.)

The old sergeant bellowed, "HOLD OUT YOUR MUG! NOW DRINK IT DOWN! THAT'S AN ORDER!" Dad choked down the unfamiliar burning liquid blinking tears between coughs. "Now listen to me, sonny. While you're in this God-forsaken war you will down your tot of the King's rum, and then you'll wrap yourself in TWO blankets and fall into your bunk. It's the one sure thing that might extend your life in this hellhole!" Dad said it was the best piece of advice he ever got in the army. The rum made you perspire heavily, and when you awoke you were dry and the outer blanket was soaked in your sweat.

From Our Listeners: Another Runner

By Joan MacKay, Prince George

On April 22, 1916, Gordon Stuart Struan Robertson, who was to become my dad, joined the Canadian Expeditionary Force in Fort William, Ontario, as a private assigned to the 94th Battalion. He was eighteen years old. He shipped out from Halifax, June 28, 1916, on the Olympic, arriving in Liverpool on July 6. He was transferred to the 32nd Battalion, proceeding to France on August 17, and was reassigned to the 28th Battalion. He seems to have been stationed at Ripon, France. He was a "runner" in the trenches and later on had the use of a motorcycle! The going rate of pay was a cool twenty dollars per month.

On September 17, two months after arriving, he was wounded in the head by a piece of shrapnel from a shell which killed his best friend/cousin next to him in the hole. The piece lodged behind his right ear, staying there for the rest of his life. He was admitted to No. 2 Australian General Hospital in Wimereux, France, convalesced in Bologna and rejoined his unit December 9.

On April 6, 1917, he wrote: "Last fall, just before the 15th of September, we were billeted in a barn. A great many of the fellows had written their names and the time that they thought the war would end. It varied from one month to two years from September. I put down 12th of July, 1917. By the look of things now, it should finish about then." April 11, 1917 (two days after the Battle of Vimy Ridge), Dad wrote, "By now I suppose you will know with what success the drive started and the Canadians helped start it. The whole affair was a walk-over and why old Fritz doesn't quit is more than I can make out." April 30: "We are by now in support of a detachment of Canadians who went over the top a few days ago. Needless to say, it was a success—as it generally is when the Canadians attempt it..."

April 23, 1917: "At last spring weather! The last few days have been bright and warm but up 'til then we had snow storms and everything was unpleasant. We had a bath this morning and it certainly felt good. I was mud from head to foot, outside and inside. The warm sun dried the mud off our clothes so we could scrape it off and the warm water and soap soon took the dirt off our bodies."

Dad, Gordon, was awarded the Good Conduct Badge on April 22, 1918. He finally left the war, France and Europe on SS *Lapland* out of Liverpool bound for Canada as Corporal Robertson on June 2, 1919, just one month shy of the three years since he'd arrived.

E.O. Wheeler, Mountaineer

By Wade Davis

E.O. Wheeler was the son of famed surveyor A.O. Wheeler, the man who first mapped the Rogers Pass. Edward Oliver Wheeler was awarded the Military Cross and membership in the French Legion of Honour, and after the war joined George Mallory's expeditions to Mount Everest. Wheeler is the subject of a new book being written by BC's Wade Davis, who told us more about what he considers a great, unsung Canadian hero.

Mallory for some reason had a great dislike of Canadians, but Oliver Wheeler, who was held in some disdain in 1921, was in fact an extraordinary man, and in the end Mallory came around to him. Wheeler's father, Arthur, founded the Alpine Club of Canada. At a time when George Mallory was doing gymnastics at Winchester College, Oliver Wheeler was climbing first ascents in the Canadian Rockies—mountains that now bear his name.

Wheeler then went off to RMC, the highest-rated candidate for our military college. He graduated having won every single major award. He then went off to train as a Royal Engineer, and he was with the 7th Meerut Division at the outbreak of hostilities and immediately was dispatched to France. By the time the Indian contingent reached the battlefield, the topography of Armageddon had come into place and the trenches reached from the Swiss border to the English Channel. Now curiously I found Oliver Wheeler—who went on to become Surveyor General of India, knighted in World War II for his contribution in the creation of eighty million maps that more than anything kept the Japanese out of India—also found the route to the mountain, the route up the East Rongbuk Glacier to the North Col, the route climbers follow to this day from the Tibetan side. That's often credited by the British in particular to George Mallory, but it was Oliver Wheeler.

Wheeler had been seconded to the expedition in 1921 with a mission of mapping the inner massif of the mountain with a new photo-topographical survey technique his father had invented in the Canadian Rockies. And so it was Oliver Wheeler who spent more time alone on the mountain exposed to the wrath of the mountain than anyone else in 1921. Ironically when it came time to assault the North Col in 1921, the reconnaissance mission, who does Mallory turn to? To accompany him to the highest point that human beings had ever reached? None other than Oliver Wheeler. They crested that North Col and they were met with a wind so ferocious that Oliver Wheeler said he thought he was going to suffocate and die. He survived it by remembering how he had survived artillery fire at the front by breathing between the blasts of the shellfire. And that night as they retreated from the North Col, having established a world height record at that time, George Mallory in this wonderful moment stayed up all night saving Wheeler's life by rubbing his legs with whale oil.

The fascinating thing about Oliver Wheeler is that British historians say there was only one diary, one journal kept in 1921 as these Brits walked across Everest, four hundred miles into the unknown to come to close quarters with the mountain that no human being—no European that is—had ever embraced directly.

Now I found Oliver Wheeler's son, a wonderful man, John Wheeler living not four blocks from the house I was born in in Vancouver. When I went to see Mr. Wheeler, over the course of a lovely afternoon he suddenly pulled two treasures off his book shelf, two fat journals that his father had kept as he marched across Tibet with Mallory in 1921. These were treasures not only for their content but for what you can read between the lines. On the day that Arthur Kellis dies and is buried, the entire journal entry from Oliver Wheeler reads, "Well, they buried the old boy in the morning, thought it'd be the afternoon, terribly sorry to have missed it, but I do hate funerals."

How on earth do you miss the interment of one of the climbers you're walking across Tibet with? I knew the answer had to lie in the Western Front. When Wheeler reached the front in the fall of 1914, the entire British Expeditionary Force had been wiped out, so the entire British sector of the line was held by the Canadians in the north and the Indian army in the south. By that time both sides had begun to sap each other, building perpendicular trenches from the main trench lines to get close, or raid, or toss bombs.

It came to the attention of Wheeler's command on November 4, 1914, that the Germans had put two saps within thirty feet of their front line. As a Royal Engineer he was given the order to go over the top and bury that sap and to do so in a way that would dissuade the Germans from ever trying that tactic again. He goes over the top, all hell breaks loose, he's got 125 men with him—machine-gun fire, artillery. To their horror they discover the saps are full of Germans about to attack them. The result is a melee of hand-to-hand combat of the worst sort. Eventually the Indians push the Germans back, but not before the entire trench is filled three bodies deep, chest-to-chest of dying boys of both sides flailing about as Wheeler would write, "Like trout in my creel."

He tried to get his wounded out, but he did have to bury men alive, and he never knew how many he actually buried alive. So when he says on Everest, "I do hate funerals," you begin to see the impact of that war on the lives of these men.

On the day he died in Vernon on April 16, 1962, there's one single word in his journal, a journal he has kept since he was a boy in 1903. That word indisputably written in his own hand is a single word that says, "Died." Imagine the discipline to be able to bring yourself to that point in a long series of journals and still be able to sign off in that way.

Finding the Mark at Home and at the Front

The Okanagan's Allan Brooks: Rifleman and Renowned Ornithologist

Allan Brooks was born in India in 1869 where his father, who was an engineer on the Indian Railways, shared his love of ornithology. The family came to Canada when Brooks was twelve and moved to Chilliwack, where he began his extensive private collection of bird specimens.

Allan Brooks.
Image Courtesy: Vernon Museum and
Archives -- Photo No. 16089

In 1899, Brooks moved to Okanagan Landing and built a reputation as an illustrator and big-game hunter. Along the way, he illustrated *Birds of Washington* and *Birds of California.*

Before the outbreak of war in 1914, he went to England as a member of the Canadian Rifle Team to compete at Bisley. He was still in England when war broke out but came back to Canada to sign up because of his militia connections. Brooks returned to England with the 9th Battalion of the first contingent. He was forty-five and was quickly made a captain and then major while serving in France. Brooks was mentioned in dispatches three times and received the Distinguished Service Order, eventually becoming chief instructor at the Second Army sniping, observation and scouting school.

His DSO citation read:

For conspicuous gallantry in the operations of 2nd and 3rd September in front of Arras. As brigade observing officer he showed great daring and initiative, pushing forward at all times with the most advanced troops under the heaviest fire. Taking a wire with him, he kept brigade headquarters well informed of the situation, and enabled the commander to make decisions that saved many lives. When the enemy were retiring he pushed forward over 500 yards in front of the infantry and telephoned back information from a long distance in front of our advance. During the two days he personally killed twenty of the enemy by sniping shots.

Tobin's Tigers stayed occupied with sports—including the classic tug of war.
Stuart Thomson photo, City of Vancouver Archives, CVA 99-157

Even at the front, Brooks continued to sketch local wildlife and record how birds and wildlife responded to the shellfire. After the war he returned to the Okanagan where he resumed painting and collecting bird specimens. Major Brooks died in 1946 and his collection of nine thousand bird skins ended up at the University of California. The Allan Brooks Nature Centre at Vernon keeps his legacy alive. Robert Bateman said of Brooks that he was one of the "foremost realistic bird painters of the early twentieth century" and cites him as a major influence and inspiration.

The BC Regiment's Distinguished William Hart-McHarg

A trip to the BC Regiment's drill hall on Beatty Street quickly confirms the honoured place of Lieutenant-Colonel William Hart-McHarg in the history of the Duke of Connaught's Own. He was born to a military family in barracks in Ireland in 1869 and immigrated to Canada before the turn of the century. Hart-McHarg studied law in Winnipeg and moved west, first to Rossland where he became a lieutenant in the newly formed 102nd Rocky Mountain Rangers. He served in the South African War and then settled in Vancouver, where he joined the Duke of Connaught's. Hart-McHarg, like Allan Brooks, was an outstanding shot and was repeatedly selected to compete at Bisley. In 1913, he won the Kaiser Cup, making him world champion.

When the 7th Battalion was organized to fight in the Great War, Hart-McHarg became commanding officer, leading them at Neuve Chapelle and Ypres. But it was at Ypres that his luck ran out. According to his obituary, the 7th Battalion was holding down a position near St. Julien on Friday, April 23, 1915. After some heavy shelling by the enemy, Hart-McHarg and his second-in-command, Major Victor Odlum (another Vancouver officer who would later take over the battalion), set out to reconnoitre the area but came under fire. Hart-McHarg was hit and Odlum went for help. He brought back a medic and Hart-McHarg was treated in a shell hole. They managed to get him to a hospital but he died of his wounds the next day.

It was later revealed that illness had reduced him to a diet of biscuits and milk while he was at the front, but he was determined to serve under difficult circumstances. In a moment of candour, he told a friend that he had only a few years to live. Military service had been central in his life and he seemed to be devoted to distinguishing himself as a soldier and leader before the illness could incapacitate him. The famous *Brooding Soldier* monument now marks the battleground where Hart-McHarg and many other Canadians fell in the Second Battle of Ypres.

William Hart-McHarg.
Herbert Welford photo, City of Vancouver Archives, CVA 371-2749

Sergeant Andrew Ross: A Scottish Rugby Hero

He served in a British Columbia regiment, but in Scotland he'll always be remembered for his competitive spirit in rugby. Andrew Ross was born in Edinburgh and between 1905 and 1909, he played five times for Scotland, winning two and losing three.

Ross trained as an engineer and after working as assistant engineer for the Edinburgh Municipal Electric Station he caught the travelling bug and headed for Vancouver. He was in the Canadian North when word of the war reached him. This is an excerpt from one of his letters:

> November 29, 1914—We arrived in Vancouver from Albert Bay on the 11th of this month, and have started training...In this Second Canadian Contingent most of the men are splendid shots. At 200 yards yesterday A Company were shooting. Twelve men made the highest possible and about 70 per cent of the Company did not drop more than five points. I had eight bulls and two inners...

Andrew Ross, rugby hero.
Courtesy of Scottish Rugby

The work in camp is hard, but we all like it, as we have to get into good condition for the British Army.

> Hastings Park, Vancouver, January 8, 1915—A man feels that it's worth his while giving up his life to save millions of homes, such as ours, from the fate of poor old Belgium…We don't want to have to stay too long in England drilling, so it is with a jolly good will we go into our drills here. You find that nearly every man has his drill book in his tunic pocket, and reads it up at odd moments.

Serving with the 29th, Tobin's Tigers, Ross wrote from the front in September 1915:

Our line varies from 30 to 250 yards from the Germans…The Germans occasionally give us a "hymn of hate" in the shape of shrapnel morning and evening. The star shells at night are fine. In fact, if you keep your head down and listen to the crack of the rifles, and watch the incessant stream of star shells, you would think you were at a firework show.

In April 1916 the corporal of his section wrote:

On the morning of the 6th April we were serving together in the trenches. While attending devotedly and most courageously, under very heavy artillery fire, to our wounded men, he was himself hit, and falling over a man he was dressing, died instantly. Quite reckless as regarding his own life, he exposed it to save, as his quick attention undoubtedly did, the lives of a great number of our men.

His commanding officer wrote:

He was killed while doing his duty like man, on the morning of 6th April. No man could do more. He was a splendid character and was loved alike by his Officers and men, all of whom feel his loss most keenly.

Tommy Burns: Boxer and Soldier

He wasn't from British Columbia and his real name wasn't Tommy Burns, but he did have some interesting BC connections.

Burns was the only Canadian-born World Heavyweight Championship boxer. Born into a German Canadian family in Ontario in 1881, he started a career in prizefighting in 1900 and then changed his name to something sounding more Scottish. Wikipedia says, "At a time when most white fighters adhered to the so-called colour line, refusing to fight African Americans, Burns had half a dozen contests with black boxers prior to his clash with the legendary Jack Johnson." During World War I he joined the Canadian Army, serving as a physical fitness instructor. That might explain this trip to Vancouver. He fought a bit after the war but his glory days were behind him. The Depression wiped out his savings and he went into the ministry. He died of a heart attack on a visit to Vancouver in 1955 and was buried in a pauper's grave in Burnaby.

Tommy Burns is now in the International Boxing Hall of Fame and a special plaque marks his grave.

Boxer Tommy Burns filled out his uniform while promoting recruitment at Hastings Park in Vancouver.
Stuart Thomson photo, Vancouver Public Library 8722

From Our Listeners: There's Trouble in the Balkans

By John Edmond, Ottawa

Cecil Harlow Edmond, my father, was born in Tenby, a pretty seaside town in Pembrokeshire, South Wales, on December 21, 1883. The family had deep roots in Pembrokeshire and Glamorganshire, with ancestors prominent in Swansea to the east, and some admitted to the Gild of Freemen of Haverfordwest, to the west. Nevertheless, Cecil ("Jack," to his family) grew up in genteel poverty, as his father had left, so that at age sixteen, in 1900, he enlisted as a cavalry trooper in the Royal Sussex Regiment to serve in the Boer War. When it ended in May 1902, he returned to Wales, with a still-unsated appetite for adventure. He and a friend, Frank Mason (later killed in World War I), saw a poster for "sunny Alberta" and, wanting to replicate South Africa's climate, set out for Canada late in 1902. Reaching Calgary in the dead of winter, they saw deep snow from the train window and decided to carry on westward!

Soon my father discovered an entrepreneurial spirit, becoming deeply involved in exploiting the burgeoning resource economy of the coast: first in fishing, then in land and timber. In the course of various timber and logging enterprises, he became friends with magnates such as Alvo von Alvensleben, the German aristocrat interned in the US in 1917, whose legacy is "Edgewood" (Crofton House School) and Wigwam Inn. Venturing into the interior, he was struck by the vast untapped land resources of the Chilcotin plateau, which he spent much of the pre-war years exploring. By this time he had a home in Victoria, but his vision was to establish a chain of ranch lands from the northwest of the Chilcotin, near Anahim Lake. In pursuit of his dream, he spent weeks on horseback, sometimes in the company of his friend Chief Nemiah of the Tsilhqot'in Indians, with his pack train, "staking" land (as could then be done). Years later, he owned a cruiser which he named Nemiah.

This adventure consumed much of the early second decade of the century. One day in August of 1914, he was riding eastward, returning to his base at the Gang Ranch, when he put in a telephone call on the primitive line that had just reached that remote area. He wanted to call Victoria. As he explained, calls had to be relayed onward at each "station" on the line. He reached Hanceville, where Mrs. Norman Lee, the matriarch of the long-time Chilcotin family, had charge of the line. Her greeting was ominous and prophetic: "There's trouble in the Balkans, Mr. Edmond." He arrived in Victoria in a few days to the full truth: Britain and Canada were at war with Germany.

The 67th Battalion (Western Scots) organized in Victoria to be part of the Canadian Expeditionary Force. As with most men of his day, duty to King and country was clear, and my father promptly joined as a junior officer. Shortly, however, his background in logging became known, and he found himself in Northumberland, in northern England, running a Canadian Forestry Corps logging operation that fed timber to the war effort. This was hardly to his liking; he wanted to "see action." He spent his leaves in London, at the War Office, trying to find a way to get over to France. The Royal Flying Corps turned him down; at six feet two, he wouldn't fit into their aircraft.

Things looked up, though, when he heard of some sort of new mobile equipment called "tanks." Senior British officers were not pleased that he knew of this still-secret weapon; nevertheless he was permitted to transfer to the "Imperial" forces. He was assigned to command "A" company, 9th Tank Battalion, at the rank of captain, and immediately shipped to France. With his then moustache, his resemblance to Field Marshall Lord Kitchener was so striking that the nickname "Kitch" stuck with him in later life.

I know little of his role in the war, and nothing of the ghastly scenes he must have witnessed. "Bodies" never figured in his accounts; he spoke only of tanks that had been "knocked out" by "Jerry." To hear him, the war was simply a grand adventure of camaraderie, devoted to "scrounging" for fare not found in rations— fine provisions and perhaps good wine, to be shared with the entire company. This was not callous; it was simply coping.

Just a week before Armistice, he was engaged in an action near the Franco-Belgian border, for which he was awarded the Military Cross by George V. His conduct was gazetted thus:

For marked gallantry during the attack on Mormal Forest on 4th November, 1918. One Tank of his section had its sponson burst in near the front line. He improvised an iron plate and sent it into action. Another Tank had its crew gassed, and he immediately got together a crew of infantry and led them into action. Owing to his fine example he brought his section into action under a very heavy barrage and at a critical time.

These were the resourceful acts of a true British Columbian: having coaxed "donkey engines" to work in coast logging, improvisation of an iron plate would be second nature, and the formalities of infantry vs. tank crew trivial in the face of a challenge.

To my father, war meant companionship and adventure, for only that explains why, in 1919, he volunteered to join the proposed White Russian campaign against the new Bolshevik regime, only to have the enterprise he sought to join disallowed by Prime Minister Lloyd George.

He left the British service with the rank of major, returning to Victoria. He started Western Construction Co. to build houses, notably on Newport Avenue in Oak Bay. He soon reverted to logging, successfully until the collapse of the market with the Depression of the 1930s. With intimate knowledge of his areas of the province, he promoted various ideas for mining, timber and land development. His foremost dream, though, was to see the Chilko–Homathko hydro potential developed. This scheme involved diverting the waters of Chilko Lake on the high Chilcotin Plateau westward by a tunnel to drop over three hundred metres to Tatlayoko Lake, draining to Bute Inlet, where industry would locate. This potential he had reported to the province in the course of his Chilcotin explorations. For this, two geographic features were named after him: a Chilko Lake tributary, Edmond Creek, and its source, Edmond Glacier. His Bute Development Ltd. attracted interest, but the hydro project was never developed.

His devotion to the preservation of history, in particular artifacts of the CPR's Empress of Japan, is recorded in Larissa Buijs's Golden Inheritance, the story of the Chung Collection at UBC.

My father died in Vancouver August 10, 1970. He possessed knowledge and love of British Columbia's coast and Cariboo–Chilcotin to a rare degree; his entrepreneurial dreams large but mostly unrealized. I believe he may, paradoxically, have been happiest meeting the challenges of leading "A" Company of the 9th Tank Battalion, to which he brought a British Columbian's initiative.

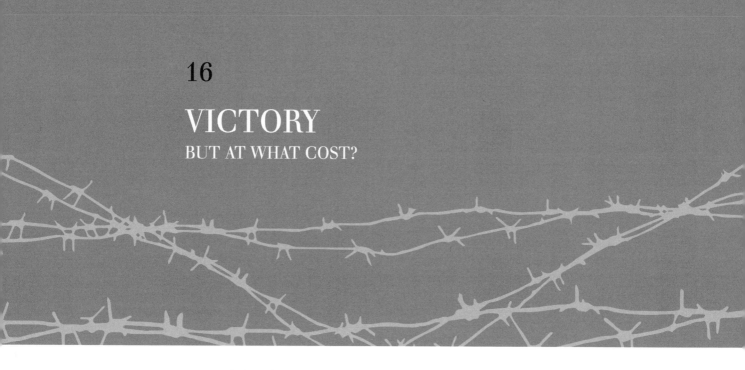

16

VICTORY
BUT AT WHAT COST?

For Britain and France, it was a victory that was all but indistinguishable from defeat. Just being able to endure it was seen as heroic.—*Geoff Dyer*

When World War I was over, the men and women who took part could be forgiven for wondering whether it was all worth it. Even after the Armistice, many languished overseas, waiting for demobilization and transport home. There were riots in England as Canadian soldiers sat out another winter in cold barracks with bad food. This was not a new world fit for heroes, but was more of the same.

Teetering governments hoping to prop up their support gave women the vote, but money was tight and genuine reform was in short supply. The "temporary" income tax introduced during the war never went away.

A hero's welcome. Canadian artists paid tribute to the returning soldiers.
Courtesy of Don Stewart

Many of those who returned to British Columbia just wanted to return to their old jobs and home life. But as BC historian Margaret Ormsby wrote, "Most of the large companies, burdened with stockpiles of manufactured goods, were firing rather than hiring. The worst conditions prevailed in Vancouver. In the mining camps of the Interior, there were almost no jobs."

Who was to blame? In this anniversary year, the historians can't even agree on who started the war or why it happened. Canada's Margaret MacMillan concludes that those who took us into the war could fairly be accused of a "failure of imagination in not seeing how destructive such a conflict would be."

The mud of the Western Front, the punishing artillery, the poisonous gas, the machine guns and flame throwers, the bombing from above and the explosions from tunnels below, the prospect of being blown to bits for the sake of a muddy stretch of trench that could be lost tomorrow—all these horrors left an indelible mark on a generation and their offspring.

Below: A victory poem. The Angel of Victory statue was designed by Montreal's Coeur de Lion MacCarthy for the Canadian Pacific Railway, which lost 1,116 employees in the war. This statue still stands in front of the CPR Station on Vancouver's Water Street. Montreal and Winnipeg also have copies of the statue.
Courtesy of Don Stewart

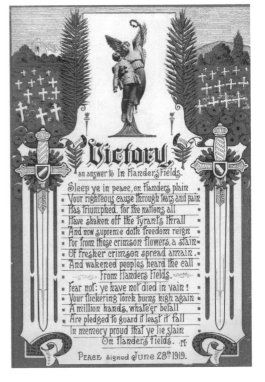

Influenza

The postwar influenza outbreak killed more than fifty million people worldwide. Fifty thousand Canadians died, with over four thousand in BC. One thousand were First Nations, a stunning reminder of the smallpox epidemic that wiped out tens of thousands of Native people in BC just decades earlier.

The so-called Spanish flu was universal in its reach, spreading around the globe, stretching medical resources already stretched thin by four years of war and visiting upon the civilian population another shocking death toll just as the nightmare seemed to be ending.

Mark Humphries, a history professor at Memorial University in Newfoundland, believes the influenza epidemic may have a British Columbia connection. Humphries has written that the flu most likely emerged in China in the winter of 1917–18, "diffusing across the world as previously isolated populations came into contact with one another on the battlefields of Europe."

How did it spread? Humphries believes it can be traced to the Chinese Labour Corps, the men recruited by the British government in Asia, transported to British Columbia by ship and then sent by rail across Canada to supply much-needed labour on the Western Front. Some of those men were already sick with a mysterious illness before they left home. While some quarantine efforts were made, they were insufficient. The Spanish flu probably had nothing to do with Spain.

Soldier Settlements

After the optimistic years under Premier Richard McBride, the new premier, John Oliver, ushered in a long period of sobriety, politically and practically. Alcohol was prohibited for about four years, from 1917 to 1921, and the political climate was pretty tame too. Oliver was a prosperous farmer, and he assumed the farming life was just the thing for returning soldiers. "He had taken it for granted, without either enquiry or consultation, that the soldiers would prefer to settle on the land," wrote Margaret Ormsby.

The Oliver government quickly moved ahead with plans to reclaim the wetlands of the Sumas Prairie in the Fraser Valley, to irrigate the desert in the south Okanagan and to establish soldier settlements at Merville on Vancouver Island, at Creston in the Kootenays and at Telkwa in the north.

But as the song goes, how are you going to keep them down on the farm after they've seen Paree? "When only a few of the soldiers took advantage of his offer of low-priced land, [Oliver] felt the rebuff keenly," said Ormsby. "He had dreamed of providing a farm for every hero."

A statue of Premier John Oliver stands in front of the Oliver town hall.
Courtesy of Greg Dickson

The town of Oliver in the South Okanagan is named after "Honest John" Oliver. There's a statue of him in front of the old municipal hall. Today, the town is the centre of the Okanagan fruit and wine industry. But it wasn't really built up by returning soldiers. "When it was realized that only a small portion of the land would be taken up by returning veterans the government decided to give everyone a chance to buy land," wrote Julie Cancela in her book about the irrigation project called *The Ditch*.

The move to broaden the market for orchards came after considerable government investment to build a network of concrete ditches, siphons and flumes. Bringing water to the desert and laying out the orchards was expensive, probably close to five million dollars. But the good news was that it put local men to work at a decent wage. Men made about five dollars a day and the project took until 1927 to complete. It employed hundreds and made it possible for some of those men to be the first to buy parcels of land.

The soldier settlement of Merville on Vancouver Island with its stump farms was probably less successful. The returning soldiers named the community for a French village where they fought. Writer Jack Hodgins grew up there and wrote about it in his book *Broken Ground*. The land wasn't much friendlier for farming than the war-torn landscape they had left behind. There were huge trees and stumps to be cleared—often using explosives, which must have been a shock to men already terrorized by the sound of artillery.

"For those returned Soldiers who were 'rewarded' with land for farming, clearing the stumps must have seemed like a continuation of war," Hodgins says. "Some were wounded by

explosives. And of course many more were wounded or killed in the logging camps. Most of them ended up in the logging camps because it became clear that very few of them would ever make a living off their farms. The land was suitable only for timber."

The Prince of Wales Visits

When the Prince of Wales visited British Columbia in 1919 to pay tribute to the province's veterans, one of the places he went was Merville. A Pathé newsreel from the visit shows the stumps and the explosions. It looks like a battleground.

The Prince toured all over the province, meeting servicemen in the cities, visiting veteran convalescent homes on the coast and in the interior, travelling by steamboat up the Okanagan and through the Kootenays. Men from all over Canada took their discharge in British Columbia. Many ended up in veterans' hospitals in BC and struggled for years with their injuries, and the complications from gas and shrapnel. But the royal tour was a triumph of public relations, providing the public with a glimpse of a glamorous royal who would be caught up in a scandalous abdication crisis on the eve of another world war.

General Currie's Image Problem

For Victoria's Arthur Currie, Armistice ended the fighting but did not end his personal struggles. For years afterwards, he was in court defending his reputation and his decision to sacrifice Canadian lives in the last months of the war. Also haunting Currie was a very poor decision he made before the war to salvage his failing real estate business. While he may have been a dedicated commander, he was a reckless businessman, and to get out of a tight spot when the Victoria real estate market collapsed in 1913, he "borrowed" over ten thousand dollars in regimental money—and used it to pay off some debts.

To compound his problems, the embezzlement was not a secret in political circles. Prime Minister Borden and some of his key ministers knew about it, and while they admired Currie's leadership abilities, they were very concerned that if the fraud became public knowledge, Currie would be ruined and they would be looking for a new commander for the Canadian Corps. Some of Currie's enemies also knew of it, most prominently Minister of Militia and Defence Sam Hughes, who started the war as a personal friend and supporter, but turned on Currie as the general rose and Hughes fell.

Currie was strangely negligent in correcting the impropriety even when his own pay packet improved as he rose through the ranks and had an opportunity to pay the money back. "It is difficult to reconcile Currie's reckless personal behavior in relation to this impropriety with that of the public general who approached war in a methodical, careful, and informed manner," wrote Tim Cook in his biography.

The whole episode is a blot on the Currie reputation and suggests a personal sense of entitlement, a belief that his personal sacrifices in leading the Canadian Corps provided some exemption from scrutiny of his finances. Mercifully, at one point during the war, two of Currie's subordinate officers who were successful businessmen stepped in and lent him the money to pay back the debt. Victor Odlum and David Watson rescued Currie from scandal but also put him a tight spot because he must have known that if he moved to demote either man, they could reveal his secret.

Sam Hughes made Currie but came to hate him. Why didn't Hughes expose the fraud? He was certainly prepared to destroy the Currie reputation in other ways at the closing of the war. Hughes became convinced that Currie had recklessly sacrificed Canadian soldiers in the final one hundred days. Hughes's mind was also poisoned by envy. It was understandable. Hughes had been removed from office at the height of his powers. Once he was the admired strongman of the Canadian government's war effort, but Prime Minister Borden came to distrust Hughes's eccentric and erratic ways and demoted him. He spent the remaining years as a humble backbencher, powerless beyond the occasionally stinging criticisms he was able to deliver in Parliament. At the same time, his nemesis Currie had gone from strength to strength so that by the end of the war he was one of the most respected generals on the Western Front.

Hughes was ill by this time and died in 1921. But before his death, he kept up a steady barrage of criticism, laying the blame for the high death toll in the final months of the war on Currie's doorstep. "I created General Arthur Currie," he told the House of Commons, but as a creator he was not happy with the result. "I have no hesitation in saying that many Canadians would be above the sod today if he had not carried out his tactics and strategy in relation to [the Battle of] Cambrai."

Hughes could keep up the accusations unchallenged because he also knew the more devastating story of Currie's embezzlement. So Currie remained silent as the stinging criticisms spread in the media. There was little he could do. And when Hughes was dead, the rumours continued to fly. It was not until 1927, when a newspaper editorial appeared in the *Port Hope Evening Guide,* that he finally decided enough was enough. The newspaper wrote:

> It was the last day; the last hour, and almost the last minute [of the war], when to glorify the Canadian Headquarter staff, the Commander-in-Chief [Currie] conceived the mad idea that it would be a fine thing to say that the Canadians fired the last shot…But the penalty that was paid in useless waste of human life was appalling.

Currie decided to sue for fifty thousand dollars. The trial dragged on through 1928 and

General Sir Samuel Hughes watches the departure of the Canadian Expeditionary Force.
Library and Archives Canada / C-002468

rehashed much of the rumour and innuendo. In the end it was a win for Currie but a hollow one. A jury found the newspaper guilty of libel but awarded Currie only five hundred dollars in damages. The war, the trial and the public humiliation shortened Currie's life considerably. He died in November 1933, just a few weeks after Armistice Day. He was only fifty-seven years old.

The pretty little cottage that the Currie family lived in is still standing in Victoria. It has been restored to its former glory and there is talk of erecting a statue in his honor. But most British Columbians have forgotten that this struggling real estate agent was Canada's greatest battlefield general.

A Journey Back in Time

Our listeners and contributors have been united in their desire to keep the story of the Great War fresh in the minds of the next generation. Teachers like Dianne Rabel in Prince Rupert and Gina McMurchy-Barber here on the south coast have made it a central part of their curriculum. Here's Gina's story and more from people who have reconnected with the past in moving ways.

Making It Relevant

By Gina McMurchy-Barber, Surrey

Early in my career I wanted to teach my students about Canada's participation in the Great War and World War II. I grew up with a healthy respect for these periods in world history because my dad served for five years in World War II. But how to make a bunch of eleven-year-olds care when the war was so long ago, so far away and had nothing to do with their lives of Nintendo, cartoons and virtual pets was another matter.

Many of my students had been reciting "In Flanders Fields" since kindergarten, wore poppies and stood for two minutes of silence on cue at our school assemblies. But one year I hoped to achieve more—for them to be really moved by these events and to leave them with a deeper awareness and appreciation. It occurred to me the only way this could happen was to find a way to make it relevant to them. So we began to find the connections in their own family history by interviewing relatives or reading family accounts.

As we progressed toward Remembrance Day, students began to light up as places and names became more familiar in our history lessons. "My great grandfather fought in the Somme," one piped up. "My uncle collects stuff from the wars and showed me a rifle with a bayonet," another was keen to tell. One boy learned that while his Chinese great-grandfather was fighting the Japanese, his British great-grandfather was on the other side of the world fighting the Germans.

I could see the class was beginning to get it. But the best was still to come—it was to bring history to life by getting them to take parts in a play I wrote called *True Patriot Love.* As the students learned their lines they inadvertently memorized history, sang songs from the era like "Pack Up Your Troubles" and "It's a Long Way to Tipperary," acted out real people's experiences and came to some important conclusions—war was not glorious, but the people who fought and died were.

Ever since that year I have taught in different schools and different ages, but have always found that with a little effort students learn to care about the Great War when they find how it connects to them. It's harder now with many of those with direct experiences gone, but all the more reason to put our family stories in writing. A few years ago I was at a teacher conference.

At break time I was making my way through a crowd when I felt a touch on my arm. When I turned I was face to face with one of the students who had been in my class that first year I taught about the wars. She was a brand new teacher, attending her first conference. "I still remember the history lessons," she said. "What we learned from that play—it was called *True Patriot Love*...right?"

Young people can appreciate the sacrifices made by those who fought and died if they learn to see that World War I and other wars were events that touched everyone's life, including their own. That's when they can truly say, "We will never forget."

Gina McMurchy-Barber is the recipient of the Governor General's Award for Excellence in Teaching Canadian History.

Cycling into History

By Barry Bogart

Almost a hundred years after Vimy. Have we learned anything? I have completed my fourth bicycle tour in Europe. My brother has a place in the north of France near Calais—Montreuil-sur-Mer, home of Victor Hugo and locale for Les Mis. On the previous three tours I had cycled around that part of France for many, many kilometres. I never made any attempt to understand the history of the area, but I kept randomly coming across large and small gravesites.

Last spring I watched on TV a ceremony rededicating the Vimy Memorial, and it really moved me. That led me into months of research into the "War to End All Wars." It turned out that much of the action took place literally under my feet where I had cycled up through Flanders into Belgium. I took a combination of trains and bikes, which worked out very well. I went by train to Bruge, then took the LF1 Noordzeeroute south from Bruge through Nieuwpoort to Diksmuide. This part of the LF1 and a little farther on pretty well follows the front lines in World War I. But you don't realize it until you see the vast monument and cemetery in Diksmuide.

After Diksmuide I switched to the LF6 route, which follows a circle around Ypres through Poperinge. I camped near there and then doubled back through Ypres to visit the many memorials of Passchendaele. It was around there that I saw the first really big cemeteries—English, Canadian, French. Over eighty thousand buried in each. But I first saw a little one—Essex Farm—where John McCrae wrote "In Flanders Fields" just before he died (and yes, there are poppies by the roadside all around there). This was one of the more moving I saw as I walked by the Canadians who died there, their headstones decorated by students from "Regina Catholic Schools."

Along the road to Lens and on to Vimy were scores more cemeteries for the French, German and Commonwealth troops. By then I was used to it, but Vimy was still to come. I had a good climb up to Vimy Ridge, and you can see the memorial from there. Just before you arrive, there is a Café Canadien at the top where I stopped to have a café au lait (no Molson there, nor a Tim's, but I was about to be on Canadian soil).

The land around Vimy Ridge has been left scarred as it was then, by bombardments. But now sheep peacefully graze on it. There are warning signs about not walking off the paths due to the unexploded ordnance still there. (I wondered if the sheep ever found any.) The memorial itself is majestic, but mournful beyond description, rivalled only perhaps by the *Brooding Soldier* statue I saw the day before. I spent quite a lot of time there and at the nearby Canadian cemeteries. British Columbians were well represented there, sadly.

Brigadier General Henry Thoresby Hughes, Royal Canadian Engineers and Monument Builder

By Sara Carr-Harris, Victoria

Brigadier General Henry Thoresby Hughes, my grandfather, came to Canada from England in the late 1800s and worked for the CPR. He is, as far as I know, the only person to have obtained his engineering degree, by correspondence—and by lamplight at that—while working for the railway. He knew Van Horne, and he designed bridges and buildings for the CPR, the stations that had the French look about them.

About 1904, the Royal Canadian Engineers was formed and he then joined up, having married my grandmother, from Montreal. Then he was stationed in charge at Work Point Barracks, Esquimalt, in about 1907 or 1908. My grandmother was with him along with their two sons, my father and his brother, who got into mischief at the army camp. Grandfather shut them up in the jail after they lit a fire to welcome mother home from a trip on one of the big CPR ships that used to come into Victoria Harbour. I believe the fire must have got out of control because the story was that the men were having to run in their white summer drill to get the fire out!

Brigadier General Henry Thoresby Hughes had a distinguished career with the Canadian military (CMG, DSO, received from King George V, Buckingham Palace), was mentioned in dispatches and after the war was chief engineer in charge of construction of Vimy and our other Canadian World War I memorials at Bourlon Wood, Le Quesnel, Dury and Courcelette in France and St. Julien, Hill 62 (Sanctuary Wood) and Passchendaele in Belgium.

Jack Patten at Kitchener's Wood memorial in Belgium with Lieutenant-Governor Stephen Point.
Courtesy of the Patten Family

He retired to Elk Lake, Victoria, in the 1930s and died in 1947. When my father lived at Elk Lake in the 1920s, my grandfather sent him his warhorse, Bill. He was an amazing jumper and I often wondered where he came from, probably from a stable in England. However, he was full of shrapnel from the war and went lame. Bill had to be put down, much to my father's dismay as Bill was a very special horse and, I believe, the only warhorse sent to Western Canada from France.

Journeys with My Father from Menin Gate to Vimy

By Lesley Patten Elarid and her mother, Jacqueline Patten

We can truly say that the whole circuit of the Earth is girdled with the graves of our dead. In the course of my pilgrimage, I have many times asked myself whether there can be more potent advocates of peace upon Earth through the years to come, than this massed multitude of silent witnesses to the desolation of war.—*King George V, May 11, 1922*

History has always been a topic of discussion at our home, and my dad, Jack Patten, was avidly interested. From his experience as a boy during World War II in England, to his time in the Canadian Scottish Regiment on Vancouver Island, he was always reading, talking with veterans and travelling to the battlefields of Europe.

The first of nearly forty tours my father organized to Europe began in 1990. I was just sixteen at the time, taking time off school to take a bus tour with twenty-seven World War II veterans and their wives to World War battle sites. How can you beat hearing first-hand stories of the war from those who were there? Over the years, my father built strong friendships with local teachers, mayors of villages and interested local citizens in France, Belgium and the Netherlands. Everywhere we went, we were welcomed with open arms, for all that the Canadians before us had done. It seems they truly follow the act of remembrance.

Each cemetery, battlefield or local village was a memorable experience. One very moving ceremony was in Démuin, France, which has forty-two graves, most of them 16th Battalion Canadian Scottish members from Vancouver Island. A wreath was laid at Piper Paul MM's grave and some French pipers played the lament, in the company of veterans and the bulk of the small village. Everyone retired to the *mairie* (city hall) for a *vin d'honneur* at the village of Aubercourt, the final objective of the battalion on that day.

From that first trip with veterans who learned about the World War I experience, to current serving soldiers, past Lieutenant-Governors of BC and interested travellers who have accompanied us on the trips, all have been so moved by the contributions of Canadians during the wars and the well-preserved Commonwealth war graves and monuments, as well as by the local people. To stand in small fields that were once battle zones, to see the amazing signs of remembrance, all Canadians should have this experience. Some notable World War I locations include:

- The Menin Gate Memorial to the Missing is a war memorial in Ypres, Belgium, dedicated to the British and Commonwealth soldiers who were killed in the Ypres Salient of World War I and whose graves are unknown. There are over fifty thousand names listed. Each evening at eight p.m. the last post is played, a tradition that has continued since Armistice except during World War II.

- Tyne Cot Commonwealth War Graves Cemetery and Memorial to the Missing is a Commonwealth War Graves Commission burial ground that contains another thirty thousand names of soldiers whose graves are unknown. The local school children visit annually to host a picnic, so those lost can hear the sound of children's laughter and know that their sacrifice was not in vain.

- The Canadian National Vimy Memorial in France is dedicated to the memory of Canadian Expeditionary Force members killed during World War I. It also serves as the place of commemoration for World War I Canadian soldiers killed or presumed dead in France who have no known grave. The remaining trenches in the area are available for tours.

There are tours available in the region and plenty of resources for those interested in World War I, such as the Western Front Association that educates the public in the history of the Great War. It is touching and awe-inspiring to be in the area that was the scene of so much death and destruction, and yet so necessary to visit to grasp the monumental effort that took place there so many years ago.

Paying Respects

By RAY TRAVERS, VICTORIA

My son Michael Travers and I have comprehensive family history records on both my wife's and my side of our family. This research made my trip possible. I have visited the World War I battlefields where Canada served many times. The most recent trip was in November

2011 when I visited sixteen graves of close family members—with descendants of common ancestors up to five generations back. Some family members who died were Canadians and others were British. Most died from 1916 to 1918.

In November 2011, I arranged a personal local guide for my tour. Over three days from Ypres in Flanders to Albert in the Somme, I visited all sixteen graves of my extended family. On each grave I left a small wooden cross with a poppy and took a photo. Some soldiers have no grave and their names are mentioned on the Menin Gate and the Vimy Memorial.

One of the graves I visited was my mother's father (my maternal grandfather), who was an Englishman: Private Reuben Wagner (November 28, 1891–August 2, 1917), buried at Poelcapelle British Cemetery, West Flanders, Belgium. Another of the graves I visited was my dad's father (my paternal grandfather), who was a Canadian: Captain and Quartermaster Oliver Travers, MC (April 1, 1876–October 29, 1917), buried at Brandhoek New Military Cemetery, West Flanders, Belgium.

Recent family history research suggests there are another three graves of my extended family who died on the battlefields of World War I. My family is probably not unique in our losses.

On this trip, I learned there are about a thousand Commonwealth War Graves Cemeteries in Belgium and France. About one half are small and seldom visited. The Commonwealth War Graves Commission, in the tradition of an English country garden, will immaculately maintain all these cemeteries, forever.

This trip gave me a direct sense of the huge human impact of World War I on Canadians, the hard lessons learned as Canada became a nation on the battlefields—our Canadian soldiers, from Vimy forward, did not lose another battle in World War I. I also have some understanding how the hard lessons learned by our soldiers and nurses who returned from World War I helped create the Canada we know today.

Marking Sacrifice: Commonwealth War Graves Commission

The scene is stark, yet somehow comforting. Uniform grey headstones etched with names and crosses form perfectly straight rows, grass neatly clipped to their edges. Low shrubs and red brick walls create a peaceful, garden-like setting. It is a place of reflection and remembrance. Similar Commonwealth War Graves Commission (CWGC) sites are found in 153 countries, funded by six Commonwealth member countries (Australia, Canada, India, New Zealand, South Africa and the United Kingdom). They mark where Commonwealth soldiers fell in each of the two Great Wars.

Originally established as the Imperial War Graves Commission in 1917, the commission emerged from the vision of Sir Fabian Ware, who was commander of a mobile unit in the British Red Cross during the Great War. Saddened by what he saw, Ware was determined to honour those who had fallen by marking and recording the graves. After the war, he worried the gravesites would fall into disrepair and be forgotten. He made the maintenance, care and documentation of these graves his life's work.

The commission engaged prominent architects of the day and asked Rudyard Kipling to advise them on inscriptions. He selected the biblical phrase "Their Name Liveth for Evermore" for those whose identities were known, and for the unidentified, "A Soldier of the Great War Known unto God." Kipling had supported the war effort, wrote propaganda for the British government and encouraged his son to sign up with the Irish Guards. John Kipling was killed in battle at age eighteen. His father later wrote: "If any question why we died / Tell them, because our fathers lied."

The CWGC now cares for the graves and memorials of almost 1.7 million servicemen and women, Chinese labourers and Commonwealth citizens killed during conflict. Monuments to the missing include the Thiepval Memorial in France, which carries the names of over seventy-two thousand casualties from the Battle of the Somme.

There are more than 130 sites here in British Columbia where Commonwealth casualties are commemorated. From single markers like the one at St. Eugene Mission near Cranbrook to Esquimalt's Veterans' Cemetery, where eighty-one casualties are honoured. Vancouver's Mountain View Cemetery includes a special Soldier's Plot where 319 World War I soldiers are commemorated.

To locate a cemetery or to learn where a soldier is buried, visit the Commonwealth War Graves Commission website at www.cwgc.org.

From Our Listeners: My Father's Wounds

By Bev Christensen, Sorrento

It is my belief that the effect that wars have on civilians often goes unrecognized. My story which follows illustrates that point but I am certain my experience is mild compared to other children of returned World War soldiers.

This is the story of my father, Clifford Warner, who, caught up with national pride, walked to a recruiting station before he was eighteen and lied about his age so he could join the army. He was assigned to serve with the 38th Regiment and was there for two weeks before his father came and disclosed that he had lied about his age. When he turned eighteen in September 1915, he was more successful and, with minimal training, was sent overseas and spent the remainder of the war fighting in the dirty, wet trenches in France and Belgium. He was wounded twice in the leg. As was the case at that time, as soon as he was considered fit he was sent back into the trenches. When I asked him why he didn't either refuse to return to the fighting or run away, he told me that the men who did that were court-martialled and often shot.

Like most World War I veterans he never talked about his experiences in the army. But one time when he was staying with me on the dairy farm after I was married, I asked him, "If there was another war and you were considered fit to fight, would you join up voluntarily again?" Without hesitation he replied, "I would run so far back into the bush they'd never find me."

A relative told me that when my dad's younger brother, John Fernandez, joined up too their mother asked my dad, who had already enlisted, to take care of him because John was considered to be somewhat frail and not as strong as her other strapping sons. John was killed at Courcelette. This was a battle leading toward the big battle at Vimy Ridge. As was too often the case in that terrible war, his body was never found. Probably he had either been blown to pieces or shot and fell into the mud and was pushed down into the mud by the wagons, horses and men passing over him. His name appears on the Vimy Memorial in France. My dream has been to visit that monument and place a red poppy beside his name.

I don't think my father ever got over his brother's death. Remembrance Day ceremonies were very important to him. If you looked at the front of veteren's parades held in Prince George in those days, you would see my dad marching straight and tall in memory of his brother and those other men he knew who never returned from Europe. A gentle man, whom I seldom heard swearing, I think he might have suffered from what we would today diagnose as battle stress syndrome because, as a teenager, from my bedroom which was located directly over my parents' bedroom, I could hear him when he roared swear words while having nightmares and my mother trying to shush him into silence.

My father loved dogs so we always had a family dog as children. But he hated cats. That didn't deter me from wanting one of my best friend's grandmother's kittens, a fluffy, white one with blue eyes. So I took it home and childishly I thought I would keep it in my bedroom and my dad would never know it was there. Everything was fine until I had to leave my room to join the family at the supper table right next to my bedroom. Of course, as soon as I left the kitten began mewing. My dad sat up stiffly in his chair. "Is there a cat in this house?" he demanded. "Oh yes, Dad. It is such a cute little kitten. If I can keep it I will take care of it. Oh please, please Dad, let me keep that kitten."

"If I find that kitten in this house I'll tie it to the clothesline by its tail, pour gasoline over it and light it on fire," he said. Horrifying words from my usually gentle father. Naturally the kitten was returned immediately.

Years later, when I had a family of my own and my father was staying with me while my mother helped my brother John's wife, Marilyn, care for a new baby, my dad sat at the kitchen table staring at one of the many farm cats we had on our dairy farm. I reminded him of the little white kitten with blue eyes that I had wanted as a child and the terrible threat he had issued against it. "Why did you do that?" I asked.

"It was because, when we went into the bombed-out villages in Europe during the war, the cats and the pigs were eating the bodies of the people and the soldiers who had died."

Then, finally, I understood why he did not like cats.

From Our Listeners: Mystery Soldier

By Yvonne Laviolette, Courtenay

Yvonne told us this story after buying an old locked trunk that, after being opened, revealed bits and pieces of the story of soldier William Rodger, who lived in nearby Cumberland.

I have always been a bit of a collector and love a good mystery and history. After reading the letters in the trunk it became clear that William Rodger had no family. There are many letters from his mother and his sister imploring him to write back to them in Scotland. One last letter came from a law office informing him of his sister's death and asking him to "settle her affairs" as he is the last known living relative.

The first entry into the trunk by date is his letter of recommendation from the Glen Elgin Scotch Distillery in Glasgow dated April 28, 1910. He then travelled to Canada and when war broke out he enlisted in the army in Vernon, BC. Overseas he worked as a bomb storage technician and there are indeed pictures of World War I Europe taken from a high vantage point that look like the earth has craters from bombs. He fought mostly in Belgium. When he returned from war, it seems he worked in mining towns around BC. When he signed up, his civilian occupation was listed as locomotive fireman. So I am assuming that is what he was doing in Cumberland. Judging from the photos he must have worked in some capacity on the dam installation at Brilliant, BC. There are numerous photographs of that dam in many stages of construction.

William Rodger wasn't a decorated officer, but he was a man who went to war and did his part. He should be honoured and not locked away in a box and forgotten about. One can see by the way he kept his World War I memorabilia that he was proud of his service. We can't imagine the horrors of Europe in World War I. We should all be proud of him. It's sad that he has no family to honour him. I have been adding to the trunk. I now have his war record service record and his death certificate. The trunk will eventually end up in a military museum.

I have included one of the photos he must have taken (at right). The date on the back is April 27, 1924. I see that it is the date of the unveiling of the cenotaph at Victory Square in Vancouver. So this is the ceremony of the unveiling.

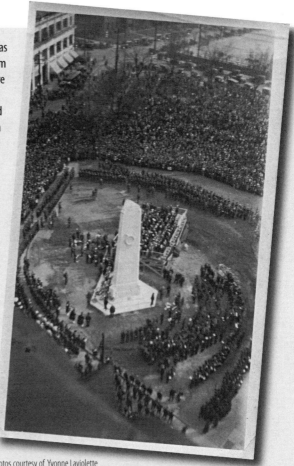

Photos courtesy of Yvonne Laviolette

A City Goes to War: Victoria's War Story on the Web

We were thrilled when we discovered a new online project about Victoria's war effort. A City Goes to War is a University of Victoria online project managed by PhD history student Jim Kempling, who is also a retired infantry colonel.

Says Kempling, "In most of our cities across the country people really have no idea what it was like in their own home town during the First World War. Victoria was the hometown of Sir Arthur Currie who led the Canadian Corps, yet if you asked most people on the street they would have no idea that he was a high school teacher or real estate agent in Victoria before World War I. That's what we're trying to recapture for people."

A City Goes to War includes two thousand primary source documents, photos, letters, newspaper articles and a searchable database of over six thousand service records of people from Victoria who served in the Great War. A timeline tracks happenings in Victoria, British Columbia and Canada leading up to and through the war years. There is also a teaching package for high schools that challenges students to create their own "Fakebook" page and explore the lives of people in Victoria during the war years. This digital model is available to other universities and cities wanting to tell local stories to commemorate the hundredth anniversary. Visit www.acitygoestowar.ca.

Our Journey into the Great War

For the past two years, we've lived in the past, and travelled to battlefields in Europe and cenotaphs here at home. We've spent time in museums, met with the descendants of veterans and treasured the stories they shared with us online. We've come to know our own family stories better and we hope others have too. This book is our tribute to all those touched by the war years.

Terms of Engagement

By Mark Rennie Forsythe

This Great War project has propelled me on a fascinating personal journey, and judging from CBC listeners' contributions, this has also been true for many others. Some family stories in these pages are finely detailed and intricately documented; others are like frayed strands to be tugged at a hundred years later. As you'll read below, I've come to learn about my great-uncle Albert Rennie, someone I knew nothing about while growing up. I've also recently learned that Albert's older brother, Robert Charles Rennie, also served. He survived the war but died before his time in 1934.

There have been surprises. Our chapter about BC's Victoria Cross winners includes Robert Hill Hanna, from County Down in Ireland. He moved to BC in about 1904, worked in logging camps and signed up with Vancouver's 29th Battalion—Tobin's Tigers. Hanna would later receive the VC for bravery at the battle for Hill 70 in France, the same fight that cost my great-uncle Albert Rennie his life. On closer inspection, Robert Hanna came from Kilkeel, Ireland, the same coastal town my Forsythe ancestors emigrated from. A search of my family tree finds him connected through marriage, and to top it off, Robert Hill Hanna lived at Mount Lehman, just a short drive from where I now live in the Fraser Valley.

My grandfather Albert Forsythe enlisted with the 122nd Battalion near his home in Severn Bridge, Ontario. The nineteen-year-old "lumberman" worked at the local sawmill and was probably well suited for the "Muskoka Cracker Jacks," as the 122nd dubbed themselves. They were off to Europe to fight the Kaiser as they sang, to "Crack the logjam." They would later become part of the Canadian Forestry Corps, cutting timber for tunnels, dugouts, railways, duck walks for muddy trenches and plank roads. Twenty thousand Canadian soldiers were involved in this part of the war effort.

I did not hear my grandfather utter a word about his experiences; he died when I was a young boy, so I never got to ask him the questions that appear so obvious now. Albert's eldest son, Hugh, later served during World War II and while stationed in England met his future bride, my aunt Doreen. This World War I project has helped me reconnect with her and my Forsythe cousins. A most wonderful gift.

My Search for Albert Ernest Rennie

Height…5 ft 8 1/2 in.
Girth when fully expanded…37 ½ in.
Complexion…Ruddy
Eyes…Brown
Hair…Brown
Do you understand the nature and terms of your engagement?…Yes.

My middle name is Rennie, attached in tribute to my paternal grandmother, Helen (Rennie) Forsythe. As a very young child I remember cigarette smoke curling above her head like a halo, and a love that flowed like a deep, underground spring. I did wonder why my middle name wasn't a more typical James, Michael or John. Rennie was formal. Adult. My parents' marriage ended when I was four years old and my grandmother Helen died when I was nine, so links with my father's family became more tenuous.

We did visit our father and his new family, and Aunt Dora and Uncle Joe's near Orillia. Dora was my grandmother's sister and also a Rennie; she and Joe lived about a two-minute walk away from a decommissioned hydro plant that harnessed the Severn River at Wasdell Falls. Aunt Dora was a champion baker who ruled her kitchen with generous panache; even the dog Daisie benefitted, treated to chicken livers cooked on the stove top. Uncle Joe was a gentle soul with an easy chuckle who rolled his own cigarettes and built their sturdy white house perched atop a jutting slab of granite. He was also responsible for the old hydro plant, which to an eight-year-old was like visiting Dr. Frankenstein's laboratory with its huge green turbines, ringed ceramic insulators and big copper switches.

Water spilled through gates inside the power house where we shuffled slowly across a narrow metal ramp above water crashing below. It was frightening—and thrilling. The roiling water made the building shudder and the sound reverberated up concrete walls to a high ceiling. I remember hearing fragments of a story about a drowned body, trapped against the dam's workings. The river seemed a malevolent force, but we swam and fished in the tame waters below the dam.

By the time I was nineteen, both Uncle Joe and Aunt Dora had died, and I had moved to British Columbia. My relationship with my father was paper-thin; we spoke with each on the phone—awkwardly—about once a year. I knew very little of his family history, especially the part that contained my middle name, which was also his middle name. Some years later I returned to Ontario with my own young family and visited the family graveyard. My aunt, uncle and father are buried in a plot beside Dora's parents, George and Isabel Rennie, and I was surprised to see another Rennie's name inscribed on the side of their headstone, green lichen beginning to cloud the letters of his name: Albert Ernest Rennie. Killed in Action in France. August 5th, 1917. Aged 21 years.

Private Albert Ernest Rennie.
Courtesy of Mark Forsythe

I don't recall hearing a word about this great-uncle, lost in the Great War. My brother Paul (with the better memory) does remember seeing Albert's photo staring out from the top of Aunt Dora's piano and asking her about the young man in the military uniform. "He was my brother, he died in the war." And that was all she would say. Our half-sister Laura informs me Albert's name appears on a plaque inside Soldiers' Memorial Hospital at Orillia, built to honour the men killed in World War I. Our mother also worked there as a nurse, and almost forty years after Albert was killed, that's where I was born and given the Rennie name. With the approach of another Remembrance Day, I feel compelled to learn more about Albert. How might I honour his short life? I know so little. It's like walking down a narrow forest path and having it come to an abrupt end. Where to next?

I dive into searching the online Canadian war records and find that Albert E. Rennie enlisted with the 157th Overseas Battalion in February 1916 for the Canadian Expeditionary Force. The enlistment paper tells me he was a nineteen-year-old farmer living at a Mrs. Watkins's home on West Street in Orillia. At that time the town had an opera house, an "Insane Asylum" and Stephen Leacock, who lived at Brewery Bay where he dredged up Orillia stories for his classic *Sunshine Sketches of a Little Town.* I imagine this young boarder Albert, setting out from Mrs. Watkins's each morning to work on a nearby farm. Leacock's fictional Mariposa was drawn from Orillia, which he thought was like so many other small towns, "with the same square streets and the same maple trees and the same churches and hotels." What was Albert thinking when he stepped into the registration office to sign the attestation papers with his stilted, compact script? Did he understand what "Terms of Engagement" truly meant? At this point in the war, perhaps he did. It had raged for almost two years with millions killed, a far cry from earlier expectations that the war would be over before Christmas 1914. The farm boy with the ruddy complexion was to be trained as a warrior. Would I trade places with him?

I came of age during the angry backlash to the Vietnam War and growing opposition to an expanding arsenal of nuclear weapons. Neil Young's "Ohio," John Lennon's "Imagine," Creedence Clearwater Revival's "Fortunate Son" and Bob Dylan's "Blowin' in the Wind" were spinning on my turntable. During my mid-teens, my father suggested I join the military as had his father, older brother and one of my cousins. His pitch: "Good discipline, and a free education." I didn't give it a second thought. I was reading Joseph Heller's *Catch-22* and Dalton Trumbo's *Johnny Got His Gun*. (The pacifist novel was inspired by the Prince of Wales's visit to a Canadian soldier who had lost all of his senses and limbs.) My generation's ethos was to question the glorification of war and the military-industrial complex and to "make love, not war."

Albert came of age answering the call to fight for "King and Country." By 1916 more than three hundred thousand young Canadians had signed up, many of them members of immigrant families from Great Britain. The colonial imperative was clear: stand up for Mother Country. Some were also drawn by adventure, others to a regular paycheque. After intensive training in Quebec and England, Albert and his Canadian troops were sent to the Western Front of Belgium and France. The front was oozing with mud so thick that it could add twenty-five kilograms to boots and uniforms. There were also the rat-infested trenches, a deafening roar of constant shelling, sniper fire, flame throwers and, to top it off, the risk of deadly mustard gas. Attacks and counterattacks came non-stop; the Western Front battle lines hardly budged over four years. On both sides the slaughter was horrific: sixteen million military and civilian deaths, twenty million wounded. Of the more than six hundred thousand Canadians who joined the Great War, sixty-seven thousand of them died and 173,000 were wounded. These are numbers so large, it is beyond our ken to grasp them.

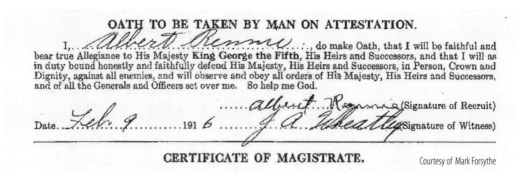

Courtesy of Mark Forsythe

There's a note scrawled across Albert's attestation paper indicating that he was transferred from the 157th Overseas Battalion to the 76th Battalion. I've located the regimental bugle call in the front pages of a battalion history; I slowly pluck out the notes on my guitar. G marching up an octave, back-stepping two notes, then, a return to G. It feels eerie to play this. Did these notes fill my great-uncle with courage, or dread? In April 1917 the Canadians experienced their most important victory at Vimy Ridge, the first major Allied victory of the war. Albert (now with the 18th Battalion) was part of the attack recorded in the Confidential War Diary of the 18th Battalion, now in the National Archives of Canada:

> At Zero hour, viz 5:30 am, the advance was made. Simultaneously with the opening up of the Artillery Barrage the Battalion left the "Jumping-Off" trenches and attacked the German front lines.

French and British troops had previously tried in vain to take Vimy, but it was the Canadians who won this vital high ground. It was the first important victory of the war; it also gave the former colony a new sense of itself. Canadian troops were lauded by the British prime minister, David Lloyd George, who wrote in his memoirs, "They were marked out as storm troops; for the remainder of the war they were brought along to head the assault in one great battle after another." The victory came at a terrible cost to the Canadians: 3,598 killed and 7,004 wounded. By early August, Albert and his comrades had moved on to a new battleground, preparing for the fight in trenches named Corkscrew, Cyclist, Cavalry and Cornwall. Military historian and author Mark Zuehlke pinpointed the battalion on the day Albert was killed: August 5th, 1917. "The Canadians were preparing for an attack in the area of Lens, France, against an objective called Hill 70. The attack was supposed to happen on August 4 but was pushed back by foul weather. So it went in on August 15. I suspect your uncle was killed by shellfire or on a patrol."

Lens was the next big test for Albert and fellow Canadian troops. Its rail link supplied the Germans, and it possessed coal supplies in high demand for manufacturing. They prepared for the attack by practising on mock German positions, so that each man would know his job. The battalion's war diary for August 5 speaks to the preparations, adding one poignant note: "Quiet day for the Battalion. The Battalion furnished carrying parties of 350 men for carrying Trench Mortar Batteries to their gun positions. Casualties numbering 1 o.r. [other ranks] killed and 3 o.rs. wounded."

This reference stopped me in my tracks. It could very well be the death of twenty-one-year-old Albert E. Rennie, killed between battles during preparations for the push on Hill 70. Albert was gone but his mates were soon in the thick of it, and by August 15, ten Canadian battalions had attacked Hill 70, repulsing twenty-one counterattacks, finally claiming it on August 18. The Canadians took Hill 70, but not the larger objective of Lens. The war diary chronicle makes for a chilling read about what these soldiers faced and includes handwritten messages dispatched from the trenches:

> From the information we have from two prisoners we have just brought in we have every reason to expect a counterattack tonight. I need a few S.O.S. flares.
>
> Cannot something be done to keep the German planes away. What's the matter with our air service?
>
> Have only about 40 men in shape to carry on…can you send more reinforcements. Some shell shock cases carrying on.
>
> Heavy barrage is required, every reason to believe they are coming over.

Part of my search to learn more about Albert Rennie has included renewing connections with Ontario cousins. I learn on the phone that Gail has named one of her sons Travis Albert. Her mother, Doreen, married my father's older brother Hugh, who served during World War II. I think she's smiling as she tells me that Hugh was also demoted for returning late from their honeymoon. I ask if she knows anything about Albert Rennie. "I just know they called him Ab." Her mother-in-law Helen (Albert's younger sister) did not speak about him. With so much loss tearing through families, perhaps it was too difficult to speak the pain.

Albert's mother, Isabel, likely learned of his death in August 1917. Just two months later, she died of heart failure. She was only fifty-seven. Her heart was surely broken. It wasn't until 1922 that Memorial Medals were given to the mothers and widows of dead soldiers. Albert's were sent to his father, George. Aunt Doreen is the keeper of a silver cross that bears the sovereign's crown, three maple leaves linked by laurel and the royal cipher "GRI" in the middle.

His name is stamped into the reverse side below his registration number: 643344. A purple ribbon is now faded and frayed.

Albert is buried not far from Lens, France, in the small village of Sains-en-Gohelle, beside hundreds of other Canadian and British troops. What if he had escaped the grim odds and returned home, fallen in love, planted crops and watched the Severn River flow past his family home? He most certainly would have tasted his sister Dora's blue-ribbon baking—deep pies and butter tarts—and experienced her crushing bear hugs, the ones I came to cherish as a child. His sister Helen, my grandmother, would have graced his life with care and tenderness that mark all the stories I hear about her. On this Remembrance Day I will remember Albert and a life that might have been. After all, I am a Rennie.

Back side of Rennie medal.
Courtesy of Mark Forsythe

He Never Made It to Europe

BY GREG DICKSON

Like Mark, my Great War odyssey began with a search for a great-uncle who never came home. His younger brother, my grandfather, survived Vimy Ridge and returned to Canada to raise a family. But Theo Dickson only made it as far as training camp in England before a sudden illness killed him at only twenty-two years of age. He left behind some wonderful letters and he was always fondly remembered by the family. His name is on the cenotaph in Vernon, but bodies were not sent home in those days and he was buried in a military cemetery in Wiltshire—too far away for family to visit or leave flowers.

I was determined to pay my respects. So in the spring of 2014, my wife Sheryl and I headed off for a holiday in the south of England. We saw Salisbury Cathedral and Stonehenge and the famous chalk hills. We visited Lawrence of Arabia's cottage and grave in Dorset. And then we found Theo's grave near Tidworth, a small town north of Salisbury. Tidworth is still a busy military base, and soldiers are everywhere. But just a little ways out of town, nestled in the Wiltshire Hills and surrounded by farmland, is a very peaceful cemetery.

I was worried that it would be one of those headstone jungles with crosses as far as the eye can see. But it turned out to be an intimate and well-cared-for place. The sun was shining and the hills were green and pretty in that English way.

I felt sorry for Theo, buried so far from his family. But he was lucky not to see the carnage of the Western Front. We left a Canadian poppy on his grave and took a moment to remember the brother who never made it home.

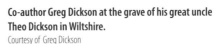

Co-author Greg Dickson at the grave of his great uncle Theo Dickson in Wiltshire.
Courtesy of Greg Dickson

A Message from the Canadian Letters and Images Project

By Dr. Stephen Davies, Project Director

We at the Canadian Letters and Images Project feel very fortunate to have been chosen by *BC Almanac* and the CBC to be supported by the proceeds of the sales of this book.

The Canadian Letters and Images Project at Vancouver Island University is an online archive of the Canadian war experience, both home front and battlefront, from any period in Canada's past. The project began as a means to put a human face to war and to remind us that war is ultimately about people, most of them ordinary and largely forgotten. Through the digitization of contemporary letters, diaries, photographs and other related materials, the Canadian Letters and Images Project permits Canadians to tell their story, and Canada's story, in their own words and images. Since its inception in August 2000, we have digitized more than fifteen thousand letters from Canadians across the country, as well as thousands of photographs, scores of diaries and a sweeping range of miscellaneous items connected to the war experience. These are all freely available to anyone through the project website at www.canadianletters.ca.

What makes this project unique is that as an online archive we do not keep any of the materials. We ask only to borrow the materials from Canadians across the country for copying and scanning, and then return them to the families. In this manner we have brought into the public domain valuable archival materials that otherwise would never have been seen. We hope that readers of this book will contact us if they have any materials they could share in this manner.

Wartime letters are like voices from the past, connecting generations across time. Correspondence helps us to put a human face to war, to poignantly remind us that those largely forgotten Canadians are far more than statistics or names on a cenotaph. The letters remind us that they too were once young, with loves and dreams, hopes and ambitions.

Correspondence permits us to share the experiences of war as the participants themselves saw it, history in the raw, without a lens of later interpretation. Such are the letters of a young soldier from Kamloops, British Columbia, Sydney Amyas Winterbottom. On April 23, 1917, he described his experiences at Vimy Ridge:

Dearest Mom and Dad:

Well, I suppose you have guessed by now, I went over the top on the first day of the big push. Our battalion were very lucky as regards to casualties, only 16 killed. . . Well I will try to describe this push. On the evening of the eighth of April, we moved into our jumping off trenches. . . About Five in the morning, the first division of Canadians went over the top. They didn't charge as the length to our objective was two and a half miles. They simply walked until they were near the point and then charged. . . We went over about eight o'clock. You should have seen how Fritz's trenches were smashed by our gunfire. We kept going always behind our barrage of shrapnel. All we had to do was follow up the barrage. It did the work. . .

But soldiers' letters are not just about battle. They encompass the full range of Canadian wartime experience. The same letter is also revealing about one of the most fundamental aspects of soldiering, the connection of soldier to home and loved ones:

I felt all through it that I was jake because I knew you all at home and the relatives had prayed for my safety. Therefore I knew I was fine and dandy. I received your nice parcel of louse proof underwear, cigs, and gum. Thanks ever so much for them. If I return home don't expect to see the lad who left you as I have changed. A little older looking I guess. I also enjoy a good cigar and drink of beer once in a while. But otherwise I'm the same. . . I hope to be back home toward September to have that deer hunt. . .

With fondest love

Lovingly, Sid

Winterbottom survived the Battle of Vimy Ridge. But he was killed a few months later in Canada's other great battle of 1917, Passchendaele. Sydney Amyas Winterbottom was only twenty-one.

The financial support provided by the sales of this book will greatly enhance the work of the project. As a not-for-profit project, without any government or corporate funding, the Canadian Letters and Images Project relies solely on the generosity of Canadians to support our work. Over 80 percent of all funds we raise go directly back into the project as student wages. Students are the backbone of this project, which provides them with a unique hands-on archival experience as a part of their education. This is an ongoing project, but we do not have the resources to do everything that needs to be done. The support we will receive from the sales of this book will permit us to hire and train more students, which in turn means we can then bring even more of these unique and important materials online for all Canadians at www.canadianletters.ca.

Hastings Park in Vancouver was another place where men gathered for drills.
Stuart Thomson photo, Vancouver Public Library 17401

OUR OWN
THE REGIMENTS

When World War I broke out, Canada's minister of militia decided to mobilize by raising numbered battalions rather than by maintaining the existing militia regiments intact. That decision has led to some confusion in the numbering system and some duplication. Canada ultimately offered four divisions under the Canadian Corps. Here are some of the regiments and battalions mentioned in this book. Thanks to the Department of National Defence site and Wikipedia for background.

2nd and 11th Canadian Mounted Rifles (BC Dragoons)—see also BC Horse

This reserve force regiment originated in Vernon on April 1, 1911, when two four-squadron regiments designated the "British Columbia Horse" were authorized to be formed. It was redesignated the 1st Regiment, British Columbia Horse, on December 1, 1911, and 30th Regiment, British Columbia Horse, on April 15, 1912.

The 2nd Canadian Mounted Rifles Battalion was authorized on November 7, 1914, as the 2nd Regiment, Canadian Mounted Rifles, Canadian Expeditionary Force (CEF). It disembarked in France on September 22, 1915, as part of the 1st Canadian Mounted Rifles Brigade. It fought as part of the 8th Canadian Infantry Brigade, 3rd Canadian Division, in France and Flanders until the end of the war.

The 11th Regiment, Canadian Mounted Rifles, CEF, was authorized on November 7, 1914. The regiment was converted to infantry and redesignated the 11th "Overseas" Canadian Mounted Rifles Battalion, CEF, on April 23, 1916. Its personnel were absorbed by the 24th Reserve Battalion, CEF, on May 18, 1917, to provide reinforcements for the Canadian Corps in the field. Now perpetuated as the BC Dragoons.

From Our Listeners: Signaller Edward Francis Hill

By Ian Haynes, Victoria

My great-uncle Edward Francis Hill was born about the turn of the century in Bath, England. He was the younger brother of my grandmother, Mrs. R.H. Simmons (née Hill), born Gladys Hill, January 1889 in Bath, England. He joined the Canadian Field Artillery as a gunner during World War I. At the time of his death he was a signaller with the 3rd Brigade, Canadian Field Artillery. He died on September 2, 1918, at the Battle of Drocourt–Quéant Line.

At Drocourt–Quéant the 3rd Brigade recounted that visual signalling was too dangerous, as German machine gunners on the flanks were able to see and fire upon the signallers handling the lamps, so the formation had to rely on pigeons and runners.

Edward Francis Hill is buried at the Vis-en-Artois British Cemetery, Haucourt Pas de Calais, France.

With help from Robyn Rossworn, Armstrong

From Our Listeners: Gunner William Forrest Maxwell Sr.

By Judy Lam Maxwell, Vancouver

I remember my grandpa as very curmudgeonly. I don't ever remember Grandpa—or even Dad—saying that he was in World War I when he was alive. I don't think I even knew that grandpa was a Great War veteran until sometime after his death in 1982. He never talked about it, period. With the centenary of the war coming up, I decided to ask my dad a lot of questions about Grandpa's experiences in the war.

Dad's father, William Forrest Maxwell Sr., was born in Vancouver on February 2, 1896. Grandpa was the sixth son of Reverend George Ritchie Maxwell, British Columbia's first Liberal member of parliament, Burrard riding, and the leading representative of the Liberal–Labour alliance. Great-grandpa Maxwell died in 1898 when my grandpa was just two years old, and his mother was left to raise seven children on her own. As the sole breadwinner, Mary Forrest Maxwell became a cleaning lady to provide for them and they lived very modestly.

William grew up in Vancouver and went to King Edward High School, where the Vancouver General Hospital is now located at 12th Avenue and Oak Street (the school later relocated to 33rd and Oak and became Eric Hamber Secondary School). After completing his grade twelve, William went to the University of British Columbia and studied in the faculty of science. During his studies in 1915, William and eight other classmates received a blessing from the university to take a leave of absence and join the war effort. They left Vancouver and headed for Kingston, Ontario, where they enlisted in December 1915. Grandpa and his classmates were part of the first graduating class of UBC in absentia. Grandpa was assigned No. 304597, in the 46th Battery (later the 33rd Battery), Canadian Field Artillery of the Canadian Expeditionary Force that went to France. Grandpa spent three years in Passchendaele, Belgium—on the Western Front—where, ultimately, the Allies lost close to 260,000 casualties, including an estimated sixteen thousand Canadians, to the Germans. Grandpa was one of a scant few who survived.

As a member of the Pacific Chapter of the Western Front Association, I've brought my dad to social events and on one occasion I discovered a fascinating tidbit of information about my grandpa. While attending a "dugout" in a member's basement, the topic of field artillery came up in conversation and my dad told the group that he thought that Grandpa was a sniper. This was the first time I had heard this fascinating story. Dad went on to say that after the war, Grandpa used to meet up with some of his war buddies at the Legion and that they were all snipers: Roy Eden, Clem Morgan, Fraser Stanford and a couple of others. Dad also said that when he was a teenager, he went shooting with Grandpa in the University Endowment Lands and that Grandpa was a crack shot. If Grandpa was a gunner in the field artillery, he would have had hearing loss because they didn't use earplugs in those days. Grandpa had had perfect hearing, so I think Dad is right about Grandpa being a sniper. It makes sense.

At the end of the war, William was given an honourable discharge in 1919 and returned to Vancouver for a short time. A group of wartime friends pooled their money and bought a homestead around Quesnel flats, the entry point to Barkerville. From 1919 to 1927, William worked on the railway and in the mines, inspected homesteads on horseback (he carried a gun), herded cattle and so on to make ends meet. It wasn't until 1927 that William moved on with his life and became a teacher. He settled back in Vancouver in 1931 and started a family.

My educated guess is that Grandpa was always haunted by his experiences in Passchendaele: seeing soldiers drowning in mud, witnessing comrades being German targets for artillery and machine-gun fire, eating bad food and drinking water tasting like gasoline. Passchendaele was known as one of the disasters of World War I, and I can appreciate why Grandpa escaped reality and lived in the bush of northern British Columbia for over ten years. This solace was his way of regaining composure after such a nightmare of killing and death and destruction. W.F. Maxwell Sr. lived until he was eighty-six.

Duke of Connaught's Own Rifles

The 6th Regiment, The Duke of Connaught's Own Rifles, was placed on active service on August 6, 1914, for local protection duties. The 6th was one of the regiments involved in the expulsion of the *Komagata Maru* in Vancouver Harbour just before the Great War broke out.

Today the commanding officer of the Duke of Connaught's Own Rifles is Lieutenant-Colonel Harjit Sajjan, the first Sikh to head a Canadian regiment. "When I was growing up," he told the *Globe and Mail*, "I didn't even think I was allowed to join the military."

Irish Fusiliers

The 11th Regiment Irish Fusiliers of Canada was placed on active service on August 6, 1914, for local protection duties. Also involved in the expulsion of the *Komagata Maru*. Now perpetuated in the BC Regiment.

1st British Columbia (7th Battalion)

The 7th Battalion was authorized on August 10, 1914. It disembarked in France in early 1915 where it fought as part of the 2nd Infantry Brigade, 1st Canadian Division. The 7th saw action in every major battle from Neuve Chapelle to the campaign of the final hundred days. Over fifteen hundred members were killed and the battalion won three Victoria Crosses (Bellew, O'Rourke and Rayfield).

Tobin's Tigers (29th Battalion)

The 29th Battalion was authorized on November 7, 1914. It disembarked in France in September 1915, where it fought as part of the 6th Infantry Brigade, 2nd Canadian Division. Over four thousand served with the 29th, commanded by a veteran of the Boer War, Lieutenant-Colonel Henry Seymour Tobin. Six hundred men were killed and more than fourteen hundred wounded. They would proudly become known as Tobin's Tigers. The battalion's honours include one Victoria Cross (Hanna). Henry Randolph Notman Clyne served with the 29th and described the experiences—at the Somme, Ypres, Vimy, Hill 70, Amiens and beyond—in his 1964 book, *Vancouver's 29th:*

> Our first long winter campaign against a welter of mud and caved-in trenches now began...Shelling was suspended by both sides throughout Christmas Day, and in the evening the enemy began singing and even waved across "no man's land." Later, the Germans erected a large notice board. The light was insufficient to read its contents but this did not affect its use as a fine target for sentries' rifles.

30th from Vancouver Island

The 30th Battalion was authorized on October 27, 1914, drawing men from Vancouver Island and the Interior. It included men from the Nanaimo Independent Rifle Company, the 68th Earl Grey's Own Rifles, the 102nd Rocky Mountain Rangers, the Grand Forks Independent Rifle Company and 107th East Kootenay Regiment. Over 290 men were killed and the battalion's honours included a Victoria Cross (Prince Rupert's Cy Peck).

30th and 31st BC Horse

The 30th BC Horse was initially under the command of Lieutenant-Colonel C.L. Bott, a veteran of the South African War. The regiment, with headquarters in Vernon, consisted of "A" Squadron from Lumby and Coldstream, "B" Squadron from Vernon, "C" Squadron from Armstrong and Enderby, and "D" squadron out of Kelowna. At the outbreak of war in 1914, the 30th BC Horse was mobilized and brought up to strength. (The 31st BC Horse was headquartered in Merritt.) Orders were received in November that the 30th BCH would amalgamate with an independent Squadron of Horse at Willows Camp in Victoria, BC, to

Opposite: For those who surrendered, the war was over. The chances of survival in a POW camp were much better than in the trenches.
Searching POWs, CWM 19930012-752, George Metcalf Archival Collection, © Canadian War Museum

From Our Listeners: POW Sidney Percy Jones

By Diane Jones, Vernon

He was a kind, gentle man. We all miss him very much.

My father-in-law, Sidney Percy Jones, was born December 16, 1896, in Deptford, Kent, England. He immigrated to Canada with his parents and six siblings in the spring of 1911 aboard SS *Corsican*. The family lived in Regina until the death of the second-eldest son, Ernest, in 1912. Sidney decided to leave Regina but returned to join the Canadian Army in October 1914. His army number was 73668. He was eighteen years of age and five feet eight inches tall.

The battalion trained in Canada until April 29, 1915, when it sailed from Montreal to England on SS *Northland*. On September 7, we find Sidney in Otter Pool Army Camp, where he forfeited one day's pay for being absent.

He embarked for France ten days later and disembarked at Boulogne, France. He went into action at the battle of Ypres, where he went missing in action on June 6, 1916.

He was unofficially reported wounded and a POW at Reserve Lazarett 5 Hanover, which was a military hospital for POWs. By mid-August he was officially reported as a POW at nearby Celle Lager Prisoner of War Camp. In October, Sidney was transferred to Soltau and then in November 1916 was moved to Hameln, Hanover.

Sidney often told the story of pouring boiling water on his foot so he would be hospitalized and wouldn't have to work in the salt mines. Unfortunately he chose November 10, 1918, to injure himself, the day before Armistice. Because of the injuries, his return home was delayed.

He arrived at Ripon, North Yorkshire, in England on December 22, 1918. He had served in France for nine months and was a POW for two and a half years. In the early 1970s I asked him some questions about World War I and he spoke easily about the war. I didn't know at the time that he had not spoken about the war except for the boiling water incident. My mother-in-law and husband had not heard these stories before.

We have his medals and a letter from Buckingham Palace dated 1918 and signed by King George V, or his scribe.

form an overseas unit, the 2nd Canadian Mounted Rifles. The 2nd CMR Regiment won ten battle honours. Two members of the regiment, Captain John MacGregor and Major George Randolph Pearkes, won the Victoria Cross. A third VC, Gordon Flowerdew, started with the BC Horse but was serving with Lord Strathcona's Horse when he was posthumously awarded the medal.

From Our Listeners: Chaplain Montgomery

By Helen Ruth Montgomery Yerxa, Vancouver

Grandfather Montgomery was a chaplain at the front during World War I. Six of his sons and one daughter, a nursing sister, all served at the front as well. My father couldn't pass the medical examination so stayed home to care for his mother and two sisters.

One of my uncles, who was in London at the time, met with my grandfather, who was on leave. He told his son how drained he was and how difficult it was to bring news to the mothers of the casualties or deaths of their sons. It was a terrible strain.

The miracle was that all six sons, one daughter and Grandfather all returned to Canada. I have one of those old personal postcards people used to have printed. My grandfather was in the middle surrounded by his six sons. I cherish it and the story it tells.

Courtesy of Helen Ruth Montgomery Yerxa

From Our Listeners: My Dad, Major Arthur Grosvenor Piddington

By Helen Piddington (Campbell), Blind Channel

My father died at age eighty, in 1960, a veteran of the Great War, the war to end all wars: 1914–18.

He graduated from the Royal Military College in Kingston as a top student in 1900. Canada had no army then so he could choose a British regiment. He chose the Royal Horse Artillery (RHA). Before leaving home, his father made him promise that when he died, Dad would return to Canada and look after his two unmarried sisters. He died early in 1906, so Dad kept his promise and returned to Canada. His senior officers were appalled.

When the war was declared in 1914, he tried to join the RHA. Still in disgrace for putting his father before his regiment, he was demoted to the Royal Field Artillery and sent to Salonika in northern Greece. He fought there for five years under terrible conditions, coming home with PTSD (known then as shell shock), unable to speak for months and prone to rage from the absurdity of all he had witnessed, especially the terrible waste of lives—so many were killed by friendly fire. With no more appetite for war, he grew apples for market in the Eastern Townships of Quebec until the family moved west in 1924, where he grew most of our food but could not, would not, kill a chicken.

When I returned from France in 1966, to set up a printmaking studio in West Vancouver, I spent as much time as I could with Mum, on Vancouver Island. She enjoyed living alone but loved being driven on adventures down strange roads in areas unknown to both of us. Once, not far from Duncan, we came upon a place that seemed frozen in time. Roads were just passable for our ancient Hillman, but the land was covered with wooden barns and houses—all of them bleached silvery grey—ghostly from years of neglect. There wasn't a soul to be seen! What had happened?

"I think I know," said Mum. "This area was pre-empted by young Englishmen in the early 1900s but, before they could get the land producing enough to send for their families, the Great War was declared. So all of them downed their tools: returned to England, then left for the front—most of them never returning!"

So for all those years, this land had been untouched, unused. Huge maples, alders and cedars filled fields and empty spaces. Orchards had trees growing to great heights, some with scraggy fruit. Driveways were impassable, choked with growth. They had chosen good land! But why had no one else claimed it?

With the bustling town of Duncan so close, we found this silent, empty space troubling and I have never been able to get those ghostly valleys and hillsides out of my head.

50th Gordon Highlanders (Victoria)

Lieutenant-Colonel Arthur Currie, of the 5th Regiment Canadian Garrison Artillery, was appointed to command the unit before the war. He later went on to command the Canadian Corps. Attempts were made by the 50th to raise an overseas battalion of its own, but without success. But they remained a militia unit, filling guard duties and sending drafts to newly raised battalions such as the 30th, 48th and 67th (Western Scots).

54th Kootenay

The 54th was raised with headquarters at Nelson. According to the popular 54th website, "a full quota of men was easily recruited and on the 15th of June 1915, the Battalion assembled in camp at Vernon, BC, for the first time. A brigade was formed here consisting of the 47th Battalion, the 54th Battalion, the 11th CMR, and, later, the Bond Battalion, all under Col. Duff Stuart."

The 54th Battalion served in the 11th Infantry Brigade, 4th Division. The 24th Field Artillery Regiment, RCA, perpetuates the 54th Battalion (Kootenay), CEF, and the 225th Battalion (Kootenay).

62nd Hulme's Huskies

The 62nd Battalion was authorized on April 20, 1915, and raised men in southern BC. It provided reinforcements for the Canadian Corps in the field until July 6, 1916, when its personnel were absorbed by the 30th Reserve Battalion, CEF.

67th Western Scots

The 67th was authorized on April 20, 1915, and embarked for Britain on April 1, 1916, where it was converted to a pioneer battalion and redesignated as the 67th Canadian (Pioneer) Battalion, CEF, on May 15, 1916. It disembarked in France on August 14, 1916, where it served as part of the 4th Canadian Division in France and Flanders until April 28, 1917, when its personnel were absorbed by the Canadian Corps in the field.

A Vancouver crowd sees off the departing 62nd Battalion.
City of Vancouver Archives, Stuart Thomson fonds, CVA 99-1092

Earl Grey's Own Rifles (68th Regiment)

The 120th Independent Field Battery, RCA, originated in Prince Rupert, British Columbia, on May 1, 1914, when the Earl Grey's Own Rifles were authorized to be formed. It was redesignated the 68th Regiment (Earl Grey's Own Rifles) on November 2, 1914, and the North British Columbia Regiment on March 12, 1920.

Andrew J. Turner worked for the CPR before signing up with the 72nd Battalion, Seaforth Highlanders.
Courtesy of Don Stewart

Seventy Twa, 72nd Regiment Seaforth Highlanders

The Seaforth Highlanders of Canada was first established on November 24, 1910, by a group of Vancouverites of Scottish descent. Upon official affiliation with the Seaforth Highlanders of the British Imperial Army, the 72nd Highlanders of Canada was redesignated the 72nd Seaforth Highlanders of Canada on April 15, 1912, and the 72nd Regiment Seaforth Highlanders of Canada on December 16, 1912. Over forty officers and sixteen hundred other ranks were drafted to other Canadian infantry units, in particular the 16th Battalion, CEF. In 1916 the regiment sailed for France as the 72nd Battalion, CEF, and very soon Seaforths were committed to battle. The 72nd quickly gained a reputation among friend and foe for its professional conduct and, particularly, for patrolling and aggressive trench raids. (VC recipient Piper Richardson served for six months in the cadet corps of the 72nd Regiment.)

88th Regiment Victoria Fusiliers

The 88th Regiment was officially authorized and established as a Canadian Militia Regiment on September 3, 1912. The 88th Regiment Victoria Fusiliers and the 50th Regiment were placed on active service on August 10, 1914, for local protective duty. These regiments contributed to the 7th and 16th Battalions, Canadian Expeditionary Force.

On August 28, 1914, the *Daily Colonist* wrote: "Five hundred Victoria volunteers will leave this morning for Valcartier, Quebec, preliminary to sailing for the front. They will include the representatives of the 50th Gordon Highlanders and the 88th Regiment of Fusiliers. The pipers will provide music for their corps to the dock while the band of 88th Fusiliers will play their contingent from Esquimalt to the boat." (VC recipient Piper Richardson served with the 16th Battalion.)

Warden's Warriors, the 102nd North British Columbia

The 102nd Battalion was authorized on December 22, 1915, and was raised in Comox, recruiting in northern British Columbia. It disembarked in France in August 1916, where it fought as part of the 11th Infantry Brigade, 4th Canadian Division. The 102nd fought at the Somme. Over 670 men lost their lives during the war and honours included a Victoria Cross (Graham Lyall).

102nd Rocky Mountain Rangers—see also the 30th Battalion

On July 1, 1898, five independent rifle companies were formed in the interior of British Columbia at Kamloops, Nelson, Kaslo, Rossland and Revelstoke. The independent companies were renamed the Rocky Mountain Rangers in 1900 but remained independent companies. In 1916 the unit raised the 172nd Battalion, CEF, for overseas deployment. On arrival overseas the battalion was dispersed to augment other Canadian infantry units but received battle honours for its outstanding service. On the home front, the 102nd staffed internment camps at Revelstoke, Mara Lake and Vernon. The 102nd also provided substantial numbers to the 54th (Kootenay) Battalion.

Western Irish, 121st Battalion

The 121st Battalion was authorized on December 22, 1915. It provided reinforcements for the Canadian Corps in the field until January 10, 1917, when its personnel were absorbed by the 16th Reserve Battalion, CEF.

104th Regiment Westminster Fusiliers and the 131st Battalion (Westminster)

The 104th Regiment Westminster Fusiliers of Canada was placed on active service on August 6, 1914, for local protection duties. The regiment raised the 47th Battalion (British Columbia), CEF, which was authorized on November 7, 1914. It disembarked in France on August 11, 1916, where it fought as part of the 10th Infantry Brigade, 4th Canadian Division, in France and Flanders until the end of the war. A member of the 47th Battalion, Corporal Filip Konowal, received the Victoria Cross.

From Our Listeners: Hugh and Jean Smith

By Linda Moore, North Vancouver

World War I interrupted my grandparents' plans to marry and immigrate to Canada, postponing their eventual arrival in Vancouver for twelve years! Talk about a very long engagement.

They gave me a bundle of postcards when I was ten years old that spanned the years 1910 to 1919. The postcard craze was in full swing, the Instagram and text messages of its day. Having tucked the collection away in various drawers since first receiving them, a few years ago I wondered why I was holding onto them. Were they really worth anything? I started to catalogue them across dates and places. Hugh's travels across Canada, his war experience and my grandparents' courtship sprang to life! What a treasure these cards became!

Early in 1913, Hugh made his way alone to Canada, as did many young men to establish themselves in the promising Dominion of Canada. Postcards between Jean and Hugh showed images of life on the two continents. He got a job with the Menzies family on Pender Island in 1914 working with prize-winning Jersey cows. In March 1915, on his twenty-sixth birthday, Hugh, along with five other fellows from Pender, signed up with the CEF. As a farmer, farrier and shoesmith, it made sense that Hugh joined the 11th Canadian Mounted Regiment (CMR). He knew horses extremely well from his life in Scotland, where he was known as a horse-whisperer who could calm these magnificent animals when danger was near.

October 1, 1915, from Vernon Camp: "Just a card to let you see Jean that I am still soldiering. I just got back from Pender yesterday. I was rather sorry to leave but I will soon get down to it again. Will write you soon."

January 1917: Hugh was with the 2nd Division Ammunition Column in France, preparing for the battle of Vimy Ridge. They worked under the cover of night skies, trudging uphill through the mud and driving rain, using light rail lines and wooden walkways, coaxing warhorses and mules, to deliver ammunition to the front line. This work was an essential link to the Canadians' breakthrough at Vimy.

April 11, 1917: Jean turned thirty-one years old. Hugh had purchased one of the intricate hand-embroidered silk cards that the French and Belgian women were making at the time, providing something special for the men at the front who were writing to family and loved ones. The hope expressed in the design is clear: 1914–1917, with the flags of the Allies of the time. A poem inside includes the words "May every breeze that fans thy brow, my fondest blessing whisper now."

However, the war didn't end at Vimy. Hugh proposed to Jean on his annual leave in October 1917. Another long year later, November 5, 1918, they were married in Scotland. While Canadian soldiers returned home, Hugh stayed with the Occupation forces for yet another six months just so he could finally be reunited with Jean in Scotland. They immigrated to Canada with their three children in October 1927, and settled in Vancouver.

In spite of the tumultuous times that my grandparents endured, what I remember is their constant peaceful and loving presence. In Vancouver and Victoria they grew abundant gardens. In the peaceful light today in my community garden, I often remember picking soft red raspberries and collecting warm eggs with my grandparents. Knowing what I do about them gives me strength to deal with inevitable conflicts that I encounter in today's world. What would I do without the garden? Surely, finding peace within is the key.

Left: Courtesy of Linda Moore

Below: HMCS *Rainbow* leaving Portsmouth for Canada. City of Vancouver Archives, LP 21

The 131st Battalion (Westminster), CEF, was authorized on December 22, 1915, and embarked for Britain on October 31, 1916, where its personnel were absorbed by the 30th Battalion, CEF, on November 14, 1916, to provide reinforcements for the Canadian Corps in the field.

158th

The 158th Battalion, which was authorized on December 22, 1915, as the 158th "Overseas" Battalion, CEF, embarked for Britain on November 14, 1916. It provided reinforcements for the Canadian Corps in the field until January 4, 1917, when its personnel were absorbed by the 1st Reserve Battalion, CEF. The battalion was disbanded on July 27, 1917.

225th Battalion (Kootenay)

The 225th Battalion, CEF, was based in Fernie and began recruiting in early 1916 in Fernie, Cranbrook, Nelson and Grand Forks. After sailing to England in January 1917, the battalion was absorbed into the 16th Reserve Battalion on February 6, 1917.

Other Prominent Units in Which British Columbians Served

Lord Strathcona's Horse

In January 1900, Donald Smith (Lord Strathcona and Mount Royal) offered to raise and equip a mounted regiment at his own expense to serve in the South African or "Boer" War. His regiment was recruited largely from the cowboys and frontiersmen of Western Canada and members of the North West Mounted Police (NWMP). Command of Strathcona's Horse was given to the now famous superintendent of the NWMP, Sir Sam Steele.

At the outbreak of World War I, the regiment was mobilized and trained in England. In March 1917, the regiment again saw action during the defence of the Somme. During the last great German offensive in 1918 when the British and French armies were on the verge of being split, Lieutenant Gordon Flowerdew won the regiment's third Victoria Cross. On March 30, 1918, at Moreuil Wood, Lieutenant Flowerdew led his hundred-man squadron on a charge that defeated a superior German force of three hundred men supported by machine guns *(courtesy of the Canadian Army website)*.

Princess Patricia's Canadian Light Infantry

PPCLI was founded for service in World War I on August 10, 1914, and paraded for the first time at Lansdowne Park, Ottawa, Ontario, on August 23, 1914. Hamilton Gault, a prominent Montreal businessman, raised the regiment out of his own funds, making the PPCLI the last privately raised regiment in Canada.

The regiment embarked for Great Britain on September 27, 1914. It landed in France with the 80th Brigade, 27th Division of the British Expeditionary Force, on December 21, 1914, and on November 25, 1915, it joined the Canadian Corps as part of the 7th Infantry Brigade, 3rd Canadian Division, with which it fought in France and Flanders until the end of the war.

10th Battalion, the 50th Battalion, the 191st and the 192nd

These southern Alberta battalions earned a place in our memory for accepting Japanese and Chinese Canadians who were turned away from British Columbia regiments.

From Our Listeners: The Stewart Family—The Brotherhood—For King and Country

By Jean Wawryk (née Nicoll)

My grandfather Frank Stewart and two brothers Robert and Jack answered the call for King and Country when World War I was declared. Before that the Stewart family had lived in Nova Scotia, but when my grandpa's mother passed away at a young age from TB the family moved to Dodsland, Saskatchewan, to homestead. His father, John Stewart, was left to raise five children on his own. The other children in the family were Gordon and a beloved daughter, Amy. They worked hard together developing homesteads. The boys took on extra jobs to earn a living. They were a family.

War would change all of that.

Lieutenant Robert William Stewart enlisted December 31, 1915. He was with the 42nd Battalion (Black Watch Highlanders). He died on March 25, 1917, mortally wounded while carrying a man to a place of safety. Robert was twenty-six. He is buried in Aubigny Communal Cemetery, France. Robert and his battalion were part of the battle for Vimy Ridge.

Lieutenant Jack Albert Stewart enlisted May 15, 1915. He was with the 8th Battalion (Black Devils—Winnipeg Rifles). Jack was wounded twice, recovered and sent back to the front. He was wounded a third time during the battle of Hill 70. He succumbed to his wounds six months after his last hospitalization. He is buried in Longuenesse (St. Omer) Souvenir Cemetery, Pas de Calais, France. He was twenty-three. Both brothers went in as privates. Both were promoted to the rank of lieutenants because of acts of bravery.

Private Frank Desmond Stewart, my grandfather, enlisted December 21, 1916. He was eighteen years old. He was with the 249th Battalion (1st Canadian Mounted Rifles) and was wounded in the Battle of Amiens on August 10, 1918. It was the third day of the "Drive." He was wounded in his legs and taken to a field hospital back of the lines. He was there for a month, then sent to England for an extended period of time.

From Liverpool Frank was sent home on a hospital ship to Canada. He was stationed the first winter in 1918 in Whitby, Ontario, for recovery and rehabilitation. Later he was sent to Regina to be fitted with an artificial leg. Grandpa came home an amputee, right leg below the knee. He was twenty.

When he returned to Dodsland, Saskatchewan, he took over his brother's farm and married my grandma, Barbara Shanks. They had three sons and one daughter, my mother. My parents are both from Saskatchewan. They met and married in Vancouver. They stayed and raised a family in Chilliwack.

I have very fond memories of my parents taking my siblings and me to Grandma and Grandpa's for visits on the farm. They would come and stay with us on the West Coast on numerous occasions as well. I can remember hearing the sound of Grandpa walking on our hardwood floors. A thump and then nothing, another thump and then nothing. His peg leg. I never thought to ask any questions about the war. He never mentioned it. He was Grandpa and I loved him very much. He passed away at the age of ninety-two in 1990.

I miss him.

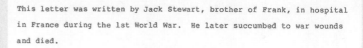

This letter was written by Jack Stewart, brother of Frank, in hospital in France during the 1st World War. He later succumbed to war wounds and died.

September 3rd *1917*

Dear Father, (John Stewart)

Only a short note today as I am feeling pretty rotten and ready and willing to declare peace, war or an election or to get married or anything else real foolish.

I am now going to give you our daily routine. We get woke up at 5 to get our face and hands washed, then about 5.45 we have the beds made, the nurses talking away at 100 to the minute and me laying on my back with a silly grin on my face as though I enjoyed it, whereas I am ready to swear at anything that comes in sight.

At 7.45 we get breakfast then wait impatiently for the paper boy to come round at about 10.30 after that say about 11.30 I get my leg dressed. While this is being done I grit my teeth and make faces as though I had just taken a mouthful of castor oil.

At 12.45 we have lunch which is generally chicken without potatoes. We have not seen any potatoes for about two weeks.

After lunch we get another wash and the beds made again and at 4 we get tea which consists of bread, butter and jam.

At 6.30 we get dinner which is usually chicken again, then we stare at the ceiling until time to go to sleep.

Of course we get our mail which comes sometime during the afternoon. I have not heard from our Battn yet but understand that we had about 75 left out of 900 so you see that they were in a bad spot. But they got what they wanted and still hold it and always will.

Love to all,

Jack

Both images courtesy of Jean Wawryk

From Our Listeners: John E. Wheeler

By John Stonier, Surrey

In 1957 I was working on the construction of the paper mill at Crofton on Vancouver Island. We had rented a waterfront cottage nearby in Chemainus, on Dogwood Road. One of our neighbours was a retired bachelor, John Edward Wheeler. He was friendly and we got on well, visiting on weekends.

On one occasion I noticed something addressed to Lieutenant John E. Wheeler and asked him about his time in the army. His story about enlisting in the army went something like this:

Shortly after World War I began, Mr. Wheeler and seven of his friends from Walhachin decided to join the army and fight for their mother country.

They all wanted to be in the same unit and made an informal pact to join up as a group. In 1914, you had to get a medical certificate of fitness to take to the recruiting office. After failing to get the required certificate for the entire group in Vancouver and Victoria, they decided to try again in Kamloops. The doctor there lined up the eight of them (Mr. Wheeler was eighth) and began his examinations. After examining five or six, he said, "You all look fit to me" and filled in and signed all the required forms.

With the necessary forms in hand they went to the nearest recruiting office and joined the army.

Three months later they were in England. Once in England they were taught one of the essentials of war: dismantling and assembling rifles, and then to the firing range for target practice. This was Mr. Wheeler's downfall for he could not hit the target board, never mind the target. After an eye examination, he was deemed unfit for the infantry and transferred to a supply division. He must have excelled in his new position as he was discharged at the end of World War I as a lieutenant. Mr. Wheeler died in Chemainus in late December 1958 or January 1959.

From Our Listeners: Reginald George Woods, 29th Battalion, CEF

By Chris Woods, Watton, Norfolk, United Kingdom

My father (and I) were born and brought up in Brighton, on the English Channel coast of Sussex. My grandfather was a shoemaker from Northamptonshire and moved to Brighton around 1885, where he continued making and selling his boots and shoes. My grandparents had eight children of whom two died in early childhood, two died in World War I and the others lived a normal lifespan.

Three children left England for much of their life, one to live in Africa, another to serve with the Indian Army and Reginald, who left at age fourteen. He sailed on SS *Lake Manitoba* for Canada in the company of some neighbours who were bakers and confectioners and who were immigrating to Prince Albert in Saskatchewan. They sailed in March 1907; his boarding pass shows that he was classed as an adult, a labourer, and his passenger record shows him as a schoolboy with five dollars.

I lost track of Reginald after they landed in St. John's, New Brunswick, and I could not find him in the 1911 census. He reappears in his 1914 attestation paper, which records he joined the 72nd Battalion Seaforth Highlanders in Vancouver 1912. At that time this was a militia unit and maybe at only five feet five he was their mascot!

On November 14, 1914, Reginald joined the 29th Vancouver Infantry Battalion, British Columbia Regiment. I am guessing but at that time the 72nd Battalion appears to have been designated for homeland security while the 29th was preparing to join the Canadian Expeditionary Force. Reginald may have seen this as a way of returning to Europe and possibly seeing his family in Brighton. In this, it appears he was successful.

On March 14, 1915, Private Woods 76088 (possibly serving as a batman) and his battalion entrained from Vancouver on May 14, 1915, sailed from Montreal on RMS *Missanabie* and disembarked at Devonport on May 30. They travelled by train to Shorncliffe in Kent near Folkestone for training. Reginald went on for training with grenades and Lewis gun in 1916. He was missed in Brighton and my father, aged twelve, wrote to his older brother's commanding officer asking if he could come home for Christmas. Reginald was granted leave in England from December 22, 1916, to January 5, 1917.

This was the last time the family was to see Reginald. He received a good conduct badge in February, the same month his brother—a lieutenant in the Royal Field Artillery—was killed in action in France. Reginald was wounded in action during the attack on Hill 70, Lens (Vimy Ridge), on August 21, taken to No. 18 General Hospital (Camiers) and died September 3, 1917, at the base hospital in Etaples.

He was buried at Etaples cemetery and later his mother was sent the Canadian Memorial Cross.

Left: Reginald Woods served with Tobin's Tigers, Vancouver's 29th Battalion. Courtesy of Chris Woods

Right: Reginald Woods' grave at Etaples, France. Courtesy of Chris Woods

Pioneer Battalions

Their work was varied but consisted of consolidating positions captured by the infantry, tunnelling, mining, wiring, railroad work, deep dugout work and laying out, building and keeping trenches in repair.

Canadian Army Medical Corps

The Corps was founded in 1904 but the Great War led to a huge expansion and eventually more than half of Canada's physicians served overseas to handle the mounting casualties. According to the Canadian War Museum, "in total, 21,453 men and women proudly wore the CAMC badge. Many of these doctors and stretcher-bearers served close to the front, and the medical service suffered 1,325 casualties during the war." The survival rate of patients getting to the Canadian Hospitals was nearly 90 percent, one reason why the Canadian medical service was singled out by name for the special notice of the King as having "displayed marked efficiency and devotion to duty."

Canadian Railway Troops

Canadian railway units played a major role in the construction and maintenance of railways of all gauges, including light railways, for the five British Army areas in France and Belgium.

Canadian Engineers

Throughout most of the war, each division had three field companies of engineers and one pioneer battalion. Assignments included bridge work, general engineering, tunnelling and mining.

Forestry Corps

The Forestry Corps was formed in 1916 to meet the incredible demand for duckboards, timber shoring and other wood products. The British government in its wisdom decided nobody was more experienced in the Empire to harvest timber than the Canadians. Over thirty-five thousand Canadians served in the Forestry Corps. Many members were First Nations and also underaged volunteers.

University Battalions

The 196th Western Universities Battalion had recruits primarily from the Universities of Manitoba, Saskatchewan, Alberta and British Columbia, as well as Brandon College. Students from the universities, wanting to maintain their university identity, lobbied the Minister of Militia and convinced him to authorize the formation of a western university battalion.

From Our Listeners: J.J. Carney

By Jim Carney Jr., Vancouver

John James (Jim) Carney was born in 1894 on the Simpson cattle ranch in the southern Okanagan Valley of BC. He was the eldest of four siblings. His parents, John Joseph and Bridget (née Casey), were first-generation Irish Canadians, born in Ontario of Irish immigrant parents. After completing high school Jim earned a teaching certificate at the Provincial Normal School in Vancouver and taught for two years in Flagstone, a small farming and logging community—long gone—in the southeast corner of BC near the US border.

On February 7, 1916, just twenty-one years old, he enlisted in the Rocky Mountain Rangers, joining the 172nd Battalion of the Canadian Expeditionary Force. The 172nd spent the summer of 1916 training, living in tents. On May 15 he was promoted to acting corporal. On October 25 the battalion departed Halifax on RMS *Mauretania*, arriving in Southampton, England, on October 31, and Camp Bramshott in Hampshire, the primary staging base for all British and colonial troops headed for Europe, the next day.

Over the next three months Bramshott suffered outbreaks of both German measles and mumps; Jim fell victim to both, spending several weeks in the isolation hospital at Aldershot. He remained at Bramshott until May as an instructor in physical drill and bayonet fighting.

On May 5, 1917, Jim volunteered to join the 72nd Battalion of the Seaforth Highlanders of Canada, a Vancouver-based kilted regiment then fighting in northern France near the Belgian border. He spent two weeks at the sprawling Allied hospital and staging area of Etaples, France, before joining the 72nd Battalion in early June.

For sixteen months (May 1917 to August 1918), Jim saw extensive action along the Western Front. He had arrived in France just one month after the iconic Canadian victory at Vimy Ridge, which broke the seemingly intractable position of the German army in northwest Europe. Vimy Ridge was part of a broader conflict known as the Arras Offensive. The Seaforths, a component of the 4th Division of the Canadian Corps, were a major force in that campaign, culminating in what is now known as "Canada's Hundred Days" (August 8 to November 11, 1918).

Carney participated in the holding of Vimy Ridge after its initial capture and subsequent battles in the Arras (France) and Ypres Salient (Flanders/Belgium), including Belleau Wood (June 1 to 26, 1918), as the Allies pushed north (though mercifully not Passchendaele). Most notable was the Battle of Amiens (August 8 to 26, 1918), strategically perhaps as significant as Vimy Ridge, for which Jim (and many other Canadians) was recommended for the Military Medal—a high-level award for "conspicuous gallantry"—which he received on May 12, 1919. (The equivalent for officers was the Military Cross.)

Sent to Officers' Training School at Bexhill, Seaford, England, on August 31, 1918, he was promoted to lieutenant on November 5, 1918. In those years, given the rigidly class-conscious British military system, an enlisted man from the colonies receiving a commission in the field was exceptional.

Following the Armistice of November 11, 1918, Lieutenant Carney was sent back to Etaples in January 1919 on "conducting" duty. He returned to England in May 1919 and, after several months in various hospitals primarily due to knee injuries and intestinal infections, on August 19 was "recommended for invaliding to Canada," departing on September 11 on the hospital ship *Araguaya*. He arrived in

Images this page courtesy of John Edmond

SHANGHAI MUNICIPAL POLICE.
CURFEW PASS No. 6273

Mr. J.J. Carney

Employed by Public Health Dept.,
S. M. C.
is exempted from the orders pertaining to curfew, whilst in the performance of his duties.

Date 8 JUNE 1938

for Commissioner of Police.

Halifax on September 19, where he was again committed to hospital until October 9, 1919. He was twenty-five years old.

Jim returned to Vancouver and taught for two years but in 1922 went to China, volunteering as a "stoker" (shovelling coal into the ship's boilers) on SS *Canadian Inventor*. He spent the next seventeen years with the Shanghai municipal council, first as a policeman and later as a public health inspector, while also volunteering in the Shanghai Volunteer Corps, a British-led militia force. In 1935 he married Dora May Sanders, a young Canadian journalist, born in Capetown, South Africa, of English-Irish parents. They had four children, twins Jim ("JJ") and Pat, Norah and Thomas.

Following evacuation in 1937, a return to Shanghai in 1938 and a final return to Canada in October 1939, Jim Carney enrolled in the Ontario Veterinary College in Guelph, Ontario, graduating in 1945 as a doctor of veterinary medicine (DVM).

From 1945 to 1962 Dr. Carney was employed by the government of British Columbia as a livestock inspector in Victoria–Saanich (1945–49), the West Kootenays (based in Nelson, 1949–60) and the Fraser Valley (Abbotsford, 1961–62). He and his wife, Dora, spent much of their retirement years on Saturna Island. Dr. Carney died in June 1976 at Shaughnessy Hospital, Vancouver, at the age of eighty-two. Dora died in 1986 on Saturna.

From Our Listeners: Walter John Hallam, #476612, Canadian Field Artillery

Robert Hallam dropped off a thick envelope here at CBC containing photocopies of various documents, with a chronology and commentary connected to his father's Great War experiences. Walter John Hallam first enlisted with the militia at Fort Rodd Hill near Victoria in 1914. The following year he volunteered with the Canadian Expeditionary Force at Esquimalt. His attestation papers indicate that he was a blacksmith by trade, with a scar on his left index finger and on the right forearm. He was twenty-three years, seven months old.

Robert writes: "He arrived at the front probably in April 1916 and saw limited action at the Somme. While sitting there on the bank of the river with two others, the middle soldier was shot dead in the mouth by a sniper. This is about the time he gave his stripes back. He said, 'There was no sense in getting killed for fifteen cents.'"

Assigned to the 10th Battery 1st Division Canadian Field Artillery, Walter delivered ammunition to the eighteen-pound guns near the front by a team of horses and caisson (two-wheeled carts). Robert writes this was "an extremely dangerous job, especially never before having been on a horse." His battery moved on to the Vimy Ridge assault and was among the first to reach the top on the first morning of the attack.

The mud and horrors of Passchendaele began for the Canadians later that fall, as Robert says, "Not his idea of a good time." Colonel G.W.L. Nicholson's *The Gunners of Canada* points to a sky-high attrition rate: "Casualties began occurring in the first 24 hours and mounted steadily during the next four weeks. The 10th Battery CFA was to suffer casualties of 200 per cent during the Passchendaele battle." Walter survived.

Then in April 1918 a shell exploded near him and his horse. The animal reared, landed on him and in the process injured Walter's leg. He thought this could be the ticket back to England, but it was not to be. He was sent to hospital at Etaples. "The British had a supply dump next to the Canadian hospital at Etaples. The Germans bombed; they got the hospital, too. On return to the hospital after running to the fields, he saw that everything had been destroyed."

After Walter was patched up he was sent back to the battery to cook in the trailer kitchen. Robert picks up the story: "Sounds good, all is well. Not so. On July 18, 1918, after leaving his post in the trailer to relieve himself, a 5.9-inch shell blew up the trailer; on his return it was gone.

"Shortly after, in October 1918 my dad saw Raymond Brewster of Victoria coming up the road. Remember Victoria was then a relatively small town and he knew the premier's son well. 'Why the hell are you here?' Dad asked. Fresh from a bombproof job in London, Brewster wanted to be able to say he had been at the front. Dad liked telling the story, always getting from me the comment 'That's terrible.' He would then say, 'Well, Brewster gave his life for his country.' On November 1, 1918, while in an observation tower, Brewster was hit and the tower blown to pieces."

The toll was terribly high for Walter's 10th Battery; by the end of the war they had suffered a 180 percent casualty rate. When he returned home he hit the road for a dozen years. He gold-panned on the Rogue River in Oregon and explored the western states. As he told his son, "You can't run away from your trouble; eventually you just get tired." When Pierre Berton phoned to ask about his war experiences, Walter didn't mince words: "We all volunteered, the horses did not." And that was that.

Robert concludes: "In the end there was something special about the relationship between the men he served with. Lieutenant Thomas Grantham Norris, a childhood friend, was one of those. The two men were from different worlds. Norris was a Supreme Court judge and Dad was an industrial blacksmith but on his deathbed Norris wanted to talk to Dad. They had been part of the most feared army on the Western Front...My dad died in 1990 at the age of ninety-eight a happy man. He held his end up."

Walter John Hallam.
Courtesy of Robert Hallam

From Our Listeners: Victoria's Fighting Gillespie Family

By Murray Thom, Victoria

In 1914, George Gillespie, manager of the Bank of BC, had seven sons and one married daughter. By the end of that year, five of those sons and the son-in-law were commissioned in uniform, either in the 50th Battalion Highland Regiment, Victoria, or in British Army regiments. Hebden (thirty-six) was a local business man, Alexander (thirty-four) was a BC land surveyor, and Kenneth (thirty-three) was a bank clerk. Hebden, Dugald (thirty), Ronald (twenty-four), Sholto (twenty-three) and Erroll (twenty-one) were all associated with the local militia, the 50th Regiment of the Gordon Highlanders, which became part of the 16th Battalion Canadian Scottish, CEF. Florence was married to Eric Colbourne, a registered BC land surveyor working with Alexander.

When war against Germany was declared, son-in-law Eric Colbourne returned to Britain and was commissioned as a second lieutenant with the 3rd Royal Berkshire Regiment. Later in 1914, Sholto Gillespie left Victoria and journeyed to Scotland with his buddy George Tyson, independent of any military unit. Sholto was commissioned in the Argyle and Sutherland Highlanders. After training with the 4th Battalion in England he joined the 91st Battalion, May 1915, in the trenches of Flanders where his cousin, Douglas Gillespie, was also fighting with the 90th Battalion next to the 91st. In June 1915, Douglas and Sholto learned that Eric had been awarded the Military Cross for an action close by at Cuinchy but had died of his wounds. On September 25, 1915, Douglas was killed in a charge against the German trenches. In 1916, Sholto was transferred with the 1st Battalion of the Argyles to the Balkan–Macedonian front near Salonika. In 1917 it was reported in the Victoria *Daily Colonist* that he had been wounded and was in the hospital in Salonika.

Hebden, a major, had been transferred to the Canadian Field Artillery, 15th Brigade, and was in England. Ronald, a lieutenant in the Gordon Highlanders, had been taken prisoner in January 1915 and, in spite of a desperate attempt to escape with a buddy by jumping from the top of a fifty-foot wall at the fortress of Lille, was still a prisoner in 1917. On the escape attempt, his buddy had broken his leg and Ronald assisted him and they returned to the fortress to turn themselves in. Erroll, a lieutenant in the 50th Gordon Highlanders, was transferred to the Machine Gun Corps and served in the trenches in France in 1917 and through to 1918.

Dugald was commissioned as a provisional first lieutenant in the 50th Gordon Highlanders and served in Canada. Florence, the widow of Eric Colbourne, served with a nursing unit attached to the Serbian Army in Salonika. It was in Salonika where she was surprised and pleased to meet her brother Sholto, who had been wounded and hospitalized there.

With the exception of the loss of the two Scottish cousins and the brother-in-law, all the other Gillespie highlander soldiers returned to civilian life after the war. Ronald was posted to Siberia with the British Military Mission, having learned Russian while a prisoner of war. He then ended up in China as a manager with Imperial Chemical Industries UK, where he was later joined by Sholto. Florence took up residence in England while Hebden, Dugald and Erroll all returned to Canada.

I am married to the older daughter of the second-youngest Gillespie son. As an introduction for my eleven-year-old grandson to the forthcoming hundredth anniversary of World War I, we visited the Commonwealth cemeteries and memorials marking the resting places of the Gillespie casualties in both world wars.

One final note of British Columbian interest: the Gillespie son-in-law, Eric Colbourne, was a registered BC land surveyor. Colbourne Creek, north of Prince George, is named in his honour. He was awarded the Military Cross posthumously for his action in June 1915.

Acknowledgements

We'd like to thank some of the BC historians who covered this ground before us. There is no better account of British Columbia during the war years than the chapters in Margaret Ormsby's *British Columbia: A History*. She wrote that book in 1958 but it still stands out for its insights. Patricia Roy helped us with her book *Boundless Optimism: Richard McBride's British Columbia*. The late Terry Reksten's *Illustrated History of British Columbia* has a wonderful chapter on wartime BC. Jean Barman graciously agreed to contribute to our chapter on women in wartime. Maureen Duffus led the way on nursing sisters. Andrea Malysh in Vernon reviewed and assisted with background on the internment camp chapter. Michael Kluckner and Nelson Riis brought Walhachin back to life. Teacher Dianne Rabel and her students contributed stories and kept sending ideas from Prince Rupert. Greg Nesteroff was generous with his writing from the Kootenays. Sue Dahlo sent wonderful stories and photos from the Boundary country. Chuck Tasaka in Nanaimo and Linda Reid in Vancouver helped with the Japanese-Canadian story. To Lorne Adamson in Vernon and Brian Milthorp from Quesnel, thanks for research and transcriptions. To Cam Cathcart and Nick Cheng, thanks for helping us with regimental history. To Peter Broznitsky and our friends at the Western Front Association, keep up the good work. Thanks to Floyd Low and the folks at the 54th, and Don Stewart at McLeod's Books, who shared his expertise. Colin Preston at the CBC Archives in Vancouver was always there for us. Carolyn Webber in Victoria was our go-to expert on research issues and always found treasure. Thanks to Julie Ferguson for her offering on Canada's first submarines, and to Peter Johnson, who told us about the virtually unknown Chinese Labour Corps. Katherine Palmer Gordon provided context for aboriginal soldiers, and maritime historian David W. Griffiths sent us stories on the sinking of HMCS *Galiano* and the hospital ship *Llandovery Castle*. Simon Fraser University piper Kevin MacLean shared his experiences in Europe, where he honoured Piper James Richardson and others lost in battle. Thank you, Robert Taylor, author of *The Ones Who Have to Pay: The Soldiers–Poets of Victoria BC in the Great War 1914–1918*, and Mel Rothenburger of Kamloops for his thoughts on aboriginal war hero George McLean. And thanks to Wade Davis who has written so eloquently about the Western Front in *Into the Silence*.

The authors would like to thank the staff at Harbour Publishing for guiding us through another project. Stephen Ullstrom was a wizard at locating numerous archival images; our patient and wise editor Maureen Nicholson kept asking all the right questions.

Mark would like to thank his *BC Almanac* producer Anne Penman for allowing him the time to dig into this project. Our families have been patient and tried to prevent us from becoming "war bores." On that point, we hope they were successful.

Mark Forsythe and Greg Dickson

For Further Reading

Barman, Jean. *The West beyond the West: A History of British Columbia*. Revised. University of Toronto Press, 1996.

Barrett, Anthony, and Rhodri Windsor Liscombe. *Francis Rattenbury and British Columbia: Architecture and Challenge in the Imperial Age*. UBC Press, 1983.

Berton, Pierre. *Vimy*. Random House, 1985.

Bishop, Arthur. *True Canadian Battles That Forged Our Nation*. Key Porter, 2008.

Borden, Robert Laird. *His Memoirs*. Macmillan, 1938.

Bumsted, J.M. *A History of the Canadian Peoples*. 4th ed. Oxford University Press, 2003.

Cancela, Julie. *The Ditch: Lifeline of a Community*. Oliver Heritage Society Museum and Archives, 1986.

Clyne, H.R.N. *Vancouver's 29th*. Tobin's Tigers Association, 1964.

Cook, Tim. *The Madman and the Butcher*. Penguin Canada, 2011.

Davis, Wade. *Into the Silence: The Great War, Mallory and the Conquest of Everest*. Alfred A. Knopf, 2011.

Drew, George Alexander. *Canada's Fighting Airmen*. MacLean Publishing, 1930.

Duffus, Maureen. *Battlefront Nurses in WWI: The Canadian Army Medical Corps in England, France and Salonika, 1914–1919*. Town and Gown Press, 2009.

Eagle, Raymond. *In the Service of the Crown: The Story of Budge and Nancy Bell-Irving*. Golden Dog Press, 2000

Evans, Hubert. *The New Front Line*. Macmillan, 1926.

Ferguson, Julie. *Through a Canadian Periscope: The Story of the Canadian Submarine Service*. Centennial 2nd ed. Dundurn, 2014.

Francis, Daniel. Ed. *Encyclopedia of British Columbia*. Harbour Publishing, 2000.

Francis, R.D., Richard Jones, and Donald Smith. *Destinies: Canadian History since Confederation*. Nelson Education, 2008.

Fussell, Paul. *The Great War and Modern Memory*. Oxford University Press, 1975.

Gamble, Len. *So Far from Home: The Stories of Armstrong's Fallen in the Great War, 1914–1918*. Self-published, 2008.

Granatstein, Jack, and Desmond Morton. *Marching to Armageddon: Canadians and the Great War 1914–1919*. Lester & Orpen Dennys, 1989.

Gray, John MacLachlan. *Billy Bishop Goes to War*. Talonbooks, 1982.

Harris, John Norman. *Knights of the Air: Canadian Aces of World War I*. MacMillan, 1958.

Hodgins, Jack. *Broken Ground*. McClelland & Stewart, 1998.

Ito, Roy. *We Went to War: The Story of the Japanese Canadians Who Served*. Canada's Wings, 1984.

Johnson, Peter. *Quarantined: Life and Death at William Head Station, 1872–1959*. Heritage House, 2013.

Kingwell, Mark, and Christopher Moore. *Canada: Our Century*. Doubleday Canada, 1999.

Kluckner, Michael. *Vanishing British Columbia*. UBC Press, 2005.

Kordan, Bohdan S. *Enemy Aliens, Prisoners of War: Internment in Canada during the Great War*. McGill-Queen's University Press, 2002.

Lamb, W. Kaye. "Building Submarines for Russia in Burrard Inlet." *BC Studies*, Autumn 1986.

Leblanc, Ron, Keith Maxwell, Dwayne Snow, and Kelly Deschenes. *Swift and Strong: A Pictorial History of the British Columbia Regiment*. British Columbia Regiment, 2011.

MacMillan, Margaret. *The War That Ended Peace: The Road to 1914*. Random House, 2013.

Macphail, Andrew. *Official History of the Canadian Forces in the Great War 1914–1919*. Canadian Forces, 1925.

Mayse, Susan. *Ginger: The Life and Death of Albert Goodwin*. Harbour Publishing, 1990.

McBride, Sam. *Bravest Canadian: The Story of Fritz Peters and Two World Wars*. Granville Island Publishing, 2012.

Niven, Frederick. *A Lover of the Land and Other Poems*. Boni & Liveright, 1925.

Ormsby, Margaret A. *British Columbia: A History*. MacMillan, 1958.

Ralph, Wayne. *Barker, VC: The Classic Story of a Legendary First World War Hero*. Grub Street, 1999.

Rayment, Hugh, and Patrick Sherlock. *Camp Vernon: A Century of Canadian Military History*. Kettle Valley Publishing, 2004.

Reksten, Terry. *The Illustrated History of British Columbia*. Douglas & McIntyre, 2001; 2005.

Riis, Nelson. "The Walhachin Myth: A Study in Settlement Abandonment," in Richard Mackie and Graeme Wynn, *Home Truths*. Harbour Publishing, 2012.

Rothenburger, Mel. *The Wild McLeans*. Orca Book Publishers, 1993.

Roy, Patricia E. *Boundless Optimism: Richard McBride's British Columbia*. University of British Columbia Press, 2012.

Roy, Patricia E., and John Herd Thompson. *British Columbia: Land of Promises*. Oxford University Press, 2005.

Service, Robert. *Rhymes of a Red Cross Man*. Retrieved from www.gutenberg.org.

Shaw, Susan Evans. *Canadians at War*. Goose Lane Editions, 2011.

Taylor, Robert. *The Ones Who Have to Pay: The Soldiers-Poets of Victoria BC in the Great War 1914–1918*. Trafford, 2013.

Tuchman, Barbara. *The Guns of August*. Ballantine Books, 1962.

Vancouver Daily Province. Various authors. *Canada in Khaki*. Published for the Canadian War Records Office, 1917.

Weir, Joan Sherman. *Walhachin: Catastrophe or Camelot?* Hancock House, 1984; 1995.

Wetherell, J.E. *The Great War in Verse and Poetry*. King's Printer for Ontario Ministry of Education, 1919.

Index